ANTHROPOLOGISTS IN A WIDER WORLD

Methodology and History in Anthropology

General Editor: David Parkin, Director of the Institute of Social and Cultural Anthropology, University of Oxford

ANTHROPOLOGISTS IN A WIDER WORLD

ESSAYS ON FIELD RESEARCH

Edited by
Paul Dresch, Wendy James and David Parkin

Berghahn Books
New York • Oxford

First published in 2000 by **Berghahn Books**

www.berghahnbooks.com

Library of Congress Cataloging-in-Publication Data
Anthropologists in a wider world : essays on field research / edited by
Paul Dresch, Wendy James, and David Parkin.
    p. cm. -- (Methodology and history in anthropology ; 6)
    "The present volume owes its origin to an 'away day' seminar
held in September, 1997, by staff at the Institute of Social and
Cultural Anthropology, University of Oxford:--Acknowledge-
ments.
    Includes bibliographical references and index.
    ISBN 1-57181-799-9 (acid-free paper)
    1. Anthropology--Field work.   2. Anthropology--Research.
3. Anthropology--Methodology.   I. Dresch, Paul.   II. James,
Wendy.   III. Parkin, David J.   IV. Methodology and history in
anthropology ; v. 7.

GN34.3.F53 A57 2000
301'.07'23--dc21

                          99-087034

British Library Cataloguing in Publication Data

A catalogue record for this book is available from the British Library.

Printed in the United States on acid-free paper.

ISBN-1-57181-799-9 hardback
1-57181-800-6 paperback

One may say (with reservations which easily suggest themselves) that in all relations of a personally differentiated sort, intensity and nuance develop in the degree in which each party, by words and by mere existence, reveals itself to the other. How much error and mere prejudice may be contained in all this knowledge is another question.

Simmel, G. 1950 *The Sociology of George Simmel* (Kurt H. Wolff trans) NY: The Free Press. p.307

*In the mind's eye, but no regrets: Himalayan village
with apricot blossom (see Chapter 12)*

CONTENTS

LIST OF FIGURES

Table

NOTES ON CONTRIBUTORS

NICHOLAS ALLEN is Reader in the Social Anthropology of South Asia at the University of Oxford, and has previously taught in the University of Durham. He has published on the ethnography of the Himalayas (dealing especially with language, ritual and myth), on the evolution of systems of kinship and marriage, on aspects of the Durkheimian tradition, and on Indo-European cultural comparativism. He is currently working on a study of the common origins of ancient Indian and ancient Greek epic.

MARCUS BANKS, Lecturer in Social Anthropology at the University of Oxford, trained as a social anthropologist at the University of Cambridge and later studied documentary film at the National Film and Television School. His publications include *Organizing Jainism in India and England*, Clarendon Press, 1992; *Ethnicity: anthropological constructions*, Routledge, 1996; and, co-edited with Howard Morphy, *Rethinking visual anthropology*, Yale University Press, 1997. He is a past Chairman of the Royal Anthropological Institute's Film Committee, has collaborated with colleagues in Hungary on studies in the history of documentary film, and is currently conducting research on documentary film from colonial India.

ROBERT BARNES is Professor of Social Anthropology at the University of Oxford and has previously taught in the University of Edinburgh. He has conducted research and published on eastern Indonesian, North American and Taiwanese cultures. He has also jointly edited books on hierarchy and on indigenous peoples of Asia.

PAUL DRESCH is a Lecturer in Social Anthropology at the University of Oxford. He was taught, long ago, by Edwin Ardener and Albert Hourani. He was a Junior Research Fellow at St. John's College, Oxford, 1982-4, and then taught at the University of Michigan, Ann Arbor, 1984-9, before coming back to Oxford. His major fieldwork was in Yemen (Dresch 1989) and he has since been working both on Yemeni history and on the ethnography of the Arab Gulf. For lack of funds and time to visit the Gulf and Yemen as often as he would wish, he goes back and forth to Paris.

ROGER GOODMAN is a Lecturer in the Social Anthropology of Japan at the University of Oxford, and is also affiliated to the Nissan Centre there. His most recent publications include: *Japan's 'International Youth'* (Oxford, 1993); *The East Asian welfare model* (a joint project with Gordon White and Huck-ju Kwon at the Institute of Development Studies, University of Sussex; Routledge, 1998); and *Children of the Japanese State* (forthcoming). During 1998-9, he was Visiting Professor at the National Museum of Ethnology in Osaka, Japan.

WENDY JAMES, Professor of Social Anthropology at the University of Oxford, has carried out ethnographic research in the Sudan and Ethiopia. She has taught in the Universities of Khartoum (Sudan), Aarhus (Denmark), and Bergen (Norway). Her publications on Africa include *The listening ebony: moral knowledge, religion and power among the Uduk of Sudan*, Clarendon Press, 1988; and she has worked on several edited volumes, including *The pursuit of certainty: religious and cultural formulations*, Routledge, 1995, and, with N.J. Allen, on *Marcel Mauss: a centenary tribute*, Berghahn, 1998. Among her current projects is a volume in press on Ethiopia, edited together with colleagues from the USA, Japan and Italy.

HÉLÈNE LA RUE is Lecturer in Ethnomusicology, and also Curator of the Bate Collection and the musical collections in the Pitt Rivers Museum, at the University of Oxford. Her fieldwork has been carried out in Japan, China and Europe, and has been concerned principally with festivals and celebrations. She is Director of the National Database and Register of Musical Instruments and is engaged in an ongoing project to identify and catalogue all musical instruments and related material in collections accessible to the public in the United Kingdom.

LOUELLA MATSUNAGA is a Lecturer in Anthropology with reference to Japan at Oxford Brookes University, having also taught at Oxford University's Institute of Social and Cultural Anthropology. Her research interests include work and the company in Japan, Japanese new religious movements, and the Japanese community in the UK. Two of her articles on Japanese new religious movements in the UK are included in P.B. Clarke (ed.) *Japanese New Religions in Global Perspective* (Curzon, forthcoming) and she has a book in press entitled *The changing face of Japanese retail: working in a chain store,* Routledge, forthcoming.

MICHAEL O'HANLON's first fieldwork among the Wahgi people in the New Guinea Highlands was from 1979 to 1981, when he focused in particular on the moral and political implications with which Wahgi credit their elaborate traditions of self-adornment. Subsequently he joined the British Museum and made further trips to the Wahgi people in 1986 and again in 1990. He mounted an exhibition of Waghi artefacts at the British Museum, a process described in his book *Paradise: portraying the New Guinea Highlands,* British Museum Press, 1993. His other books include *Reading the skin,* British Museum Press, 1989 and *The anthropology of landscape,* Oxford, 1995, co-edited with Eric Hirsch. Since 1998, Michael O'Hanlon has been Director of the Pitt Rivers Museum at Oxford University.

DAVID PARKIN, Professor and Director of the Institute of Social and Cultural Anthropology at the University of Oxford, has carried out field research in East Africa since 1962, much of it while at the School of Oriental and African Studies, London University. Current interests include Islam, medical anthropology, socio-material prosthesis, and cross-cultural rhetorics. Recent publications include *Sacred void: spatial images of work and ritual among the Giriama of Kenya,* Cambridge, 1991, and *Autorité et pouvoir chez l es Swahili* (co-edited), Paris, 1998, the latter resulting from on-going collaboration with French colleagues.

FRANK N. PIEKE is a Lecturer in the Modern Politics and Society of China at the University of Oxford, and also affiliated to the University's Centre for Modern Chinese Studies. He has published two monographs: *The social position of the Dutch Chinese* was published in Dutch in 1988 and translated into Chinese in 1992, and *The ordinary and the extraordinary: an anthropological study of Chinese reform and the 1989 People's Movement in Beijing* was published by Kegan Paul International in 1996. His current research interests are the social and political changes in the Chinese countryside and Chinese migration and emigration, and his most recent publications in these fields are *The Chinese in Europe* (edited with G. Benton), Macmillan, 1998, and *Internal and international migration: Chinese perspectives* (edited with H. Mallee), Curzon, 1999. Frank Pieke's general anthropological interests revolve around the issues of social action, agency and personhood.

PETER RIVIÈRE is Professor of Social Anthropology at the University of Oxford. He has had an interest in the northeast corner of South America since he first went there in 1957. As well as his field research among the Trio Indians of Surinam and the Brazilian frontiersmen of Roraima, he has published a comparative work on the native peoples of the region (*Individual and society in Guiana,* Cambridge, 1984) and a book on the nineteenth-century British-Brazilian boundary dispute (*Absent-minded imperialism,* Tauris, 1995). He is currently working on other aspects of the history of the area, including a volume for the Hakluyt Society on the nineteenth-century scientific traveller, Sir Robert Schomburgk.

ACKNOWLEDGEMENTS

The present volume owes its origin to an 'away-day' seminar held in September, 1997, by staff at the Institute of Social and Cultural Anthropology, University of Oxford. This seminar was supported by a grant from the Teaching and Learning Network for Anthropology (itself funded by the Higher Education Funding Council for England and Wales). A second round of discussions was held in March, 1998. In preparing the text of the revised papers for publication, the editors would like to acknowledge the very helpful assistance provided by staff of the Institute, Isabella Birkin, Mike Morris and, especially, Gina Burrows.

INTRODUCTION

FIELDWORK AND THE PASSAGE OF TIME

Paul Dresch and Wendy James

To research, write, and teach good anthropology does not depend only on first-hand fieldwork. A moment's reflection reminds us that the world is full of 'sources' on the forms of human life and experience, both linguistic and nonlinguistic, to the point indeed of overwhelming a scholar. Historians cannot keep up, and on most topics have to restrict themselves to processing a fragment of what is available. Our concerns overlap with theirs. Nor should we forget the importance in anthropology of earlier desk-bound writers for whom the advancement of professional fieldwork was one element among many in the larger project of comparative 'human sciences'. Marcel Mauss, from his Paris study, was a vigorous proponent of more and better fieldwork, but this was by no means to replace the use of existing historical, linguistic, archaeological and museological sources.[1]

While even today most would admit, perhaps, that the talent for doing good fieldwork does not come naturally or equally to everybody, to perform it has often been a distinctive requirement, at times almost seeming to define our discipline. This has had the effect of diluting expectations and cheapening, in a sense, the currency: all kinds of neighbouring subjects are prone now to adding a little 'fieldwork' or descriptive observation to their research practice, while funding for the classic two years' full immersion for the mainstream anthropologist – in Britain, at least – has virtually disappeared. The emphasis has slipped towards fieldwork of less than a year as part of a student's educational experience. The slippage helps fuel arguments for a return to older standards, and the idea of fieldwork as the defining purpose of anthropology is thereby reinforced among those who might wish to debate wider issues.

Nick Allen takes a sceptical look at this situation in our concluding chapter, arguing that we do not need to have everybody in the field for years on end and that anthropological understanding need not rest on fieldwork per se or on the quality of personal engagement. At the same time, not all anthropology (perhaps not very much, in fact) can be built on existing sources, and the need for extended study is one 'we continually have to defend from bureaucratic rationalizers and the enemies of academic freedom' (Barnes 1988: 247).

Anthropologists sometimes fetishise fieldwork, it is true, though the term was never theirs alone: archaeologists and geographers, for instance, do fieldwork and have done so for a long time. In recent years, however, anthropologists in particular have come to feel increasingly uncomfortable about spreading practices of rapid field assessment in economics and development studies, the taping of informants in social psychology, the interviewing of consumers in market research and the holding of 'focus-group' discussions to investigate the opinions of voters or television viewers. These practices, described as fieldwork or ethnography, suggest that directed research can be more immediately productive than enquiry seeking quietly the local terms of life. Some anthropologists no doubt feel their turf has been invaded. Others, however, have more serious concerns and ask themselves what it is that justifies a patient engagement of the kind anthropology pioneered, for simply going somewhere – whether halfway around the globe or a few miles from your office – does not define fieldwork as anthropologists do it, nor does staying somewhere longer than do most economists.

In 1997 modest funds were made available in the UK to enable anthropology departments to discuss the teaching of methods.[2] This was welcomed in view of the general dearth of funding for research that might use those methods, particularly overseas. (The comparison with France gives pause for thought; one wonders on occasion what value British governments place on the world around them.) Life 'in the field' is a method not easily taught, if indeed it can be 'taught' at all, and some mystique adheres to the practice which for students can translate into plain mystery. The mystery can usually be dispersed by spelling out the implications of enquiry in different settings, at odds though the results may be with simpler visions of methodology. A group of us at Oxford took the opportunity to hold a small conference on fieldwork and then developed draft papers through a further meeting and discussions among ourselves.[3] This volume is the outcome.

The literature on fieldwork is now large, and some of the issues raised are examined by David Parkin at the end of the book. The dominant concerns of much recent debate, however, have been focused away from what used to be confidently called 'method' and concentrated rather upon the role and responses of the fieldworker as an individual apprehending the world through their particular perspective, personal experience, and imagination.[4] Feminist arguments have been effective and powerful here. Our effort in this volume is a complementary one, to redress the balance and consider again the continuing presence of an intransigent historical world and the challenge this presents to sustained description and interpretation. The passage of time in retrospect diminishes the significance of the individual researcher but emphasises the materiality of the world we live in; neither fieldwork nor anthropology, nor yet the lives of those who do such things, is adequately represented by the motif of some brief encounter.

Anthropology and the passage of time

All of the contributors to the present volume, like most anthropologists, have long-term interests in the areas on which they write, and specific episodes of personal fieldwork are only part of the general story. The 'arrival scenes' made much of in critical accounts of classic monographs (see James's response in chapter 3) are a minor preface to engagements that may extend over decades and involve, in sometimes interesting as well as compelling ways, ageing in parallel with people living different lives from ours. Everywhere has its literature, also. At the least, one has an academic literature which offers ready-made topics one might pursue or try consciously to avoid but cannot ignore. Often an indigenous literature, whether ancient or modern, both reveals and obscures far more of interest. Poetry, memoirs, local histories, newspaper pieces on current affairs, television and film, music and dance, plastic art, all are grist to the mill of understanding. These materials have to be transformed by imagination and analysis, and even years of fieldwork do not equal or replace the whole of research activity. What fieldwork may be, in the midst of this, depends on a broader view of anthropology.

In Oxford, as in many universities around the world, museums provided a starting point. Anthropology was thus taught at the Pitt Rivers Museum from the 1870s. 'Social anthropology' at Oxford later drew inspiration from developments at the LSE and Cambridge, as well as from Paris, and by the 1950s had grown away from the museum to establish a distinctive, intellectually ambitious character (James 1998: 4–10). Well before structuralism swept the humanities, anthropology in Britain earned respect from disciplines such as history, philosophy and theology. It was not primarily anthropology's field material, nor the personal experience of its authors, that helped secure this recognition but rather the way that ethnographic information was analysed. The 'exploratory' base of ethnographic testimony was vital, however. It is still vital to the work we do, as museum practice itself now testifies. Hélène La Rue's account (in chapter 10) of her work as ethnomusicologist and curator illustrates how mobile the context is in which 'collection' takes place and performance must be understood. The work of Clare Harris on Tibetan art, largely based on the productions of refugee communities, offers also a refreshing perspective on an established topic, and one which crucially depends, as does La Rue's, on insights from first-hand study – not just of the art but of people's lives (Harris 1997, 1999).

To quote David Pocock, anthropology is an 'empirical philosophy' (1988: 203). As such it is a branch of humane enquiry, a 'science' like history in so far as the enquiry is disciplined in certain ways but a different matter from, let us say, genetics or cell biology. R.G. Collingwood specified the difference in terms of the fact that human phenomena have both an outside and an inside aspect. 'In the case of nature, this distinction between the outside and the inside of an event does not arise. The events of nature are merely events, not the acts of agents whose thought the scientist endeavours to trace' (Collingwood 1993 [1946]: 214). The 'thought' signalled here is not solely that of explicit reason, nor a formula for individualism, but rather that underlying the assumptions of a period, a cultural climate, a shared tradition.[5] Evans-Pritchard, evoking Collingwood, laid out half a century ago one version of the ideal, associating anthropology with history as he conceived it:

> The thesis I have put before you, that social anthropology is a kind of historiography, and therefore ultimately of philosophy or art, implies that it studies societies as moral systems and not as natural systems, that it is interested in design rather than in process, and that it therefore seeks patterns and not scientific laws, and interprets rather than explains. These are conceptual, and not merely verbal, differences. The concepts of natural system and natural law, modelled on the constructs of the natural sciences, have dominated anthropology from its beginnings, and as we look back over the course of its growth I think we can see that they have been responsible for a false scholasticism which has led to one rigid and ambitious formulation after another. Regarded as a special kind of historiography, that is as one of the humanities, social anthropology is released from these essentially philosophical dogmas and given the opportunity, though it may seem paradoxical to say so, to be really empirical and, in the true sense of the word, scientific (Evans-Pritchard 1962 [1950]: 26).

Few would any longer argue. Others reached similar views by different routes, and in each case the passage of time in anthropology as a subject will be seen in specific ways.

The views of David Pocock and of Louis Dumont (both of whom taught at Oxford in the post-War years) can be related to Evans-Pritchard's, as they themselves made plain. Perhaps the most interesting of their practical initiatives, however, was the establishment of a journal that aimed to reconcile studies of a classical literature with enquiries in the field, *Contributions to Indian Sociology*. Literate traditions had been marginal to anthropology and vice versa in the broader philosophical or historical study of regional civilisations. Indian ethnography, it seemed, was what 'broke the jinx' (Dresch 1992: 20). If the Second World War were taken as a watershed, anthropology might surely separate in two on these grounds. The engagement of 'other cultures' with Western tradition on one side of the line was timeless and direct; on the other, and increasingly through the decades, both contextualised and nuanced. Franz Steiner's comparative analysis of the moral ideas of danger and of truth, and his efforts to develop a social anthropology of labour, also illustrate a convergence with philosophical and historical questions.[6] As a subject, however, anthropology has always worked on at least three levels, which are worth distinguishing: humanity at large, geographical or cultural areas, and ethnographic particularity. Increasing subtlety in the second domain is an index of the subject's change and maturity. The alignment of the first and last domains defines the subject itself and colours most traditions of anthropology.

Dumont wrote memorably of students' realisation, from Mauss's teaching, of themselves as social beings (Dumont 1970 [1966]: 7). Pocock developed when he taught at Sussex the distinctive idea of a 'personal anthropology', not an understanding of oneself so much as of one's shareable relation to the world.[7] Godfrey Lienhardt remained part of Oxford anthropology from the late 1940s to his death in 1993 and while his writings on the Dinka set a new standard for ethnography, his particular knack, one might think, was to treat all circumstances as equally familiar and as equally strange – all equally as 'fieldwork'. He provoked many of us to see, as he did, the life around us as no less exotic than any report from Africa.[8] The views of Rodney Needham and Edwin Ardener are cognate also, although fieldwork was a small part of the former's anthropology and a large part of the latter's. Needham's greatest contribution was surely the careful demonstration that, while terms of professional art had no necessary substance, terms of local life were a key to understanding;[9] and what some might call 'nominalist' anthropology, though Needham would not have used such terms, is now the subject's common sense. Ardener theorised our situation as analysts more explicitly than most, exploring the implications of a world in which forms of sense overlap in ways at once revealing and concealing a common, if dispersed, humanity.[10] The formula of anthropology as 'empirical philosophy' would perhaps have been acceptable to all.

The history of the discipline was integral to teaching in this tradition, for anthropology is not a subject in which unilineal schemes of progress allow 'paradigms' to wipe the slate clean in displacing predecessors. To understand an author's meaning one 'must know what the question was ... to which the thing ... said or written was meant as an answer' (Collingwood 1970 [1939]: 31), and the questions change more rapidly than do the explicit terms; but further than this, an historical awareness is needed also to understand one's own position. There is no Archimedean point to stand on, nor any polestar from which to take one's bearing. In the last twenty years an autonomous history of the subject has come to seem less attractive, and one now has to see anthropology in broader intellectual terms, sometimes leading and sometimes following the movement of thought in places where it is written, if 'professional' debates are fully to be understood (Kapferer 1990, Dresch 1992: 23–24). In parallel with this development, the false distinction between movement and stasis in different societies, which in the nineteenth century gave the subject its distinctive start, has been recuperated. Though not quite in the sense Evans-Pritchard envisaged, we have become a subset of historiography.

To take an historical view, in part, is to distinguish oneself and one's understanding from the immediacy of experience, and while immediacy is sought in fieldwork, to capture it in writing or on film is not the sole end. We should recall Lévi-Strauss's reflections, in the book which recorded his own first-hand travels in South America, on his early passions for geology, psychoanalysis and Marxism, which all sought realities behind immediate appearance. He was willing to agree that experience enveloped reality, but there was no simple continuity between the two and in fact could not be (Lévi-Strauss 1961: 61–62). Does this mean a flattening of experience, a denial of what occurs? It is true that, as Lionel Trilling said, 'to minds of a certain sensitivity "the long view" is the falsest historical view of all ... ; seen from a certain distance, it says, the corpse and the hacked limbs are not so very terrible, and eventually they even begin to compose themselves into a "meaningful pattern"'(Trilling 1955: 201). O'Hanlon's chapter, 'A view from afar', in this volume confronts the issue in making sense of a battle he stumbled into in New Guinea. The initial problem seemed a tension between voyeurism and lack of feeling. In fact the feeling required was locally of a specific kind and spectatorship an essential part of the encounter: not to have grasped the assumptions of those involved would have been the error, sacrificing local sense to an alien aesthetic of the self.

The long view – or the broad view which anthropology favours – is a necessary corrective to the feeling, which we all remember from our early teens, of being the first person on earth things have ever happened to; and the burning assumption, of course, that everyone's feelings must surely be the same as ours. A sense of history requires one to downplay one's own uniqueness and do justice to that of those one lives with. To reduce accounts of fieldwork to autobiography would be wrong intellectually as much as morally, for it obscures the means by which knowledge is produced in shared encounters and falsely objectifies what in fact one knows.

Close acquaintance

As an anthropologist one tries to make intelligible, to oneself and others, forms of human life. These are complex, for they conjoin many subjectivities and by definition no one account is adequate; yet they possess a certain objectivity despite this, for, at the least, there is a choreographed circulation of words, images, made things, formulae of interaction, which recur in a particular setting and inform the lives of people living there. This is true even in settings which no one 'owns' in a cultural sense: the etiquette of airports, for instance, would be worth study. Far more interesting, however, are those settings in which people build some enduring sense of shared position. Whether clustered in a village or spread across the internet or family visits, the imageries which characterise such particular lives involve currencies of reference held partially in common and forms of interaction which are, as the saying goes, second nature.

To stray beyond such currencies is in some degree to be unintelligible. Most of us, most of the time, pay small attention to the fact and simply live our lives, but in fieldwork one does pay attention: one notes the obvious, at home or abroad, and tries to think explicitly, 'What must be the case to get from this point in what was said [or done] to that?' (see Dresch's discussion in chapter 5). To understand forms of human life is to grasp connections, most of which remain implicit (see Banks's demonstration in chapter 9, discussing tape-recorded conversations with Jains about their past), and until one engages with people closely one does not know what those connections are.

The fact that anthropology cut its teeth, as it were, on distant places is important, for that made obvious the fact that lives may differ in ways one cannot simply 'observe' or measure. For a long time the obvious truth was denied: 'all that we may loosely call the realm of ideas was reduced to epiphenomenal status' (Pocock 1988: 204). At a later date, in reaction to empiricism, categories seemed the major issue and Durkheimian principles of 'classification' and 'collective representations' made explicit the notion that there were starting points for analysis distinct from the public language of Western capitalism.[11] In no case, in the West or elsewhere, would one now wish to stop at the level of categories or of representation in any form. In Lionel Trilling's formulation:

> Somewhere below all the explicit statements that a people makes through its art, religion, architecture, legislation, there is a dim mental region of intention of which it is very difficult to become aware. We now and then get a strong sense of its existence when we deal with the past, not by reason of its presence in the past but by reason of its absence .... The voice of multifarious intention and activity is stilled, all the buzz of implication which always surrounds us in the present (1955: 205–6).

It surrounds us in familiar circumstances, when we know what is going on or have some project that defines our presence. When we do not know – as often a tourist does not – then the buzz of implication is replaced by spectacle, a tableau of the exotic and the stuff of postcards. Connections, implications and intention are all missing.

When we fail to reflect on our position, we enter the realm of ideology, not a realm of ideas, as Trilling points out (1955: 286), but a realm where thought of any conscious or rational variety ceases. Peter Lienhardt's essay on rumour, some years ago, signalled the need to seek what lies behind and conjoins the kind of absurd narrative that people themselves half know means nothing: 'Rumours which produce integration in terms of feeling without thought are the voice of the mob before the mob itself has gathered' (Lienhardt 1975: 131). The sundry British media events of the last decade remind us how true that is. The distant and everyday exemplify routinely the same principles, however, and Maurice Bloch has portrayed the obligation to understand the inarticulate even in respect of 'kinship'. Only after some time in the field did he discover the existence of (untheorised) moieties in the marriage practices of the Zafimaniry of Madagascar: 'There is ... nothing mysterious about a kinship structure which operates without people knowing its rules ...; [it is] the product of concepts and schema which are nonverbal and about which it is not necessary to speak' (1998: 51). He also highlights ways in which historical memory cannot be condensed into verbal narrative (47–49). Somehow one must bring to light the assumptions linking narratives, actions and silences; for without those assumptions what is said explicitly cannot properly be understood.[12]

Fieldwork in the simplest sense is needed to find things out. The existing literature on many places, groups of people, or types of activity is too weak to be of analytical use (see Barnes's account in chapter

11; the very language group of the people he went to live with was misidentified). But fieldwork of the specific kind that anthropologists do, whether staying in one place for a long time or going back repeatedly over years and decades, is necessary because the 'buzz of implication' which informs real life is otherwise unheard. A tableau of the exotic may be all one has, on the model of stiffly posed photographs in formal robes.[13] Or one may have a falsely familiar tableau where roles and appearances seem immediately to make sense and one forgets the complexity of people's lives. Rayna Rapp, for instance, uncovered a tangle of silent raw feeling, duplicity and crossed motivations in her study of the 'unborn children' debate in the United States, a distinctly anthropological enquiry into people's lives in a world of public principle versus private person (Rapp 1999). One strong point of fieldwork is its wager that listening to people, wherever they may be and whatever they are doing (however much, indeed, their particular rhetoric is found sympathetic or otherwise), may be worth the time.

To sustain one's awareness of the unsaid is taxing. The ideal, as Barnes notes below in citing Evans-Pritchard, would be several return visits interspersed with episodes of rethinking: his reason for saying so is a lack of comprehension among funders and administrators of what research entails (compare Barnes 1988: 247). But the ambition of being a 'full-time ethnographer' would still entail a punctuated life, a pattern of reflection and field-enquiry arranged in discrete episodes (compare Lévi-Strauss 1977: 15–16), for to live in a particular setting for any time is to acquire the automatisms of the everyday. Joan Burke explained this after several years of combining anthropology in a Catholic mission in the Congo with vocational duties as a teaching sister: 'Such an "immersion" experience tends with time to render ... many of one's observations banal. With this goes the related problem of retracing and unpacking what have become almost "second nature" understandings' (Burke 1989: 222). To bring to mind the basis of those understandings is a large part of anthropology's business, and analysis begins often from a mismatch of expectation among different settings. The passage of political time means that, as Parkin puts it (see chapter 4), 'there is always more revelation where that came from'; but a quietly domestic time-scale produces the same effect, for the long-term fieldworker, both observing and analysing as they go along, must somehow keep track of successive resolutions of difference and familiarity which the reader of a finished monograph or a set of articles cannot experience.

To reconcile late familiarity with early mismatch, and thus to make available some part of one's knowledge to those who were not there, poses a literary challenge. Properly, a careful and nuanced form of writing links the argument of an article or book in some way with what went to make it up, and the pegs on which one sets such writing are seldom those of positivist common sense. Walter Armbrust, for instance, begins an exposition of modern Egypt from a simple quotation, of a kind we all use in our own worlds and too easily ignore in those of others; to explain what that quotation 'means' in real life requires a book embracing poetry, popular song and cinema as much as political economy (Armbrust 1996). Geschiere writes on 'witchcraft' yet speaks primarily of wealth and power in modern Cameroon (1997 [1995]). Donham's ethnography of the Ethiopian revolution (1999) moves between fragmentary vignettes of the capital and of the remote traditional kingdom of Maale to depict an unexpected pattern of collusion and dialectic between the detailed expressions of socialist fervour and such seemingly distinct forms of 'modernism' as evangelical Christianity. The visiting 'Marxist' revolutionaries were shown by local Christians where to bury the late king's bones in a low place; for Maale, whose kings were always buried in the highest mountain, this was the 'quintessentially revolutionary act ... Maale's equivalent of the beheading of Louis XVI' (ibid.: 53).

A revolution was long ago wrought in historiography by attention to numismatics, inscriptions, styles of handwriting, a range of what until the late nineteenth century was thought ephemeral. Anthropology still encounters, on occasion, criticism of a kind that historians encountered before their subject fully found its method – why bother with the length of those men's skirts or those women's trousers, or with why the tassles on people's hats are of different length? Detail is often the clue to implicit worlds, as archaeologists have always appreciated (see for example Gosden 1994, 1999). What historians, archaeologists and anthropologists have in common here is a wish to get beyond appearances, to see a dance or a document, a meal or the layout of a court as something more than spectacle, to make it intelligible to ourselves and others. Recent forms of enquiry short-circuit the process and, while claiming to give us 'knowledge' of the social world, render it opaque to understanding. If we ask what is really known, beyond stereotypes and headlines, of the inhabitants of British cities, we find the answer is almost nothing. The shops and offices and pubs are full of 'unknown citizens':

> Our researchers into public opinion are content
> That he held the proper opinions for the time of year;
> ...
> He was married and added five children to the population ...
> Was he free? Was he happy? The question is absurd:
> Had anything been wrong, we should certainly have heard. [14]

Deal with our citizen in social terms, as anthropologists do by inclination, and we realise that most of human life around the globe is a blank space.

Social forms and 'data'

In the sixty years since Auden published his poem the phenomenon he wrote of has become a still more dominant feature of 'mass' society. Yet these facts which masquerade as data (that is, as something merely given) belong to someone, and in the case of 'objective' enquiries belong to those who commissioned the research, who themselves are then enchanted by the product. One need only tune in to the morning radio to hear this happen. Vast surveys tell us what we knew already, or tell us truths which a modicum of patient listening in pubs or shops shows to be only partial or in serious respects not to be truths at all. Bureaucratic reality becomes rationalised to fit the survey form: one can sympathise, indeed, with Pieke's Chinese bureaucrats (chapter 6, below) for whom information is power and its dissemination 'propaganda work'. Yet somehow, in garbled fashion, the answers to pre-set questions must express a reality organised in different terms. Hence, as John Davis puts it for a newly revolutionary Libya, 'the spectacle of rulers putting their ears closer and closer to the ground in the hope that they would eventually hear some whisper which they would recognise as the authentic voice of the people' (Davis 1987: 135), and governmental fascination in Britain for the moment with, for instance, 'focus groups'.

Anthropologists found out a long time ago that pre-set questions give back only what one chose to ask, and the spectacle all around us of empiricism confirming its assumptions at the expense of connected thought is sobering. One remembers the line from Gaston Bachelard which Rodney Needham quoted, 'one must reflect in order to measure, not measure to reflect' (Needham 1971: xvi). Here at least is a point of method on which professionals in the subject might all agree. Again anthropology's initial experience of 'distance' was helpful in establishing the point. The lesson was taught by Edmund Leach (1961) that the very attempt to standardise terms, and thus attain objectivity of a simple kind, blocks understanding: if the case at hand involved father-daughter sex in the Trobriands not being 'incest' and the fact that among the Lakher of Burma children of one mother by different fathers could marry, then so much the clearer the demonstration that common sense among the English-speaking middle classes was 'not a necessary model for the whole of human society' (ibid.: 27).

Leach himself rejected the comparison of whole societies in favour of analysing the principles of 'partial systems'.[15] Nonetheless, the seeming boundedness of human groups and their traditions as presented in the literature of that period (in the backwash, perhaps, of empire) allowed difference to be taken as largely given and anthropology to be located in the passage of time as having grasped a fleeting opportunity which one day might disappear.

> If one ... asks what will become of anthropology when economic progress
> has transformed all peoples into modern citizens of the world, one could
> answer that at that moment anthropology will have progressed sufficiently
> that we can construct an anthropology of ourselves, which would probably
> not have been possible had the existence of societies different from us not
> forced us to come out of ourselves to look scientifically at man as a social
> being (Dumont 1972 [1952]: 21)

That elision of a particular anthropology ('we', 'ourselves') with
knowledge of humanity at large was common,[16] and aligned with
viewing much of the world as what Eric Wolf calls 'people without
history' (1982). Pocock more realistically expressed the hope of seeing
at least distinctive Indian and Japanese anthropologies (Pocock 1971:
x–xi), if not other sundry versions too, to complement those grounded
in Euro-American experience. To some extent, in fact, this has happened. Increasingly one has Japanese colleagues 'in the field', for
instance, though still sadly fewer studying Britain, France or the
United States than these latter countries have working in Japan.[17] The
ambition of a true 'science of humanity', existing in the exchange of
reflection and investigation, remains unfulfilled and of its nature can
never be completed. Yet it deserves pursuing.

There is more at stake, as one can see, than 'qualitative method'.
The very image of 'method' perhaps suggests a scientistic model
whereby progress is made by refining a single set of terms applicable to
all cases and adapted to circumstance primarily in their mode of application. One conceptualises, in a system of that kind, tests the model by
experiment or research and reconceptualises in the light of experience
to attain a better fit of facts to model. In anthropology this vision of
research works poorly:

> ... the two processes of experimentation and conceptualisation are not sep-
> arate. If there is a difference between scientific experience in general and
> this, it is that in anthropology experience is not determined solely by an
> hypothesis but itself reacts on the concepts themselves and in fact con-
> tributes to the construction of scientific concepts. The identification of
> observer and observed results in experience taking hold of the observer
> himself (Dumont 1972: 20)

The term 'science' here has a value not usual in English, and 'experience' is conceived broadly; but the argument applies equally to what
some might assume would be thoroughly distinct activities – the pursuit of anthropology in general and the conduct of field research. Each
demands a constant realignment of terms, to reveal tacit interconnections and to discover the analyst's position in a broader world.

Integration in the world economy has not, of course, meant
homogenisation of what once appeared 'other cultures': if anything,

rather the opposite has happened, with groups defining themselves against their neighbours with increasing ferocity, as it often seems, yet in oddly uniform terms of difference. The modern situation resembles in some respects the 'archaic' terrain that Lévi-Strauss once depicted for Lowland South America: '... an established semantic environment whose elements [are] used in all kinds of combinations – not so much ... in a spirit of imitation but rather to allow small but numerous communities to express their different originalities by manipulating the resources of ... a common conception of the world' (Lévi-Strauss 1969 [1958]: 8). The theme has been explored elsewhere by James, Boddy, Dresch, Just and others (see James, ed.: 1995) in an attempt to face up to what presents itself as raw distinction and yet plainly derives from larger patterns of expectation.

The depth of difference apparent in anthropology's earlier imaginings is not so easy to penetrate as once it was. Difference at ethnographic level is entirely real, however, and postcolonial realities add some urgency to requests for careful and detailed fieldwork. Standardised terms ('democracy', 'pluralism' 'civil society') are traded among governments as chiefs and empire-builders in tales of precolonial times used to swap glass beads, or for that matter opera-hats, beyond the actualities of rum for gold and slaves for muskets.[18] As Jean Bayart puts it (1993), the political language of the present world is like a 'pidgin'. The users of such language, for all that they share terms, bring to them very different assumptions which demand exploration at both ends or all ends of shared usage: talk of 'democracy', let us say, is no more self-explanatory in the case of a Washington functionary 'validating' other countries' politics, than in the case of some 'local' functionary working towards renegotiation of a loan on favourable terms at Washington's expense. The widespread acceptance of 'culture' as something possessed and celebrated raises the same issues. Laura Peers, for instance, demonstrates the complexities which run through representing 'native peoples' in Canada, whereby everyone involved, including those represented, is drawn into practical collusions in shared imagery such as that of the heritage museum (Peers 1994, 1999), the value of which on private reflection may be deeply various.

What one says is never, in any setting, self-explanatory. This was always the advantage of the term 'collective representation' over 'collective conscience', making clear that the effect and value of public forms on those involved may differ but the forms still structure a partly shared reality. In many societies, to take a basic case, the standard etiquettes of greeting, regardless of what disasters have occurred, may be of the form, 'What news?', 'The news is good'. No one with any sense would stop at recording the mere utterance. The claim that nearly everyone in China is 'Han' or nearly everyone in Japan is 'middle class'

are solidified versions of this phenomenon, and the imagery of individual virtue may work in the same way, as Pocock reports his Indian
acquaintances saying simply, 'I am a good man' (1988: 207). None of
these claims is such as to be refuted or accepted as fact but rather each
must be understood.

The phenomenon of the counters of interaction never being all of
the interaction advertised recurs everywhere, for it is part of being
human, but in the world as we find it, where factitious uniformity is
imposed both among states and within them, the necessity to 'interpret' common terms brings the inheritance of anthropology into fresh
focus. 'Social scientists on contract research are baffled, and at times
disgusted, at what appears as the "leisurely" time frame of anthropological research and the refusal, typical of many of us, to define
"issues" before, and even while, research is proceeding' (Baumann
1988: 229). But until one stays and listens, one genuinely does not
know what the 'issues' are and everything pretending otherwise is
obfuscation, an imposition of one group's vision on the complexities of
others' lives. The product of a patient engagement with social life is
that other endeavours – be they 'social studies' at home or 'international relations' abroad – seem often to be asking the wrong questions.

How good, then, is the material an anthropologist gathers? (We are
referring here to the material they produce in their tape-recordings,
notes and photographs, which later is open to multiple, though
scarcely arbitrary, reinterpretation; see Parkin's discussion in chapter
4.) Quality varies with circumstance. Length of residence and sustained revisits help, of course, in so far as one simply learns more. But
we should go a little further. Malinowski's famous 'synoptic tables',
though scarcely a fair representation of his own more perceptive practice, expressed the ambition of producing a total record of the kind
with which students often find themselves obsessed – a sort of dream
of the secret police as if recording every act and conversation would
allow complete knowledge.[19] It would not. Listening to the tapes would
take as long as recording them, and as the person-hours of analysis
multiplied so reality would slip away. This totalising model of 'observation', participant or otherwise, leads to absurdity. The question
might be posed in reply of how 'representative' an enquiry can be
which rejects the possibility of analytical closure.[20]

In practice certain patterns are widespread. One might only need to
go through a greeting ritual a few times to get the hang of it, for
instance, and the thousands of occurrences afterwards, be this Sur-
biton or Papua New Guinea, hardly each need listing. But exceptions
to the rule occur. Or one finds that the rule one had formulated, tacitly
or in a notebook, from experience was poorly drafted. Or one finds,
most often, how limited was the set of cases one had taken for the

whole: some variance of rank or age, of season or circumstance, intervenes and the significance of the greetings one had earlier learned alters. But again mere multiplication of cases is no help, for even one case may be sufficient to change one's view. All analyses involve what Ardener once called a 'guess at the programme' (1989: 47–60).[21] Very little is simply 'given'. If greetings in the city, for instance, are not those of the countryside, then country and city are distinguished and one must go on to determine in which circumstances that distinction matters: who counts as a 'peasant', as it might be, for whom on what occasion. The question of representative 'samples' is replaced by that of, often tacit, local self-definitions.

If we wish to say our lives are structured (this is one way, and only one, of saying life may be made intelligible), we must soon admit that 'there is a range of structures: some conscious, some unconscious' (Ardener 1989: 43) which inform both action and perception, and the number of possible connections among items of 'data' is in theory indefinitely large. People elsewhere are in the same position, and fieldwork thus involves the meeting of at least two sets of layered implication. At surface level, so to speak, as Bourdieu points out, conversations between enquirer and informant to start with comprise a mismatch of gaps, of things that are not worth saying (Bourdieu 1977: 18); as familiarity grows, and indeed a certain sense of complicity, the gaps in each account align with those in the other, and the exotic tends to the familiar without commentary. One lapses into new automatisms, simply 'knowing' how to greet one's neighbours and acquaintances.

The philosophy of what we know can become complex. Ardener himself invoked 'syntagmatic' against 'paradigmatic' structures, which in later, more elaborate forms lost many readers, but the basic idea is simple: before one can follow the course of events one must know the types of events at issue. The most powerful of Ardener's images for a general readership probably remains the first, the empiricist measuring of how and where the legs of chairs skid off knots in wooden floorboards and the building up of a complex analysis through masses and velocities and coefficients of friction. As Ardener points out, the simple statement, 'This is a dining room', renders the process null. 'Except on Thursday from seven until eleven when it is a dance hall.' And even when a formal dinner is going on, the Queen may not yet have 'dined' or the haggis not yet been 'piped' (Ardener 1989: 48). One definition nests inside another.

Hence, the importance of trying possible connections, of pursuing conventions in different contexts, of hearing and seeing the kind of interwoven reference that may emerge in stories, song, encounters, art and gestures – those passing hints of iconic connection that so occupy fieldworkers in the course of day-to-day enquiry. Such perceptions are a matter far more of 'recognition' than of 'observing'. To a great extent, at home or abroad, one hears and sees only what already one half knows, and fieldwork is therefore more experimental than most accounts suggest, a point on which again the imagery of 'method' makes the process more opaque to students than need be the case. To put the matter simply for the sake of clarity, one is constantly thinking the equivalent of 'There must be a word for ..' or 'There must be a way of ...'. Either one spots this and moves on, or one finds its absence and has to rethink. The process has no final conclusion, but nor does it have a fixed beginning. Few anthropological reports are simply wrong; all are provisional, inadequate. The corollary perhaps, very much as for an historian, is that there is no such thing as 'bad information' but there is endless room for misunderstanding its significance: to take an extreme possibility, what one thought was the standard form of greeting between friends (all recorded with fair accuracy) might in fact be the form used to fob off foreigners.

Cases and the subject generally

If a sense of history is indispensable to anthropologists, so is a sense of place (compare Fardon, ed., 1990, among the most solidly useful of general volumes in the last decade). Regional traditions of enquiry differ. The depiction of particularity – 'the thrill of learning singular things', in that much-quoted phrase of Leibniz – requires a certain cunning of presentation: Frake, for instance, conjures up effectively the elusive yet pungent Englishness of Norfolk (Frake 1996). Most importantly for the present purpose, however, forms of fieldwork differ with forms of life. If one thinks of anthropology as a matter of paradigms and progress on the model of the simpler sciences, this is not always understood, for it then appears that 'method' should be everywhere the same and ethnographies ideally should all look the same in consequence, which is not the case.

The point is clearly presented in Peter Rivière's chapter, which we have therefore placed at the volume's start. The morally rather self-referential world of Trio Indians in the Amazon forest was easy to learn, as it were, albeit no doubt lonely at times and not a good place to fall ill. The world of poor Brazilian cattlemen, which defined itself against a metropolitan horizon of educated city folk from which Rivière was perceived to come, proved more opaque. The contrast is not a matter simply of isolation. Tales of 'lost tribes' may obscure the fact that groups of people have deliberately moved away from larger systems of power which they know about all too well (again see Rivière). There is also the question of how people define their worlds. Bob Barnes, towards the end of the volume, thus contrasts Kédang with Lamalera, the one an integrated cosmological world well suited to the methods of late structuralism, the other a world that sees itself more in terms of historical contingency and thus demands a different kind of writing (compare Barnes 1974 and 1996). Objectively, so to speak, one is no more isolated from the wider reality of history which anthropologists try to analyse than is the other; they lie, indeed, not far apart on the same island.

If there is one example in the world of people's lives seeming utterly disconnected from our own in Euro-America, it must surely be New Guinea, and O'Hanlon notes how difficult this imagery has proved for ethnographers of the region. A literature exists, and indeed filmography, on 'warfare in the New Guinea Highlands', and O'Hanlon enountered, unexpectedly, an 'example'. The battle itself, however, spectacular though it may have been, was not informative; what mattered in retrospect was the Komblos' sense of warfare as a missing centre of their world, compromised until now by secrecy and distrust among themselves and for that reason not discussed much with outsiders. Not in the battle itself but from the fact of 'having been there' a pattern of quiet and guarded assumptions becomes something one can talk about. A survey would not detect this, nor yet would a 'focus group'; the meetings O'Hanlon depicts around a smoky fire in a leaky hut were a far better chance than many will ever gain to discover what people feel and think, yet the structure of thought and feeling only comes to light when a public event turns the world, for a moment, inside out – the New Guinea version and the version of the visitor alike.

Most of the chapters deal with fieldwork in settings more akin in some ways to Rivière's cowboys than to those of, say, Trio Indians or New Guinea Highlanders. China, Japan, India, the Arab World, all obviously define themselves both within and against larger horizons and have a keen sense of their value in world affairs (Dresch refers to 'strong models'). This is not say all 'great traditions' are in some respect the same: one might almost distinguish China and the Middle East, despite their vast size and population, as Kédang against Lamelera. Scale of itself is not definitive, nor the older contrast between 'simple' and 'complex' societies. One of Needham's great contributions to anthropology's progress a generation ago was the famous case of the Purum in northern India (Needham 1962), a second-hand analysis based on Das's fieldwork, published 1945, among precisely 303 people. When the apparently 'empirical' (but misguided) question was later asked of how many alliance groups the Purum had, the answer would have required 'something like the psychoanalysis of every Purum' (Wilder 1971: 211). Many large-scale societies and global structures, meanwhile, are run by small numbers of people (in cases, scarcely more than the Purum) whose institutions have enormous reach.[22]

When the history of the late twentieth century comes to be written, such institutions as the International Monetary Fund and the World Bank will be central to accounts of many regions, and if the experience of anthropologists is any guide, the story will prove sobering. The Cold War dominated part of the fate of many countries. 'Globalisation' requires unpacking as a project and ideology of bankers,[23] just as much as one studies the unthought facts of migration, the flow of capital, and the rise of mass communications, now celebrated as much as analysed in terms of 'transnationalism' and the like. The work of Alex de Waal on patterns of collusion in the world of humanitarian aid has already prompted ripples of shock among development anthropologists and even politicians (de Waal 1997). In fieldwork one experiences only aspects of these vast phenomena, albeit aspects that many but anthropologists ignore. One cannot see the whole, however. One can only be on guard against self-centredness, and a certain cross-cutting of experience with history deserves noting. North America and Western Europe have been fortunate in the time-span these chapters cover. For fifty years we have had no large-scale wars on our territory, and we have most of us been fairly prosperous; certain other areas, which fifty years ago were in the cloying hold of empires, have been the site of almost constant warfare.

Wendy James thus found herself committed to Uduk-speakers in the Ethiopia-Sudan border land. Already in the 1960s they defined themselves in part as an 'ethnographic remnant', as survivors of destruction by a larger world. The history then recurred in modern form, and the 'field-site', as it once seemed, was overwhelmed, destroyed and displaced by apparently endless war. Here was a set of people whom an earlier anthropology would happily have seen as proper grist to its mill, small in numbers, linguistically distinct and culturally 'traditional' looking, with an oddly self-sufficient model of who they were. But to understand that model requires a history which directly involves 'ourselves': the British officers who 'pacified' the area at the turn of the twentieth century, the Sudanese anthropology students James taught or took with her to the field, and randomly international functionaries who now deliver 'aid'.

David Parkin has had the unusual chance to do fieldwork in a good many different settings and repeatedly over long periods. The Giriama once conceived themselves, quite realistically in some ways, as self-sufficient and self-defining, and anthropology in those days knew how to respond – another 'simple society'. Changes in their lives mean the equation no longer holds. Not far away lies the Swahili world (the very term for the language is Arabic for 'lowland' or 'coastal') whose members defined themselves from the start in wider terms of Islamic religion, trade and long-range connections. Yet in the period when the Giriama become plainly part of the wider world, the Swahili speakers came to specify their worth in restrictive terms. One could thus, despite anomalous shape and colour, become an 'elder' with the Giriama; but one could not become a 'scholar' in parts of the Swahili world without becoming Muslim.

Dresch continues the theme of 'strong models', of the kind young Swahili activists deploy but which in the Arab world have been integral to self-definition since before anthropology was thought of. Such models define the position of outsiders. They are not, however, restricted to particular localities; and the anthropologist, in the modern world, thus faces problems of what to say and what not to, of when to analyse or when to continue taking part. The personal relationships on which much of fieldwork rests cannot be explained in detail without betraying confidences, and the form of such relationships is sometimes denied by those who claim to speak not only *of* the people whose lives one wants to understand but *for* them. The discussion calls into question, as do many of the papers, the empiricist model from which much discussion of method still derives – 'what empiricist anthropology treats as obstacles are social facts' – and invites comparison of both research practice and forms of writing between, for instance, regions of Africa and regions of the Middle East. If the monographs read differently, there may well be compelling reasons.

Frank Pieke on China faces a different set of silences and discretions about the everyday centred heavily upon the state, and reproduced at village level or on the city street. Demands for projects to be specified in advance play into an organised opacity, and in discharging obligations of 'contract research' one finds oneself eluding the rhetoric both of bureaucrats locally and of external funders. Pieke thus writes of 'serendipity'; one must be alert not only for the unsaid but for the chance to pursue its meaning. Early in his practical experience a widespread popular revolt against authority occurred, portrayed in the Western media and playing to that media in the name of common humanity. The image of a 'total event' is important here. Most ethnographers experience such events at some point and think about them all too little, but Tian'anmen Square and O'Hanlon's New Guinea battle, for all the difference of scale and suffering, were equally worlds for a moment turned inside out. One difference is that O'Hanlon can publish photographs of the combatants at this late date, while Pieke spent a period pretending to be Frank Niming and must still use discretion in discussing the excitement and the hopes of 1989.

Roger Goodman makes the point explicit that fieldwork abroad involves the meeting of assumptions by two societies (in his case two quite powerful and modern societies, those of Japan and Britain) about each other and about themselves. The individual may be the instrument of research; but individuals are not primarily what research reveals.

Rather, the discourse of Japan on Euro-America and that of Euro-America on Japan cross-cut in ways that invite, quite explicitly, reflection. The 'total event' of Pieke's account is meanwhile displaced by the 'total institution' in Goffman's sense (Goffman 1971). To be an anthropologist in Japan or of Japan is often in fact to be a member of a school, a company or a ministry department. Non-Japanologists will reflect not only on the extraordinary uniformity of most writing on Japan, but on the difficulty of finding critical distance in such a self-consciously coherent world.

Both Goodman and Matsunaga (in the chapter following) show how tight definition of one's role need not mean simply silence or exclusion. A local tradition exists in Japan of seeking criticism in a tactical way outside the bureaucratic unit; and different roles, each tightly defined, may coexist for each person. Matsunaga does specifically what Goodman suggested in general terms, reflecting on her interaction with Japanese society to bring to light the exchange of half-thought assumptions. Few of us have quite the courage to take on, as Matsunaga does, the implications of personal disaster: one could hardly choose a more painful case than miscarriage save the loss of a child one knew. In what way was the experience 'cultural'? The process of encountering a doctor and an unsympathetic hospital, of being denied human sympathy and care, raises questions of 'foreignness' as a way of allocating blame on both sides. With distance and the lapse of time one can see a range of constraining options within which everyone involved was trapped. To 'objectify' may not be to lose the event so much as to discover what the event was.

Marcus Banks takes up the case of a highly mobile set of people, whom he first met in Leicester if not through literature, and only later in India where the relationship between literature and people took solid form. The Jains are famous for long-range trade and labour. While the circle of speakers explain events often in fragments that require tacit knowledge of family and generation, the analyst is concerned at how to depict those fragments in a discourse where the kin-links and tacit knowledge are absent and a wider story of movement and migration requires explaining. An earlier essay (Banks 1988c) deserves reading in parallel. 'Classical' fieldwork had seemed a matter of detective work, pursuing an elusive truth that might disappear if one stated the aim too clearly; shooting a film, on the basis of that experience, worked through revealing one's goal and method, and having subjects build their accounts around an explicit project (ibid.: 259). The second exploration of semi-shared experience depends upon the first, tacitly informing the shots selected so as not to present simply spectacle to audiences elsewhere.

None of the cases can be reduced to the 'lone' fieldworker. One is not of course alone, as the geneticist might be in their laboratory or the historian in an archive, for one is living among the people one hopes to write about. The forms in which they accept, reject or ignore one's presence are open to understanding and are integral to what one learns, and those forms, as we see, are far larger than the self. As Herzfeld has pointed out, the oxymoronic image of 'participant observation' often obscured this, displacing to the mythic 'field-site' all difference and disorder alike while leaving the observer or analyst with knowledge no one else could quite hope to reproduce (Herzfeld 1987: 16–17, 63, 139–41, 164–6). Rivière's early work is a test case of one sort, for in effect there was no existing literature. The patient work of the Trio in socialising their visitor is validated, however, by later accounts from other groups whose principles of moral order prove similar. Japan might furnish the opposite case, where the visitor may acquire such familiarity with both literature and mores that they cease receiving compliments on their ability. An earlier view of fieldwork, drawing perhaps on readings of Malinowski, played down such forms of objectivity: one had to 'be there' to offer an account, and distance was the guarantee of knowledge.

Hélène La Rue turns this inside out, presenting a mode of enquiry that once separated rigorously, as a canon of method, the collection and the analysis of information. Music was recorded or transcribed. The product was then compared elsewhere with other products. Yet to be an ethnomusicologist one had to have 'collected' in distant or distinctive places. The 'field' here was something of a false quest, for the reality of musical events is performance and performance conventions are as clearly brought to light by visiting musicians as by the ethnomusicologist in distant places. The Allegri Quartet are no more real and no less so than the band from Rajasthan.

Barnes insists upon a dead-pan presentation (also Barnes 1988). The chapters which precede his show the issues underlying what he describes. Here, again, in the case of very detailed work in Indonesia, the image of the lone fieldworker collapses. One may indeed be alone or with one's family in the midst of people whom one's neighbours at home know little of, but one works within a whole subject, learning from those who have written of adjacent places and producing material from which others in turn may profit. The image of compiling a dictionary, in Barnes's chapter, is memorable. Slow and patient work in collaboration with others, though it makes little mark in general commentary on anthropology, is often the most rewarding part of the whole process.

Lessons

At the start of this introduction we invoked a tradition. To locate the tradition's worth among the humanities in general we tried to cite views old enough that they could not be suspected of too great specificity or of stemming from short-term ambition by a single discipline. Let us end, then, by seeing what has changed with the passage of half a century. Here again is Evans-Pritchard in 1950. He thought, as the public often still do, that anthropology dealt with 'primitive societies':

> I believe that during this second half of the century it will give far more attention than in the past to more complex cultures and especially to the civilisations of the Far and Near East and become, in a very general sense, the counterpart to Oriental Studies ... that is to say, it will take as its province the cultures and societies, past as well as present, of the non-European peoples of the world (1962 [1950]: 28).

In some sense that has happened, but so has a great deal more. The idea of complex societies looks antique, for what would a 'simple' society look like? The old pretence of isolation is not supportable. And what difference is there in principle between non-European and European peoples, if the numerable term peoples even be admitted? There is nowadays no shortage of good ethnography done 'at home', all of which immensely complicates the very notion that Western society adds up to something distinctive that could be opposed to the non-West. Jonathan Webber's edited collection on Jewish identities in the 'New Europe' illustrates how archaic some of the older dichotomies have become, and yet also the continuing relevance of engaged first-hand research (Webber 1994).

Several of us have cited Tim Jenkins' account based largely on experience in rural France (1994), and others of his publications touch usefully on work in Britain (1999): the specificities of research are determined by the local setting, but the arguments advanced are of general relevance. Nor should we forget the relativities of 'home'. Matsunaga married into Japan, for instance; and indeed most of us have married into or out of somewhere, as often our assorted parents and grandparents did, a pedestrian fact which provides a useful check on too grand flights of theoretical fancy about self and other. As Allen points out (below, in the last of our chapters) talk of 'difference' and the 'other' and 'cultural relativism' collapses into solipsism if taken seriously.

One can see that what once seemed 'classical' fieldwork – two years in a single village, so to speak – was and still is a special approach well adapted to particular cases, but not to all. For the reasons rehearsed earlier, an experience of explicit difference was part of anthropology's development, and on balance a useful part; the experience, within that setting, of intensive acquaintance with small communities helped extend the discipline. It is not, however, the subject's sole basis, and accounts of anthropology's history might be clearer on this point than in fact they are. Not only for a lay audience but for professionals as well at a certain period, Malinowski's closely-focused accounts of fieldwork in the very specific context of the Trobriand Islands was taken as too general an exemplar (1922, 1927, 1935). A generation ago, James was asked why she had never done 'real' fieldwork, and La Rue still mentions she has 'never had the chance'. Yet of the twelve chapters presented here by people of different ages working in very different places, how many represent a quest for some ideally alien world exemplified in a single place? And if all, in various ways, examine the particularities of people's lives in places and times, they also look beyond the range of a given locale or event in seeking the possibilities of understanding.

Nick Allen's concluding chapter argues against seeing anthropology as all fieldwork. This is surely right. One might argue, indeed, against claiming all fieldwork worth the name as somehow the preserve of anthropologists. Sinclair Lewis did 'fieldwork' to write his novels and did it well. Cardinal de Retz, the great cynic of political memoirs, was in his way a fieldworker. Those whom our ancestors in the subject dismissed as 'merely travellers' – or missionaries or administrators for that matter – were often superb, and around us as a formal discipline have always been fieldworkers whom our textbook history excludes unjustly. The defining feature is not the label 'anthropologist'. The defining feature is listening for the unsaid, looking for the visually unmarked, sensing the unrepresented, and thus seeking for connections among parts of the obvious which locally remain unstated. To that degree, fieldwork of the kind anthropologists attempt is indispensable.

NOTES

1. This point was made by Dumont 1972: 11; Mauss makes it himself in a text of about 1930 which is included (in a revised English translation) as chapter 2 in James and Allen 1998; his broad approach to methods in anthropology is discussed in James's chapter 1 of the same book.
2. We are glad to acknowledge this grant made available through the Higher Education Funding Council and the Teaching and Learning Network for Anthropology, which partially supported a one-day workshop held away from the Institute of Social and Cultural Anthropology in Oxford in September, 1997.
3. One existing base we had to build on was the special edition of the *Journal of the Anthropological Society of Oxford* in 1988 dealing with the topic of 'Second fieldwork' (including papers by Banks and Barnes among our present contributors). *JASO* 19, 1988.
4. The topic of the fieldworker's identity, and how it might be affected by the experiences of fieldwork, occupied a complementary set of seminar discussions in Oxford in the autumn of 1998, in the 'Ethnicity and Identity' series organised by Shirley Ardener, Jonathan Webber and Ian Fowler. A selection of papers from that series is being prepared for publication by Kathy Szent-Gyorgyi. Parallel concerns run through, for example, van Maanen's *Tales of the field* (1988) focusing on the exercise of writing ethnography, and Bill Watson's recent collection *Being there* (1999) which illuminates aspects of 'doing' it. Three specific personal styles of fieldwork are discussed in MacClancy (1996).

5. 'We shall never know how the flowers smelt in the garden of Epicurus, or how Niet-zsche felt the wind in his hair as he walked on the mountains', a point as valid for ethnography as history; 'but the evidence of what these men thought is in our hands' (Collingwood 1993 [1946]: 296), as too is the evidence of a great deal more, as Collingwood's own work on the persistence of Celtic art forms through the Roman occupation of Britain revealed (1932).

6. Franz Steiner's best-known publication is *Taboo* (1956), now reissued in the present series. In the first chapter, he makes a clear distiction between the broader aims of social anthropology and field observations for their own sake. When he became a student of Radcliffe-Brown in 1938, social anthropology and comparative sociol-ogy were held to be 'the same thing', but field techniques had come to dominate dis-cussion and to become 'problems' in themselves. 'Simplicity seemed to enhance observability; the emphasis was on observation and on variety ... Malinowski remained unchallenged when he confused general rules concerning the compara-tive relevance of field data with theories of society' (1956: 15). See also Steiner 1954a, 1954b, 1954c.

7. Pocock 1994. Manuscript versions of this argument passed from hand to hand for two decades before eventual publication. The idea appears also in the preface to the second edition of Pocock's first general introduction to social anthropology (1971 [1961]).

8. Lienhardt 1961. A set of essays on the anthropology of religion, specifically ori-ented to 'vernacular' Christianity, was put together as a festschrift for Godfrey Lien-hardt and reflects the way he widened the horizons of the subject (James and Johnson 1988). Some of the resonance of Lienhardt's teaching is captured in the special issue of *JASO* devoted to his memory (28/1, 1998).

9. See for example Needham 1971, 1973, 1975.

10. The major papers are collected as Ardener 1989.

11. It was a series of publications concentrated in the 1960s which really established what Pocock (1971 [1961]: 72–82) diagnosed as a shift from 'function' to 'mean-ing', traceable primarily to Evans-Pritchard's anthropology. One of the first striking publications was Leach's 'Magical hair' (1958); other key works were Needham's translation of Durkheim and Mauss's *Primitive classification* (1963), Mary Douglas's *Purity and danger* (1966), and Beidelman's 'Swazi royal ritual' (1966).

12. The 'archive' (Foucault, 1972, 1980; cf. James 1988: 2–12, 25ff) has to be deduced from fragmentary evidence; it is not available for observation, but underlies what 'makes sense' in everyday domains.

13. Anthropologists have criticised such imagery in opening up a new field of sensitiv-ities to the implications of the visual: see for example the various contributions to Banks and Morphy, 1997.

14. Auden 1976.

15. Leach 1961: 6. The same idea is developed in a very different setting by Julian Pitt-Rivers (Pitt-Rivers 1977).

16. Compare, for example, the two short concluding chapters to *Tristes tropiques* where Lévi-Strauss invokes Rousseau as a guide on our quest for the 'unshakeable basis of human society', which we should find in the image of the neolithic age, from which we have so distanced ourselves by mechanical progress (Lévi-Strauss, 1961: 381–92, esp. at 389–90).

17. The discipline is now taught in a large number of Indian universities and there is a voluminous literature by Indian anthropologists. However, while this writing largely concerns itself with Indian studies and debates about Indian society, it seems to continue and reflect the dominant themes of Western anthropology about its own methods and practical relevance. There are, for example, parallel debates over the link with history and politics on the one hand, awkwardnesses about 'tribal'

ethnography, and the claims of 'village' studies as against civilisational and textual studies on the other – here Hinduism and 'Sanskritisation'. For overviews of the background see Burghart 1990, Béteille 1996.

18. See the helpful collection on 'civil society', edited by Hann and Dunn (1996).

19. The tables are set out in Malinowski 1935. Compare Marvin Harris's extraordinary 'emic' description of Mrs Harris cooking: 'Our initial concern will be with idio-episode chains emitted by single actors ... As an example of such a chain, consider the following idio-episodes which my wife kindly permitted me to record:

> ACTOR-TYPE: Adult Female
> PLACE: Kitchen
> TIME: Early Evening
> 1. Walk to cabinet.
> 2. Pull drawer out.
> ...
> 27. a. finger turn burner control.
>   b. Put down frying pan on stove burner...' (Harris 1964: 72–73).

20. Geertz has criticised the 'Jonestown is America written small' approach (1973: 21–223). But the criticism Tonkin, McDonald and Chapman encountered (1989: 19–20) that one can't study Germany because it is too big is a different issue – a mistaking of representation for mentality.

21. Granet's lucid demonstration of Chinese etiquette makes the point (Granet 1973). Social life, the treatment of the body, the orientation of human activities and the cosmos alike are patterned through and through with right/left oppositions; but there is no clear cut dichotomy organizing the whole. For example – and this gives only a hint of the exquisite 'complication' of the domain of etiquette – while it is proper to use the right hand for eating, the side to which honour and status belongs is the left. In greeting, boys are educated to cover the right hand with the left when they bow and then present the left hand; while girls should cover the left hand and offer the right. However, in time of mourning, men make their salutations as though they were women, concealing the left and extending the right hand. The precise pattern of the greeting is more generally related to the phases of ceremonial time, and thus in China: 'A left-hander is worth as much as a right-hander. More exactly, there are cultural eras, or physiological phases of the Universe, in which it is fitting to be left-handed, and other phases in which it is appropriate to be right-handed' (Granet 1973: 45, 53).

22. See for example Robert Jackall on the personal interactions of those in US corporations (1988), Georgina Born on the human aspects of the leading music research institute in Paris (1995), Cris Shore on the bureaucrats of the European Union (1993).

23. An argument lucidly set out by William Pfaff, who summarises claims that while 'globalisation' has been popularly seen as inevitable, almost natural, this belief 'was not universally shared among political economists. It originated as the sectarian enthusiasm of a minority of writers and theorists ... and it derived more from their political hostility to "big government" than from objective economic analysis ... To millions in Asia, Russia and Latin America, deregulation of the international economy must look like a vast swindle' (Pfaff 1999).

Chapter 1

INDIANS AND COWBOYS:

TWO FIELD EXPERIENCES

Peter Rivière

It has become a commonplace of anthropology that an ethnographer's personal qualities and characteristics will have an influence on his or her ethnographic production. Sex, age, educational background, psychological make-up and other features will all bear on what type of information is collected and how it is interpreted. Then there are also such matters as whether the fieldworker is alone, with a partner, or even a family; whether separate accommodation is lived in and self-provisioning is undertaken, as opposed to a high degree of dependency when both food and shelter are provided by the host community. To these factors must be added another set of influences on the outcome – the community's degree of contact with and knowledge of the society from which the fieldworker comes. Finally, and it is a point I wish to touch on briefly at the end, there is the matter of the nature of the particular society itself and the degree to which it influences the outcome.

In this contribution I want to consider two fieldwork situations in which the reaction towards me of the host communities could not have been in greater contrast. In both cases, the personal factors were pretty similar; I worked alone, and there were only four years between the two studies. I have no particular reason to believe that my character and psychological make-up had changed much, if at all, in that interval although educationally I had achieved the right to put the initials D.Phil. after my name. In other words, the difference in the two experiences can to a very large extent be attributed to the people's experience of and attitude towards the society from which I came and their assessment of it vis-à-vis their own.

The two sessions of fieldwork I want to compare concern the Trio Indians of the Surinam/Brazilian frontier and the Brazilian ranchers and frontiersmen of Roraima. The experiences in these two settings were very different because their respective knowledge, understanding and views of the outside world were radically different, having been moulded by particular sets of social, economic and political relationships. Accordingly, as a representative of that outside world, I was perceived and treated differently. There were also radically different types of communities. The Trio, although living within a modern state and not untouched by world events, were a relatively coherent and integrated society whereas the Brazilian ranchers were constituted by a looser amalgamation of individuals and families who had washed up on the frontier.

Indians

When I first went to the Trio in 1963, they were only just beginning to enter into permanent, settled contact with the non-Amerindian world. This does not mean that they had had no earlier experience of non-Amerindians. There are many indications to suggest that the Trio are composed of a number of remnant peoples, refugees perhaps from early contact with European settlers, who had fled for safety to the headwater region of the Surinam-Brazilian border. For at least two hundred years, they had been trading with the escaped slave communities, the Bush Negroes or Maroons, from the middle reaches of the Surinam rivers for manufactured goods, in particular metal cutting tools, in return for assorted items such as hunting dogs and cassava squeezers. The Trio have a number of stories about their relations with the Bush Negroes and one concerning their first contact with Europeans, all of which suggest none too happy experiences (see Koelewjin and Rivière 1987: 265–82). Indeed, even in the 1960s the Trio were exhibiting that ambivalence about outsiders that is commonly reported among Amerindians; that is the conflict between the desire for contact and the metal goods that come with it and the fear of the sickness and death that the bearers of these goods have often brought.

Although there was almost certainly contact between the Trio and the occasional European during the first half of the eighteenth century, it is not until Schomburgk's visit to them in 1843 that we start to get any details about these people. In the first half of the twentieth century various expeditions, mainly Dutch and Brazilian boundary commissions, passed through their territory, and accounts by some of their members added to what was still a scanty knowledge. None of these people stayed long, but from 1950 onwards the Franciscan missionary, Protásio Frikel, made annual visits to the Indians on the Brazilian side of the border. Although, as he stated himself, his stay in any one place during these visits was short, the total time spent among the Trio was considerable. At about the same time there were various prospecting expeditions originating from Dutch Guiana (as Surinam then was) which had disastrous consequences for the health of the Trio. Then, in 1958, the Brazilian Air Force cut a landing strip on the area of savannah in the headwaters of the West Paru. This strip proved unsatisfactory and another was made the following year which became a small air force base and the site of initially a temporary, and then from 1963 a permanent Franciscan mission (Frikel 1971: 13–17).

On the Surinam side, the late 1950s were also marked by an opening up of the interior. This was achieved through Operation Grasshopper, which involved cutting a series of landing strips which were then permanently manned by small maintenance crews. These did not impinge on Trio territory until 1960, when the strips on the Sipaliwini savanna and at the confluence of the Tapanahoni and Paloemeu rivers were made. In 1959 the government granted permission to the American Door-to-Life Gospel Mission to work among the Trio and in the following year this organisation cut an airstrip beside the Alalaparu, a small tributary of the Sipaliwini. Missionary work began there in earnest in 1961 when another mission station was also set up at Paloemeu. The Door-to-Life Gospel mission collapsed in 1962 and its work was taken over by the West Indies Mission.

When I arrived to start my fieldwork among the Trio in August 1963, the situation was thus: three mission stations were in operation, the Roman Catholics at West Paru on the Brazilian side and the Protestants at Alalaparu and Paloemeu in Surinam.[1] In both countries the missionaries had persuaded the inhabitants of a number of villages to settle around them and this process was to continue over the next few years. Prior to this the Trio, who numbered fewer than a thousand, had lived in scattered villages of thirty to fifty people, spread over nearly 10,000 square miles. The point I wish to make is that when I arrived among the Trio they had only relatively recently started living in permanent contact with non-Amerindians and the total number of these people in their territory was very small, perhaps a couple of dozen. The non-Amerindians became the source of Western goods and their presence effectively killed off the trade with the Bush Negroes. There was no regular contact between the Trio and national populations, whose representatives, in the absence of mineral wealth, made no attempts to colonise such a remote and inaccessible region. A handful of Indians had been outside their own territory but seemed to have found the experience so strange that they had difficulty in conveying their impressions to those who stayed at home.[2] In other words, Trio direct knowledge and experience of the outside world was very limited and, with the exception of those who could speak the pidgin trading language used with Bush Negroes, they were all monolingual in Trio. Even so, I was much struck by the apparent impact that the missionaries had had in a relatively short time. Both villages contained a church into which virtually all the Indians trooped once or twice a day, a school was under way, and the idea of a daily and weekly routine had been impressed upon them. However, the apparent ease with which Amerindians adopt new ideas and practices only to revert to old ways when it suits them is historically well documented and I would be less surprised today.[3]

There was no love lost between the Roman Catholics and the Protestants and the policies of evangelisation of the two denominations were very different. It is worth examining them summarily. The Protestants worked almost exclusively in the Trio language, teaching the Trio to read and write it and translating parts of the Bible, including, in due course, the whole of the New Testament, into it. Their policy was not to interfere in the subsistence economy, but clearly drawing the Indians together into a settlement many times larger than those previously existing and imposing a daily and weekly regime so that school, church and the sabbath could be fitted in did have consequences for social, political and economic life, even if the changes that occurred were not intended by the missionaries. On the other hand the missionaries made every effort to eradicate all cultural features that they perceived as in any way being associated with Trio beliefs and practices about the spirit world. These included not simply shamanic activity but such things as drinking, smoking, dancing and flute playing. The extirpation of shamanism required that shamans give up their rattles which contained the physical embodiment of their spirit familiars. How this was to be done aroused considerable anxiety as it was feared that the familiars (the Trio term for these is the same as that for pet animals, of which the dog is the prime example) would become dangerously fierce if released from the control of their masters. One of the solutions was found by giving some of them to me on condition that I would take them far away and never return with them. This accounts for the collection of Trio shaman rattles in the Pitt Rivers Museum. The disappearance of practising shamans did not, of course, remove the shamanic world-view on which it was based. In many ways the Protestants were not that interested in preparing the Trio for incorporation into the wider Surinamese society, whereas the Franciscans took the opposite approach. Their policy seems to have been to turn the Trio into Brazilian citizens.[4] They set out to teach the Trio Portuguese and most of the scriptural teaching was conducted in that language. They introduced new modes of cultivation and taught Indians to be drivers, mechanics and electricians. Work rotas were set for which the Indians were paid in coupons. On the other hand, the priests made no attempt to ban such practices as smoking, drinking and dancing and were not overly concerned about shamanism. It might be added that people moved between the missions and whereas some undoubtedly sought what was not available where they came from (such as beer, shamanism, Western medicine and goods), others travelled fired up by evangelical zeal or what Frikel was to refer to as 'spiritual terrorism' (Frikel 1971: 79).

At this point it might be stated briefly why I chose to undertake fieldwork among the Trio. I had spent nearly twelve months in 1957–8 in South America, much of the time in the interior where I had seen quite a lot of Amerindian life, which had greatly interested me. When I arrived in Oxford as a graduate student in 1962 it was with the intention of working in Amazonia, although this was not greeted with great enthusiasm by everyone. Evans-Pritchard tried to divert my interest to Africa on the grounds that nothing was known about South America. This was true, but as far as I was concerned that was just the reason for going there. But why the Trio and why Surinam; or rather Dutch Guiana? I find my memory uncertain on this point but my attention was perhaps drawn to Carib-speaking peoples by the presence in Oxford of Audrey Colson (then Butt), whom I had first met in British Guiana in 1957 and who was at the time the only South Americanist with a post in a British university. In making plans to do fieldwork I looked for a people who were relatively remote and undisturbed but not too inaccessible nor too few, and for work among whom government permission would be forthcoming. The Trio fitted the bill very well and would, geographically, have been equally accessible in Brazil. I never tried to see how readily the Brazilian authorities would have given permission, but it could not have been easier than with the Dutch whose instantaneous response was 'yes, how interesting, but we are not responsible for you'. With hindsight I am not unhappy with my choice, not least because the Trio have been spared the ravages of contact. Even today the region remains remote. It is no more accessible than it was forty years ago and the non-Amerindian population is still minute and impermanent (see Carlin 1998: 6–9).

At the beginning of the 1960s South American ethnography was in its infancy and as late as as 1974 it was still possible accurately to subtitle a book on Native South Americans, *Ethnology of the least known continent* (Lyon 1974). When I went to the field, the existing monographs on Native Amazonians could be counted on one's fingers and none of them was of the quality of those from other ethnographic regions. For Guiana there was Gillin's *The Barama River Caribs* (1936), which had a distinctly old-fashioned feel about it, with a chapter on physical anthropology including twenty tables of anthropometric statistics. While I was in the field the situation dramatically improved with the appearance of Goldman's *The Cubeo* (1963), the first genuinely modern Amazonian ethnography. This was shortly afterwards followed by Maybury-Lewis's *Akwê-Shavante Society* (1967) and two years later by my own *Marriage among the Trio* (1969). These three works, dealing with widely separated regions, each in their way started a tradition.[5] It could be said that this was not too difficult because the field was completely open. Indeed this was one of the problems in presenting Trio ethnography – what context to set it in. This explains why the theoretical discussion in *Marriage among the Trio* is based in the literature of South India and Ceylon. On the other hand, I hope this does not explain why the discussion of Amazonian relationship terminologies has still not freed itself from the Indian sub-continent.[6]

In the early 1960s the Trio classification of outsiders was undergoing a fairly radical revision as a result of new contacts that had undermined the previous relatively simple distinctions made among non-Amerindians. For present purposes it is not necessary to consider these in detail, but basically there were *mekoro* (Bush Negroes), *karaiwa* (non-Amerindians from the south, Brazilians), and *pananakiri* (non-Amerindians from the north). The last category was beginning to disintegrate as the American missionaries distanced themselves from other *pananakiri*. Nor did my presence help as I was a further anomaly. Although I obviously shared much in common with the American missionaries, particularly in general appearance and language, I clearly differed from them in many respects. I certainly did not have the possessions they had, I did not tell the Indians what to do the whole time and the way in which I lived was very different; I lived with an Amerindian family, eating their food and sleeping in a hammock. Furthermore I was not a Christian. I assumed the missionaries told the Trio this and it is certainly true that by their fundamentalist definition I was not and am not, but it did result in persistent attempts on their part to try to convert me. At the same time, while in certain ways I could be aligned with the non-missionary *pananakiri*, a rather heterogeneous cast including Dutchmen, blacks other than Bush Negroes and almost anyone else, there were just as many, even more ways, in which I differed from them also.

Clearly I was a bit of a puzzle and furthermore, although I chose to lead a sort of Amerindian life, it was totally obvious to them that I was not equipped to do so. I could do nothing that a man of my age might be expected to do – which was virtually everything. I could not cut a garden, hunt, fish, weave baskets, make bows and arrows, et cetera. I could not even talk. They were hospitable but then there is a tradition in the area of hospitality – without which it would be very difficult to move around. It has to be said that the generosity that goes with such hospitality is seen as a prophylactic against sorcery – all strangers are suspected of being sorcerers. In other words, to some extent I was feared as a potential sorcerer whose sorcery could be defused by hospitality. I was also distrusted, as any single man is, as harbouring unacceptable intentions towards the women. On the other hand, and I only learnt this on a return visit, I was also suspected of being a total failure who had been forced to leave his own village for incompetence – you must remember that they had had no experience of the world beyond the forest and assumed that all people's livelihoods were much like theirs – and indeed in practice, as I have just explained, I could do nothing and knew nothing. In other words, there also existed the view that I was no more than a harmless idiot. At the same time they caught on to the fact that I was willing to learn and they seem to have decided, although I do not know if they made an explicit decision about it, that I should be taught to be a proper person. In other words they set out to teach me how to live. Although I was never told this in so many words I do know that I was not the only person to be singled out for education. In the late 1960s a small and isolated group of hunters-and-gatherers, the Akuriyó, who lived in the area, were tracked down with missionary encouragement, and persuaded to settle alongside the Trio. The Trio were quite explicit about their intention to educate these 'children', as they referred to them, so that in due course they would grow up to be proper people with gardens, bread, basketwork and all the other cultural attainments of Trio civilisation.

On my first arrival in the village of Alalaparu, I was assigned a house in which to live whose owners happened to be away. They consisted of an elderly man and his wife, their adult son (unmarried and who behaved oddly) and a divorced daughter who, on their return, seemed a bit put out to discover an uninvited guest, but cheered up when they discovered that I had a good supply of salt. The house, which was large for that number of residents, was open sided and ideally situated alongside the village square so that, even from the vantage point of my hammock, I could see what was going on. I remember on my first evening sitting there and watching people carrying small quantities of cooked and uncooked food across the square and thinking that once one had unravelled where the food was coming from and going to one would have a fairly good understanding of the social organisation of the village. I had planned on depending on the Trio not simply for shelter but also for food so had brought very few supplies with me. Instead I was well provided with trade goods. These included knives, machetes, hoes, assorted sizes of fishhooks, fishing line, red cloth for loin cloths and aprons, mirrors and beads. Although these last have now become part of the fictional past of interaction with 'natives', they were highly valued by the Trio who used them for a range of ornaments and elaborate female aprons. I gave quite a large proportion of my goods to the village leader for him to distribute as he thought fit,[7] but I kept back part to exchange for items for the museum collection I intended to make (which is now in the Pitt Rivers Museum) and also as payment for any particular help or services. I also had a shotgun and cartridges, rather rare equipment in the early 1960s, which I used to lend to hunters in return for a part of the game which I would then hand over to my hosts. I was normally fed by my hosts although most days there was a communal meal in the village square at which I was given my share. To begin with at these gatherings I tended to be given the best, that is to say the fattiest, pieces of meat, but when it was noticed that I used to slip the lumps of boiled pig fat to small children, rather poorer, that is say leaner, portions came my way. It was not uncommon for other families to call me to eat if I happened to pass while they were doing so and I would invariably be included when drink was circulated round the village. I later found out that there were definite advantages in being a bachelor; when, for a few weeks on a later field trip, I was joined by my wife, we were regarded as a fully functioning economic unit and expected to provide for ourselves. It was the hungriest period of fieldwork that I experienced.

As far as work was concerned the major problem was language. The missionaries, who had already made good progress with the language, provided invaluable assistance but it was mainly through unceasing exposure to it that one started being able to use it. One thing I did find out was that of the people to whom I talked most adjusted their language to my level and left me with an inflated view of my improving fluency until, that is, I found myself in conversation with someone unaware of my limitations. A particular problem were the old women, most of whom were toothless and invariably whispered with their hands in front of their mouths; this difficulty was overcome by a teenage boy who voluntarily chose to act as an interpreter, repeating audibly (and, I suspect, in a simplified version) what was said. Hunting also proved problematic in so far as I tended to be too slow and too noisy for my Indian companions – I just did not seem to be designed to move rapidly and silently through tropical undergrowth. This was resolved by abandoning a young man's role and joining up with an older man whose main activity was fishing rather than hunting. He always went armed in case some game presented itself along the trail but it was a very much more leisurely business and the outings often turned into marvellous nature walks with his pointing out to me as we went such things as where animals had been feeding. There were also many other activities such as agriculture, expeditions to collect fish poison, or canoe making in which I could actively participate. There were also a very large number of sedentary occupations, from weaving to bow making, during which it was possible to carry on prolonged conversations. What did prove invaluable was their inclusion of me into their kinship system. What I mean by this is that kinship is the idiom of all Trio relationships and by definition the Trio social world is exclusively populated by people whom you address and refer to by a kin term; for someone to be a member of your social world you must know by what term you address each other.[8] How many dozen times I must have gone through the procedure of deciding with people how we would address one another I have no idea but it is a process which leaves one with an intimate knowledge of the workings of the relationship terminology. If access to people to talk to was never a problem, privacy was. This was not simply a matter of the natural curiosity about me and my belongings which on my arrival and for some weeks afterwards was absolutely intense. Rather, it was being on permanent public display, whereby it was known where you were and what you were doing every minute of the day, that I sometimes found rather trying.

If most of the time during fieldwork I was living as a pseudo-Indian, my main non-Indian interaction was with the missionaries and their families; one at each of the villages in which I lived. Despite my regrets at how they had curtailed interesting features of Trio life, their presence undoubtedly made fieldwork very much easier in all sorts of ways. They were, for example, instrumental in introducing me into the village and helping me find a family to live with. By the time I arrived they already had over a year's experience of the Trio language and provided enormous assistance with it. They also supplied a line of communication with the outside world both by radio telephone and the monthly visits by an aircraft of the Missionary Aviation Fellowship. It must also be said that their influence with the Indians was such that without their support fieldwork would have been very difficult, perhaps impossible.

If during my first spell of fieldwork among the Trio I was very much treated as an ignoramus who needed to be taught, I found on a return field trip in 1978 my role had changed somewhat and in certain areas of knowledge, such as genealogies, I had graduated to that of expert. As a result of missionary teaching, there had been some changes in Trio cosmological ideas, particularly among the younger generation. These included such practices as burial in the floor of the house and such beliefs as the soul of the deceased going to the soul reservoir on the eastern horizon. Discussing what had become very old-fashioned ideas fascinated the young, to whom they were often new, while the older people enjoyed the reminiscences. At the same time, in the intervening years, the Trio had changed. Although they had retained some of their fearfulness of outsiders, they had become more self-confident in their dealings with strangers. By then they had had contact with a wider range of different types of non-Amerindians. Many of them had visited the city of Paramaribo and at least one had been to the United States. They had also adopted a rather take-it-or-leave-it attitude towards the outside world, although it was very much 'take' if, in their estimation, it was worth it. On the other hand they still had only the vaguest appreciation of the Western economic system and declined to understand why those with apparently so much would not give it to the Trio who had so little. At the same time the strong grasp of the missionaries had weakened, there were dissenting voices and it had been cynically noted that the wages of sin were not *immediate* death.

The point is that in the early 1960s the Trio, with their relative ignorance of the outside world, were entirely secure in and proud of their own way of life; nor fifteen years later had it been significantly undermined. The Trio saw it as perfectly reasonable to help people who fell below their standard. This made fieldwork very easy because they were only too happy to teach me. They wanted me to learn and clearly derived satisfaction when I showed signs of being able to do and understand things. If this was not confined to traditional ways, about some of which, such as the process of cursing, they were often rather reticent, at least in public, their attempts to convert me to a brand of Trio-ised fundamental Christianity was a small price to pay for a group of willing informants and teachers.

Cowboys

The other fieldwork experience, among a Brazilian ranching community, could not have been more different. This took place in the very north of Brazil, on the border with Venezuela and the new state of Guyana, in what is the modern state of Roraima but what was then the Federal Territory of Rio Branco. I had first spent a few weeks in the area in 1957 and had been fascinated by the region's sheer backwardness and remoteness from the rest of Brazil. I returned to do fieldwork in 1967 and things had not changed much. The total area of the state is 230,000 square kilometres and in 1960 the population was 28,000, grown to 40,000 by 1970. In the latter year, this gives a population density of about 0.18 to each square kilometre, almost four times lower than for the neighbouring State of Amazonas. The most unpopulated part is the south and west of the territory which is mainly covered with tropical forest. To the north and east the vegetation is mainly savannah and it is on the southern edge of this and on the banks of the Rio Branco that the single town of any size in the region, Bôa Vista, lies. In 1970 its population was 17,000 or over 40 percent of the Territory's total. Although planned on a grand scale, Bôa Vista was an open, straggling and unfinished city, with cattle wandering around in the red mud or dust of its streets. Even so, it was the government and commercial centre and what services there were in the territory, such as education and health, were located here. The next largest settlement lay some miles downriver but otherwise there was just a handful of small cow-towns and agricultural colonies scattered across the savannah. Most of the rural population lived in dispersed ranches.

The remoteness of the territory mainly resulted from the lack of communications with the outside world. There was no overland con-nection with the rest of Brazil; the Rio Branco is not a good waterway – for over six months of the year there is not enough water in it for nav-igation and the middle reaches are blocked by rapids which are only surmountable at the highest flood. There was meant to be a weekly commercial flight, by DC3, from Manaus but restrictions on flying in bad weather and at night played havoc with the timetable. Internal communications were not much better. There was a mere 700 km of unpaved road, much, if not all of which was impassable in the rainy season; as were the jeep trails that criss-crossed the savannah. At that time of year canoes and horses were more effective means of trans-port. There were a number of light aircraft available for charter but as they always flew chronically overloaded their safety record was poor. There tended to be shortages of everything, and in Bôa Vista, despite being the capital of a ranching industry, even meat.

It was in the 1970s, not long after my fieldwork, that Roraima finally began to wake up. Among other developments were the open-ing of a road link with the rest of Brazil and Venezuela and the con-struction of a proper runway to take jet aircraft. Also of considerable significance was the growth of gold and diamond mining. Whereas this pursuit had always been carried on alongside cattle ranching, in the late 1970s and 1980s there was a gold-rush which, because it involved the invasion by miners of Yanomami territory, received world-wide notoriety. By 1992 the population had risen to 216,000 and the road network increased to nearly 4,000 km, although still vir-tually all unpaved. Although I have not been there since those devel-opments occurred I am told that Bôa Vista, now with a population of nearly 120,000, has changed out of all recognition and is a modern, bustling city with paved streets and without a cow in sight. It has recently been described as 'one of Brazil's most agreeable small cities' (Hemming 1994: 59).

That I did fieldwork in Roraima came about in a not completely straightforward manner. In 1966 I was appointed to a research fel-lowship at the University of London's newly founded Institute of Latin American Studies. There was not there any enthusiasm for Amerindi-ans nor for the study of them, so I chose Roraima instead, knowing that it was an intriguing place and that there were Indians as well as cowboys. At the time, although there was historical material, ethnographic accounts of rural Brazilians and of the Amazonian frontier were rare. This was equally true of studies of ranching communities, as Tim Ingold noted in 1980 in his *Hunters, pastoralists and ranchers*, where for the last group he had to rely to a large extent on my work – not for the want of anything better but for the want of anything at all. In other words, once again I found myself in a theoretical void. In some ways this one was much easier to fill as the material conditions of existence, in particular the communications infrastructure, so obviously dominated the nature of socio-economic life in the region.

I have published only a single work as a result of that research – my book *The forgotten frontier; the ranchers of North Brazil* (1972) – although there are some unpublished papers, such as 'Pepper and salt: Amerindian and Brazilian relations in North Brazil' which is concerned with ethnic identity in the region. My research concentrated on the ranching population, who were mainly Brazilians of every conceivable racial admixture from apparently pure European through pure African to pure Amerindian, although the local classification tended to be simply *civilizado* or *caboclo*: the former a Brazilian national and the latter an Amerindian. In terms of phenotype it was often difficult to distinguish between the two, as many Amerindians had deserted their people to become *civilizados*, that is to say to live as Brazilians, speaking Portuguese, eating Brazilian food (salt beef and *farinha*) and working mainly as labourers. The term *caboclo* was used to refer to those Amerindians (Wapishiana and Macushi) who continued to live in their own settlements, speaking their own language (at least among themselves), eating native food (peppery stew and manioc bread) and practising a modified but traditional subsistence economy of slash-and-burn agriculture and fishing and hunting, the last not excluding taking the occasional cow. The relationship between *civilizado* and *caboclo* was mainly exploitative, with the latter often being forced to provide free manual labour and other services for the former under the guise of godparentage.

The first few months of fieldwork was a peripatetic affair. I based myself in Bôa Vista and obtained invitations to visit ranches. This did not prove too difficult as ranchers were in the main an extremely hospitable crowd. This allowed me to visit quite a lot of ranches of varying size and complexity. Some of these were small family-owned affairs whereas others were part of much larger organisations, one of which had its headquarters outside the territory. Although on the larger ranches there had been some attempt to develop modern methods of ranching with improved breeds of cattle, fenced paddocks and sown grass, the general level of operations was primitive. Cattle, except for an occasional inspection, were left to fend for themselves on the open savannah for most of the year and many had become semi-wild. The main annual event was the round-up which took place in the dry season, December to March. Although this was a time of long, strenuous days it was also a time of socialisation as different ranchers cooperated in turn to round up their cattle. It was also the time when the cowhands got paid. In the late 1960s the traditional form of payment (traceable back to the sixteenth century in Northeast Brazil), one calf in four drawn by lots, was still prevalent although cash wages were creeping in. This traditional form of payment partly reflected the low value of the cattle but was also favoured by cowhands since through it they could build up a herd and achieve the aspiration of becoming ranchers in their own right. A smaller round-up was also made in the wet season with the express purpose of selecting animals for market. While the flooded condition of the savannahs made these months ill-suited for such an activity, it was essential to do it then because it was the only time of the year when there was enough water in the river to ship the cattle downstream to market. Nor were the conditions under which the animals were transported any help in obtaining a decent price. The cattle were herded, often with considerable violence, into barges where, crushed together, they passed anything up to five days without food or water before reaching their destination. The lack of easy access to a market and the poor condition of the meat when it reached there were together responsible for the undeveloped state of the Roraima ranching industry, an activity which I have described as 'subsistence ranching'.

After spending some weeks visiting a variety of ranches, it became clear that this approach was of limited value and not the best use of my time. Ranches tended to be relatively isolated and very small economic and social units, often no more than a family, for all but the busiest seasons of the year. In other words there were often very few people to talk to and during the day the adult men of the house often went off, leaving me at home with the women and children who kept themselves very much to themselves. Attempts to go with the men were sometimes successful and, having ridden regularly since the age of five, I found little difficulty in adapting my style to that of the local cowponies and their tack. Indeed some of the most enjoyable days during fieldwork were spent in the saddle against a backdrop of open savannah, palm trees marking watercourses and distant blue mountains. As often as not, however, all sorts of excuses were put in the way of my accompanying the men. On some occasions the reasons given seemed genuine, such as the lack of a pony, and in retrospect I know I should have bought a horse for the duration of my stay (I had not budgeted for such a piece of equipment and am uncertain how the Ford Foundation might have reacted). At other times the difficulties seemed more artificial, although I worked out that they were intended as ways of preventing me from exerting myself. In the locals' view, nobody could possibly want to ride out in the sun or the rain when one could swing in a hammock on the ranch veranda. It was not, however, always the veranda, and where I was allowed to hang my hammock depended on the elaborateness of the ranch house and my perceived status. Space in and around the ranch house was divided between men and women (including pre-adolescent boys), and family and non-family. Non-family males would normally sleep in the bunkhouse, which in some places I did. Elsewhere and where room allowed, it was clearly decided that I was too polite or proper for such surroundings and company.

When I gave up moving from ranch to ranch on the grounds that it was a relatively unproductive means of work, I settled in one of the small cowtowns of the interior. Here I slept in a tiny room behind one of the bars and took my meals in another. Both arrangements were purely commercial and I paid in cash. In many ways this was a very much better locality from which to carry out research. The township was not populous, about a hundred permanent inhabitants, many of whom were the families of ranchers who lived there during term time in order that their children could go to the local convent school. In fact, most of the bigger ranchers had town houses and the richest rancher of the district, who was old and semi-retired, lived there the whole time. It also contained a number of shops-cum-bars, a chapel, a radio-telephone office, the local law officer, and an airstrip to which the Brazilian Air Force was meant to make fortnightly visits. Accordingly, it was the centre for a largish hinterland of outlying ranches which were fairly easy to visit for a day or two. More valuable, however, was the steady flow of visitors into town. Whereas there were good practical reasons for most visits, the opportunity was also taken to be sociable, in other words to have a drink and learn the latest news and gossip. Sitting at a bar or in the shade outside, a great deal of information was available. This sounds an ideal situation and in many ways it was, but a vast amount of what one learnt was superficial and it proved very difficult to dig deeper.

One of the reasons for this was a mixture of the way people perceived themselves and the way they perceived me in relation to them. Although they were to a remarkable degree cut off from the rest of Brazil, the Roraimaenses were far from ignorant about it. Some had made journeys to the cities of the south (the rest dreamt of Copacabana), there was radio, and illustrated magazines found their way into the area. A message they got from these various sources was that they were stupid and uneducated hicks living in the back of beyond, and well beyond the pale in Brazilian values, which draw a clear hierarchy between the civilised bustle and activity of the city and the increasing quietness and sadness as one descends into the interior.[9] The Roraimaenses were accordingly extremely suspicious of people from the urban outside world. They assumed, and probably rightly, that they were figures of fun to educated Brazilians who would look down on them and laugh at their ideas and practices. When faced with such people they tended to stay quiet, keep their opinions to themselves and say what they thought their interlocutors wanted to hear. Unfortunately I fell into the category of educated outsider, and I was referred to and often addressed as *o doutor*. This was not because I had a doctorate (they were not aware of the fact) but simply because it is common in the interior of Brazil to use this title for educated people, and it is certainly preferable to the alternative, *coronel* or colonel, with all the unfortunate connotations that term carries. Furthermore, most people just did not or declined to understand what I was trying to do. I was once asked 'Why do you want to know what we know, when you are an educated man and know so much more than we do?' In fact the serious block was their assumption that I knew better, and would not be interested in or would laugh at their ideas. Nor could they see how anyone would surrender the comfortable urban existence which I obviously usually led in order to live with them, unless there was some ulterior motive or I was a fugitive from the law. Among the rumours that went round were that I was a spy, although I cannot imagine what I was meant to be spying on. On one occasion when a party of Brazilian military personnel visited the township where I was living, one officer conducted a rather heavy-handed cross-examination of me which was clearly intended to discover whether I was a geologist carrying out a surreptitious survey. Another aspect of my local identity was the insistence that I was American despite the fact that when asked I always said I was English. This puzzled me but I never asked about it until one day I arrived back in the township to be told that a party of English visitors had arrived; they turned out to be from Guyana and black. It then emerged that the Guyanese who came across the border often called themselves English and were usually black. Accordingly, I could not be English.

Admittedly my period of fieldwork in the region was only six months but I never really managed to break through the protective shield people tended to hide behind. It was possible to get something by just watching and listening but attempts to get elucidation or local exegesis on observed events or overheard comments proved mainly fruitless.

These two brief accounts of different field situations speak for themselves but in conclusion there are two general points worth drawing attention to. The first relates to a comment I made in the introduction, which was to the effect that the Trio and the Roraimaenses constitute different types of society. This seems to me to reproduce itself in a different form. I could not have written about these two groups in the same way. I have found it much easier to write about the Trio because it is possible to do so in a more coherent way; their society has its own internal dynamics from which one could construct a model. I would have liked to have done the same thing for the frontiersmen of Roraima but could not detect anything similar. Instead I had to resort to external factors to describe what was going on. I could have written more on these people, but it would have been along the same lines; for example, on such topics as the role of credit in the development and maintenance of townships. Now it seems possible that this is not an unusual phenomenon and the nature of the ethnography produced is partly dictated by the nature of the society in question. In other words, a society collaborates in the production of a particular type of ethnographic writing.

The second point is that in Roraima, my designated position was unequivocally superior and the reaction of the locals was to close their ranks. Just how superior the educated outsider was perceived to be was demonstrated to me very forcefully when I was visited by an anthropologist from Pará who volunteered to collect some information for me. I suggested that he might make a census of the cowtown. This he did by the simple expedient of ordering the inhabitants of each house to line up outside and give their names, age and relationship to the household head – a performance that made me cringe but proved highly effective! My position among the Trio was far more equivocal. I appeared to belong to a people whose economic and technological skills were recognised as vastly superior, even if I myself apparently lacked certain of their attributes and did not behave like them. At the same time although I lived more or less like a Trio, I certainly was not one. I did not fit anywhere and perhaps this accounts for the fact of their ambivalence towards me – was I a dangerous outsider or a harmless fool? What I have to be grateful for is the fact they tried to teach me what it meant to be a Trio.

NOTES

1. For a much fuller description, see Rivière 1966 and, for developments up until 1978, Rivière 1981a. Rivière 1981b gives an account of Trio evangelisation. The most up-to-date account is Carlin 1998.
2. This is a linguistic problem more than anything else. The Trio language did not contain the words and concepts necessary to describe shops, traffic and hospital wards. I found this myself when attempting to explain certain aspects of Western life in the Trio language.
3. For a discussion of this phenomenon among the Tupinamba, see Viveiros de Castro 1992.
4. This is the continuation of a traditional practice whereby claims to territory were made by seeking the submission or friendship of an indigenous group living there.

See Farage 1991 for an account of this strategy on the Rio Branco in the eighteenth century.

5. This, I hasten to add, is not my opinion of my work. See Viveiros de Castro who writes of *Marriage among the Trio:* 'é o primeiro trabalho extenso e rigoroso dedicado a um sistema de parentesco amazônico. Ele está na origem de várias outras etnografias regionais ...e dispôs a maioria das balizas hoje utilizadas' (1993: 156).

6. I am not convinced that the question of how Dravidian are Amazonian relationship terminologies is more than an 'invented' intellectual puzzle. Even if there is an answer to it, I am not certain that it will tell us anything useful.

7. Because of the amalgamation of several villages into a single settlement, the traditional political organisation in which each village was an autonomous unit had been partly superseded by an overall leader who exerted his influence through the backing of the missionaries.

8. This does not mean that relationship terms are used consistently throughout one's social world. Consistency is high among those genealogically closely related but fades with genealogical distance. This feature is discussed in detail in Rivière 1969, Chapter V.

9. The standard Brazilian description of places in the interior is that they are *triste* and lacking in *movimento*.

Chapter 2

A VIEW FROM AFAR:

MEMORIES OF NEW GUINEA HIGHLAND WARFARE

Michael O'Hanlon

From one point of view, all fieldwork is extended fieldwork. Of course, this is not to deny that while some anthropologists spend just one period in the 'field', others make repeated trips to the same community: successively adding (perhaps in different coloured inks) to increasingly dog-eared files of genealogies; getting used to the embarrassment of failing to recognise individuals remembered as children but now grown up; and eventually being consulted over details of their own culture by the very people whose lives the anthropologist is overtly there to study. Rather, to insist that all fieldwork is extended fieldwork is to draw attention to the way in which field experience (whether the product of a single or of multiple visits) potentially metamorphoses in significance in the mind of the anthropologist, as time goes by.

Such continuing reassessment of earlier experience can be prompted by a range of factors, none mutually exclusive. Shifting theoretical perspectives within anthropology have the capacity to endow particular fieldwork episodes, hitherto seen to be of no especial significance, with a new centrality. The investigator's own developing life course – as he or she marries, has children, ages – may also lead to the reevaluation of earlier field data, if only to highlight the lacunae in it. Finally, certain fieldwork experiences may work on the anthropologist over time, rather in the way that Basso (1988) shows that Apache moral narratives can 'stalk' people's minds. The troubling quality of such experiences may stem either from their failure to articulate smoothly with the rest of fieldwork, or from an intrinsically disturbing character (Nordstrom and Robben 1995).

I have made two return trips to the Wahgi people of Papua New Guinea's Western Highlands Province, since I first began to work there in 1979. In this chapter, however, I focus on long-term fieldwork in the other sense, and reflect on the way that a single unsettling event, and my reactions to it, have – if not quite 'stalked' my thinking over the years – at least resisted the mental domestication which the passage of time generally accomplishes.[1]

On 9 September 1986 my wife Linda Frankland and I left our field-site on the North Wall of the Wahgi Valley to travel the dozen or so miles to Minj on the other side of the valley, in the hope of examining the battle shields which, we had heard, had recently been made for the warfare which had broken out in the area. We had arranged to meet en route John Burton, friend and archaeologist of the area (see, for example, Burton 1984); he was to give us a lift in the Australian National University's Toyota Hi-Lux into the small backroads which lie in the territory of the Wahgi tribes Kukika, Konumbka, Ngenika and Kamblyeka south and east of the local administrative centre of Minj (Figure 1).

A little way beyond Minj, our progress was arrested by a notice, written in capital letters in felt pen, on a large piece of cardboard which had been nailed to a stake and stuck in the road. It was arranged as follows:

NOTICE
FOR
RIOT SQUART OR POLICE
"INJUSTICE"
WHY ARRESTING KUKI-KONUMB
UKA WITH THEIR WEAPONS AND
NOT THE GENEKAS?
GENEKAS ARE THE CAUSES OF
THE WHOLE TRIBAL FIGHT AND YOU POLICE
SHOULD LOOK INTO THIS SERIOUSLY BEFORE
TAKING LEGAL ACTION. WE NOW ASK YOU
POLICE TO GO TO KOPUNG AND PUKAMIL
VILLAGES BEFORE ARRESTING US. THANK YOU!!

Dismounting from the car to examine this, we became aware of a distant clamour and, making our way southward through a screen of trees, we came across a large expanse of flattish ground on which, in the distance, a battle was in progress. On enquiring, we were told that it was between Kukika[2] and Konumbka (as on the notice, their names are sometimes paired as Kuki-Konumbka) on the one side and Ngenika ('Geneka') assisted by Kamblyeka on the other. We spent the next two and a half hours watching the fighting, following well to the rear (one

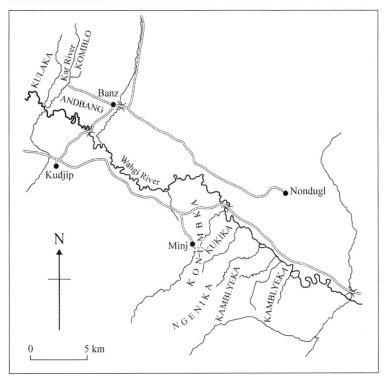

Figure 1 *Central Wahgi valley, showing approximate position of major groups*

of the senses in which I intend the word 'afar' in my title) of Kukika and Konumbka men as they gradually advanced around four hundred yards, until, just before three o'clock in the afternoon, two Land Cruisers full of men of the Riot Squad arrived, fired a number of rounds of tear gas, and the opposing forces fled.

There have, of course, been many attempts (well summarised by Knauft 1990) to explain the sporadic revival of warfare in parts of the Highlands in the 1970s and 1980s, forty years after it had been suppressed by the Australian Administration. However, as Merlan and Rumsey have noted (1991: 344), there are very few published anthropological eyewitness descriptions of such fighting, although there are some important unpublished accounts (Bruce 1992, Muke 1993) and a number of films,[3] as well, of course, as descriptions by patrol officers (for example Vial 1942) of earlier, contact-period warfare. The first, and modest, aim of this chapter is to go some way towards filling this gap in the published literature by providing a description of those few hours of fighting. My account does not even provide much basis for generalisation, for it is the only battle that I have seen at even remotely close quarters in the Wahgi area, although my long-time informants of Komblo tribe on the Valley's North Wall have given me many verbal accounts of precontact warfare and these, along with material recorded by other anthropologists, provide both a baseline and a point of comparison for my direct observations.

A further justification for offering a description, however limited, of this battle lies in its historical interest. The years since 1986 have seen major changes to Wahgi warfare, with the introduction first of home-made guns and, more recently, of manufactured weapons, dynamite and, it is rumoured, of grenades. Indeed, Burton (1990), who has also published his own briefer description of this same battle, was to see it as a watershed, the last 'traditional' Wahgi battle. Subsequent events slightly qualify this picture at the level of detail, since some Wahgi groups have since drawn back from using firearms, and have inten-tionally restricted themselves to the traditional armoury of bows and arrows, spears and axes (O'Hanlon 1995: 486ff.). Nevertheless, firearms now provide a dominant context for warfare, even in those instances when they are not actually used, lending a degree of histor-ical interest to this earlier engagement.

Reference to the passage of time evokes the second sense in which I use 'afar' in my title and the second, more reflective, intent of this chapter, alluded to at the outset. Over a decade has passed since watch-ing the battle. As the experience has sedimented itself in my memory, I have become increasingly conscious of the contradictory responses which it aroused in me. It would be idle to deny that, at one level, it gratified an ethnographic curiosity that was only saved from solitary voyeurism by the presence of hundreds of Wahgi spectators. At the same time, I found myself reluctant to exploit the opportunity, a reluc-tance which is partly reflected in the years it has taken me to write about it. Again, while the battle was an undeniably compelling spec-tacle, ethnographically I found it oddly uninformative, and not simply because of the distractingly heightened atmosphere.

My account, then, is a hybrid one. On the one hand, it is a descriptive attempt to portray a compelling and unusual event, one which took place away from my main field-site, on the periphery of the 'thick' con-text which fieldwork attempts to construct. On the other hand, this chapter is a personal rumination, written from the vantage point of two decades' involvement with the Wahgi, as to why the circumstances of my fieldwork should have led me to feel it was so important to 'see' warfare. In one sense, then, I am offering two different kinds of 'tales of the field', and in my conclusion I reflect on where they fit in terms of van Maanen's (1988) eponymous classification of fieldwork accounts.

But before attempting to develop these points, it is first necessary to sketch the impression of warfare which I had earlier constructed from informants' accounts, and then to describe the occasion itself.

Hearing about warfare

During my original period of fieldwork, six or seven years before watching the battle, my Wahgi informants had been almost obsessively keen to talk about warfare – if also anxious *not* to talk about it in certain respects, as I shall describe. Traditionally, at least in the immediate period before the first Whites entered the area in 1933, warfare had been endemic in the Wahgi, as it was in the New Guinea Highlands more generally. All Wahgi clans and tribes had experienced both formal battles, as well as the uncertainties of night-time raids and ambush. Many had known rout and subsequent periods as refugees with kin and affines elsewhere in the Valley.

This general experience of warfare had been particularly traumatic for members of Komblo tribe, the Wahgi group with whom I have carried out most of my fieldwork. In the late 1920s, Komblo's intermittent fighting against neighbouring Wahgi tribes – into whom they were also densely intermarried – had deepened in severity. After months of increasingly intense combat they were besieged on Ongmange, the massive buttress which overlooks the Kar Valley. From Ongmange, Komblo engaged in a series of bitter encounters with their massed opponents, mutually driving each other to further excesses by mutilating the corpses of the dead, while women died in night-time forays to harvest sweet potato. Finally, when all their pigs had been cooked and eaten and men were too weak from hunger to support their heavy shields any longer, Komblo fled Ongmange at night, stowing their valuables in netbags, and dressing young boys in skirts to disguise their sex in an effort to prevent their being killed should they be intercepted *en route.*

Komblo's flight must have taken place around 1932, for they say that they had only recently been expelled when the first Australian expedition to enter the area, the celebrated Leahy-Taylor patrol of 1933, arrived. Eventually, and partly through the agency of Ond Koi, a subsequently renowned Komblo man whom the Australians hired as a translator, Komblo were reinstalled on their territory by the new colonial regime (O'Hanlon 1993: 30). But though they were thus restored on their land, this experience of intense warfare against neighbours and kin, of siege, flight and repatriation, was deeply inscribed on the consciousness of those Komblo who lived through it, and was generally the first thing that each successive Komblo informant wished to tell me about when I first embarked on fieldwork among them.

But if in these respects my Komblo informants were eager to talk about this aspect of warfare, there was also much that they didn't want to talk about, and which, indeed, they actively tried to withhold from me for the first fifteen months of my original fieldwork. This has to do with the place warfare occupies in Wahgi male life. For some

Highlanders, such as the Mae Enga described by Meggitt (1977), warfare appears to be regarded broadly as a pragmatic matter, with victory and defeat seen as the outcome of secular and material factors: skill, strength and experience in fighting, superior tactics, the dependability of allies, et cetera. The impression is given that 'magic', 'ritual' and the invocation of supernatural aid, while practised in connection with warfare, are felt to be somewhat uncertain and peripheral aids.

For the Wahgi, on the other hand, and for their neighbours in the Jimi Valley, the ritual dimension of warfare was strikingly foregrounded, a contrast which has also struck other anthropologists (Reay 1987: 84ff.). This ritual dominance is apparent in a number of respects. Crucial to traditional Wahgi warfare was the practice of war magic, a complex which many Wahgi regard, indeed, as originally imported from the Jimi area. It was at the war magic house that, before battle, Wahgi clansmen were traditionally decorated in supernaturally-charged charcoal which was said to de-individualise them, making them appear indistinguishable. This process of anonymisation was merely the bodily expression of more general ideological emphases when preparing for war, all of which focused upon the construction of a solidary, undifferentiated fighting unit.

Predictably, this stress upon solidarity was underlain by considerable apprehension as to its existence. On the one hand, Wahgi men with grudges against their clansmen were, and are still, suspected of being in clandestine contact with enemy groups, ready to hand them sorcery materials which undermine a clan's capacity to fight effectively. On the other hand, as in the case of Komblo tribe, Wahgi patterns of marriage and enmity mean that the opposing side may also contain dense networks of affinal and maternal kin whose concern for each other's well-being may have led them to exchange ritual gifts (*kupol nol* – O'Hanlon 1989: 84) which, again, are thought to have the power to sap the effectiveness of the clan. Preparations for fighting were loud with clansmen's mutual urging to confess outstanding grievances or disloyalty towards each other and to disavow pacts which might undercut the effectiveness of the fighting unit. As Harrison puts it, a clan going to war – the clansmen's identities masked beneath ritually charged charcoal, their internal quarrels formally confessed – represents a political achievement: one in which the claims otherwise exerted by extra-clan kinship on clansmen as individuals are temporarily set aside (1993: 113ff.).

This thoroughgoing ritualisation of warfare extended well beyond the period of physical combat. For outstanding intra-clan betrayals, and unconfessed interclan pacts or the failure to identify maternal kin in the heat of battle, are felt to have ramifying consequences for the future, if they give rise to deaths and injuries. So long as the true circumstances surrounding such deaths remain hidden, they are thought to continue to cause sickness, infertility and further deaths down the generations, as angry ancestral ghosts smite their descendants for continuing, even inadvertently, to associate with those who brought about the deaths.

For the Wahgi, in fact, such periods of past warfare possess certain of the attributes of a stereotype of the Australian Dreamtime. As with the Dreamtime, Wahgi conceive of past warfare as a time when powerful forebears stalked the land, enacting deeds – whether in the form of betrayals, killings or pact-making – which are thought of as having profound implications for the future. If one is to remain healthy and to prosper, one must act in accord with these originary doings, separating oneself from the descendants of those who might have been implicated in the deaths of one's own close kin, giving assistance where it was rendered and repaying injury with injury. The *difference* when compared with the Australian Dreamtime is that the Wahgi version is a black-box Dreamtime: while there is general agreement that it was during this intense period of fighting and expulsion that these originating acts took place, exactly what they were is disputed and must, rather, be deduced retrospectively from sequences of misfortune and well-being in the present.

And like aspects of the Dreamtime, these matters are secret, or discussed only obliquely. The reasons for this have been explored elsewhere (O'Hanlon 1989: chap. 3); a summary here is sufficient. First, information relating to betrayals, to concealed grudges, to hidden anger or the inadvertent slaying or offending of maternal kin remains highly political; an individual possessing such information is thought able to deploy it against the clan to which it relates in any future fighting, and it may also become the basis for compensation claims should it become public. Secondly, despite the weight attributed to it, such information is also always regarded with a degree of scepticism; while at one level it explains current illnesses and deaths, at another level such illnesses and deaths themselves generate such knowledge, as individuals advance rival hypotheses from present patterns of illness, infertility and depletion as to what must have taken place in the past to produce them. Finally, such information is closely tied in with the activities of ancestral ghosts, and Wahgi tend only to discuss ghosts with considerable circumspection, for to talk about them risks invoking them with consequences that cannot be foreseen. If these reasons were not enough to exclude me from this kind of information about warfare, my Wahgi hosts suspected at times that I was in turn withholding from them the secrets of European 'power'; this being so they were doubly disinclined to share knowledge of their 'power' with me.

For much of my first period of fieldwork, then, I was the eager recipient of deeply contradictory stances towards warfare on the part of the middle-aged Komblo men who had appointed themselves my main sponsors and informants. On the one hand, the drama of these individuals' early lives of fight, flight and repatriation had been such that they felt compelled to recount it to me on every occasion. On the other hand, Komblo men felt that the fortunes of warfare were in many respects merely a playing out in the external world of the effects of underlying betrayals, covert pacts and secret alliances. And this highly-charged information – both the general principles and the politically-sensitive details of specific cases – Komblo men were initially resolved to withhold from me.

Even now, twenty years on, I find it easy to recall the sense of looming failure engendered in me, as a novice fieldworker, by my early inability to 'get' such material. That information of this kind undoubtedly existed was evident from the hints, lacunae and suppressions in Komblo men's accounts of warfare. These are among my strongest memories of early fieldwork: long evenings spent sitting on our woven *pitpit* house floor from which fleas carry out guerrilla raids on my crossed and stiffening legs, the rain hissing steadily down on the thatched roof and cascading into the drainage ditches around the house, watching the absorbed faces of men in the harsh roar and light of a pressure lamp as they recount details of warfare and its consequences. But my questions – when I can assemble them – are circumvented. They elicit only anodyne answers; or perhaps a noise outside or the intrusion into the house of some insect (both of which can be signs of the presence of ancestral ghosts) result in the subject being swiftly changed. At most, someone notes elliptically that, for example, ever since the early fighting the men of a particular subclan have always looked unimpressively slack-skinned; or that it was only when a given man moved away from his fellow clansmen to live with his maternal kin that his wife produced male children.

I will return later to the effect which Komblo men's ambivalence in discussing warfare had on me: on the one hand as the heart of their recent experience, the drama of which they were anxious to convey; on the other, something whose motivating details they were deeply uncomfortable in talking about and initially decided not to share with me.

Observing warfare

The battlefield on to which we emerged in September 1986 (seven years after those frustrating early months of my first fieldwork) is sketched in Figure 2, which also shows the movements of the two sides as the battle proceeded. In the foreground lay a considerable expanse of sweet potato garden; at its southerly end stood a screen of casuarina

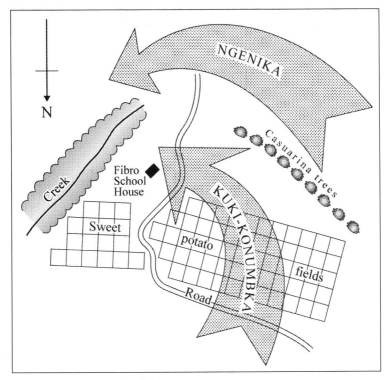

Figure 2 *Sketch of the battlefield, 1986*

trees some way beyond which the foothills of the South Wall climb sharply. To the left, beyond the road and fibreboard schoolhouse, the ground is broken by a creek. By the time of our arrival at half-past twelve, Kukika and Konumbka had pushed their Ngenika opponents south across the sweet potato gardens (now much trampled in consequence) and the fighting was taking place near the casuarina trees. From among them, billows of smoke arose at a number of points, while streams of arrows flashed from right and left across the sky.

Hundreds of spectators – women and children, as well as men – were scattered in groups watching the fighting. Some of the men were armed. Lacking as I did any knowledge of who was who among the warring groups, it was impossible to know whether such men were spectators who had thought it prudent to bring their weapons with them, or were in fact combatants biding their time. Occasionally, a man so heavily armed and decorated as to be unmistakably a combatant would walk steadily through the spectators towards the front (Figure 3).

The fighters' garb was mixed. The political and moral significance of Wahgi adornment had in fact been the subject of my original field-

Figures 3a and 3b *Shield carriers walking towards the front*

work, and the full panoply of warfare decoration – cassowary head-dress, heavy charcoal, cordyline bustle and long front apron hitched up (*misap to*) to prevent it snagging – had often been described to me. Indeed, I had frequently been told that were I ever to see men decorated for warfare I would find their appearance so terrifying that I would be forced to look away (it is the ghostly support which warriors invoke before battle which is felt to lend them their paralysing aspect). But I now found that while a few men on the battlefield were traditionally dressed, the majority wore shirts and shorts, though generally with some local component to their attire, particularly to their headgear.

Such local touches included nassa or bailer shell forehead ornaments, decorative leaves and head-nets, sometimes ornamented with minor plumes. Other combatants had forsaken traditional headgear altogether, in favour of protective innovations: one youth had donned a yellow hard-hat while another man wore a crash helmet. Charcoal was another local component of dress, applied to the face or to the skin as a whole. A number of men had smeared their faces with mud, suggesting that they were in mourning for a kinsman lost earlier in the fighting which, spectators told us, had been going on for some three weeks. But in the absence of detailed knowledge of the groups involved, it was impossible to know whether there was any more general correlation between these variations in decoration and the distinctions the Wahgi themselves make among warriors. One spectator whom I asked did say that charcoal was worn by the principal combatants (the *wal dam*: 'fathers of the thing') but my own impression is that age was as much a factor, with mature men in their thirties and forties wearing the more traditional dress, though the disguising quality of charcoal does make estimating age difficult.

Aside from fire – the torch can be a weapon, as Meggitt reminds us (1977: 54) – the offensive armoury on the battlefield comprised spears, bows and arrows, and steel axes. The Wahgi distinguish three types of spear, according to whether they are single pointed (*kula dasing*), double pointed (*kula ju pakal*) or have a carved upper shaft with triple prongs midway down, just above the handle (*kula jimben*). Occasional Wahgi spears, referred to as *kula ambonggo*, are tipped with bone, and I have been told that a variety of 'poison' (*enz kongo* – see O'Hanlon 1989: 59ff.) can be inserted into the space between head and shaft, though it is said that for this to be effective, the spearman must always rest the base of such a spear on his foot: one of a number of Wahgi proscriptions on things touching the ground. Most spears, however, are wooden pointed and all but one of those I saw that day were of the severely practical, single pointed type, though Burton (1990: 226) observed some that had been given metal points, an innovation which had of course long ago overtaken axe heads.

Wahgi bows (*opo buno*) are made either from the locally growing *koimb* or *buno* woods, or from imported black palm wood. Braces at either end, made from small drilled wooden spheres, prevent the split cane string from slipping down the stave. Arrow shafts are made from cane, and the heads either from leaf-shaped bamboo or from notched wood. Traditionally, the Wahgi do not use quivers, and bowmen go into battle clutching a bundle of arrows; today, however, occasional makeshift quivers are made using a tin can and I also saw some warriors with bundles of arrows slung transversely over the shoulder. Burton, who progressed much further towards the battle front than I dared to do, estimated that an average of ten to twenty arrows was being fired per minute (1990: 228). Since a man does not carry more than a couple of dozen arrows at most, supply can become a problem, and it is likely that the occasional women observed carrying arrows on the battlefield were bringing fresh stocks, either from home or collected on the battlefield itself.

The only defensive weapons in use were massive battle shields (*kumbrapi*). These were being carried by spearmen rather than by men armed with bows and arrows. However, it was difficult to gauge the precise number of shields on the field, since it is easiest to tell shields apart by their adornment, which in the case of Kuki-Konumbka (behind whose lines we were) faced towards their Ngenika opponents, while Ngenika shields, facing us, were too far distant to see clearly. However, I counted twenty-two shields between the two hundred or so Kuki-Konumbka warriors on the field. Two of these were made from metal rather than the traditional wood. Shield adornment, too, showed some innovation, often being executed in acrylic paint and, in at least two cases, explicitly graphically-meaningful designs had been superimposed on the traditional, more geometric, decoration. In one case, a leaping man had been painted onto a Ngenika shield, while a Kuki-Konumbka shield had a plastic strip across the top advertising Cambridge cigarettes ('Make yours a Cambridge today') with, below it, the inscriptions GIF-FO and G-4.

Elsewhere, I have described the more thorough-going transformation which was later to affect both shield use (as guns entered warfare) and shield design (O'Hanlon 1995). Shield design, in particular, underwent a process that I have dubbed the 'graphicalisation' of meaning, as men made much wider use of writing and of advertising and sporting imagery to re-express clan identities and to communicate new meanings on their shields. For example, warriors' corporate solidarity, rather than being reflected in uniform body charcoal, came in parts of the Wahgi area to be expressed in 'team' terms, through adopting a common shield design based on the local sporting trophy, the 'Cambridge Cup' (O'Hanlon 1995: 483).

In 1986, however, this development was only apparent in nascent form on shields (and, in a different way, in the roadside notice aimed at the police). I do not in fact know what the inscriptions 'GIF-FO' and 'G-4' signified and at that time was not sufficiently sensitised to what proved to be an interesting subsequent development to ask. One Wahgi man, who misread 'GIF-FO' for 'GIF-10' on a photograph I took of this Kuki-Konumbka shield, did suggest that it was a taunt that Kuki-Konumbka were superior to Ngenika as Grade 10 (sixteen-year-old) schoolchildren were superior to Grade 4 children. Though I think this is a misreading, the changes apparent by 1990, when I next observed shields, frequently included such taunts and also plays on words and numbers. For example 'GIF-FO' and 'G-4' look as though they might be versions of one another, reminiscent of the plays on 'Six 2 Six' around which one North Wall subgroup were later to coordinate their shield designs (O'Hanlon 1995: 484).

My attempts to move closer to the battle front were discouraged by concerned spectators who worried that I might get injured. Spectators do get hurt in warfare: Komblo, the tribe with whom I work on the North Wall of the Valley, tell how they were drawn into the Andbang-Kulaka conflict around the turn of the last century after Keke, a Komblo man, was killed by an arrow in the eye while watching a battle between them. At that stage, however, I did not appreciate quite how fluid a battle front can be and was seduced into moving a little closer. It became apparent that the Kuki-Konumbka strategy was to push Ngenika southward, firing houses and clumps of bamboo and felling bananas and sugar cane as they went, while conducting a holding operation on the eastern side of the battlefield, where shieldmen were spaced out at regular intervals on the high ground above the creek to prevent outflanking. From his more advanced position, Burton describes the Kuki-Konumbka warriors on the active southern front as organised into 'platoons' of up to twenty bowmen, fronted by four to six shield men (1990: 228). My own impression, however, is that manoeuvering was carried out with little explicit command and control: noncombatants were constantly shouting advice and warnings but there was a sense less of central direction than of a group of men loosely coordinating their actions in response to the changing situation.

Shortly after our arrival, the first casualty, a youth with a small arrow wound in his left abdomen, made his way to the rear, holding the extracted arrow that had inflicted it. Generally, in the case of minor wounds, individuals appeared to be left to cope by themselves. There is an excellent hospital at Kudjip, seven miles to the west, where more seriously injured men could in principle be taken. However, in 1984 a provincial government edict had imposed a K60 charge (1 Kina was then approximately 70 pence) for those seeking medical attention for battle injuries. For a year, Kudjip Hospital had resisted the surcharge until they found that battle casualties were being shipped in from neighbouring provinces to take advantage of their cheaper treatment. In 1985, therefore, the hospital imposed a levy of K20 for battle injuries, over and above the K10 basic charge for hospital treatment. Going to Kudjip or elsewhere would have been additionally difficult for wounded Ngenika men, since Kuki-Konumbka controlled access to the main road; indeed, I was later told that Ngenika had sold off all their vehicles since they could no longer get to the Highlands Highway.

At 12.52 p.m. (my notes are specific on time if on little else) there was a short-lived Ngenika counter-attack, perhaps stimulated by what was to be a sustained Kuki-Konumbka assault on the schoolhouse. *Muku niya!* ('Hurry, Hurry'), called the Kuki-Konumbka warriors, *Wa! Wa! Pi ep punom!* ('Come! Come! ... Now they're going back up!') Though not directly defended, this schoolhouse became the focus of what seemed disproportionate Kuki-Konumbka efforts to destroy it, with periodic demands that a vehicle bring up kerosene to help burn it down. Meanwhile, another Kuki-Konumbka man was being helped back towards the rear, this time apparently with serious wounds as those assisting him brusquely waved away the spectators who tried to approach; at the same time, a shield carrier was limping back, pointing out a wound in his thigh, while another man, his face taut, sat on the ground, gingerly touching a broken-off arrow head embedded in his left ankle. A 'Peace Committee', one of the men appointed by the provincial government in an effort to promote peace, observed: *Opo mam esimbel* ('It's a major battle').

However, this flurry of activity was a prelude to a break in the fighting. Earlier, women had been moving around the rear of the battlefield with bamboo tubes of water to refresh those fighting. But now there was a general move by Kuki-Konumbka men back towards rest areas at the rear of the battlefield. Koch observes in his account of Jalemo warfare that 'In the course of a day's battle the fighting deteriorates [sic] several times into phases of relative tranquillity with both sides exchanging arrows only sporadically. Small groups of warriors then gather around fires to smoke and to discuss the fortunes of the battle' (1974: 78). This appeared to be a similar moment, with an unspoken agreement on either side that no major attacks would be made while most men sat around, resting and smoking (but not eating), their shields propped upright against their spears (Figure 4a). Some of the shields bore the marks of a considerable number of arrow strikes, others hardly any at all. Women and children stood or sat around on the periphery.

At 1.40 p.m. the long cries of 'ooooh aaah!' (*konspol to*) with which Wahgi draw attention to events and harness corporate action were heard in the distance, and there was a general move up to the front again. Men were exhorting each other to fight better and to get a move on, swearing in English and Pidgin, a linguistic shift also made when men are drunk (see, for example, Grossman 1982: 67; Josephides and Schiltz 1982: 79), though I saw no beer or other alcohol. Older men were distributing arrows, handing three or four to each man. The battle resumed, rumours now circulating that Kukika had killed Kui, a Kopanaka man presumably enrolled as a Ngenika ally. Meanwhile, renewed attention was being given to destroying the schoolhouse, and a stream of Kuki-Konumbka carrying dismantled parts of the building made their way to the rear. Women, too, were harvesting the abandoned Ngenika sweet potato gardens, despite the occasional shouts of

Figure 4a *A break in the battle*

Amb kep na-wakiya! ('Stop digging up sweet potato, you women!') from men concerned that the harvesters would be vulnerable in the event of a Ngenika counter-attack.

However, Ngenika continued to be pressed hard, the fighting now swinging round to the creek in the east, across which Kuki-Konumbka warriors attacked, while the line of defending Ngenika shields was visible amid the smoke on the creek's further lip (Figure 4b). Kuki-Konumbka women expressed delight at the Ngenika retreat, while one

Figure 4b *Ngenika shields beyond the ridge (copyright John Burton)*

Kuki-Konumbka youth armed with bow and arrows appeared on the reverse side of slope, perilously unsupported by shieldmen, dodging and kicking up his heels in the military prance known as *opo kumbo* ('war wall'), as he fired grass and bamboo. Elsewhere, there was a burst of *konspol to* cheering as the structure of the schoolhouse finally collapsed. A few drops of rain began to fall.

At this stage (2.52 p.m.) the Riot Squad Landcruisers arrived; in the confusion, the exact sequence of events was difficult to establish. There had been cries warning of a Ngenika counter-attack a few moments earlier. Whether for this reason, or because they had spotted the approaching vehicles, the front line of Kuki-Konumbka men began to fall back with startling rapidity. Meanwhile, other Kuki-Konumbka warriors, apparently unaware of the Riot Squad's proximity and concerned to dispel the rumours of a Ngenika counter-attack and halt the retreat, were yelling *Gend! Gend!* ('Lies! Lies!'). Ngenika themselves, seeing some of their opponents drawing back, now advanced with equal rapidity, which briefly left Burton, my wife and me near the shifting centre of the battle. I recall running over the hummocky ground, my camera bumping awkwardly on my chest, noticing an arrow drop disconcertingly close by, and feeling profoundly stupid, before the oncoming Ngenika men too saw the Riot Squad vehicles and fled. No attempt was made by either side to engage the Riot Squad, who by that point had earned a reputation for entering conflicts less as peace-makers, than as a third force which disinterestedly burned the dwellings and slaughtered the pigs of both sides (Reay 1982: 633).

A view from afar

A number of points of contrast stand out when comparing what I had been told about past warfare by my Komblo informants on the North Wall of the valley with what was observed on this South Wall battlefield. For example, most warriors wore smaller amounts of the supernaturally-charged charcoal than I had anticipated; indeed many were dressed in less martial a fashion than men feel to be necessary when merely making aggressive compensation payments (see e.g. O'Hanlon 1989, plates 14–15). Again, men's earlier verbal accounts had tended to present women as passive in warfare, and had not prepared me either for their role as arrow-suppliers, or for their intermittently evident emotional commitment.[4] Of course, such contrasts in turn beg the question of whether these are differences between cultural norm and social practice, or between practices North and South of the Wahgi River, or reflect the fact that most of what I knew about warfare derived from my Komblo informants whose own immediate experience of fighting was largely in the precontact era. These points cannot be pursued here, though it is worth noting that the Wahgi themselves tend to present warfare into the mid-1980s as broadly the same kind of thing as precontact warfare, and emphasise that the major historical disjunction came with the introduction of guns at the end of that decade (see Reay 1982: 630; Muke 1993: 256; see also Meggitt 1977: 181).

But mildly illuminating though watching the battle was in these respects, it was far more compelling as a spectacle than it was anthropologically informative. Our field notes of the occasion are thin, at least in relation to the weight of the remembered experience. Subsequent enquiries did fill in a little of the background. Back at my North Wall field-site, informants told us that the fighting had begun after a drunken young Konumbka man had struck a Ngenika big man; Konumbka were slow in making the compensation payment of money and pigs, and, at a meeting to discuss this, Ngenika men had in turn hit a Konumbka youth who had subsequently died of his injuries. At that point the war began, the death toll reportedly reaching fourteen by mid-September. However, this account itself is certainly a simplification; it does not cover how Kukika became involved: indeed speaking of 'Ngenika', 'Kukika', 'Konumbka' as though they constituted solidary blocks, while it does follow local usage, conceals a much more complex situation in which some of the constituent clans will have been more heavily involved, while others are likely to have had divided loyalties depending on their previous histories, the extent of marriage ties between them, and the degree of co-investment in commercial enterprises.

Of course, there are reasons for my relatively impoverished understanding of the battle. While South Wall groups belong to the same cultural area as those on the North Wall, I know few individuals there, have comparatively little knowledge of local group structure and history, and find it very difficult to understand the South Wall dialect of mid-Wahgi. It also seemed unsafe to move around the battlefield, so I saw only one area of it; nor, for practical reasons, was it possible for me to return to the battlefield on a later occasion to interview participants. Moreover, the combatants themselves were understandably in a heightened state and I think I was myself in a mild state of shock. Ottenberg makes a useful distinction between written field notes and 'head notes': those mental impressions which are not written down because they seem to be too numerous or too obvious to need to do so (1990: 144). Looking back over my notes I find that I have made no record of – and found myself unable to photograph – the two mental images which remain as my most powerful impressions: watching the seriously wounded man being carried from the battlefield while his companions unambiguously waved spectators away, and standing over another wounded man, listening to his intake of breath as he touched the broken arrow shaft in his ankle, steeling himself to pull it out. Indeed, the sole Komblo spectator I encountered on the battlefield, a man too young to have taken part in Komblo's own pre-contact warfare, also seemed somewhat stunned and remarked to me that this was the first time he, too, had seen a battle.

The combination of the participants' self-absorption, and of my neither being able fully to understand the South Wall dialect nor knowing the local context, gave the battle a distanced, filmic quality, reducing it for much of the time largely to its visual dimension. To that extent it had some of the properties which MacDougall identifies as characteristic of anthropology's early interest in photographs and other visual imagery which 'appeared to show everything, and yet ... remained annoyingly mute' (1997: 277). MacDougall's comment itself reflects the recent upsurge of critical interest in the visual: an upsurge in which 'visualism' has, of course, been analysed – in Gell's phrase – as 'a culpable offence' for its voyeurism and incarnation of asymmetrical power relations (1995: 236).

I certainly felt intermittently intrusive while watching the battle (one reason for my notes being thin, for I felt awkward in pressing my enquiries), and I am all too aware in writing about the battle now that I risk sounding as though what was significant about an event at which people were being injured and killed was whether or not it was anthropologically informative. As it happens, I think my awkwardness in this respect is part of a fieldworker's uncomfortable Eurocentric baggage, for I had little sense that the Wahgi participants themselves felt that our presence was voyeuristic – indeed, spectatorship is intrinsic to Wahgi warfare, for combatants expect spectators to assess their appearance before a battle. An unimpressive appearance is thought to presage defeat, and may prompt further bouts of communal confession in an effort to locate the undisclosed breaches of corporate solidarity responsible for the warriors' poor appearance.

John Burton mentions similar qualms, referring to speculation that the presence of film-makers may actually have contributed to the warfare recorded in *Dead Birds*, the well-known film featuring Dani fighting (1990: 232). Burton is quite clear (and I agree with him) that in the Wahgi case our own presence made not the slightest difference to what was going on, and far from being in a position to influence it, I felt at times under speculative scrutiny from young men who, knowing that they were already acting illegally in being on the battlefield, perhaps wondered whether they might not also relieve the rubber-necking Whites of their Toyota, wallets and cameras. Certainly, this was the opinion of my normally imperturbable sponsor back on the North Wall who, alarmed by our failure to return until early evening, warned us never to repeat the exercise for that reason.

A colleague to whom I mentioned that I was writing a paper describing this battle similarly sounded a note of caution, less about whether it was insensitive to attend such an event (he made no comment in this regard), but whether it was an appropriate subject to publish on. Isn't it rather voyeuristic, he asked. His immediate reaction reflects, of course, the concerns of the last decade or so with issues of representation. 'Traditionally', the anthropologist would have been more likely to conceive of himself ('he' was perhaps more often 'he', then) as a dispassionate observer, eager to record details of an activity which, as I have said, has infrequently been seen by New Guinea Highland anthropologists. More recently, however, anthropologists' sharper awareness of how they create their object of study through the selective choice of topic, and the responsibility that they consequently have when they portray the lives of those without comparable power to represent themselves, have combined to exert a degree of self-censorship towards describing things which might reflect discreditably upon 'their' people.

Put most strongly, the argument would be that in choosing to describe this battle – as opposed to more common and less extreme occasions – the anthropologist risks endorsing an already prevalent stereotype of Highlanders not only as exotic, but also as prone to violence, and unable to govern their own affairs. While some limited description of warfare might be justifiable as evidence in making a theoretical point, the argument might continue, the extensive and largely atheoretical description which I have given is truly voyeuristic. To give such a description is especially unfortunate when local people are not themselves able to represent alternative versions of their lives. These are powerful and emotionally appealing arguments, and it is in part precisely such reasons which have kept me from publishing an account of the event to date, aside from a brief reference in an earlier book.

Are there any counter-arguments? The first is whether the recent anthropological preoccupation with equity in matters of representation reflects an inflated and introverted view of anthropologists' own influence and importance. Take the present example. The Wahgi themselves clearly know that they periodically engage in warfare, and often talk about it, as well as about how to stop it. Accounts of the subject regularly appear and are debated in Papua New Guinea newspapers and in television programmes seen by tens of thousands of viewers. A locally produced official publication is similarly explicit. The *Handbook of the Western Highlands Province and its Government: celebrating 10 years of Provincial Government* (Mell 1987) looks at first sight to be the kind of anodyne bit of bureaucratic self-promotion which it would be in Britain, with its subheadings for such topics as 'Building a foundation for the future', 'The cabinet of Premier Kapal' and 'The provincial engineering unit'. Yet it also includes a contemporary photograph captioned 'Preparation before partaking in a tribal fight', along with the statement that 'Western Highlands is among some few provinces ... that have experienced a lot of tribal fighting. There were some years in which there reported continuous fightings which has led to the use of firearms which substituted traditional weaponry [*sic*]. Tribal incidents have proved hard to bring to an end.' Moreover, Wahgi scholars themselves have begun to produce analyses of warfare – treated as an integral part of local culture (Muke 1993).

Does it make sense in these circumstances for anthropologists to adopt the kind of self-denying ordinance reflected in my colleague's caution to me, and in my own reluctance to date to describe this occasion? I don't know. But it could be argued that in glossing over such uncomfortable aspects of local practice, anthropologists collude with its perpetrators (in the case of warfare, broadly with men) at the expense of its victims (women, whose capacity to feed their families and visit their kin suffers disproportionately, and children, whose schooling is disrupted). At its worst, self-censorship in this regard can look as though anthropologists are embarrassed – ethnocentrically so – on behalf of the people they work with, an oddly paternalistic position to end up in.

But despite my intermittent feeling of intrusiveness in watching this battle and in writing about it now, and despite its uninformativeness, I would be dishonest if I did not also admit that I felt that it was valuable to have seen it, disturbing though it was. In his edited volume James Carrier (1992) has taken Melanesian anthropologists to task for exoticism, for the extent to which they have mistakenly constituted the peoples they study as different, pristine and largely unaffected by historical process. Contributors to Carrier's volume, such as Keesing and Jolly (1992: 227), acknowledge the degree to which they were themselves drawn to work in traditionalist enclaves in Melanesia by the romance of studying seemingly untouched peoples. Carrier delineates the intellectual devices – 'authenticity', 'essentialisation', 'isolationism and passivism', 'unidimensionality', 'mirroring' – through which, he suggests, Melanesian anthropologists have misrepresented their subjects, introducing a kind of 'covert hierarchisation' (1992: 12) in which some aspects of culture – the 'traditional', the exotic – come to be seen as somehow more real, more typical and more noteworthy than others.

I think few anthropologists who began their Melanesian fieldwork as I did in the 1970s can read Carrier's account without some degree of self-recognition. After all, it cannot merely be accidental that such people chose to study the cultural construction of female initiation or personal adornment in the New Guinea Highlands rather than, say, afternoon bingo in Lowestoft. But to admit to a degree of satisfaction in having seen this battle reflects not just the misplaced search for pristinity which was a factor in first attracting many anthropologists to the region. After all, by 1986, there had already been considerable debate – of which I was well aware – as to whether the renewal of fighting in the Highlands was evidence of the persistence of traditional cultural practices, or resulted rather from distinctively modern strains produced by cash-cropping, land shortage and the breakdown of traditional structures of trade, exchange and authority (Strathern 1977, Good 1979, Podolefsky 1984). And the 'modernity' of the battle itself, with its crash helmets, its calls for kerosene and its notice to the Riot Squad, could hardly fail to register with even the most tunnel-visioned exoticist.

Rather, my feeling that observing this battle was a significant ethnographic experience largely derived – I now realise – from the way in which Wahgi men in general, and men of Komblo tribe in particular, had constituted warfare and its consequences, both as the absent core to their culture, and as a realm from aspects of which they initially excluded me. As I attempted to describe at the outset of this chapter, Komblo men saw the increasingly severe warfare immediately before contact as a defining moment in their own sense of themselves. They had had to come to terms not only with the multitude of deaths in the fighting itself, but also with the stigma of having been expelled as refugees, forced to hand over their prepubescent daughters as wives to their hosts:

in return for tumbledown houses,
in return for overgrown sweet potato gardens.

It had also been during this intense period of fighting that people believe took place the betrayals of fellow clansmen, the inadvertent killing of kin, the making and breaching of pacts which continue to resonate as death, depletion, infertility and affliction in the present. If these formative experiences led Komblo men to have a doubly ritual attitude towards warfare, it also had consequences for me. Komblo men's reiteration of the significance of this period, their constant relating of the events of the present to this originary time, and their initial exclusion of me from the details of it, engendered an enduring sense, despite myself, of having somehow missed a vital dimension to culture, endowing warfare with a mistaken sense of concreteness, as though it were an artefact which, if only I could finally see it, would impart the missing sense of lived experience. It was this, I now understand, which engendered the conflicting emotions I have tried to describe: of simultaneously being troublingly pleased to have seen that battle, yet disappointed by its inevitable failure to yield greater insight into a fetishised past.

Conclusion

In his pithy study of the literary and rhetorical devices used in writing up the results of fieldwork, van Maanen distinguishes three sorts of tales – 'realist', 'confessional' and 'impressionist' – and he delineates their characteristic forms and strategies. In realist tales, he says, the fieldworker is 'self-cast as a busy but unseen little fellow who is confident that the world as represented in the writing is the real one' (1988: 64). Realist tales are marked by closure; a problem posed at the opening of the text is seen to be more or less resolved by its close. In 'confessional' tales, in contrast, the narrator emerges centre-stage, admitting biases and inadequacies as 'a way of building an ironic self-portrait with which the readers can identify' (ibid.: 75). 'Confessional' tales may feature shock or surprise and describe a shift in point of view, often towards one said to be that of the natives themselves, though for all their purported striptease, confessional tales are no less constructed than 'realist' ones. 'Impressionist tales' often similarly feature such a shift in perspective or understanding, and (like some confessional tales) may become the starting point for reflective or meditative themes. 'Impressionist' tales differ, however, both in the fact that the events described are generally extraordinary rather than mundane, and in the balance that is kept between realistic objectivism and the 'self-absorbed mandates' (ibid.: 73) of 'confessional' tales.

I am not sure where to place my own tale in terms of van Maanen's typology. It would seem to have elements of all three; indeed, van Maanen acknowledges that the modes are by no means mutually exclusive. 'Confessional' tales often complement 'realist' ones, he notes: though for reasons I don't understand he regards the very specific character of the events and people in 'impressionist' tales as fitting less happily into realist or confessional writing (ibid.: 108). The account I have provided of the battle itself is a factual one, and to that extent 'realist', but the event itself had something of the exceptional quality which van Maanen associates rather with 'impressionist' tales. Indeed one could imagine that a coldly realist mode of expression might, in some circumstances, make a tale more arresting than adopting an 'impressionistic' rhetorical style. And, of course, this chapter has also been a piece of confessional writing, reflecting upon an event that I once witnessed which I found disturbing and dense with sensory impressions, but which took place in circumstances which seemed to deprive it of a theoretical context – until I saw a way of making that very lack a context in its own right.

NOTES

1. Earlier versions of this account have been presented at the Universities of Oxford and Edinburgh, at University College London, and at the Australian National University. Among those others whose advice is gratefully acknowledged, but who are entirely exonerated from responsibility for the defects in a paper which I have not found easy to write, are: John Burton, James Carrier, Linda Frankland, Wendy James, Peter Loizos, David Parkin, Jay Ruby, Jeffrey Ruoff, Jonathan Spencer and Andrew Strathern.
2. This is the group I have elsewhere referred to as 'Koleka' (e.g. O'Hanlon 1995: 479), this being the North Wall pronunciation.
3. E.g. Connolly and Anderson's *Black Harvest* (1992).
4. Reay states that in one battle in 1979–80 in the Minj area women took an even more active role, hurling stones at the opposing side, but that this was so effective that men intervened to prevent them, since they (the men) 'needed to take the credit for all the deaths on the other side' (1982: 631). Presumably, some kind of immunity must have been extended to the women in question, to allow them to get close enough to hit any warrior with a thrown stone. This is reminiscent of the situation among the Kapauku Papuans, where women also collect arrows on the battlefield for their husbands but additionally are granted an immunity which allows them to function as scouts and to protect the flanks of advancing forces (Pospisil 1963: 59).

Chapter 3

BEYOND THE FIRST ENCOUNTER:

TRANSFORMATIONS OF 'THE FIELD' IN NORTH EAST AFRICA

Wendy James

Fieldwork is usually discussed in an imaginative present; it is pictured in a here-and-now frame, an encapsulated moment of encounter. 'Observation' as seeing, and even 'participation' as doing, are actively engaged in the moment, and it is the quality of that moment which is conventionally supposed to define our distinctive scholarly insight as anthropologists. Left out of this picture are equally important aspects of 'fieldwork' which escape the momentary frame: these are most obviously rooted in the processes of language, and especially in those aspects of our conversational engagement with 'informants' which even on a short visit exceed the moment. This language-based side of fieldwork is concerned less with active observing, than with receptive listening; less with participation, than with memory, reflection, and thinking about a situation from a certain distance, through a plurality of methods beyond 'fieldwork' as such and more like those of the historian. Seeing and doing is of the experienced moment, cast in a conceptual or ethnographic present, but inevitably it too becomes recast in memory (see David Parkin's discussion in chapter 4). Listening, from the start, is necessarily set in time. It draws on memory and anticipates replies, whether in the direct question-and-answer mode of a bilateral conversation, or in more passive mode amidst a storm of voices.[1]

James Clifford wrote: 'We notice how much has been said, in criticism and praise, of the ethnographic gaze. But what of the ethnographic ear?' (Clifford 1986: 12). There is some interesting and pertinent discussion in Gemma Fiumara's recent book on the 'listening' side of language, where the active agency of speaking, writing, opining and defining is set conceptually against the receptive nature of interpretation and understanding (Fiumara 1990). 'Observing', we might add, implies one active person; 'listening' requires at least two, and as a method most effectively comes into its own in a community, a shared and larger situation. As ethnographer one is rarely an independent observer; one is nearly always a dependent listener, trying to catch at least one but often many more than one other voice, indeed to capture both sides of a conversation or argument between various others, to engage in a discourse with many levels. There is not only speech; there are silences, there are actions and events. One is listening as a temporary film extra might have to in the middle of an epic drama; from where do I come in, what side am I on, what is my cue and how do I avoid making a fool of myself?

Over time, the sense of being historically placed in a developing situation can intensify. At the start of fieldwork one naively has the impression of embarking on a short adventure story, to be nicely rounded off with one's own chosen moment of farewell. In my case it soon became clear that the story was not really mine, and certainly not under my control. The field was a moving target: 'observing' it was rather like trying to capture shifting scenery from a series of moving escalators. I found I understood more by listening than by observing. Moreover, long-term fieldwork can never be a passive matter of returning to re-observe the same scene. Quite apart from the ethnographer's own ageing and changing circumstances, the choreography of internal discourse and action in any community will transform itself through local memory over decades. Succeeding generations of contrasting ethnographies about the same locality can later be interpreted as different 'takes' on a changing local plot, as Borofsky has shown for the island communities of Puka Puka (Borofsky 1987). Even for a lone scholar working in a relatively peaceful and stable part of the world, repeat visits must be more than 'checking up on the ethnographic facts' or observing 'social change'; they must include listening and responding to changing reflections on a past now shared with the ethnographer. In more turbulent circumstances, there are likely to have been several dramatic turns in the local story and the ethnographer may be cast in a different role, pick up different cues and have to revise old interpretations.

My own experience of fieldwork has been rather like being dragged from the audience to play a series of different bit parts in an endlessly unfolding action serial. I have got to know some of the other actors personally. In most cases they have no option but to play out the tragedies and semi-comic ironies of their allocated roles, even to the death. I have a lot of sympathy for them, and want to understand better what is driving the whole story. I have made efforts from time to time to spread and diversify my research, to abandon North East Africa and go to India, or to the pueblos of Colorado and New Mexico, for example; but circumstances have drawn me back again and again over thirty-five years to the Uduk-speaking communities of the Sudan-Ethiopian border. My relationship with them has become more intense with each encounter, not because of its intrinsic nature or through positive friendship (in some ways the discomfort and sense of personal distance has increased more than the effective feeling of friendship) but because of the changing politics of a wider situation which has thrown us together in unexpected ways.

The focus of my research was originally in some vague way the internal 'society and culture' of the Uduk, but very soon it became a question of how their lives were set in time: what had happened in the past, as an illumination of the present. It then became a question of space; since they were displaced wholesale in 1987, my efforts have been devoted, on and off, to finding out where they were, under whose 'protection' if any, and when, if ever, they will be able to 'go home'. The story of the last decade and more has become a trekking out of one socio-political space and into another, as the very shape of these spaces has changed with the waxing and waning of the influence of governments, guerrilla movements and international powers (a story sketched in James 1996). The dominant questions have become: what is happening to them right now, and why, who is to blame and what is to happen next? As of late 1999, the primary homeland of the Uduk people in the Sudan is empty of civilians, as it was in 1899. Some are serving in the Sudan government forces, some in the Sudan People's Liberation Army (SPLA). The rural population who survive are stranded in a couple of temporary refugee schemes across the border in Ethiopia, one of them almost exactly a place of refuge in the previous century. The local district town of Kurmuk, which adjoins the frontier, has been taken for the third time by forces of the SPLA, who still hold it; and there is no visible solution to the Sudanese civil war.

Induction

I had been captivated by the writings of Professor (later Sir Edward) Evans-Pritchard while still an undergraduate reading geography. As a graduate student, I was later taught mainly by him and by Godfrey Lienhardt, but it was not my original intention to follow the existing links of Oxford anthropology to the Sudan. I had been committed to the idea of studying in some part of Africa since I was a teenager, intrigued by my father's stories of Uganda (he was seconded to Makerere University College in the 1950s). I had myself spent a few months in the then still British-run territory of Tanganyika, and would have loved to return to East Africa. I belonged to the 'postwar baby boom' in British anthropology, a generation of graduate students whose numbers were suddenly rising in the early 1960s just as the sources of funding which had supported the subject in the late colonial period began to dry up. My generation had been warned that there were more of us than could be funded from the usual sources, and so we might think of applying for jobs as well as for research funds. Armed only with a Diploma and B.Litt. in anthropology, I was given a lecturership in the University of Khartoum at the age of twenty-four, being reassured at the interview in London that I would be able to do field research for my doctorate as a part of this employment.

The first modern civil war in the Sudan (1955–72) was escalating at the time when I first arrived to teach in Khartoum, and textbook conditions for studying 'the south' were out of the question. Given my primary interest in the civilisations of Africa, I considered the marginal area of the Nuba Hills, bordering the predominantly Arabic-speaking and Islamic northern regions of the Sudan, as a possible location, and began to seek advice. Ian Cunnison, then head of the Department of Social Anthropology and Sociology, more or less ruled this out. The first reason he gave was that it would be too difficult for a woman (not only on grounds that it would be physically tough in that area but also that it was becoming politically tense). The second was that we were already expecting a new colleague who was coming specifically with a view to doing research in the Nuba Hills (Jim Faris). After considering various other possibilities I decided on a preliminary trip to the southern Blue Nile. Nobody could then have realised that this would be no less tough and politically complicated. Ian also suggested, when I came back and discussed possibilities, that I should choose a reasonably large group, not a very small one, for my research – suggesting a figure of 30,000 minimum. In the end I chose to stick with the Uduk – who were many fewer than this, probably around 10,000 at that time. I can now see some of the reasons why Ian gave me the advice he did, and how I might have had an easier time following it. At the time, I thought I had given myself a modest and manageable topic for study, the society and culture of a people who had recently had missionaries and for whom therefore there were language materials; they included a few English-speaking Christians, they broadly shared the cultural history of the 'south' but for arbitrary administrative reasons were included in 'the north' and were therefore accessible to me. If they had been a much larger group – say the Ingessana whom I nearly chose (compare Jedrej

1995, Okazaki 1997) – I would probably have remained within their embrace, their cultural world, in classic ethnographic mode, my ambition restricted to the interpretation of this world. There would have been a relatively cosy closure between me and this self-contained 'field', plausibly fulfilling that promise of completeness which an older anthropology had seemed to offer. Would I have seen beyond what I would have taken for its own horizons?

In the event, even in the 1960s I could see that 'the Uduk world' was an untenable fiction. They were such a small, dispersed and vulnerable set of communities, that they knew this themselves; their memories and fears reached out beyond any apparent cultural bounds, and they relativised their own identity in the present. They had to be seen as part of a wider regional and historical formation. Over the years I have come to see very clearly that my own presence among them was a minor sideshow of the same history: as a young Westerner making the most of an opportunity for ethnographic intimacy with a 'southern' community after the first intensification of civil war had conveniently absented the missionaries but before the resurgence of war in the mid-1980s physically destroyed the whole area.

The first encounter

The relationship between myself and the Uduk people took on a very particular character from the start, linked to the specific starting date of late 1965/early 1966, and developing through the series of fairly short visits I was able to make up to mid-1969 when my contract with the University of Khartoum came to an end. Had I arrived two or three years earlier, there would have been foreign missionaries (mostly American women) resident at Chali, a station of the evangelical Sudan Interior Mission devoted mainly to converting the Uduk. I believe that I would have chosen a different area to settle in, and a different language to learn. At the least, I would have settled as far as possible from Chali. Had I arrived two or three years later, when the civil war had intensified, it is possible that the authorities would not have allowed me to conduct research in this area at all. As it was, the missionaries were deported in early 1964, and I established myself less than two years later in a hamlet a few miles from Chali (just far enough away, I thought, from the old mission) and embarked on 'fieldwork' in the classic sense.

It was important and in fact easy to establish that I was not a missionary – accepting local beer made this clear – and I soon found myself welcomed as a convenient ear for grumbles about the tough puritan discipline of the mission days. Many of these stories came from those in the outlying hamlets who had some experience of mission

school but after falling by the wayside had returned home. Looking
back, I now believe that a kind of conspiratorial intimacy was born
between me and my particular range of close friends and informants
at this time, a pact of sympathy against the authoritarian regime of
the old mission; and on the basis of this original intimacy, I came to
share their (discreetly bolshie) attitudes to money-making merchants,
supercilious nomad Arabs, overbearing policemen and, in due course
(on a revisit in the early 1980s), the presence of patrolling soldiers.
Eventually the political story of the independent Sudan and its struggles to redefine its national identity in an Islamic mould came to dominate and reshape my relation to the Uduk people as a whole, and to
redefine my relation to former friends and institutions in the Sudan,
north and south – even to the point (in the early 1990s) where I found
myself working in mutual sympathy with the former mission body,
latterly renamed as the Society of International Missionaries (still
abbreviated as SIM). Over time, a particular and perhaps precariously
narrow 'field' relationship seeded at a sensitive time has developed in
unexpected ways.

Fitting in the fieldwork: Sudan, 1964–9

Right through my five years with the University of Khartoum, fieldwork meant fitting visits in and around my teaching and examining
duties. After leading two excursions of some weeks each with student
teams to the slums of Port Sudan (a project our department was invited
to undertake as a contribution to tackling the welfare problems of rapid
urbanisation), I managed nearly a year and a half in my own chosen
'field' – that is, the Uduk villages of the southern Blue Nile – but this
consisted of specified terms of research leave and part-vacations spread
over a longer span of several years. I was always conscious of having to
keep an eye on something else. The longest single period was of six
months, and for part of that time I had a Sudanese student with me for
'fieldwork training'. Although I had the advantage of coming and
going and turning up again unexpectedly in the Uduk villages, and thus
establishing the impression that I was an old friend, I rarely had the feeling myself of being on more than a provisional quick visit, and envied
those contemporaries who were able to stay a year, or two years, on a
honeymoon field research project, untrammelled by other duties and
able to luxuriate in local culture, Malinowskian style.

    Later on, I remember being interviewed for a position at the LSE
and defending my apparently weak commitment to fieldwork. The
panel asked why I hadn't ever stayed a complete agricultural year in
my field area, and I was grilled about this quite pointedly. My excuse

about the start of the Khartoum University academic year clashing with the harvest season in Udukland seemed rather lame even to myself, and I still greatly regret never having celebrated the first fruits with them, or joined their rounds of glad feasting at this time. A professional fieldworker should obviously have been there. Later on I did not feel so bad about this, and now I do not wish to apologise. There is no such thing as completeness in fieldwork. What I may have missed as regards the October-December season in the southern Blue Nile, as a first-time fieldworker, I have now made up for in unexpected ways. Disruptions and discontinuities were not always visible in the field notes of an earlier era, nor in monographs, but they are present in life, and current circumstances in the war zones of Africa and elsewhere now dictate that they are made visible in our notes. 'Displacement', 'violence', 'memory' and so on have even become standard topics in the teaching of anthropology. The older assumptions (on which I was brought up) that what we were studying were essentially the principles of 'order' in society, and the regularity of the ways in which people understand the world, have been themselves displaced.

My first fieldwork itself was shaped by the security situation, though I did not realise at the time that my frustrations were a kind of fieldwork in themselves. Deliberately acting as sensitively as I could, in the course of my initial tours of the southern Blue Nile I avoided making a beeline for the former mission at Chali among the Uduk, right on the frontier with the south and the (first) civil war, though I knew of its existence. When the local (Muslim) officials in the district town of Kurmuk invited me to join them on a visit there on Christmas Day, 1965, I accepted. Immediately liking the feel of the place, and seeing what appeared a wonderful opportunity for research, I arranged to stay on, and engaged a language teacher in proper fieldworking style. After the first few weeks I was apprehended by the police, and had to return to Kurmuk, where restrictions were placed on my movements for a week. The authorities assumed I must be some sort of returning missionary and would have got rid of me altogether if I had not been employed by Khartoum University, then a respected and prestigious institution.

When I returned on the next occasion I took care to bring a suitcase full of permissions and a Sudanese student. His role, in part, was to explain to the local authorities (in Arabic, and as a fellow-national) the importance of academic field studies in social anthropology as a part of the national development effort. This worked and certainly made it possible for me to stay on for a few months. I had by now moved to my chosen hamlet at some distance from the old mission and the police station. But I never knew, on this or any of my subsequent visits, when the authorities would again ask me to leave. The local police always kept an eye on me, walking over the few miles from the station to visit my hut and check up unexpectedly, sometimes at six o'clock in the morning. I tried to keep up friendly relations with them, the high point being when I was able to send them over a bag of tomatoes from my own vegetable patch. At no point was I ever sure how much longer I would have to do my fieldwork. There was even an organised delegation of Muslim merchants protesting to the Kurmuk district authorities at my presence in the rainy season of 1966 – they thought I was a covert missionary. While I was actually there among the Uduk I was always conscious of the need to make the most of the time. I think this is why I decided to take large boxes of batteries and record as much verbal material as I could (on three-inch reels – this was before cassette recorders). It seemed very important to capture whatever I could in the way of stories, conversations, songs, et cetera, so that I would have plenty of texts to mull over later.

I think this strategy worked; I have always used a tape-recorder (as well as still and 8 mm film camera, and more recently a video camera). 'My informants' are pretty well used to this and in the refugee camps today they expect me to take photographs and make tapes to send to their relatives elsewhere. This method of working has become even more necessary in the short and pressured revisits I have made in recent years. I believe it was not common in anthropology when I started, but it has left me with a tremendous archive of spoken material from Uduk informants, in many cases arising from conversation with the same individuals at different places, and different times, which I have drawn on in all my writing and hope to go on using in my work. I think, moreover, that there were some other 'plus' features to the whole strained situation in which I carried out my original fieldwork. I was never able to think of it as something self-contained, insulated from my 'normal' life. In the original fieldwork I was not (nor was I seen to be) from outer space, but from a secure position in the country itself; my findings were fed back into my teaching at the University, and throughout my five years working in the country at that time I inevitably picked up very much more about its history, ethnography and current politics than an average visiting researcher could have. Moreover, I was teaching regularly, both general anthropology courses from the first year up to the optional honours degree year, and also courses on the Sudan itself, both ethnographic coverage and problem-oriented courses on social change. My use of Uduk ethnography in my teaching led to various reactions from students and colleagues; conversations over this made me realise that my own work was adding to the 'visibility' of the Uduk, already regarded as an anomalous group of Christians in the North, a political 'visibility' which eventually became tragic.

Whatever good it did me, the five years' experience of teaching in Khartoum has complicated the way I see social anthropology, the historical vulnerability of its 'theory' and the political entanglements of its research practices. Living in Khartoum, mixing with a growingly significant range of 'others' (i.e., colleagues, students and friends) who were debating the nature of their own country and their own future, was (in retrospect) central to my 'fieldwork'. Before I ever accepted the job in Khartoum and gave up the idea of research in Nigeria, Uganda or elsewhere, I had been told quite firmly in the Kings Arms (mainly by Peter Lienhardt, though Godfrey backed him up) that it would be good for me to have to learn some Arabic and to teach students. I did attend Arabic classes for a year, and I made a point of seeing what parts of the country I could, though these opportunities were not many. My regular movements mainly by vehicle, but also in part by donkey and on foot between the southern Blue Nile and the capital city, made me very conscious of the escalating civil war and rising tension in the country as a whole. Nationality and gender were relevant here: as a British person, one was often welcomed in the remoter areas of the Sudan at that time – especially the non-Islamic ones. Older people gave a flattering appraisal of the former 'English' rule, and the Uduk in particular remembered being given peace by the 'English Turks' at the turn of the century (indeed in the current war they ask why the 'English' don't do more to help them). As a woman, I felt more comfortable in the villages of the southern Blue Nile than I had done in the northern Sudan, especially among the matrilineal Uduk where women wielded personal freedoms unknown in most parts of the country. In Khartoum, as one of the very few single women teaching in the University, I suppose I represented some kind of progressive modernity, but at the same time had to listen to friendly but firm advice from my women students about my dress – they insisted on sleeves and longer hemlines, because the young men were already 'talking about' me.

As the civil war intensified, I became clearly identifiable as someone sympathetic to the southern cause. Friendships with northern Sudanese in Khartoum, and even teacher/pupil relations, became more and more uneasy. This period seemed to coincide with a rise in public Islamic consciousness and a new conservatism about the place of women, both aspects of northern Sudanese society I found impinging on me, personally and professionally. I remember taking a class one day on the Somali; we were using Ioan Lewis's contrast between the ecology, and corresponding forms of religious organisation, of northern and southern Somalia. A young man put up his hand; he didn't understand what I had just explained. I went over the argument again carefully. The student rather too firmly declared that he still did not understand how variations in Islam could be explained by geography. I asked for a show of hands by those who shared this problem, and the show was decisive. Realising that they were denying me, as a young female Westerner, the right to 'explain' variations in Islamic belief on the basis of any kind of social science, I said we'd better leave it there for today, gathered up my books and walked out. I had come up against what Paul Dresch in this book (chapter 5) dubs a 'strong model' in which there is a proper place for strangers and limits to what they can do or say.

My actual 'fieldwork' visits to the Blue Nile villages were in a way a release from these rising tensions in Khartoum. On looking back now after so many years, I realise that the real challenge for me, as a personal question and as an academic one, lay not in the relative 'safe haven' of my professional fieldwork but in my encounter with Khartoum as a city and with what was happening in Sudanese society at the centre. The Uduk and other small communities out in the bush were facing these national-level changes too. While it was a worrying outlook even in the late 1960s, it could not then have been imagined that a couple of decades later appalling numbers of people would die as a result of continuing war, and hundreds of thousands (including all the rural Uduk) would have left the country altogether and become refugees.

Getting away from the Uduk: Ethiopia, 1974–5

I had realised the need to avoid 'boxing in' my research around one small community before my five years in the University of Khartoum were up, though on my return to Oxford I wrote a fairly conventional thesis. After a period attending conferences and teaching in Fredrik Barth's department in Bergen, mainly arguing about 'theory' in anthropology (see for example James 1970, 1973a, 1973b), I saw my next opportunity for 'fieldwork', which came in the mid-1970s, as a chance to open things up. I wanted initially to go to western Ethiopia, and to study the series of minority groups in the hills and valleys of the escarpment, such as the Koma, Mao and Gumuz. Only some of these groups were linguistically related to the Uduk, but all shared a comparable historical experience and one which I could relate to those of the peoples on the Sudan side. However, I saw this project as a way of moving into 'Ethiopian studies' more widely. I did not want to be identified for ever as a 'one-tribe' anthropologist, or even a 'tribal' specialist as such, and in the hope of embarking on a series of research projects which would give me the chance to write about Ethiopian civilisation as a whole, I organised Amharic classes in Oxford. A few others joined in, and we studied for about six months. I got a grant from the old SSRC (Social Science Research Council), and as a result was able to spend a term's sabbatical and a couple of long vacations in Ethiopia in 1974 and 1975. This was a fruitful period in itself, though this research could not be completed because of Ethiopia's socialist revolution which was gathering steam at the time and which eventually led to the repressive regime of Mengistu Haile Mariam.

I believe that the ethnographic work I did then has some value (see the references in James 1986, 1988) but, as with my Sudanese experience, the greatest value for me of this period of 'fieldwork' was the entry it provided into understanding something of the history and current experiences of Ethiopia as a whole. *Faute de mieux*, I and other colleagues who had been doing fieldwork in rural Ethiopia in the early 1970s and were unable to return decided to make the most of our 'peripheral' perspectives on the imperial period, and produced a book on this theme which was surprisingly well received (Donham and James 1986). While my own paper in this book was devoted to my field enquiries among the Gumuz of the Blue Nile, a people who lived on both sides of the international border, what attracted comment was the way in which, collectively, we had related 'fieldwork' research to a wider framework of historical and political analysis. This Ethiopian interlude in my work provided, as it turned out, a basis on which I could claim some competence, in the 1990s, to carry out 'real' historical research (see James, Baumann and Johnson 1996) and also to take on what used to be called 'applied anthropology', reporting on refugee issues affecting the border.

Return to the Sudan, and touching base with the Uduk: 1982–3

Because of the 1974 socialist revolution in Ethiopia and its violent aftermath, ordinary research projects by outsiders, and even by Ethiopian nationals, became almost impossible for nearly twenty years. It was certainly out of the question for me to return there for a long while. On the Sudan side, which I still know very much better than the Ethiopian, I had one further sabbatical leave opportunity for a different kind of fieldwork, in the southern city of Juba. This had been established as the regional capital of the Southern Sudan by the peace agreement of 1972. By 1982 my husband Douglas Johnson, already a historian of the region, was employed there as a civil servant on an archives project. Though we had small children with us, I was able to start on a study of the town itself and the social history of 'southern Arabic'. This research, which I expected to develop into a wider set of studies on the urban communities of the Sudan and Uganda, was again cut short, by the abolition of the Southern Regional government and the renewed outbreak of civil war in 1983. But though our work was unfinished and our departure premature, I did have the chance to visit areas of the Southern Sudan I had never

seen before, as we travelled through (for me) romantic and atmos-
pheric regions where the Nuer and Dinka and Azande peoples lived.

I was also drawn back into the orbit of the Uduk, through the unexpected opportunity of a revisit to the southern Blue Nile, with husband and children in tow. This was a short but extremely productive
opportunity for my writing. It was also a visit which clarified some of
the difficulties and rewards of 'long-term' fieldwork. We arrived (by
road from 'the south'), Douglas inexplicably a civil servant from Juba,
with myself as his wife trying to explain to the newly established and
very suspicious garrison in Chali in a very rough Arabic dialect the
reason why we had come. We finally got through to some sort of temporary understanding on the main basis that I had once taught in the
University of Khartoum. I was extremely relieved and happy, in a way,
to be back in my old hamlet, and my old friends were delighted at my
new family circumstances. There were tensions, however, symbolised
by ominous lorry tracks around the settlement, where I had never seen
vehicle tracks except my own. The people said that the soldiers came
up regularly, looking for labourers.

Flight of the Uduk: tracing the dispersal, 1987–99

My first ethnography of the Uduk was built around the theme of
uncertainty and insecurity, as the people looked to the past (James
1979). I came to realise as I was writing it that the people had understood better than I had at the time how fragile too was the social peace
of the 'present' during the first civil war of the independent Sudan. By
1987–8, and the publication of my second full-length ethnography
(James 1988), renewed civil war was raging and the news was confirmed of the total destruction of villages in the southernmost Blue
Nile. Thousands of people had fled under fire across the border to
Ethiopia. My 'field' in the narrow sense had disappeared, and been
replaced by an international arena of conflict and crisis. The story of
the people, which I tried to follow from then on, had to be framed
within the perspective of internal events in Ethiopia, and the international relations between that country and the Sudan. Their common
border at this time was one of the last frontiers of the Cold War.

I was on my way to Addis Ababa in late 1989, partly to find out from
the UNHCR office (United Nations Commissioner for Refugees) there
whether I could visit the refugee camp where most of the Uduk were said
to be, when I saw on the airline television news that the Berlin Wall had
fallen. Part of western Ethiopia had already gone too, to the control of
the anti-Mengistu forces. I was not surprised to find out in Addis Ababa
that I could not visit the camp. From then onwards, as I have described

elsewhere, the surviving core of the Uduk-speaking people have crossed the international border several more times. After a third attempt to seek asylum in Ethiopia, at the time of writing they are mostly in two separate refugee schemes in the southwest of the country (James 1996). Some have been in refugee camps in Kenya and Uganda as well as in Ethiopia; they have redefined their relationship to the SPLA and its own internal factions on several occasions, and there are even today young men fighting on pretty well all sides of the current civil war. Individuals over the last decade have reached as far as Alexandria and Nairobi under their own steam, and others have arrived in places such as Dallas and Salt Lake City through international refugee resettlement programmes. To give any account of this dispersal I have to take account of changing political relations not only across North East Africa, but also of US policies; of UN policies and especially of its funding priorities; the projects of the missionary organisation (SIM), which maintains a key relationship with the scattered Uduk communities mainly through its offices in the capital cities of Addis Ababa and Khartoum (where it still holds freehold property). The missionaries have by now moved back into educational activities for the refugees, and into centre stage as far as my 'field' is concerned; I have exchanged information with them and now get on very well with them as individuals. I have a long-standing plan to visit the Billy Graham archive centre in the US, where I believe there are some records of the SIM and their work among the Uduk. I would now like to write more sympathetically about their commitment than I ever thought would be possible for me. The people themselves now nearly all claim to be Christians, and partly because of this the old 'conspiratorial' feeling I shared with them has had to take on new forms.

The anthropologist turned consultant: 1991–4

Though I had not anticipated it at the time, the renewed contact of 1983 made it very much easier to reestablish *rapport* several years later on, in a series of short encounters with displaced groups in exile after the wholesale flight of 1987. A brief visit was made to Khartoum in the summer of 1988, when I saw something of those who had been stranded there by the war. The main part of the rural population of the southern Blue Nile were on and off in Ethiopia and inaccessible to me until 1991, when many thousands of them had shown up, back across the Sudanese border, in the crumbling town of Nasir in eastern Nuer country, where the UN flag now flew (Figure 5). They had arrived there under duress, as a result of the shifts and turns of a war which had carried them southwards in the wake of the SPLA, retreating first from the Sudan government onslaughts and then from the collapse of

Figure 5a *Getting to 'the field', Upper Nile, 1990s style*

Figure 5b *UN headquarters at Nasir, 1991*

Mengistu's regime in Ethiopia. Twice during the Oxford long vacation that year, I had the opportunity to report on some of the stranded communities in Nasir to the Nairobi-based UN Operation Lifeline Sudan. The Uduk were struggling to keep going in very difficult circumstances (see Figure 6). On two later occasions (1992, 1994) I reported from Gambela to the UN in Addis Ababa after 'the Uduk' – by now quite famous in aid circles – had returned again to Ethiopia. An invitation from *Disappearing World*, which resulted partly from David Turton's knowledge of my activities, brought me back in 1993 to my long-term 'field', now a new transit camp for asylum seekers, to do a bit more private 'fieldwork' in the course of making a documentary film about displacement, bereavement and memory. All these projects helped me realise how one's own research, even of the most intimate 'psychological' kind, is embedded in events affecting a whole region over time. In fact I was caught up in a violent incident and had to help bring in the military authorities; relations were strikingly transformed for a moment as between Uduk and Nuer in the camp. I wrote this up as a study of the forms of fear (James 1997). The time in question now included the end of the Cold War, a new generation of small wars in the Middle East and the Horn of Africa, and the entrenchment of a particularly nasty militant Islamic regime in Khartoum. This regime is still prosecuting a *jihad* (holy war) against people of the kind I originally chose to study, though attempting (as of the last year or so) to improve its image with the West; the US, meanwhile, classifies it as a regime guilty of state terrorism, has engineered many international sanctions, and in 1998 used long-distance missiles to destroy a factory in Khartoum.

'Fieldwork', at least in Africa, has lost its innocence. While anthropology has ironically gained a firmer foothold in African universities since the 1960s, fieldwork can no longer be talked about straightforwardly as social science. Who is in charge, anyway, of the spaces in which anthropologists seek to work, whether they are local nationals or outsiders? In these postcolonial days, funding applications from wheresoever have to be addressed to the quite different expectations of international academic peer-review and of institutional or political gatekeepers in Africa. There was perhaps a time when applications for funding were couched in terms of a search for new places and people to describe: filling in the ethnographic record. But even my own first requests for Ford Foundation research money available to my faculty in the University of Khartoum had to be phrased in terms of development priorities; there was a strong reference to the imminent completion of the Blue Nile Dam at Roseires, and the consequent need to survey the rural communities of the area. While today's applications to Western funding bodies may refer to more whimsical themes of

Figure 6a *Bible-study in a camp at Nasir*

Figure 6b *Improvising 'hearth stones' from Nile mud*

identity, memory, reflexivity and so on, to public bodies in most 'developing' countries a demonstrably pragmatic line is likely to produce better results. What does a fieldworker do, what use is it, and to whom is the benefit?

I remember trying to explain my original project in the women's quarters of a very hospitable merchant's family in a small town on the border with Ethiopia, a town long associated with slave-trading. They could not understand why someone like me, a teacher from the University, should be going to the 'Burun' villages to live (a blanket term for all the miscellaneous locals between the Ethiopian border mountains and the Nilotic plains to the west). I pointed out that there were no books at all about the 'Burun', the way they lived, cultivated the land, and their interesting customs, and that teachers and students in the University wanted to have books about all parts of the Sudan and all Sudanese people. This seemed to work. 'Yes,' said one sharp old lady abruptly, 'it is quite true: the Burun are very clever. The sons of the *'abid* [slaves] are *extremely* clever. I have seen that for myself.' An extended silence ensued. Later, in the town of Kurmuk, I was explaining to a group of (male) officials and merchants over tea one evening what I planned to do. I had already been speaking to one old trader who had been given administrative responsibility over the 'Burun' areas in (I think) the 1920s. I thought I would use the justification of fieldwork as 'history', so that it did not look too political. I had misjudged what was political on this old slaving frontier. There were no books about the history of the Burun, I explained, and this was why the University had sent me to do this study. 'But the Burun', I was told quite stiffly, 'the Burun do not have any history. And you said before you were studying anthropology. You did not say you were studying history. What is it you are really after?'

In the course of my more recent 'field' trips, I have had to explain to various UN and aid agencies what research I had already done, and what advice I could therefore offer. The modern assumption is that one can supply information about 'culture'. A couple of nurses, Scandinavian I think, approached me in Nasir in a tent full of exhausted mothers and babies, some half-dead. 'You're an anthropologist? We're so glad you've come. You can tell us about their culture. We have a problem with these women here. They won't breast-feed. Is there something in their culture about this?' A Finnish journalist interviewed me, asking whether it was true that these people had such a rich cultural knowledge of the bush and the forest, they had never starved before? She was very keen to hear about indigenous cultural knowledge, but could not see that while it had been useful to scattered hamlets in the forested hills, it did not help 20,000 people stranded together on muddy flats amidst the swamps of the Upper Nile. And yet whenever I did try to explain 'cultural' matters, such as matriliny and the relative autonomy of women, to whatever authorities were registering people and allocating plots and resources in one displaced camp or another, they were not so keen on listening. According to standard UNHCR and development agency practice, households are registered wherever possible under the names of men and their dependants, and male household heads are grouped according to former village units which are supposed to stay together. Authorities then tend to become totally confused with the matrilineal comings and goings – why should a young man who was registered to receive rations in his father's village suddenly move elsewhere? Nor can they understand the visibly large proportion of female headed households (and the tolerance of changing personal relationships). A group of refugees in the Gambela scheme agreed disgustedly with my diagnosis. 'You're right! That's quite true. The UN knows *nothing* about mothers' brothers.'

The UNHCR office in Addis Ababa included a senior official who was also a trained anthropologist. He was supportive of my work, and I think knew very well that whatever I wrote in the way of a report, the UN was itself a part of the longer trajectory of the story that concerned me. The PR official also was quite helpful later, understanding my interest in 'Uduk culture' and sending me a video tape of some musical performances which had been put on in Addis Ababa as part of Refugee Day, 1994. I knew that some of the Uduk had gone up to Addis to take part in this, and looked forward to seeing the tape. Unfortunately, they don't appear (except for a glimpse in the grand finale and curtain) – the show was hogged by Nuer and Somali.

The Uduk were once so remote that the Anglo-Egyptian government in the Sudan (i.e., the Brits) decided that if American fundamentalist missionaries were allowed to work there, at least they could not cause significant disruption. Ironically, and partly because of that historic decision which rested on a recognition of the people's vulnerability, the Uduk have become a lens through which the major shapes of regional historical and religious transformation can be brought into clear focus. They have responded sensitively and flexibly to a whole series of modern 'global' discourses concerning nationalism and 'ethnicity', the world religions, culture, refugees, heritage, identity and so on. Pursuing the evidence to write about this well is what my 'fieldwork' has now become. I am obliged to try to put to critical use the fact that my research has remained for so long a series of provisional and partial approaches, fragmentary and dislocated encounters, guesses as what is going on and speculating (along with all categories of 'informants') what on earth will happen next. Here I have found Tim Jenkins' recent paper on fieldwork extremely helpful; complete accounts in conscious language may be made up on the hoof as the ethnographer elicits explanations from the informant, but beyond this, the social reality even of a stable community is itself a series of partial and hesitant encounters between parties with incomplete knowledge. Ordinary life shares with 'fieldwork' an element of 'apprenticeship', and the ethnographer has to learn much as a child learns (Jenkins 1994). If these observations are appropriate to everyday life and its academic study, how much more so to the visibly shifting ground and conscious uncertainties of a war zone.

Since acting as a consultant to the UNHCR and playing a part in the decision-making process which led to the setting up of a substantial refugee scheme near Gambela, and subsequently reporting on its progress, I have found myself not only an apprentice, but a practitioner – I have become in a way part of my own field of study. In so far as a relatively quiet space has opened for the core of the people, though of very limited extent and constrained in time, I have found myself playing a role in the making of this space. This position itself places a burden on me, and on my relationship with specific persons I used to know well. As not only a 'friend' of the people in general, but someone who had at one time a minor but effective voice with the UN, the refugees have come to expect miracles of me. It is very difficult to see how I can go back again (even to see personal friends) except in the role of consultant at a strategically-lucky time when I might be listened to. The task of offering advice and recommendations would be more tricky than before because the scheme has settled in, and UNHCR's view of its needs are not identical with those of the Ethiopian authorities. Meanwhile my various links with people in the diaspora remind me of the many levels of relative trust and distrust in which people of a war zone have to live, drawing on memories and hopes rooted far below the public allegiances of the moment.

Concluding commentary

Recent critiques have tended to privilege the idea of personal encounter as the essence of fieldwork. The very terms in which our fieldworking practices as a whole are discussed have converged on a defining phenomenological moment as the key to the whole endeavour. The word 'ethnography' is a case in point. I am sure that when I was a student, it did not have the abstract and elevated sense it now has – an essentialised category. An ethnography was a type of book, rather than a timeless mode of encountering and enciphering the world. There were useful and less useful ethnographies, a few excellent and imaginatively theoretical accounts among a range of bread-and-butter work, but all were valued as primary contributions to the general comparative and

analytical aims of social anthropology. Now, 'ethnography' is appropri-
ated in a more limited and specific way as one term among others for a
range of positivistic methods used by sociologists and psychologists – it
is added on to measurement and experiment as a means of recording
data. In its modern-day technical sense it scarcely acknowledges the
moral or conscious agency of those being studied, let alone the analytical imagination of the scholar, as the best of the traditional full-length
monographs, in my view, often did.

The idea of 'ethnography' as a method 'in the present' also tends to
encourage a simplistic notion of 'culture'; this runs right through
Writing culture, for example where Evans-Pritchard is said to suffer in
Nuerland as he crosses 'cultural boundaries' (Rosaldo 1986: 88–89).
Ethnography, presumably as a writable mode of experience, is said to
exist at the boundaries of cultures. It is true that Talal Asad suggests
that the idea of anthropology as the 'translation of culture' can be
traced back to Oxford, for example to John Beattie's *Other cultures*
(Asad 1986: 142, referring to Beattie 1964). But I believe this attack
is slightly off-target. The content and scope of Beattie's book is far
more world-historical than the title might suggest (well-informed people assumed at the time that 'other cultures' was a formulation supposed to appeal to the American student market). Tom Beidelman's
1971 collection for Evans-Pritchard was actually entitled *The translation of culture*; but very few of the essays even in this book speak to that
essentialised image of cultural difference that Asad is rightly concerned to criticise. I am quite sure that recent critics of mid-century
British social anthropology as 'culture-translation' have missed its
openness to historical analysis (compare for example Pocock 1971 –
first edition published in 1961 – and Lienhardt 1964; even Evans-
Pritchard 1937). Asad's arguments about the role of strong languages
feeding upon weaker in the disciplinary practice of anthropology are
true and well taken, as is his general advocacy of the need for academic analysis to reveal the underlying structures of domination in the
real world. Oxford anthropology has not been entirely innocent in this
respect, at least in its role as Asad's *alma mater*.

To some extent the idea of distinction and pure difference in 'culture' is linked with its twin image of fieldwork as a primary encounter
between opposites. The privileged scene imagined by both champions
and critics of fieldwork is that of the young scholar, newly arrived in a
foreign place (the *locus classicus* has to be Mary Louise Pratt's essay in
Clifford and Marcus 1986). Thus the questions that have come to
dominate the whole debate about 'ethnography' presuppose a fresh
starting point on both sides, on the part of the youngster leaving home
for the first time and also on the part of the community who find they
are cast in the role of host, teacher, friend and lover. The encounter,

later celebrated in anecdote, and these days also in professional writing, is emotional, mysterious; full first of silly misunderstandings, but later transformed to an elevated epiphany of understanding. The metaphor of the youthful courtship and love affair goes quite a long way. Novels are full of it, as ethnographies are of the scholar virgin's first encounters. But neither the novel about first love, nor the personal confessions about first fieldwork, are an adequate framework for appreciating the extended drama of a lifetime's loves, the history of a marriage, or a lifetime's struggles with the writer's 'others'. These are far from deriving their singularity from some oppositional relation to the person of the scholar; they are necessarily plural and mutually constitutive among themselves, something which historians (perhaps our closest academic cousins) take for granted.

Like historical research, good fieldwork is itself set in time. Repeated contact with a given field area or region is becoming more common in anthropology. Several of us (I am including students in the collective pronoun) have 'been there' in various different capacities – for example, as teachers, lecturers, project advisers, journalists, film makers, or political groupies. Some of us can claim to have gone more 'native' than others in the regions we study, by nationality or through marriage and affinal links (compare Louella Matsunaga's chapter in this volume). In fact most of us have become known figures in the regions we study, and have acquired an habitual status, long-term friends and so on not necessarily very different from those we have 'at home'. Even fellow academics are increasingly out there in the field, as colleagues and inevitably also as 'informants'. Some of the most delicate relationships I think one has to negotiate, whether as a foreigner or a national of the country concerned, often concern local intellectuals. Here I would include not only those actually employed in universities, but also local writers, editors, publishers, politicians, aid personnel et cetera – in fact the local intelligentsia, even down to secondary school children. Even if they are not formally 'gatekeepers' who can refuse one a permit, they are there in the bar, they are there on the bus to one's fieldwork village, they even show up around the camp fire in the evening while visiting their relatives. Are they part of 'the field'? They perhaps are, but they are also fellow interpreters of the social scene, and they do have their own opinions of what we seem to be well paid to do. Moreover, they have been trained in respected educational and academic contexts, and sometimes in long-established and authoritarian disciplines which do not necessarily have much respect for the whimsies of (post-) modern Western liberal anthropology, including the over-valued *naïveté* of first encounter. I think we should demystify this image of our selves and our method, and take a humbler approach to the hard work necessary 'in the field' to provide those analytical accounts of human life and experience which might outlast in their significance the emotional ups and downs of the author in producing them.

NOTE

1. I would like to acknowledge the helpful discussion which followed my presentation of a version of this paper at the seminar series held at Oxford in the autumn of 1998 on 'The identity of the fieldworker', organised by Shirley Ardener, Jonathan Webber and Ian Fowler.

Chapter 4

TEMPLATES, EVOCATIONS AND THE LONG-TERM FIELDWORKER

David Parkin

The various deconstructions of concept and method during the so-called crisis of representation in anthropology in the 1980s nevertheless soon set up new oppositions, one of which is that between experimental and experiential ethnographies (Poewe 1996; Olivier de Sardan 1992). This can essentially be glossed as a distinction between problems of writing and problems of actually doing fieldwork. According to Poewe (1996: 177–8), experimental ethnography is that first propounded by Clifford and Marcus (1986) and Marcus and Fischer (1986). It has also been called the literary critique (Fardon 1990), because, as is by now well known, it sees the 'facts' produced by fieldwork as shaped if not determined by the particular styles of writing and reading used by the ethnographer. Recognising the inevitability of this and of the impossibility of any other than skewed representations of societies which are studied, the proponents of the literary critique wish to experiment with different writing styles in order to include within the finished article or book the voices of the people under observation. What is striking about their approach is how little they actually say about fieldwork itself, as distinct from its representation.

Experiential ethnography, by contrast, seeks understanding through the engagement of selfhood in anthropological problems and especially through fieldwork experiences (Poewe 1996). In older language, we might say that experiential ethnography gets its knowledge from fieldwork and is inductive, allowing epistemological principles and problems to emerge from that experience and from a comparative reading of existing ethnographies.

Poewe (1996: 200) concedes that the two types of approach partially overlap, the one associated with so-called postmodernism and the other being of more traditional anthropological provenance. The first tries to find the best way of getting facts represented in text and the second asks how we arrive at the recognition of something as a fact from our involvement in the field. A third, nowadays less favoured approach is that of the fieldworker as impartial observer, participating if at all as at a distance, and objectively analysing social facts and institutions on the positivistic assumption that the anthropologist's presence in the field does not affect that which they observe. In so far as quantitative measurement is often part of fieldwork at some stage, there are at least elements of this approach in modern ethnography, but henceforth I do not deal with it.

Remembering fieldwork

Of course, once we take account of long-term fieldwork over many years among the same people and/or in the same region among related peoples, we are likely to conclude that we alternate at different points between, on the one hand, trying to represent adequately facts we are confident of and, on the other, losing our confidence in what we had earlier been sure about, wondering how we ever came to such a firm conclusion. We may start out very experientially but later develop experimental yearnings, and vice versa.

It seems to me that what is at root here is not so much a distinction between experimental and experiential ethnography, but rather the problem of fieldwork memory. This may take two directions. On the one hand, old field notes and what the writer remembers about the events to which they refer may take on the character of a template (cf. Ardener 1970), providing a generative model on which subsequent data are collected and interpreted.[1] Alternatively, the notes may have new meaning in the light of more recent theories and interpretations, and evoke experiences of the events rather than providing a ready-made explanation of them. Evocation is ambiguous and so precludes precise factual recall (Sperber 1974: 117–49; see also Maranh 1993). This is convenient if earlier assertions are no longer intellectually or ideologically tenable. By contrast, the notion of template presupposes an underlying paradigm of behavioural or cognitive consistency, around which elaboration may or may not occur. It oozes confidence, being foundational and yet flexibly contoured. Long-term fieldwork is increasingly a play between the paradigmatic and evocative, between the remembered facts and assertions we later build on and the events whose description and explanation no longer fit current theories and social and personal circumstances but which remain significant in an indeterminate way.

Why are we confident about our description and memory of some past fieldwork experiences and not others? I do not think that this is simply a matter of remembering some events better. It is more to do with the biography of remembered events: how they fare in the long passage from initial experience to theoretical placement. Let me begin to try and answer this question by contrasting one confidently remembered social fact from my own past fieldwork with a much less certain one.

In the late 1960s in an agricultural area of the Giriama of Kenya, I was told unambiguously, and recorded the fact, that certain aspects of Giriama relationships were terminologically divisible into three: respect/fear (*ku-ogoha*) between adjacent generations; joking/play (*ku-tseyana*) between same and alternate generations; and an intermediary respectful playfulness, translatable as clowning (*ku-imiria*), which was definitely not the same as joking and characterised the relationship with the mother's brother – who 'is a kind of father whom one must respect, and not joke with as one might in exchanging obscenities with a grandfather ... and from whom one could take things ... and even clown with' (Parkin 1991: 93–94). Seven years later, the same close friends were living in a mainly cattle-keeping area of Giriama country. They insisted that there were only respect and joking relationships and that they could never have said otherwise: *ku-ogoha* was contrasted with *ku-tseyana*. They continued to say that one could help oneself to a mother's brother's chicken and goats but not clown with him, for this would have been too disrespectful. The shift in their views clearly accorded greater formality towards the mother's brother who was treated even more like a father, except for the permitted 'theft' of animals or food.

I had recorded their remarks verbatim, and could only conclude that their views had changed but that my observations had been correct at the time. I am confident that what they said was different on the two occasions and so can reasonably claim that their views had indeed changed. That much appears factually correct. I might also speculate that the shift towards greater formality in the mother's brother relationship might be related to their residential shift from a farming to a cattle-keeping area, with the possible implication of more marked patriliny in the latter. That I do not know what many or all other Giriama would have said on the matter, nor whether they would have altered their views in the same way, is a problem of representative evidence but not one of confidence in one's memory and interpretation: the opposition between respect and joking terms and relationships remains a paradigmatic template which can be altered to include or exclude clowning.

My contrary example is also drawn from the Giriama farming area, and in particular a section of it densely covered with coconut palms, which are central to the subsistence and cash crop economy, and produce palm wine, which is extensively consumed on a daily basis and at rituals, especially funerals (Parkin 1972). During my first period of fieldwork among these Giriama in 1966–7, I recorded in my notes a whole number of binary oppositions reverberating through the society, several of them linked to the material and symbolic use of palm trees. I also believed at the time that I was not imposing such oppositions as a result of having read structuralism. The consistency and symmetrical elegance of the symbolic and practical oppositions were so startling that I had to examine carefully whether I was exaggerating what I saw. But I believed that this was not the case and that they were a central part of the reality I observed.

After fieldwork, when I was back in London writing up, a seminar paper presented possibly in late 1967 or early 1968 by James Fox on Indonesian (Roti) attitudes to palm trees and binary symbolism, premised on right:left :: life:death, was so uncannily like my own East African coastal data that I was literally left speechless: how could you convey that sense of comparative wonderment in the face of sceptics who at the time would dismiss the possibility of marked Indonesian effects on East African coastal society? It was not a good time to venture diffusionist explanations. Nowadays, I would risk ridicule and speak up, for the possibility of traceable Indonesian influence seems more likely in the light of recent discoveries indicating much more trans-oceanic sea travel than was allowed for in earlier Eurocentric descriptions. The theoretical and the personal do here converge in that discomforting lack of intellectual courage.

But now it may be too late to demonstrate the parallel, for so-called modernisation among the Giriama may have removed the facts on which the parallel was based. One cannot demonstrate what is no longer there and one's field notes may well be judged as having been unduly influenced by the Lévi-Straussian structuralism of the 1960s. Moreover the sense of wonderment at possible Indonesian influence occurred at a seminar, the intellectual evocation of which is quite different from that of the published, factually detailed document (rendered as Fox 1971). Nor can I now be sure that the binary oppositions and dichotomies I recorded were any more unusual than those recorded in other African societies, which even non-Africanists have observed (Needham 1960; 1967). My notes can still evoke the sense of wonderment, but there is insufficient evidence allowing me to see the facts on which it is based. Were, then, those binary oppositions part of a template rather than evocation, and part therefore of a transformative model of Indonesian and African symbolism now lost beyond recall? Was the anthropological circle in which I move so opposed, not only to diffusionist, but also to structuralist interpretations of geographically dispersed binarisms as manifestations of *l'esprit humain?*

Even if new and convincing archaeological evidence of possible Indonesian settlement were forthcoming, it would be unlikely to resolve the question of how much the binarism I had observed was African, Indonesian or something of both. And yet, given the current strength of the archaeological turn, and of bolder suggestions of the extensiveness of Austronesian migrations, as from Madagascar for example, the evocation is retained as possibly part of new ethnographic discoveries and theory. It is in this sense that evocation untidily works towards possibilities rather than a definite outcome of enquiry.

This is much more than a contrast of more as against less factual evidence. It is also that of confident and unconfident memories and interpretation, a difference which is not reducible to facts. Thus, proof of Austronesian arrivals and settlement could not by itself demonstrate that such people were responsible for the particular versions of Giriama binary symbolism. In the absence of such demonstration, my experience of this facet of fieldwork will remain evocative. By contrast, the shift from three-part to two-part characterisations of generational relationships among my small group of Giriama friends is undeniable. As such, and despite its limited representativeness, it can be used as a model for investigating the mother's brother relationship as a possible pivot and index of alternations of 'weak' and 'strong' patriliny, or, as among nearby related peoples, of matriliny and patriliny, among whom I perceive a kind of template allowing for such shifts.

Age in fieldwork

What these cases have in common is to offer the returning and recurrent fieldworker, inscribed within his or her very process of ageing, possible reinterpretations of data, the more likely and definite in the paradigmatic than in the evocative example. That is to say, long-term fieldwork, especially in same or cognate areas, is a cumulative exercise of interpretation in which the changing perceptions of the fieldworker are part of a personal unfolding life history. Political and social as well as theoretical changes, including the experience and analysis of so-called globalisation, are commonly seen as 'causes' of microscopic change: for example, the village becomes dependent on cash-cropping and labour migration by young males. Other changing influences are the extent to which a locality becomes literate, learns English (or other metropolitan language) in addition to its mother tongue, produces its own anthropologists and other intellectuals, has local people rather than outsiders as administrative officers (or the reverse), sees the foreign researcher as a source of bounty and/or of customary wisdom, and so on.

As far as these kinds of change are concerned, the long-term fieldworker may have been able to see the before- and after-effects, for example having lived in the community when no English was spoken, and having experienced the shift towards increased use of this language and of media also using it, or of experiencing distaste for the later practice by some ethnographers of paying informants in cash on an hourly basis (justified by 'new' fieldworkers as 'egalitarian' and sometimes welcomed by local people) instead of the earlier practice of reciprocating in kind rather than cash (now condemned as 'patronising' but sometimes preferred under certain circumstances by locals). In this sense the fieldworker, while affected and to some extent involved in these changes, stands outside them. One can compare as part of one's observations their nature and consequences but need not regard them as part of oneself.

Yet, the longer-term fieldworker's own ageing process has an inner as well as outer aspect. This is so whether the period is ten or thirty years. As in the above examples, fieldworkers can put themselves in the position of external observer and see changes as they grow older. At the same time, their ageing is also constitutive of their role in the society they are observing. It is also constitutive of their career as anthropologist and of their receptivity to changing ideas as to what may be regarded as a relevant field of anthropological enquiry and unit of study.

With regard to the latter, the historical movement in anthropology towards the study of regions rather than small localities and then of diasporas rather than regions, has for a certain generation, to which I happen to belong, coincided with our having reached an age or seniority conferring marked respect in many of the societies we work in. The shift to the study of regions rather than bounded localities is likely to be accompanied by the experience of working in increasingly heterogeneous and dispersed social formations. Thus, long-term fieldworkers' prolonged familiarity with a fieldwork site does not necessarily make it simpler to analyse. The very familiarity invites a probing which may recast experience.

The analytical rejection in anthropology of the fictitious, sealed-off single, homogeneous 'tribal' society as the object of study in favour of activities that dissolve boundaries or render them provisional and even nonexistent, is rather like moving from template to evocation. A template generates models of itself for further application, and so is easily isomorphic with the simple idea of homogeneous society. A complex society, analysed in terms of greater population density and interactional scale and as made up of overlapping and recursive loops and counter-loops and connectedness, cannot so easily be traced back onto a template. It is more likely to generate evocations than paradigmatic models. Conceptually, we see not one society but a region of many overlapping ones and of cross-cutting socio-cultural influences. While the outsider's distinction between homogeneous and complex society risks being subjective and fictional, and may sometimes ignore indigenous perceptions of interactional scale and density, it is also part of anthropology's shift from studying societies as timelessly replicating themselves to analysing them as changing so dramatically that it is difficult to see the continuities.

This increasingly comprehensive vision, as fieldwork spreads out to and perhaps beyond a region, makes it difficult to study the experience of ageing from within a single trajectory, which ideally would be done in a single, homogeneous group of people organised within a recognisably similar system of events and structures over time. And yet, although we cannot fully study others' ageing if we are not ageing with them, our own ageing process invariably affects the way we are treated by those who have heard of us from work elsewhere in the region. They will at least make deductions from seeing, or having reported to them, changes in the fieldworker's physical appearance. Their responses, which may include new stories about the fieldworker, then become part of the fieldworker's own changing perspectives.

Societies differ, of course, in the manner and extent to which ageing determines position, so that for the fieldworker who has done extensive work in increasingly 'complex' societies (i.e., those of greater interactional scale and density), his or her diversity of experience reflects in snapshot form some of these differences. The realisation that all societies are heterogeneous to some degree and not homogeneous, coupled with the influential Manchester School's encouragement from the 1950s and 1960s onwards to study complex societies, has run in parallel with this cross-cultural social ageing. It has discouraged early faith in paradigms in favour of less tidy evocations of past fieldwork experiences.

Let me again illustrate this with examples. As time went on during my intermittent years among the Giriama, I became well known for my genealogical and customary knowledge, much of it committed to writing of course. I came to be regarded as a kind of guardian of such knowledge, with young people in particular sometimes consulting me on clan relations, much of which was rapidly being forgotten. At the same time, I became more and more interested in neighbouring peoples who are linguistically and culturally related to the Giriama and therefore part of a larger regional social entity. Many had converted to Islam a generation or so earlier. Among these new Muslims a clan- or lineal descent-based notion of tradition was suppressed, the better to forget their non-Islamic origins.

This emerging contrast became stronger the more I worked in Muslim Swahili-speaking society, moving from the recently converted to those for whom ancestors had only ever been Muslim. The contrast was between non-Muslim Giriama for whom traditional knowledge based on elderhood continues through the generations, and Muslim Swahili for whom knowledge was the timeless one of Qur'anic revelation to which historical narrative was only a revelatory supplement. One can be incorporated among either people, provided one plays by the rules. Among the non-Muslim Giriama these are customary, animistic and egalitarian. Among the Muslim Swahili they are monotheistically religious and hierarchical, with often a disdain for customary, allegedly pre-Islamic practices and beliefs. Each people venerates what they regard as men of wisdom. New Giriama scholars have emerged as counterparts to the long-standing clerics of the Swahili Islamic *ulama.*

This shapes their attitudes to the outsider who lives among them. Giriama see me as having come up the ranks of generation and so as deserving of epistemological seniority through the experience of having lived, observed and practised among them. They gloss over the fact that I have not in fact lived among them continuously over the last thirty-two years, being more like the long-term, distantly resident migrant worker, who may spend even less time than myself overall in the rural homestead. What is important here is the personalised iconic quality, which requires that the fiction of my continuous residence among them be preserved.

By contrast, for me to reach anywhere near the same ranking and regard among Swahili Muslims, long residence and even some textual erudition would never be enough. At the least I would need to have come from, or spent a long period at, an Islamic college in the Middle East, to have a reading and speaking knowledge of Arabic and not just Swahili, and to be able to point to an illustrious line of Islamic teachers, the most recent of whom would be my own teacher.

These are assumptions about knowledge acquisition which are more than just there to be analysed. They determine one's very status and impose limits on one's fieldwork. Among the non-Muslim Giriama I can be incorporated as someone who knows things by the very fact of my becoming an older person. Being old is, barring exceptional cases of idiocy or outrageous behaviour, ipso facto the prerequisite of wisdom. Is it not the case that it is the grandparents who tell the moral fables, know the medicines and have ritual powers and secular skills of mediation and arbitration? Of course one must be taught as well as observe such crafts. But such learning is also mediated through the very process of social ageing.

Among the Muslim Swahili, however, I can only be incorporated or internalised as a Muslim sage from a position of having first been externalised as a full product of the wider, global Islamic world. This can be a cumulative process, and sometimes takes many years. But there are also many examples of young sheikhs in their thirties who have come to prominence while still young and whose authority rests on pre-eminent Islamic scholarship, probably much of it learned abroad. The Zanzibari radical movement of 1992–3 was led by such sheikhs, and, more generally, Islamic radicalism is often driven by the demands of youth (Parkin 1995). Old age is of course respected among the Swahili, and the elderly may be asked for advice and help, but for their wisdom to be acknowledged as markedly as among the non-Muslim Giriama it would need to be expressed as a gift of Islamic learning. The fieldworker as such could not achieve such a position and would need, in fact, to abandon this status and actually become a pious life-serving Muslim. These are not differences that could have been foreseen before a very long period of fieldwork. Nor could they have been deduced. They are certainly more a product of experiential than experimental ethnography, and of inductive more than deductive methods.

This indeterminacy in ethnographic fact-finding, for example in not knowing how much one's ageing process will or will not confer social wisdom, seems to increase the more and longer we work in the same area or region. It is not, however, a case of, over time, not seeing the wood for the trees, nor is it like trying to reconcile what quantum theory sees as the indefiniteness of the microphysical world with the definiteness of the macrophysical world. Nor is it a postmodern problem of, so to speak, making it up as we go along. Rather, I think it is a problem of, through time, inserting oneself into the only likely positions allowable: a knowing sage among non-Muslims as against a forever inadequately trained Muslim among the Swahili.

Paradoxically, the fieldworker is not always able to fit the facts of a society into ever neater analytical categories the longer they work there. It is the field itself, if I may reify, which may increasingly control the fieldworker's social placement to a degree greater than when fieldwork was first carried out. One's social position has, after all, been negotiated and settled and requires very special events to remake it, for it is now the product of others' social investment of time and effort. It is as if, while the anthropologist's theoretical reliance on initial paradigms gives way to evocations prompted by fieldwork notes and experience, the people among whom he or she works are creating for themselves a structure of certainties into which the fieldworker is fitted and upon which future expectations of his/her role are based. They make for the fieldworker a social template at the same time as he or she may be modifying or abandoning the one initially formed for them.

Most anthropologists, in Africa at least, experience having to be located in a set of kinship and relationship terms and statuses early during fieldwork. My own placing occurred among the non-Muslim Giriama in 1966 as follows:

> I was allocated the site of a house whose construction had just been started and which belonged to the homestead head's eldest son, who was working in Dar es Salaam....
>
> Through partial identification, then, I was already provisionally cast in the role of son of the homestead head.... But confirmation was needed, for people in and around the homestead were still uncertain how to address me. I came to know well a man of my own age from another homestead. He prided himself on his fearlessness, being prepared to joke with and even insult chiefs and headmen, yet stopping short of visibly incurring their wrath.
>
> In a typically daring conversation one day, he called my wife *hawe*, meaning grandmother but also used by a man of his brother's wife. People were embarrassed and asked each other questions. Were he and I, then, no more than peers? Was I no higher in status than that? Should he address my wife in that familiar way? I joked back and people concluded, therefore, that his judgement was in fact perfectly sound. My status was settled. We were peers or 'brothers'. I was then called Karisa, son of Muramba, the homestead head, and given his MwaMweni clanship (Parkin 1991: 45).

This fixing of kinship and generational status defined my roles in customary events, rituals and everyday life, but was clearly based on a negotiation of the position in which, initially, I was allowed to participate. It is the beginning of the template which people create for the fieldworker, who, at the same time, is also seeking firm 'structures' on which to base an understanding of the society. That is to say, the people build logically relevant new statuses onto the fieldworker's initial position, so reinforcing those initial assumptions about generation and kinship. But the fieldworker does the opposite to his or her own early 'theoretical' model of the society, picking at it selectively over the years, seeing some aspects as worthy of retention as templates but others as the source of uncertainty.

Theory changes

Is this dismantling of templates an intrinsic and inevitable feature of long-term fieldwork? Or is it more to do with the recent anthropological turn to the study of dispersed populations, diasporas, forced human displacement and migration? Do models of such crises give way to appeals for empathetic understanding rather than explanation, much reinforced by media using rapid communication technology? Or is it that theory corrects itself, so to speak: the model cannot account for socio-geographical spread and complexity and so must alter or be discarded? Theories do not of course correct themselves, but nor do they die simply because the facts to which they are applied change. Such choices belong to their practitioners, who themselves work under the influence of interests and aesthetic perspectives determining theoretical 'elegance'.

Inadequate, too, is the tautology that theories change because the conditions under which they are produced change. For instance, it was not inevitable that wider regional fieldwork would lead to explanations in terms of overlapping and sometimes fuzzy categories and diasporas, as has become the case in recent theory (Hannerz 1992). An alternative direction might have been to analyse regions as the structured replication of discrete social units premised on an original idea of the self-sealed social entity, as indeed happened in the early colonial demarcation of regions as internally constituted by separable 'tribes'. In fact, even nowadays, United Nations and United States world governance is still largely premised on the idea of nation-states as the building blocks of higher-level alliances rather than on the clash or coordination of activities and interests straddling national and supernational boundaries. In other words a theory of, so to speak, replicated monothetic classification still prevails over one of polythetic classification, to use Needham's distinction (1975). Of course theory invites reflection on the logic of its argument, but in anthropology it is the memories and mis-memories of long-term regional fieldwork which challenge argument, doing so through an alternation of templates and evocations, as fieldworkers continue over years to visit one or more field-sites within a region.

So far, I have spoken of 'facts' confidently recorded as such in field notes later evoking uncertainty, and of other 'facts' as hinting at behavioural templates which, despite their generative, labile and not immediately visible nature, do not cause uncertainty. I have also described how long-term fieldworkers gradually become 'templated' by people while they themselves treat much of what they remember from earlier field notes as no longer shaping theory and as little more than evocative. But alternation also occurs: templates may become evocations as our confidence in them wanes, but evocations may become more believable exemplars of behaviour if they seem to fit the explanation of new events. Again, I provide an example.

Over time I worked more and more among Muslims whose grandparents had been non-Muslim and who could still speak and understand the non-Muslim vernacular, despite now speaking almost entirely in the 'Muslim' language of Swahili. They recognised this degree of sameness with non-Muslims from whom, for reasons of religion and style (*adabu*), they tried to distance themselves. On some parts of the Kenya coast, Muslim and non-Muslim homesteads are interspersed yet members of one group rarely enter the others' homes. Having worked in a neighbouring non-Muslim area for some years, speaking their vernacular, and then later among Muslims speaking Swahili, and being known to both, I did visit both kinds of homestead. On one occasion a young non-Muslim Giriama man accompanied me on a visit to a Muslim homestead of my acquaintance. He was shocked to see the divorced wife of a man of the homestead chatting amiably with her former husband while visiting her children there. Among his own people, where divorce is much rarer (or was at the time) and bridewealth much more valuable, there is only hostility or at least total distance between divorcees. The distinction was for me a standard, expected fact arising from differences in brother-sister ties, marriage stability and rules governing father-right and bridewealth payments, of the kind commonly taught to first-year undergraduates. Moreover, the Muslims prefer first marriages to be between cousins, except those of one's father's brother. For the young Giriama man such friendliness between ex-spouses somehow blurred exogamous clan boundaries which ought to be kept unambiguous: complementing this, other Giriama have said that their Muslim neighbours 'are lost' because they do not have clearly delineated exogamous clans or descent groups.

In the local distinction made between Muslim and non-Muslim on the Kenya coast, non-Muslims included such up-country people as the powerful Christian Kikuyu and Luo as well as long-established coastal non-Muslims (i.e., Mijikenda), a few of whom were becoming Christian though most remained animists. In fact, the up-country Kikuyu and Luo were first seen by the non-Muslim coastal people in the 1960s, 1970s and early 1980s as closer to themselves in not being Muslim and even as opposed to coastal Muslims, from whom the up-country people bought land and property to set themselves up in business. The distinction between Muslim and non-Muslim at the coast was fundamental during this period and evoked a whole number of other associations: mosque versus church; Swahili versus the vernacular speech; Swahili versus European dress; Islamic versus secular politics; and so on.

Much later, from August until November 1997, hundreds of non-coastal people were massacred or forced 'back' up-country, allegedly by coastal residents, even though many of the victims had been born at the coast and were perfectly fluent in Swahili. A report by the private Kenya Human Rights Commission (1997) suggested that government agents and not local people were responsible for the outrage. Whatever the truth, the deaths certainly occurred and were popularly regarded as a manifestation of conflict between coast and up-country. Few up-country people remained by December 1997 when I was there.

Tourism was halted and the cash economy came to a virtual halt. This had been preceded by national political calls by the then government for a federal Kenya in which coastal peoples would enjoy the autonomy they had sought in an earlier generation. The Kenya Luo and Kikuyu had opposed federalism and so were in opposition not just to the ruling government but to coastal peoples also, both Muslim and non-Muslim. What I had once observed as conflict between coastal Muslim and non-Muslim now appeared as cultural, as coastal people generally forged a common identity in opposition to up-country people who had been acquiring coastal land and businesses: the popularly and sometimes politically expressed divisions between Muslims and non-Muslims on the coast had given way to a division between all coastal people and all up-country people, between coastal Kenya and the rest of the country. Major regional or territorial strife of the kind familiar in modern African states, thrown into relief by the coastal massacres, thus assumed the status of a recognisable and widespread behavioural template which replaced my earlier evocative memories of Muslims differentiating themselves from non-Muslims.

This example illustrates not just the incompleteness of long-term fieldwork but more its exponential incompleteness. There is always more revelation where that came from. The changing theories and intellectual styles within which we work, the altered global politics and the increasing presence in the field of persons wishing and able to question our reasons for being anthropologists, are undoubtedly factors which shape how we observe and write. But I think we should not forget that it is a feature of the utmost significance that long-term fieldwork in a region produces experiences whose remembering and mis-remembering make up a kind of logic of its own, based on alternations of template and evocation.

Fieldwork and pre-existing texts

Although a characteristic of all fieldwork, I believe that this process of alternating remembering and mis-remembering is most distinctive or salient when fieldwork has been carried out in a society for which ethnographic records are nonexistent or sparse, or treated as such. Without such records fieldworkers are their own archive and lack recourse to other sources for either corroboration or being reminded.

For instance, my experience of fieldwork on the East African coast was shaped by the fact that I started among the non-Muslim Giriama in 1966 and that no other anthropologist had worked among them. A district officer in 1911 had written a useful if restricted ethnographic account (Champion 1967), as had a famous Giriama politician (Ngala 1949), and there had been some very limited accounts by missionaries and travellers (see bibliographies in Prins 1952; Spear 1978; Brantley 1981; Willis 1993). For the most part, then, my developing perspectives on Giriama were relatively unaffected by previous writings on them. This sense of ethnographic discovery, unmediated by other work, carried through into my later studies of the ethno-linguistically related Swahili-speaking peoples, who are mainly Muslim. Despite the fact that a large literature exists on the Swahili, I have always tagged this on, so to speak, to my own fieldwork-based analyses as it has seemed relevant: in moving gradually from a study of the non-Muslim Giriama to the Muslim Swahili I have preserved that sense of textually unmediated, fieldwork-based ethnography. This 'slide' from the study of the one to the other group is evident in my use of the term, 'intermediary Swahili' to refer to recently converted Muslims who have renounced their coastal vernaculars and non-Muslim beliefs and customs in favour of the Swahili language and way of life, and who are typical of earlier generations who have in this way augmented the Swahili-speaking peoples (Parkin 1985).

This is mentioned as a fact rather than justification, and in order to make the contrast with fieldwork among the Kenya Luo, whom I studied first as migrant workers in Uganda and later in Kenya. The Kenya Luo and other Luo-speaking peoples had already been much written about when I started my fieldwork in Kampala, Uganda. They are part of the Nilotic language and culture group, who include the Nuer, Dinka, Shilluk and Anuak of the Sudan, and so are central to many of the founding debates in social anthropology, including discussions of lineage formation, its definition of territorial attachment, feud, egalitarianism and uncentralised political organisation, bridewealth exchanges and transhumant pastoralism, to name a few. On the Kenya Luo and closely related Alur alone, Evans-Pritchard (1965) and Southall (1952, 1953) had shortly beforehand written extensively and influentially when I began fieldwork in 1962, and other scholars had begun studies of the Luo. Even earlier a prominent Luo had written in detail on Luo customs (Mboya 1938). Although my study was the first to focus on urban Luo (cf. Southall and Gutkind 1957), it would have been impossible not to have known this and other extensive literature and, taken together with the general theoretical background in social anthropology to which many Nilotic studies had contributed, not to have had one's perspectives shaped by it.

Only two major periods of fieldwork were undertaken among urban Kenya Luo, totalling no more than three years: 1962–4 and 1968–9, with a first study of the Giriama curiously 'sandwiched' in between for fifteen months over 1966–7. The problem of juggling three languages, Giriama and Swahili on the one hand, and Luo on the other, and of managing such contrasting field venues, persuaded me from 1969 to concentrate on Giriama- and then Swahili-speaking peoples, having benefited at a relatively early age from considerable exposure to the Swahili language. Comprising three years within the seven-year period 1962–7, fieldwork among Luo was intense. It was also extensive, for, while focusing on urban-dwelling Luo in Kampala and Nairobi, I spent some time in their home province of Nyanza, based in the homestead of a family with ramifying ties in town and the rural area (Parkin 1969; 1978). By contrast, fieldwork among the Giriama and then Swahili unfolded at a more leisurely pace: fifteen months 1966–7, vacation periods in the early and mid-1970s, a further fifteen months in 1977–8 and vacation periods during most of the 1980s and 1990s.

There are, of course, many possible reasons for this contrast, some of them of a practical nature as already mentioned. It is difficult, however, to resist the conclusion that one important factor in the brief but intense engagement with the Luo was the fact that the voluminous past and burgeoning literature afforded fewer possibilities of an ethnographic experience unmediated by textual sources. It inhibited the possibility of discovering and appropriating many 'facts' as entirely one's own, and so made less salient the process of alternating remembering and mis-remembering that characterised, and still characterises, the life-long study of the Giriama and Swahili-speaking peoples.

A special feature of working in documented societies is that discrepancies may appear between what is in print and the fieldworker's own findings. Does this provoke the same dilemma as when it is one's own field notes which are inconsistent? My response is that the clash between facts derived from one's own fieldwork experience and those in print does not personalise the dilemma to the same extent. It may well be a matter of concern and even of major investigation to reconcile another's printed version with one's own findings. But such divergence is neither confined to an on-going fieldwork career nor sealed within a self-referential nexus of authorial responsibility. Either one's own data or those of the writer are wrong, or perhaps the passage of time has seen a shift, which in itself can excite study. But what are not evidently inconsistent here are one's own findings and powers of scrutiny.

With regard to my pointing out to Luo some discrepancies between what they themselves said at different times, I would sometimes be urged to seek verification from the available literature. Much cited was Chief Paulo Mboya, whose book on traditions and customary practices (1938) was known by many Luo, as well as work by European authors. My own image of Luo society was also partly drawn from these sources and influenced my interpretations. This is not to say that these interpretations were inaccurate. I think on the whole they were not. The point is that my Luo data might sometimes confirm or create templates or evoke uncertain patterns, as among the Giriama. The distinction between these two alternatives, however, lay under the shadow of the literature on Luo and of the theoretical influence of the lineage model in anthropology, which might sometimes be used to decide which of the possibilities the data best fitted. One can here at least understand the unconventional appeal by some anthropologists to their students to ignore the literature on a people before doing fieldwork among them.

I end with this case of the Luo, for it is evident that, increasingly, the groups studied by future ethnographers will already have been studied and documented in recent times by anthropologists trained in modern techniques. Some will themselves be from the society being studied or from somewhere other than Euro-America. The modern call for multi-vocal/perspectival/site fieldwork and ethnography recognises this and constitutes a colossal challenge (see the epilogue to this volume). By contrast, the apparently unique and personalised relationship of fieldworker to a field-site and its people has undoubted echoes of the colonial officer and 'his people', the former protected by a distinctive status from outside interference and the latter restricted in the extent to which they are likely to be involved in the practice and products of fieldwork. By current standards it is also inevitably narrow in its analytical reliance on the one fieldworker, as distinct from many, both outside and indigenous.

But what is the aim behind experimenting with simultaneous multi-site and multi-perspectival fieldwork, in which issues are debated as part of the fieldwork? Is it that poetic licence or straight inaccuracy on the part of ethnographers is likely to be curbed when two or more fieldworkers collaborate in studying the same society? If so, this would seem to satisfy the search for socio-cultural truths, for neither fieldworker would be allowed by the other to intentionally fabricate data for persuasive effect.

On the other hand, it is doubtful whether fieldworkers normally act in such bad faith: an aspect of fieldwork that is often forgotten is the sense of personal commitment and engagement it confers on the lone fieldworker. It is remarkable how much we regard fieldworkers as seeking and reproducing their findings in good faith, however much we may disagree with their interpretations and methods of enquiry. Nor do I think we are mistaken in this general regard. What prevents a fieldworker from wilfully falsifying the data is precisely the sense of self that is invested in a long-term, demanding, and usually difficult human enterprise and set of relationships. To lie about the data is to betray that selfhood as much as it is to betray people with whom the fieldworker has over time established ties which are as much based on emotion as on objective analysis. To that extent, lone fieldwork is indeed a self-focused activity but one which, like the work of the artist, seeks to draw out from contrasting worlds of humanity a common understanding of the reasons for difference.

Conclusion

My points are as follows. When we re-read our field notes or make return visits to the field, we not only alternate between being certain and uncertain of our data, we shift between their generative influence on further investigation or their evocation of fieldwork experiences about which we are insufficiently sure to take further. I also suggest that while this is a feature of all long-term fieldwork, it is especially marked for societies about which nothing or little has been written, for we become our own sole archive. In better documented societies we can always try to find evidence to resolve an uncertainty and, while this may be inadequate, our perception is of a repository of information on that society which is, so to speak, shared with other scholars and chroniclers and so mediates our on-going fieldwork experience and interpretations.

This perception of a single-society, multi-authored archive shared with others is perhaps also becoming increasingly typical of modern fieldwork for another reason. This is because, from impression, more ethnographers, from a wide range of nationalities and from the country in question, carry out studies of the same areas simultaneously or on the heels of each other, often too rapidly for substantial fieldwork results to have been published. These different ethnographers may in fact have quite different interests, but this does not seem to limit our vision of an expanding store of knowledge of a particular society which both directs and constrains what will in due course be written about it.

Perceptually, at least, the day of the lone fieldworker is largely over. But the notion of long-term fieldwork seems likely to continue, if somewhat differently. Ethnographers may nowadays more often carry out long-term fieldwork in short vacation periods spread over years than in larger blocks of time, as was possible when funding was more plentiful and universities allowed such absences. The spreading popularity of the discipline and world-wide governmental financial restrictions on purely academic research may here be combining to create effects greater than those resulting from intellectual debate.

NOTE

1. The sense of template here is not in fact the same as that of the carpenter, who uses, say, a wooden and therefore rigid pattern to copy precise outlines on walls, floors, cupboards or whatever. Template as used by Ardener refers rather to an arc of actions, movements, words and sentiments, none of which is likely to be exactly reproduced. I provide an example of a paradigmatic template in Parkin 1987: 63.

Chapter 5

WILDERNESS OF MIRRORS:

TRUTH AND VULNERABILITY IN MIDDLE EASTERN FIELDWORK

Paul Dresch

Two weeks before the meeting which led to these papers I was chewing *qat* near the Edgware Road. I wanted to understand more of South Yemen's past, and was chewing with relatives of an ex-ruler who, at the British collapse in Aden, had been driven into exile by the NLF (National Liberation Front). Only recently had some returned. Towards the end of the chew, but before 'the hour of Solomon' when people are lost in their own thoughts, I asked my host an obvious solidary question (after all, I hold a British passport). How could the British have so mis-handled things that, having failed to do a deal with myriad acronyms, they lost South Yemen to the NLF, the group most at odds with London's government? I was looked at with plain suspicion. The British from the start had planned it that way. It was obvious that X (the name of a famous radical, a Minister post-independence, a bugbear of colonialists before that) worked for British Intelligence. Whatever one says at that point is somehow wrong. By tacit assent to viewing history as conspiracy, I joined the conspiracy at hand.

A little later, in the hour of Solomon which *qat* brings on, I reflected that fieldwork was often like this. The experience was not well described as simply 'dialogue'. Nor was it 'data collection'. It was more like a trade in secrets, though in a curious way. The more thriller-like the material, the less difficult to gather, to the point where one was constantly being told things unfit for print: the more mundane and empirical the published facts, by contrast, the more collecting them resembled clandestine intrigue. Fieldwork itself, meanwhile, is obscured by 'metropolitan theory'. The process and the product are not trusted. To explore the issues I shall need to examine more than personal experience, and I shall need a metaphor.

Wilderness of Mirrors (Martin 1980) is the title of a book on Cold War paranoia. If Black Spy, to follow *Mad Magazine*, deserted and told all he knew of his colleagues' shenanigans then White Spy locked him up or sent him back to be shot and believed no word of it. Calculation was inverted by imaginings of ubiquitous deception plots: the fuller the information, therefore, the less it could possibly be true.

The terrain imagined

When Western authors took a detailed interest in the Middle East, fifty years either side of 1800, they entered existing rhetorics. In a first round of experience the emphasis fell on courts and on urban life, with a bias of quality towards female writers. In a second round the emphasis and approbation fell more on a tribal world in literature dominated by male authors. The latter style of writing prefigures all but recent anthropology.[1] Morier on Persia, Elphinstone on Afghanistan, Burckhardt on Arabia, strike familiar chords. Both Elphinstone and Burckhardt highlight moral concerns by argument through direct contrast and both put a surprising emphasis on 'refuge'. Burckhardt's largely second-hand account of Badu is organised around this theme (1830: 87, 92, 100, 187ff.) as if the local world comprised morally discrete spaces.

At an early stage of my interest in Upper Yemen I found myself from first-hand experience saying much the same. Although 'honour' had fallen under ban among Mediterraneanists, such terms were salient and their use consistent. To make sense of usage one had to assume what I called a 'peace' (Dresch 1981), a structure of privacy, control and vulnerability which underpinned each collective name. Tribes north of Sanaa were a pattern of such structures. Their geographical boundaries remain rather stable (something fieldwork does not show), and families rise and fall, people migrate, great political movements sweep the area, largely in other terms (Dresch 1989).

Martha Mundy, the most accomplished of Western fieldworkers in Yemen, denounces the account fiercely (Mundy 1995). All terms not applicable to agrarian society world-wide are suspect, she argues, for difference which is not of degree but of kind is ideology,[2] disguising the secret of exploitation. A less ferocious disagreement, which appeared before I published work of substance, came from Lila Abu Lughod.

Again difference is problematic. It exists, she seems to think, but one should not say so: 'Why privilege this aspect of society ...? If in defense anthropologists want to argue that segmentary opposition is a widespread principle of Arab social life, they will have to show its relevance in nontribal contexts' (Abu Lughod 1989: 284). I am not so convinced as she that the Arab World must be all or nothing. 'But,' to echo Tom Wolfe's famous line on Marshall Macluhan's fame, 'what if it's true?'[3]

If it is true, or thinking in some way makes it so, we shall find a world in which privacy is highly structured and integral to the definition of social groups. One belongs, as an outsider, to none of these. We should therefore expect, as with Herzfeld's Greece (Herzfeld 1987), that anything an ethnographer might want to know will by definition be something they should not, and if they do know they should at least keep quiet beyond the family circle. We might also expect a twist, however. If, to take an old formulation, oppositions are 'nested', a structure will be found in whose nodes and interstices fieldworkers from elsewhere might thrive in distinctive ways. Whatever the specific pattern, caution about private truth seems basic: to list what elsewhere might be public knowledge will be problematic, as indeed it often is in Middle Eastern cases.

At the start of an argument I did not anticipate I sketched one salient principle in the form of a couple of opposed cones, each of which had an outside of repute and an inside of vulnerability (Dresch 1986). That relation is often coded as male and female. The sex of the fieldworker is not wholly determinant (women have usually more options than do men) but commonly sex and symbolism line up with practicalities: one knows most intensely a small space, usually female if we impose labels, or less intensely a wider one, usually male. What Abu Lughod decries as harem theory and segmentation theory (Abu Lughod 1989, cf. Mundy 1995: 4) diverge in short-term experience.[4] Longer-term considerations echo the same forms, however. Abu Lughod's account of poetry among the Awlad 'Ali (Abu Lughod 1986) thus consists of two discrete halves. A review of conventional (male-centred) views of honour and genealogy precedes consideration of women using what politely can be misrecognised as mere quotation, and part two follows strictly from the truth-value of part one. One lesson of the book is that crossing the halves is dangerous. The subject matter itself is 'secret', which leaves the reader with a sense of intimacy and the writer with a problem locally, for the gatherer of secrets is in Arabic *jasus*, a spy.

Assumptions of oblique secrecy encompass more than pyjama-parties. They inform in rather genial ways local politics, and Burckhardt relates how the Imam Sa'ud was told that the Meccans, in defiance of what was thought God's law, were smoking tobacco in their homes: '"Do you not know," replied the chief, "that it is written, 'Do not spy out the secrets of the houses of the faithful'?" Having quoted this sentence of the Koran [*la tajassasu ... ba'dukum ba'dan*, presumably, though Qur'an 24:61 may be at issue], he ordered the informant to be bastinadoed' (Burckhardt 1830: 303). Anthropologists soon take the point that reality, beyond prescriptions of texts, must be approached obliquely – 'fieldwork is an apprenticeship of signs, a process of entry into a particular world' (Jenkins 1994: 445), and there is much in this particular world one should not ask directly. To establish one's facts on, for instance, kin-links and thus acquire a measure of common sense one works through 'contacts' and 'introductions' (even 'cut-outs' if truth be told) and endless quiet implication. To describe the process in foreign terms would be to sound very like a spy.

The social everywhere involves selective privacy, and privacy is always layered. Local protocols are learned in fieldwork. *Qat* chews in Yemen are a godsend, for instance, and café tables in Greece spare ethnographers leaping dangerously from crag to crag; but one could not, I imagine, gather details of particular practice in either case. The questions appropriate to such settings are not those of a private family setting (late at night when the chew is over, legs out in front of you like an old lady) nor those of, say, a public conference (endless *mujamalah*, which means 'courtesy', 'flattery', or in many a context 'polite waffle').[5] Mistakenly identifying contexts – as if, so to speak, a café table meant the same thing everywhere – will produce confusion, and generic advice on 'fieldwork methods' is therefore vacuous, for what empiricist anthropology sees as obstacles are social facts. Shift context, as in publication, and the facts do not change but they are realigned and in a sense are tested.

One of the women with whom Abu Lughod did her fieldwork exclaims, '"You've scandalised us"; for her, a book about particular people and everyday life in her community might seem little more than a public display of family secrets' (Abu Lughod 1993: 41). Individual persons, it goes without saying, should be spared embarrassment, and forms of etiquette vary among among cases. But everyday life as a 'family secret'? That is more arresting. It is not an image one encounters in all ethnography, though it colours much work on the Mediterranean and on the Middle East.

In the fieldworker's paradise of Ghana the proverb runs, 'One does not reveal another's back': in other words, one can talk of oneself but not of one's kin or neighbours. Personal openness seems common and writing on West Africa (indeed on much of Africa) presents itself in these terms as oddly straightforward. In the Arab World, by contrast, one 'covers' from view one's own affairs.[6] According to context these encompass a great deal, including in fits of hubris the affairs of all Arabs everywhere. One's neighbour's affairs, in another context, are theirs to cover; to speak of them oneself, though not in the neighbours' presence, is normal, while facts that belong to no one – or, most alarmingly, to the state – are fair game. As fieldworker in such a case you scribble something from politeness (details of the room, your thoughts on the encounter) but not what is freely offered, for it is 'dangerous' and strictly 'not your business'. On the other hand, much you want in your notebooks is not to be discussed publicly. The quotation from Imam Sa'ud takes us part of the way. To cite the quotation, however, is itself to reveal something usually left unstated: that these tacit understandings exist at all.[7]

Lest it be thought the problem applies only to people much concerned with agnatic descent (which would not describe most of Yemen, I should stress; and rural Yemen twenty years ago is what I shall focus on), let us note for instance Egypt in the form of its minor bureaucrats. Again a certain caution about the everyday is evident. 'Basically if you ask permission to do fieldwork outside of intellectual circles they'll say no. You can't do fieldwork outside of Cairo. You can't study minorities. If your work involves talking to poor or middle-class people they get real antsy.' My informant goes on to say what is true of most places, though true in very different ways: 'The odd thing about Egypt is that you can often do pretty much what you want without asking permission.' How and why become a secret themselves, the experience of old hands.

The terrain experienced

To suggest that some areas are more difficult than others, or less transparent, is uncomfortable in ethnographic company. The paucity of results in certain parts of the world is plain, however, and the imagery in this case is of long standing. Here is Evans-Pritchard:

> In present circumstances I would not, though I speak Arabic, care to try to do research in most of the Arab lands. Even were I given permission to do so, there would be constant supervision and interference. In such countries the anthropologist is regarded as a spy, his knowledge likely to be used in certain circumstances by the Intelligence of his country; and he is also resented as a busybody prying into other people's affairs (Evans-Pritchard 1973: 9).

The substance of that distinction remains unclear, for Evans-Pritchard fails to analyse his problem. Yet his experience in 'the Arab lands' produced no anthropology. *The Sanusi of Cyrenaica* (1949) is a chronicle of a would-be ruling family, interesting in its domestication of the tale to Western forms and more so in its political success, but the people with whom he lived for a time are sketched in functionalist caricature.[8]

Before the nationalist carapace takes form we find a dearth of ethnographic detail.

The carapace of states is now itself a fieldwork site where one
encounters motifs at once parochial and far-reaching. Passing through
Kuwait many years before 1990, for example, I was found to be carrying a large box of Yemeni books and was asked with deep suspicion,
'Why do you know Arabic?' Border officials are strange everywhere.[9]
Their silliness at Los Angeles does not involve asking 'Why do you know
English?' Much as in Greece (Herzfeld 1987: 45, 52; Just 1995: 297),
language in the Arab World is marked as of political and moral worth,
yet Arabic, let us not forget, quite unlike Demotic Greek, is one of the
world's great languages, for Muslims the language in which God
addressed humanity. Enormous encouragement greets one's first
efforts. Progress brings one to other forms. As a French colleague with
experience of Egypt puts it, 'when you speak about thirty words it's
tat'kallam 'arabi kwayyis (you speak Arabic well), when you speak two
hundred it's *'awiz ayy bi-zabt* (what *exactly* are you after here)?'[10]

The 'margins' to which anthropology is sometimes drawn are easier. A long conversation with an old man far from Yemen's capital
many years ago covered all sorts of matters to do with Western politics
and marriage practice, and an hour of detailed chat in which he mas-
tered my family connections, though politeness forbade my enquiring
of his, ended with him asking, 'What's this boy speaking, then, Arabic
or Foreign?'[11] Even then, the thirty words against two hundred argument applied. Knowledge itself was problematic. To be worth talking to
one has to know things, but the question then arises of how on earth
one knows them. The usual congratulatory form, 'You're a bright
boy', 'You're a sharp lad' (as some might wish, you have 'command' of
material), was *anta khatir*. The word *khatir* means 'dangerous'.

To arrange different cases in segmentary order might not be difficult.
It would not be useful. Rather, all of them turn on a simple idea of privacy and of precedence which the confessional mode of fieldwork narrative, with its wish to place the fieldworker's character at the centre of
a story, tends somewhat to obscure. Within obvious limits, the phenomena at hand are structural. As Roger Goodman points out in this volume
(chapter 7), the fieldworker is the instrument of research and detects the
assumptions informing their position in the world vis-à-vis that of people they encounter. Mediterranean ethnography provides parallels.

Pitt-Rivers is one of few anthropologists who, analytically instead of
squashing argument, sees his fieldwork experience as 'not without significance'. Buying drinks in Andalusia is his example:

> [I]t was not long before I was permitted to return such hospitality to mem-
> bers of the plebeian community and even to play the role of patron ... but I

was never permitted to pay for wine we had drunk together by men of the upper class ...; they would simply remind me that I was a foreigner and that they would be ashamed to let me pay in their town; or they would promise that next time I should be allowed to pay – a 'next time' which never came (Pitt-Rivers 1977: 105).

The same will apply in some degree anywhere. The kerfuffles over coffee and the like in 'Arab lands' can be splendid. But in much of the Arab World, on the principles Pitt-Rivers describes, visiting patterns denote hierarchy and one is simply not visited in formal terms.[12] In more pressing ways than who buys the drinks, one remains the eternal guest and only locally defined sets of persons can act as hosts. The sets in turn are defined in some degree against each other. Women ethnographers, when committed to a locally female role and thus grasped within the sets opposed, are better off in this respect than men, in other respects worse off: tales of tearful parting from claustrophobically intense friendships are common. Men, or sometimes women playing locally the male position, are either harmless and no one takes them seriously (in which case no one talks to them, no fieldwork is possible) or in some degree are matter out of place. One must manage one's connections carefully to avoid harm to others and yet keep oneself in play.[13] The fact that hospitality is a form of control should not obscure people's generosity; nor should formality obscure trust and friendship. The forms of friendship remain private, however – quite intensely so over years and decades – and do not expand to generalised social roles, for one group's assimilated guest remains the other's stranger. Hence the partisanship which Abu Lughod reports: 'This is your girl who wrote this!' (1993: 41).

An older anthropology is awash with folk-tales of fieldworkers' integration, which sound a different note: one is spliced to a marriage class, located in a clan, accorded an appropriate totem. Such moves in New Guinea perhaps or (pagan) Africa denote models of society wherein the moral world is largely a local world and in a sense pretends to self-sufficiency. One may as a misfit be a sorcerer or just as plausibly be made kin. Elsewhere there are 'strong models' of people's worth in a larger universe. Outsiders have a place in these before they ever arrive, and their position is negotiable thereafter only within limits. China and Japan, I suspect, would be good examples. The Arab World surely is. It happens to stress, as parts of rural Europe do, the rhetoric of foreigner as guest or protégé, ideally dependent and controlled, such that fieldworkers are anomalous unless immobile or well connected.

Pitt-Rivers, speaking of Franco's Spain, describes the interstitial in terms familiar to many who have worked in the Middle East. You are not a beggar, nor yet, to take his other extreme, Ulysses. What are you,

then? 'The threat which I embodied was represented in the belief that
I was a spy, which was discarded only after months of evident ineptness in that role' (Pitt-Rivers 1977: 105). One regrets he does not follow up the theme. Ineptness is in the eye of beholders, and one doubts
that even in Spain at the time such talk of the contemporary sorcerer
evaporated quite so evenly. Nor is the law of hospitality the only issue.
The logic of the stranger is entangled with that of world domination
and one's imaginary position can be absurd, for the threat of the outsider may be no greater than their apparent promise.

At a properly 'remote' place, a friend of many years' standing was
politicking with some success. Rulers had received him, large quantities of money had changed hands, and late at night, by the light of a
swinging oil lamp (he had perfectly good electric lighting, but circumstances were what they were) he told me his message should reach
'the powers' as if we were somewhere in the years between Fashoda
and Agadir. What, said I, the Americans? 'No, no, the Americans do
not understand. I mean the British and the French. The British *know*'.
My suggestion that not even the French, more adventurous in such
regards, would be interested fell on deaf ears – 'Paul, *you* must be our
Lawrence.' The world has changed since the Great War, yet someone of
power in fairly local terms took this nonsense seriously, for money was
much in evidence. What if others thought I was Lawrence or (more to
my own taste) Sandy Arbuthnot? 'Participation' is not an option;
'observation', the other half of that tired phrase, will be equated with
participation anyway, and one's nape-hairs prickle.

Pitt-Rivers himself, moving among the different anthropologies of
Britain, the United States and France, seems to have been the perpet-
ual stranger, and a Parisian colleague expressed doubts about 'what he
was *really* doing there'. The pattern of evasions and silences so familiar from fieldwork forced the question in the end (it was that or
silence), 'You mean he was working for the CIA?!' The final shift of eye
contact said, Yes. An Englishman of means, once married into His-
panic aristocracy, a name in American circles, dinner guest of Parisian
luminaries, now married to the French editor of *Reader's Digest*, and
intrigued by *rural* Europe – *'awiz ayy bi-zabt?* What *was* he doing
there?[14] The teller of the tale comes off as a trifle paranoid. The subject
of the tale need not be much alarmed, one feels, for the logic of the
stranger takes its value from specific circumstance.

States in the West, save in times of panic, draw lines around their
secrets. They worry about particular sites and documents, not forms of
hospitality, and anthropologists are merely marginal wherever they
may come from and almost whatever they may do. Not all states are
like this. And the Arab World's certainty about who is who (the phenomenon of the strong model) is complemented by concern for pri-

vacy among those within the model's bounds. The fieldworker's position and that of locals are therefore not dissimilar. People who enter within a cone of privacy and may claim to know what is going on are the people who do not matter and are thus told little; the people who matter, save those who are family, are not inside the cone. The suspicion keeps arising among neighbours that what one hears is illusory and what is real is somehow not being heard. Structurally, one is living in a wilderness of mirrors. An attempt to grasp the system as a whole, which is what the fieldworker may well be doing, suggests access to deeper secrets or a wish to gain such access.

The word *khatir* is used of others than foreign bookworms. Nor is 'dangerous' a bad thing to be, though for foreigners the tag is unwanted and uncomfortable: it means sharp, perceptive, someone not taken in by appearances. Prolonged immersion is required to feel what is going on, however. So too is some approximation to equality. Fixed positions simply halt discussion, after which it is all *mujamalah*: 'polite waffle' or otherwise, in a low-key American sense, 'bullshit'. Archaeologists, notoriously, gain impressions of instant rapport, situated as they are in rankings of employment and state prestige. So do short-term business visitors. The quieter wind-drifting anthropologist feels like Heyerdahl on his raft, surrounded by life that passengers on liners say is not there.

Of all people why us?

Conflicting orders of privacy, and thus of self-esteem, are a large part of what we study and part of what everywhere we live. Views of fieldwork, wherever done, as 'collecting data' are at odds with practice. In Yemen, for instance, I found it impossible to tape what elsewhere would pass as 'interviews'. To do so, as I explained (Dresch 1989, introduction), would violate a local sense of context, of what could properly be said to whom. All I had on tape, as of late 1983, were a few set pieces. Lila Abu Lughod, across the gender divide in another setting, found much the same (1986: 24; 1993, introduction).

There is, however, one account which rests on a taped record and at the same time addresses interiorisation of the world's disputes in fieldwork. Andrew Shryock's book on Jordan (1997) features a wide range of characters, including an overwhelming local figure whose bid for influence rests partly on a doctorate in anthropology from Cambridge.[15] Alternative histories are at issue. The state has its written version. Tribes have their different oral claims. Those with great histories once held power, and if the fieldworker is the agent of American policy then it is they, in their opinion, he should rightly speak to (ibid.: 178);

those with lesser histories are less forthcoming (ibid.: 165). What used to be described as social structure – a rather public phenomenon— is a structure of disagreement, among other things of selective privacy. The tape-recorder acts 'as a divining rod of spoken authority' (ibid.: 147). One question the book does not address is, what was it about the politics of Jordan which made this a subject one could tape at all? The lack of recorded texts in other work (Davis 1987 on Libya, Dresch 1989 on Yemen) appeared evidence of mere obtuseness among older anthropologists, or perhaps lack of moral fibre.

Urged on by the author some years before the book, I resolved to tape more. I selected a very public occasion, the annual gathering around the tomb of al-Husayn at Raydah, attended by holiday crowds from Sanaa and thus not likely, I thought, to draw suspicion of hole-in-the-corner methods. Out came the tape-recorder. Smiles all around from neighbours in the crowd. Shyness seemed indeed my problem. Thirty minutes later, however, I was in Raydah prison with the local bad boys in their chains and shackles, who in the usual way of rural Yemenis were charming – *tafaddal, makan-ak* ('please, do sit here'). The secret police who took me off as darkness fell were less fun.[16] Precisely by trying not to seem a spy (*jasus*) here I was in the labyrinth of National Security.

What fieldworker, beyond the new constraints of working in one's own state-boundaries on an internal subject class, has no stories of official botherment? But ethnographers of the Middle East show fondness for the genre and often swap *mukhabarat* stories, the generic term for secret police. The Raydah incident in my case involved being driven off by dishonest persons to security headquarters in the capital, where a character out of Graham Greene beat the table until soon before dawn and accused me of 'spying' (on what, one may wonder; in the nature of the case, wrong side of the desk, one cannot ask); a later episode further south, precipitated by the fact that tourists arrive in groups by expensive four-wheel-drive vehicles and ethnographers arrive on a truck-load of onions, was more alarming. But I was not the only one.[17] What is the divining rod telling us?

Were security, in some John Le Carré sense, the issue one would expect political scientists to be in constant trouble. They write about things which in that sort of world might matter; and some of them, conspicuous in their own academic circles, do 'participant observation' of dreadful kinds.[18] Rarely do they get arrested. Anthropologists meanwhile fossick in local detail. Other subjects suppose we ask about people's sex-lives (we rarely do, but if material arises on the nature of the self or such we write it down) and the room for offence is vast. Yet most ethnographers manage the immediate sense of trespass without much upset. They still encounter police authority. If one studies, say, 'political parties' one attracts less trouble.

Tim Jenkins makes a general point about state modernism with reference to the French countryside: 'The "official" point of view ... tends to see all "local" phenomena as in some sense survivals' (Jenkins 1994: 448), and thus potentially an embarrassment if one lacks the self-confidence of elites in Paris. The Middle East as a whole, perhaps, (certainly the Arab World) is placed often in the position of French peasants. Mundy thus worries lest one 'primitivise' through mere description: on this ground she and Abu Lughod agree, though otherwise their work differs fundamentally. Not everyone thinks this way. Contemporary phenomena for most of us are as modern as one another, and rhetorics of modernity, wherever found (be it France or Arabia), are facts among many; but they are salient, effective facts. Egypt's powerful rhetoric of 'authenticity' against 'modernity', for instance, equates much of the real with the folkloric. Literature on the Gulf divides, on similar grounds, between abstractions of international relations theory (an unrealistic view of life) and an imagery of coffee-pots and camels. Surveys and statistics become the mark of 'scientific' knowledge, while qualitative approaches to the contemporary world are left to novelists and the everyday becomes difficult to speak of (Raban 1987: 126–7). What anthropology might be, apart from vulgar snooping, can be very hard to get across.

In the contemporary world state empiricism is a constant problem, so is modernist ideology. The self-promotion of secret policemen is also common. Allied to nested rhetorics of privacy, however, the mix becomes deeply complex, and the distinction is hard to draw between *jasus* in the Qur'anic sense (someone who snoops in household business) and 'spy' in the modern sense, someone violating the integrity of a state-centred collectivity. The extraneous (*'awiz ayy*, what do you want here?) and the interstitial (*anta khatir*, you're 'dangerous') turn equally and always on the ambiguities to which our earlier citation of Imam Sa'ud pointed, that everyone knows, or thinks they know, but no-one should ever say, and talk of 'spying' thus recurs precisely where no intelligence service would have an interest.[19] As Abu Lughod shows (1986, 1993), the most obvious is the most sensitive.

Wilderness of Mirrors

An unwary reader of Herzfeld's *Anthropology through the looking-glass* (1987) might gain the impression that only states stand between the rest of us and comradely good-fellowship. In fact, he makes clear, our problems are less simple. Rhetorics of privacy and precedence are deployed in kaleidoscopic variety – the chips of coloured glass are shaken this way and that, the mirrors remain constant – and to ask how the system of mirrors works is suspect. These optical metaphors are themselves a 'device of misrecognition' (Jenkins 1994: 440) which protects forms of self-esteem. Herzfeld (1987) and Just (1995) thus show how central the idea of 'Europe' is to discussions of matters Greek, how convoluted it can make ethnography, and elsewhere in Europe's fringe (say Portugal) has the same capacity. Terms offered every day 'in the field' are excised from the literature if they are not also used in committees at Strasbourg or Geneva, for the local is problematic.

The same idea, though centred on the West at large, haunts discussion of the Middle East, perhaps particularly the Arab World. Difference which is not of degree but of kind can only be ideology, for at base we are all supposed to be engaged in the same global project of modernity. Said's *Orientalism* thus remains much cited: 'the felt tendencies of contemporary culture in the Near East are guided by European and American models' (1978: 323).[20] Twenty years later, with the passage of time, it is hard to be certain what was meant. The models even then were numerous, the responses have proved diverse; the position of elites was never that of the poor, and so forth. 'Felt tendencies' suggests something basic. Unfortunately the status of such tendencies is prescribed before one starts enquiring, for all forms but the generic national are 'Third World ideas' (ibid.) which lead nowhere, and the local is thus an error.

The local *mukhabarat* and the transnational intelligentsia decry the same issues. Anthropology, correspondingly, encounters at conferences what it does in *qat* chews or recording poetry at tombs. The idea that everyday life itself is a secret informs more than the affairs of household-clusters, and fieldwork, distinctively, is rooted in the everyday along with much of anthropology's interest, whether studying peasants, local notables or the managers of national states. In the wilderness of mirrors it cannot be trusted. Whatever is presented by 'informants' if it purports to be distinctive news from one side can only be deception of the other's making. 'Orientalism' must have spread to the Orient itself (ibid.: 322). Two recent cases of fieldwork's reception will make the point.

Leila Fawaz depicts Michael Gilsenan's ethnography of Akkar (northern Lebanon) as a 'hall of mirrors'. That indeed is how he writes it up. Definitions of the region itself were heavily overdetermined for those within and outside alike, the local powers worked self-consciously by illusion and veiled threat, the peasantry and retainers could only respond with 'finesse', with the assertion that all was *kizb* ('mendacity'), the world an elaborate lie. The case is exemplary, for Gilsenan spent two decades thinking what to write and picks his way among the problems with fawn-like delicacy.[21] 'When they asked what he was doing in their area he lied and said that he was working for a doctorate. Gilsenan felt guilty about lying and in my opinion, rightly so, as no genuine relation could follow from that...' (Fawaz 1997: 79). Plainly the confessional mode is ill-advised here. But which genuine relation would one choose? Join the peasants, where one survives by lying or gets one's legs broken; join the lords perhaps. For that matter, join Beirut's intellectual *crème*. There was no neutral ground to stand on, any more than in less stressful cases (Jenkins 1994). 'The book focuses on violence, a perfectly legitimate and a very interesting topic, but [one] that can be offensive to those from the region and to others if it does not also consider other features of traditional rural life' (Fawaz 1997: 79). The review stops short, but only just, of saying, 'What about the charm of folk-dancing, our beaches and famous ski-resorts?' The everyday should not be spoken of.

'Traditional rural life' may raise a smile among anthropologists, and one can visualise these imagined folk deploying their own analysis: who writes what in which journal might perhaps be explained in family terms, by bids for lordly prominence, or by some form of *kizb* (that is, lying and illusion) among editors. Segmentation (Abu Lughod 1989) is not the issue. Those kind of settings, typical of the tribal worlds in which she and I have both worked, are in fact where the problems are least intense (the phenomenon of each unit discussing those next door accounts for more of the whole than with official culture-keepers; the reference point of 'the West' is often less important), though to note this is itself to invite controversy. Rather, what one can and cannot say seem ordered by larger structures, which one encounters part by part but consistently in different settings. The only constant is the theme of prestige and privacy. Nor are these structures localised to a mythic 'field-site', as one soon finds in book reviews and conferences.

We reach a stage where anthropology's predictive power is scarcely less than that of particle physics. Shryock's book on Jordan, to take our second case, thus locates against his Badu-centred model Palestinians, Arab Christians, and, not least, cosmopolitan intellectuals with an interest in political science of a certain genre whose denial of local reality is predicted to follow the patterns of Said's book (Shryock 1997: 72, 178, 307, 315 and passim). In the longest and most vituperative review I know of, Joseph Massad appears like a physicist's prediction (Massad 1997). The very structures of privacy are inverted, to the point where one is forced to consider whether the reviewer has or has not a foreskin (ibid.: 105). The fieldwork meanwhile, no matter what one records verbatim with whatever care, must be simply wrong – or more exactly, disinformation.[22] Black Spy and White Spy are as one.

Unlike physicists (one cannot speak for spies), anthropologists crave the unpredictable. The Arab World itself retains autonomy in large degree, and people have lives of moral interest. We must press on. Fieldwork is not the mode of 'intellectual conquerors' (ibid.: 104). It is quieter. Only by patient listening in sometimes difficult settings do we hear what is being said, for 'the employment of the "official" account, or of any abstraction, may be defined in one perspective as a refusal of experience' (Jenkins 1994: 446), and the ordering of such accounts, wherever found, is therefore integral to understanding. Here fieldwork, in the sense anthropologists recognise, has genuinely odd features.

Fieldwork as will and representation

Discussions of fieldwork vacillate between 'method', as if the world were flat (certainly as if no people lived there), and 'anecdote' best left for bar-room stories. Occasionally anthropologists return from the experience as wrecks and transmute this to jollity (Nigel Barley comes to mind), but generalities tend the other way, to the agonistic, and even so collected a person as Leach thus refers to fieldwork as commonly 'traumatic', which is nonsense.[23] What, then, do you tell your reviewers or the local *mukhabarat* who ask 'what are you *really* doing here?' Or, as I was asked for hours on end – I translate a bit literally – 'What are the reasons that lie behind? (*ma hiy al-asbab al-khalfiyyah?*)'

One used to be able to say, 'I am studying the so-and-so.' The implications are absurd to administrators but intelligible to anthropologists: 'I had no interest in witchcraft when I went to Zandeland, but the Azande had; so I had to let myself be guided by them. I had no particular interest in cows when I went to Nuerland, but the Nuer had, so willy-nilly I had to become cattle-minded' (Evans-Pritchard 1973: 2). The case is overstated. But the moderns are in broadly the same position. My own contribution thus far (Dresch 1989) was built around the seeming fixity of certain forms of historiography and tribal boundaries, neither of which I went looking for or suspected as possibilities; indeed my mind was filled, in so far as one can recover an earlier common sense, with Althusserian notions of uneven shifts, structural determinance and class conflict. Shryock (1997) says his analysis of oral history was not his first intention. Abu Lughod's work on poetry arose from local facts (Abu Lughod 1986: 23–24). Why, then, is the process demanding and description difficult? The answer is plain, I think. Wherever fieldwork is done, be it Washington or Wadi Halfa, one is listening for the unsaid.

Jenkins spells out how the position of the foreign ethnographer is in some ways no different from that of a person born there. Wherever one was born an analytical temperament must be handled carefully, as linguists know well already. 'Discourse analysis' in their world, which begins with writing down all the 'ums' and 'ers' in a conversation and proceeds, just as we do, to ask, 'What must be the case to get from this point in what was said to that?', is notoriously problematic with those one records. All social life depends on tacit spacers and assumptions.[24] To say what those assumptions are in the course of conversation is to be unsociable, indeed to be psychopathic, and one cannot say at home or abroad, to officials or to people in the street, 'I shall listen between the lines of what you say.' The assumption one does so is the basis of conversation, however, and to map the more detailed assumptions used is to map the social.

We have seen what sometimes happens when the result is published. Yet if the claim is made that something should or should not be said, is or is not true, that in turn must be analysed in the same way as the material with which one started, and 'the field', so to speak, expands indefinitely. It is not undifferentiated. One must always think who is speaking, what their relation (if any) is to those spoken of, and what is not being said by whom, which if only spelled out upsets a whole constituency in academic life. It is plain where the feeling comes from, therefore, of there being *asbab khalfiyya*, 'reasons which lie behind'. The counters of interaction are essentialised images; they are not the interaction itself. Answers to the question 'What *exactly* are you after here?' must always be intrusive or else evasive.

The necessary papers and initial enquiries 'in the field' about my own purpose years ago were met with something on my part about 'customs and traditions' (*'adat wa-taqalid*), not because of a wish to deceive but because my Arabic was then so limited.[25] The odd thing in retrospect is how how easily that unfolded into real life. John Davis (1987) very reasonably wrote his proposal on Libya in terms of long-distance trade, not the everyday life of Libyans, for what could be said of the everyday that was not in *The Green Book*? But plainly 'conversation' developed, for he wrote a sympathetic monograph. Sometimes to call oneself an anthropologist is to give offence. 'So I have for many years,' said Evans-Pritchard, 'advised students about to embark on fieldwork to claim that they are historians or linguists' (1973: 9).

Presumably that is now forbidden. State empiricism is no monopoly of the Third World. In the margins of the ESRC's application forms (Britain's Economic and Social Research Council), for instance, one finds: 'honesty to subjects about the purpose ...; how ... ethical questions will be dealt with; ... which professional code of conduct will be referred to'. Such dicta are not realistic. Moral relations never work by codes save at the level of pure *mujamalah* (that is, put politely, of sheer 'waffle').[26] The model informing such dicta perhaps is survey work; the target, as it were, is the powerless mass of social security claimants or dependants of the health service, labelled with disdain for their position now as 'clients' as if somehow they had volunteered to have their souls raked over. This is not our world. Anthropologists, in the nature of the job and whomever they work with, deal with persons who retain autonomy. The agenda is largely set by one's hosts, the forms of interaction are under their control, and where this is not so, little useful comes of it.

Those parts of the world with strong models of their moral worth make the point in obvious ways, for no code can specify how one encounters them. Initiation into a world of signs, to use Jenkins's image, is in any case a process one cannot legislate, for tacit agreement has always its own logic: the Imam Sa'ud did not sanction tobacco, in Burckhardt's tale, nor yet did he allow it said the Meccans smoked. There are forms of honesty other than those of the zealot who was bastinadoed and whose insistence on absolutes contravened the very code invoked, as the Association of Social Anthropologists do when in the style of our time they confuse methodology with manners at the cost of all moral sense: 'Once the methodological advantages (of covert observation, of deception, of with-holding information) have been achieved, it is rarely defensible to allow that omission to stand' (ASA 1987: 4). The 'method' recommended seems to be that one deceives people, gets what one wants and tells them at the end, 'Surprise!' None of my acquaintances in anthropology describes what they do in that way. The choice of terms in parentheses meanwhile is chilling – as if the worst fears of one's hosts abroad were true and really we were all spies. To run the absolutes of such prescription through a world informed by indirection would produce disaster.

Home truths

Different structurings of privacy are the stuff of life. One feels one's way. To explain in print how it is done, in this case or that, is to bring to light what everyone left unsaid, and of necessity, therefore, one skirts key issues: only the passage of time allows the parties involved to pretend that the world has changed and that what first defined them has become a story. Marriages and friendships, let alone anthropology, are sustained by quiet acceptance. If one can suggest, however, that 'observation' and 'data collection' (even 'dialogue') are poor descriptions of what anthropologists do, and that all are in a sense evasions, the effort may be worth while. Anthropology instead is much like the rest of life. During fieldwork, the anthropologist changes from a position of misinterpreting the offers made, or the roles available, to one of having to decide whether or not to take them up (Jenkins 1994: 443). The longer the fieldwork lasts, which is only to say the longer one's interest and connections last (usually several decades), the more obviously true the description is.

In the case of 'strong models' the offers made are limited in distinctive ways and they recur with scant regard for contexts defined by others. That is their nature. In certain contexts of its own devising, anthropology sets as firm demands. With the passing of the steam age, contexts overlap and one is therefore going to encounter offers one cannot properly accept, as much at conferences or in publication as among the mountains, and choices one cannot properly avoid, not least between explaining and taking part. Not all the roles on offer are compatible. Nor is fieldwork the whole of anthropology. It is not by itself, where I have worked, a 'sufficient way of gaining knowledge about other people' (ibid.: 434). It is, however, indispensable to doing so and within its limits the knowledge produced is, as Jenkins goes on to say, 'sincere and reliable (and so testable)'.

NOTES

1. The division into periods is not exact. The wonderful Chevalier d'Arvieux (origin, I think, of that Victorian clunker, 'Farewell my Arab steed') wrote his book in the seventeenth century, published in 1718. The best of the women authors are those of the late eighteenth century (see Melman 1995, where the rhetoric of lit. crit. should not discourage one). For an excellent analysis of later (British) male fascination with 'the noble Badu' see Tidrick 1989. Why the shift? In part because of shrinking distance: to write of court affairs with the candour of former 'ladies of quality' would these days have one declared *persona non grata*.

2. For a detailed and sympathetic review of Mundy's work see Bédoucha 1997. The virtues of the different arguments must be judged by those interested; what is relevant for the present purpose is the form of argument.

3. Gilsenan (1990: 222), also discussing anthropology of the Middle East, makes a similar point with a line from Synge.

4. The problems are accentuated by the fact that most work is done by very young people. Long-term constraints in one's homeland, never mind abroad, remain mysterious: for all the work we have on 'gender', therefore, the family remains too little analysed. As for my own fieldwork, my wife was based in the capital and I was often out and about; unintentionally we mimicked the system of many Yemeni friends, but that is more for her to write of. For other matters see Dresch 1989, intro.

5. Conferences on the contemporary Middle East seem more striking in this respect than those on most topics. What is said on formal panels bears often no relation to what is said in coffee breaks. The very terms used are different.

6. Thanks to Stefano Boni for *obi nhyre obi kyre*. Despite acute distrust of the local Forest Service, only about 6 people out of 200 preferred not to answer Stefano's survey questions on land tenure and inheritance, asked by a comparative stranger. An amateurish approximation to the detail gathered takes years in many Middle Eastern settings.

   As Herzfeld suggests (1987: 64), 'covering' and 'exposure' might replace honour and shame. So might such terms as secrecy, domination, evasion, prestige and dishonesty; but all turn on the same assumptions as the original terms thirty years ago. His 'looking glass' motif meanwhile recurs in the titles of pyschology books, but twice conspicuously elsewhere: Raban (1979), on Arabia, and Verrier (1983) on Britain's clandestine relations with the Middle East. It is not so popular for books on Africa.

7. A general discussion of secrets would take us far afield, by way of Simmel. But such concerns were popularised in anthropology by Bourdieu (1977 [1972]), whose examples, one might note, were Middle Eastern.

8. Apart from *The Sanusi* (and where is the rest of even that?) Evans-Pritchard produced only lists as dull as previous Italian lists. He lived in Cairo for a time. He knew Lebanon in the war; but the only trace is in others' memoirs (Maugham 1947), where we find him intriguing against the French and shooting bottles off a wall with his revolver.

9. Arab friends are often treated abominably at the borders of Western states, and the popular imagination affects all of us. American airlines on the transatlantic route were at one time a rich source. A Lebanese friend on an American passport was held up by TWA at London with the marvellously Zen question, 'Why were you born in Beirut?' Stamps in my own passport at Delta's check-in led to the charming query, 'Do you *know* any of these people?' Stupidity does not flow one way.

10. The language and suspicion theme recurs in Amitav Ghosh's travel book (1992: 199, 338). Ghosh plays off the exclusions of the modern world (much dwelt on in terms we all experience) against the genial exchange of mediaeval traders. The traders are still there. How specific the exclusions are to a Eurocentric world one may doubt. His thesis on the Egyptian delta lies dormant on Oxford shelves.

11. *'arabi aw 'ajami*. The term *'ajami* sometimes means Persian but Yemenis at the turn of the century used it of Turkish, and those less exposed to the transnational world used it until recently of Generic Foreign.

12. One's attachments grew close and have proved long-lasting. The only formal visits from men, however, with the water-pipes stoked and the carpets spread, were contrived events near the end of sustained periods. Women used to drift up the stairs and laugh at me swabbing down the courtyard, children would wander in and out, we were on more than 'borrowing sugar' terms with a crowd of neighbours, my wife was taken along to births, marriages and deaths constantly – but a formal 'visit' remained a contradiction.

13. 'Cf. Dresch (1989: xii and xiv) on ... the epistemological virtues of association with [major] shaykhs' (Mundy 1995: 207). That is not quite what I intended. But one does need, as it were, protectors, and I remain very grateful to mine for allowing me to get on with things: without them I would have had to do a 'village study'. Mundy herself used the good name of a noted antiquarian with excellent government connections. Others have aligned themselves with liberals in local academic life and the latter have sometimes paid a price.

14. Were the story true, one's estimate of the CIA would need revising; but, as in a hundred field situations, how on earth does one respond? Dinner-jacket, sardonic grin? 'The name's Pitt-Rivers ... Julian Pitt-Rivers.' Irony gets one nowhere, but French academics would repay more study. I do not vouch for the biographical details.

15. This is the point to confess for the record that I acted as one of 'Dr Ahmad's' examiners. Small world.

16. Again compare Ghosh (1992: 333ff.). Suspicion, it seems, is everywhere (ibid. 112, 125, 199), linked with a parochialism the author finds constantly upsetting (ibid. 50, 62, 169, 235). In practice he was surely more resilient than his book persona. But his account, as a citizen of India, is worth pursuing to dismiss the illusion that somehow everything boils down to East and West.

17. One cannot tell others' stories without their permission. Suffice it to say, then, that anthropologists get more of this than others and that, strikingly, sex is not a key determinant, though position coded locally in gendered terms is: if one stays within someone's protected space one is usually left alone.

18. One person, whom it sometimes seemed one could not get off a plane in the Arab World without passing, worked for a time on Yemen. He then addressed an important Saudi audience, saying Yemen was in effect two countries liable to fragment if pushed. The hypothesis was tested (May 1994) with large casualties. He remains *persona grata* everywhere. It goes without saying that *politologues* one admires do not play these games; but those who do are in control of substantial jobs and funding.

19. Unfortunately the literature on spying does not concentrate on the Middle East. But if open secrets are so sensitive, are the classical objects of espionage (secret minutes and the like) perhaps easy to get hold of? And if they are, do they matter much?

20. The fame of Said's work is interesting. Although academic orientalism is central to his interests he nowhere addresses it directly, thus missing the important point: it was not that such people as Goldziher imposed a painter's fantasy on the Muslim World but that they adopted so fully one local view – they became (Sunni) *ulema*.

    The moral judgements on travellers, meanwhile, those fieldworkers of another age, are strange. Lane, residing in Cairo, behaved by his own lights as a gentleman and is condemned for *not* taking a local concubine: 'thus he preserves his authoritative position as mock participant' (ibid. 163). Flaubert, by contrast, behaved abominably (ibid.: 184ff.) and somehow comes out of it rather well.

21. See Gilsenan 1997, where references will be found to very careful papers between the fieldwork and the monograph.

22. Direct local speech may thus be 'internalized Orientalist dicta' (Massad 1997: 105). If locals want to pretend they are less honest than foreigners, for instance, they must have got it off Glubb Pasha; but the theme recurs elsewhere than Jordan before Glubb was born (Doughty, in *Arabia Deserta* (1936), not only reports the cultural figure but deconstructs it rather nicely too: 'The Engleys are not thus! nay, I have seen them full of policy ...').

23. Leach's remark is at the start of *Rethinking Anthropology* (1961: 1). Nigel Barley's works begin with Barley 1983.

24. For a wonderful example of close-range linguistics see Beeman (1986) on Iran. There is nothing that good on an Arab case; but nor in the Arab World is the logic of manners theorised as explicitly as in Iran.

25. Abu Lughod, whose Arabic I would think was better than mine by far, reports using the same catch-phrase at the start of fieldwork (Abu Lughod 1986: 14). What else could one say that made any sense?

26. Herzfeld (1987: 68 and passim) deals well with the question in ethnographic context. The more general problem of 'ethics' is discussed by Pocock 1988 and deserves more thought than it receives, for such language as a form of control is everywhere.

Chapter 6

SERENDIPITY: REFLECTIONS ON FIELDWORK IN CHINA

Frank N. Pieke

As Max Weber wrote long ago, science as a vocation demands from its practitioners the ability to negotiate the tension between control and creativity and a devotion to progress that is never fulfilled: 'In science, each of us knows that what he has accomplished will be antiquated in ten, twenty, fifty years. That is the fate to which science is subjected; it is the very *meaning* of scientific work, to which it is devoted in quite a specific sense. Every scientific "fulfilment" raises new "questions"; it *asks* to be "surpassed" and outdated' (Weber 1946: 138; italics in original). Science as a discipline is thus a specific creative process and a special kind of institution at the same time: a discursive community of scholars who are committed to the open-ended production of knowledge through systematic induction and deduction. Discarding the notion that reality is law-governed and knowledge is finite, such a science is committed to the discovery (or creation) of facts and their interpretation (Weber 1949).

Serendipity is at the heart of this endeavour. Popperian positivism can do no more than declare the formulation of new ideas in science as 'nonscientific' inspired conjecture. Nonpositivist science, however, considers the pursuit of new, unexpected insights the essence of science. It is as systematic, and definitely more reflexive and honest about the nature of the scientific enterprise, as positivist science.

Serendipity in this enterprise is less random and more proactive than suggested by the standard gloss of the term, 'the faculty of making happy and unexpected discoveries by accident' (*The Concise Oxford*

Dictionary, eighth edition, 1990). In this chapter, I first of all argue that science systematically *creates* the conditions for serendipitous discoveries. Secondly, science *capitalises* on accidents by systematically harnessing them into an evolving pattern of discovery. In other words, serendipity describes the creative tension between structuration and event, and that balance between control and creativity which defines science as a vocation within a discursive community.

Below I describe various levels of serendipity in my past and ongoing research projects.[1] When doing research, I found that inevitably many factors beyond my immediate control influenced my work, some of which proved serendipitous in their own right, while others were at least instructive. Serendipity, I have come to appreciate, not only informs the ethnographic exploration of events, cases and cultures. It is often just as important in guiding concept formation, comparison and generalisation. Finally, serendipity often has a decisive impact on the selection of research topics, and thus ultimately on the long-term direction of both an individual academic career and anthropology in general as a discipline.

Serendipity and fieldwork in China

Until 1978, the People's Republic of China was the world's largest *terra incognita* in the social sciences, the ultimate frontier of first-hand investigation. Since the late 1950s, political scientists and national security specialists had led the way in building up a respectable establishment of modern China specialists and China watchers in the United States.[2] Whether hawks or doves, these scholars were united in their conviction (largely correct, we can now tell with the benefit of hindsight) that the information coming out of China mostly consisted of lies or carefully encrypted truth. Understanding China thus in large part consisted of exposing falsehood and decoding obscure messages. The truth was not plain for everybody to see. The Vietnam war bred a new generation of China specialists, who thought China to be the source of Maoist deliverance from the evils of capitalism and imperialism. With very few exceptions, these youthful enthusiasts have now changed their views.

Both groups of scholars suffered from an acute dearth of information about what was actually going on in China. Getting there and seeing China with one's own eyes attained an almost mythical quality. Real life in China was a carefully hidden secret that somehow, China specialists believed, held the key to understanding what, according to some, was the miracle of Chinese socialism or, according to others, the ugly reality of Chinese totalitarianism.

Anthropologists were, on the whole, not among the China-watching crowd. The (at least) two generations of China anthropologists who entered the academic establishment between 1949 and 1978 subscribed to the Malinowskian dogma that research needed first-hand fieldwork and accepted that China was therefore beyond the reach of anthropological inquiry. Following Maurice Freedman and Arthur Wolf, they did their fieldwork in Hong Kong, Taiwan, or among the overseas Chinese (usually in Southeast Asia). With only very few exceptions, the People's Republic of China simply did not exist as far as anthropology was concerned.

When China opened up to foreign researchers after 1978, anthropologists were therefore somewhat slow to enter the fray. Yet anthropology could not escape the deeply ingrained belief that the reality of normal, workaday life in China is a powerful and dangerous mystery. Doing fieldwork in China has a taste of forbidden fruit; despite the drudgery of endless negotiations and gatekeeping rituals (banquets!), fieldworkers in China relive at least some of the excitement of the small child sneaking up to the apple-stand in the neighbourhood greengrocer's.

What lends much currency to this perception is that Chinese officials, too, 'treat everyday life as a secret'. This is by no means unique to China, and indeed I have borrowed the phrase from my colleague Paul Dresch's contribution on the Middle East to this book (chapter 5). In the case of China, the reasons for this secrecy seem to me an outgrowth both of established bureaucratic practice and of the specifics of Maoist ideology and politics.

To begin with the latter, Mao of course was a great believer in the power of the word and the willpower of human beings. Together, they should be able to overcome objective obstacles to the attainment of full communism. As reality fell farther and farther behind purported achievements, the need to restrict information became ever more vital; lies and secrecy not only covered up an unsavoury truth, but also, and perhaps even more importantly, were a prime means to bring about change. This reached an all-time high during the Great Leap Forward (1958–61), when cadres were actively encouraged – if not outright ordered – to lie until an estimated twenty million people had died of starvation.

In addition to this, and the reason why reality still is a secret despite twenty years of 'reform and opening up to the outside world', there is the innate tendency of bureaucratic actors anywhere in the world to dissimulate. In his pathbreaking work on the politics of economic behaviour in planned economies, János Kornai developed the concept of the 'soft budget constraint' to explain how resources are allocated in the course of bureaucratic negotiation processes. Access to information is a key instrument for bureaucratic actors in manipulating the outcome of these processes. Just like other resources (money, labour, raw materials), information is withheld and hoarded in bureaucracies (Kornai 1980).

Withholding accurate information and spreading carefully doctored disinformation are indeed a prime way to exercise power among bureaucratics in China. Conversely, giving full and total access to hoarded information renders a Chinese bureaucratic actor defenceless against conflicting claims and attacks and irrelevant as a gatekeeper. From the perspective of the people who give or deny us access to the field in China, the facts of everyday life, no matter how trivial, therefore matter a great deal.

That normal life is such a powerful secret in China ought to make anthropology particularly dangerous. Anthropology more than any other discipline makes it its business to understand in detail what happens at the grass-roots level. That we do not meet more suspicion than we already do is probably because most people in China either do not know what anthropology is, or have an understanding of the discipline at odds with the self-perception of Western anthropologists. In China (as in many other parts of the world) anthropology either draws a blank, or conjures up images of colonial exploitation and the investigation of the physique or queer customs of primitives by members of a dominant group or culture. During my fieldwork, which usually takes place through or in direct cooperation with Chinese academics, I therefore find that I have to invest a great deal of time dispelling incorrect (at least from my point of view) notions about our discipline and convincing Chinese colleagues, counterparts and bureaucratic gatekeepers of the virtues of long-term efforts to study a society of which one is not a member and whose language one speaks only imperfectly.

Needless to say, my efforts at self-interested proselytising have met with varying degrees of success, but explaining anthropology in terms that make sense to Chinese social scientists and officials is nevertheless essential to gain access to informants and field-sites. When doing this, one is often faced with suspicions born from the secrecy of everyday life. There is little one can do about this apart from stating one's methods and objectives in very general terms. This suspicion is, after all, not a matter of some misunderstanding of what anthropologists are up to, but, quite on the contrary, an acutely accurate understanding of our work. The problem is rather that what to us seems unexceptional comes across as subversive to gatekeepers steeped in the game of information hoarding. On a more salutary note, confronting healthy Chinese scepticism has often forced me to question some of anthropology's more outrageous claims to achieve intercultural translation and dialogue through full immersion in an alien environment. And, when discussing my own anthropological fieldwork with Chinese social scientists, I have also come across more constructive images and even a genuine interest in our discipline.[3] Let me illustrate these rather general points by recounting my first real fieldwork experience in China.

Fieldwork: Beijing 1988–9

In 1988, when I arrived in Beijing for my doctoral fieldwork, I had already discovered that research in China is not straightforward.[4] The problems of explaining and justifying anthropological fieldwork begin with the difficulty of obtaining official permission. In general, it is essential to have a Chinese organisation which is willing to act as official host. By acting as the fieldworker's temporary work unit, this organisation can help overcome the many hurdles that bureaucracy puts in the way of the proposed project. In the case of my fieldwork in 1988 and 1989, the Institute of Sociology at the Chinese Academy of Social Sciences in Beijing agreed to receive me, thanks to the support of one of the researchers there who happened to be a friend and former student of mine.

The Academy is a ministry-level organisation and therefore fairly independent. Yet ever since its foundation in 1977 the Academy has been controversial. Its research institutes provide a haven for independently-minded intellectuals, many of them with a personal history of criticism of the regime and ensuing persecution, and before June 1989 some of its institutes were undiluted think-tanks for radical leaders. With official patronage these intellectuals have been able to carve out their own liberalised niche in the bureaucratic social structure, but, as I was soon to find out, at the price of isolation from the other parts of that structure.

My position in China was made even more difficult because the Institute of Sociology had been the official host of Stephen Mosher, a Stanford anthropology graduate student denied re-entry into China in 1980 after what the authorities considered to be repeated breaches of trust (Pieke 1987). Subsequently, the Institute had been pressing the leadership of the Academy for permission to invite other foreigners to conduct fieldwork, but this had been given only in the summer of 1988. This meant that I was living in a fish bowl. Engaging in behaviour that might cause the Institute trouble would effectively have closed the door on future foreign anthropologists.

Being aware of the problematic nature of fieldwork by foreigners, I arrived with a research proposal already strongly adapted to suit Chinese sensitivities. I had chosen the social structure of a 'work unit' (a factory, institute or government organisation) as the topic of my research. This, I hoped, would give me the opportunity to interview both ordinary members and cadres of such a unit. Moreover, this topic could accommodate a broad range of subjects, such as the organisational structure of the work unit and its relationships with other parts of the bureaucracy, the structure of individual families belonging to the unit, or informal decision-making processes. Unfortunately, things in China turned out to be worse than expected. Upon arrival I was asked to translate my fieldwork proposal into Chinese. Subsequently, the foreign affairs officer at the Institute completely rewrote the proposal, adapting it so as not to offend the bureaucrats who would have to approve it.

In the end the Institute's efforts proved unsuccessful and permission was not granted because 'the conditions at the basic level are not satisfactory'. Fortunately, I was considered somewhat of a test case and had already spent much time in Beijing, so my friend felt obliged to come up with an alternative. The four or five researchers at the Institute with whom I had become friendly, he suggested, should together have enough friends and acquaintances to act as my interviewees for a while. After all, the municipal authorities had not refused to grant permission, but had merely said conditions were not satisfactory. This network-centred approach worked, and I succeeded in interviewing about forty-five families, many of them several times, in the three-month period between mid-February and mid-May 1989.

Under these circumstances, a community or geographical area was no longer the locus of activities, but instead people from all over Beijing would be interviewed. More importantly, I could only do this by shifting the focus of the interviews away from the social structure and networks in one community to family and individual strategies for pursuing one's interests at work and in private life. Methodologically, this meant that the subjective reality of my informants in the context of concrete events became my primary concern. The constraints of my situation had forced me to focus on practice and become more of a postmodern (or at any rate poststructuralist) anthropologist than I had intended to be.

The outbreak in mid-April of the People's Movement (I prefer this term over 'Tian'anmen 1989' or 'June 4' that are often employed as a shorthand reference to what was in reality a nationwide movement that lasted for almost two months) obliged me to change the focus of my research once more. During the interviews many people had talked about hardship and the inequities caused by the reforms, but there was no indication that these tensions could lead to widespread social unrest in the near future. Yet, this was precisely what happened.

During the first stages of the movement, I remained merely an interested bystander. I tried to follow what was happening, but felt that the movement would either quickly be suppressed or else lose its force. During the student demonstrations of 27 April and 4 May, however, the movement showed for the first time that it could mobilise large segments of the population, and I decided to devote more of my time to observing the demonstrations, taping speeches, collecting pamphlets, and asking questions about the movement in interviews and informal conversations.

Under the impact of the student hunger-strike that began on 13 May, the demonstrations turned into a true mass movement, culminating in the demonstrations of 17 and 18 May when the people of Beijing openly defied the government. At this juncture, the movement had become the only topic of conversation. It halted the normal flow of life, becoming what I propose to call a *total event*. A total event imposes its interpretive frame upon the whole of society. Normally, an event is intricately tied up with the myriad of other events which constitute its context. A total event, however, is autonomous. Instead of the normal dialectic between event and context, a total event creates its own context and determines the meaning and significance of all other happenings. Non-participation or neutrality cease to be legitimate options. All social actors are drawn into the arena, while all fundamental problems and conflicts in society are expressed in terms of the interpretive frame of the total event.

The compelling force of a total event extends even to peripheral social actors such as foreign anthropologists. During the movement, I felt thus that I had no option but to study it. Once again, therefore, Beijing society was determining the subject and method of my research. But this time it was different. It was not me trying to find ways and means to wring opportunities from an indifferent society and a positively unwilling municipal bureaucracy. The initiative was pulled out of my hands, and the Chinese themselves started deciding what my fieldwork would be about.[5]

Very quickly foreign observers became vitally important to the movement. My personal experience with the initial stages was limited because my friends at the Institute asked me to avoid involvement. They did not allow me to take pictures in the Square, talk to the students, or go to their campuses. Suspicious activities on my part could well be used as a pretext to crack down on my research. Having spent the first fifteen weeks of my stay seeking appropriate permission, I was prepared to listen to that argument. Fortunately, by the first week of May my friends had relaxed their standpoint considerably. They still did not want me to talk to, let alone interview, student activists, but at least I could take pictures, collect documents and tape speeches.

In the new context of the People's Movement, my roles as social scientist and student of China were redefined as witness and historiographer. Producing a record of the righteous struggle against unjust rulers is an extremely important item on the political agenda of Chinese remonstrants. All participants in the movement knew this and never stopped me from observing, photographing or taping any aspect of the movement.

The declaration of martial law on 20 May and the subsequent attempts of the army to gain control of Beijing by force heightened the drama of the movement. Violence, suppression, and martyrdom were felt to be inevitable. The new atmosphere pervading the city also had a very strong impact on me. I was no longer only an observer. The catastrophe that was about to happen changed me into a participant. Although undeniably a foreigner, the threat of violence from a common enemy made me part of the people whom I had come to understand and respect during my seven months of fieldwork.

The People's Movement was so all-absorbing that it left a vacuum after its suppression on the night of 4 June. My involvement in the movement had given me meaningful things to do at home. Moreover, it became clear to me that staying behind in Beijing until September, as I had originally planned, would be pointless. The city was clearly preparing for a prolonged period of vicious repression and rectification. Under these conditions finding people to interview would be almost impossible, and very dangerous to them.

Even back home, I was not completely free from the constraints imposed by Chinese society. The Chinese Academy of Social Sciences had played a very active role during the movement. Early on my hosts had told me that my writing about the movement would be detrimental to them in surviving the political campaign that would inevitably follow its suppression and, so they added, would make it very difficult to receive me or other fieldworkers in future. In the end, it was decided that I had best write under a pseudonym. As a result, Frank Niming was born, who published several articles and a book about the movement before his retirement in 1993.

Experiencing the People's Movement in the context of a long-term fieldwork project involved me to an unexpected extent in Beijing society and culture. Moreover, my experiences show that anthropological fieldworkers can become more than just peripheral actors in the community or events they study. When the stakes are raised, their observations and experiences are not only interesting to themselves or to other social scientists, but can be important to the people they study as well. The anthropologist's writings can provide a way for the local people to decontextualise the events making up their lives, and invest them with a future relevance for their own society. By helping the anthropologist write the events of their culture, the people studied ensure that their own point of view can survive the forgetfulness of public opinion and the vicissitudes of military suppression and political control.

Before setting out for the field, I had already been steeped in the criticisms levelled by anthropologists against conventional, Malinowskian fieldwork. Fieldwork, I had come to agree, should indeed be more than harvesting data. Anthropologists should leave their methodological ivory tower and engage in an intersubjective and equal dialogue with the people studied. Yet I had no real picture of what this would mean in terms of daily activities. The immediate challenge was to be granted, in the first place, an opportunity to talk to a member of that elusive category 'the natives'. Indeed, the time-honoured strategy to grab the data and run appeared to make all the sense in the world.

Nonetheless, I came to appreciate the value of dialogical anthropology even during the difficult fieldwork I had embarked upon. Caught in a situation that made a traditional community study and much initial structuring impossible, I was forced to translate and rethink an abstract epistemological choice into a strategy to become an anthropologist of a society seemingly designed to frustrate fieldworkers. I came to understand that dialogical anthropology was much more than sitting on a bench in the village square exchanging ideas and information with the 'natives'. Dialogical fieldwork should be a dialogue with the entire social reality encountered, a chain of events heard about, observed and, above all, experienced. The efforts of the ethnographer to make sense of what, at first sight, seem to be random accidents are similar to the creative interpretive work native actors engage in to make sense of their world. Earlier events provide (part of) the interpretation of later ones, and take on new meaning in the light of later experiences.

In the context of my fieldwork, the decision to study the movement was only natural, indeed almost inevitable, and I thought of it more as a continuation of my earlier work than as a new project. I set out to study the movement as I had studied the local dynamics of the reforms. I was essentially under the same constraints and used many of the same strategies. During the earlier stages, my exposure to the movement was largely determined by the help provided and the constraints imposed by my host organisation. Accordingly, one of the limitations I imposed upon myself was never to participate in the demonstrations I was following, because this might do much harm to my project, my hosts and future fieldworkers.

The People's Movement offered a unique opportunity to an anthropologist whose focus is on events rather than on the reconstruction of a structure or culture which is assumed to exist outside observable reality. Processes, which have to be teased out with great difficulty when studying more mundane (or past) events, were there for everybody to see. First, the People's Movement, purposely designed as a public event, took place largely in the streets. Second, the People's Movement consisted of a clearly demarcated sequence of sub-events, which followed more or less logically from one another. The events developed their own internal moral order and history, making it possible to analyse the movement as one macro-event. Third, and most important, the movement was a total event, subjecting all other events in society to its interpretive frame, and could therefore be studied as an autonomous phenomenon. Here I was no longer dealing with ordinary adaptations of the social order with their largely unseen and unintended effects, but with the construction of an alternative order that challenged the existing state of affairs. The People's Movement was studying Chinese society and history while it was being made, and for a brief period I was allowed to be a participant in that process. Despite its tragic conclusion, I will therefore always think of the Movement as the moment when I was in a full sense what I had hoped for years to become: an anthropologist of the Chinese people.

Fieldwork: Raoyang 1994

Serendipity is the essence of fieldwork research, yet many researchers may object that in the real world of professional academic research, there is little time and often even less patience for such exploits. Social research is funded by foundations, research councils or government organisations who expect clear answers to simple questions. In other words, the rewards expected from the rigours of positivism may be a figment of the methodological imagination, but nevertheless are a rock-solid social fact that constrains the work of all but a happy few who do not need to write research proposals to survive.

I certainly have had my share of these constraints and appreciate how frustrating it can be having to work on things that I considered tangential to my own research interests. Yet it is not quite as bleak as that. Instead of considering the demands for contract research a necessary evil, they can also be thought of as serendipitous opportunities, events shaping a research career that are of the same order as the accidents making up a single research project. This may perhaps sound unduly Daoist, but allowing such events to happen certainly helped me discover things and ponder issues that I would otherwise never have considered. Ultimately, I have found that many such contract projects tie back into my main long-term research interests, providing me with information and points of comparison that have much enriched my understanding of Chinese culture and society. External funding may be intended to make academics do things they do not necessarily want to do, but our task is to use external money in ways unforeseen and unintended. These two objectives need not be contradictory: indeed, I would argue, they logically follow from each other. Here, I briefly review one such experience.

After 1989, my next fieldwork experience in China took place in 1994. In the spring of that year, I spent three months in Raoyang county, 235 km south of Beijing.[6] The project and circumstances could hardly have been more different. I arrived in Raoyang as the tutor of a group of six mature students of the International Centre for Development Oriented Research in Agriculture (ICRA) in Wageningen, the Netherlands.[7] In Beijing the six students were joined by a group member/liaison and an interpreter from the Centre for Integrated Agricultural Development (CIAD, the Chinese counterpart, see below). In Raoyang one further member joined us, an agricultural researcher from Hengshui prefecture of which Raoyang county is a part. The students were being trained in so-called rapid rural assessment, a method for the quick identification of development bottlenecks that is as much favoured by development organisations as it has been derided by more 'serious' social scientists working in development studies (Brandjes et al. 1994). Very quickly, I discovered that I was operating in a minefield of conflicting expectations, and (after several mistakes) again found that virtually the only way to make any sense of it was to follow the Dao.

In Raoyang, we stayed in Beiliuman village in Liuman township, whose success at greenhouse vegetable production made it somewhat of a local model of agricultural development. Here we were quickly caught in a web of competing interests. It transpired that the group had been allowed into Raoyang county as a personal favour from an official in Hengshui prefecture (rather than Raoyang county) granted to the head of CIAD in Beijing.[8] The government of Raoyang county, however, had little patience with my students after they found out that they would not be the expected source of Dutch agricultural technology and development aid, and felt cheated by both CIAD and Hengshui prefecture. Perceiving the students as guests of Raoyang county, Liuman township, too, made it its mission to be as uncooperative as possible, consistently referring the group to the county for assistance. As we have seen, the county thought of the group as guests of Hengshui prefecture and referred them to their patron there. This person, in turn, was less than enthusiastic. He assisted the group simply as a personal favour granted to someone else and could therefore not fully mobilise his official bureaucratic weight as an official in the prefecture. Moreover, as a mere bureau head in the prefecture he held the same rank as the head and vice-heads of Raoyang county and was therefore unable simply to order them to comply.

The fact that the group got any work done at all had to do with the cooperation of Beiliuman village cadres, who knew we were guests of Raoyang county rather than Liuman township, but appeared unaware of or uninterested in the county's lukewarm attitude towards us. Even more importantly, Beiliuman farmers turned out to be very friendly and happy to spare us a few moments in their (genuinely) busy schedules. Farmers in this village are very proud of their entrepreneurial success. Entrepreneurship was the defining feature of a new sense of local pride and identity that was pitted against the township and county governments, and farmers were keen to tell us about it.

Despite the initial problems, the group thus gradually found a way to do some useful work. Yet frustrated by the lack of cooperation, about halfway through their stay the group decided that it would not matter if they antagonised the county even more. Determined not be locked into a model village, they wanted to do a comparative study of Luotun, the poorest village in Raoyang county. This village was located in Niucun township, a two-hour bicycle ride from Liuman. Located in the bed of the Hutuo river, Luotun's fields had been covered by several metres of sand during massive floods in 1954 and 1963, making them unsuited for the cultivation of the area's main crops of wheat, sorghum and cotton. As a result, Luotun had to depend on food aid from the national government for most of the collective period until the early 1980s.

With the reforms, the Maoist preoccupation with grain production gave way to more flexible agricultural policies. After Luotun village cadres had turned down offers to relocate the population of the village to surrounding areas, Niucun township cadres decided that the cultivation of peanuts would be the second-best solution. The county provided loans and technical assistance to the Luotun farmers and, most importantly, allowed them to pay for their grain quota in cash earned by the sale of the peanut crop. Although still poor, Luotun farmers could now at least feed themselves.

In the late 1980s, however, Luotun village leaders became aware of other and more lucrative alternatives. Fruit production seemed especially promising, given the relatively small amounts of irrigation water needed. A plan to develop fruit orchards was drafted and submitted to the township and county authorities. These, however, turned the proposal down on the grounds that Luotun's flood-prone fields were unsuited to long-term investment in wells and orchards. They argued that Luotun should be grateful for the county's earlier efforts to start up peanut farming. Angrily, they put Luotun at the bottom of the county's and the township's priority list for agricultural investment.

To Luotun cadres our research provided a more than welcome opportunity to vent their grievances against the county and hopefully to be heard by higher authorities in Hengshui, Shijiazhuang (capital of Hebei province), or even Beijing. We were received with open arms, and cadres and villagers turned out to be willing, if not positively eager, to tell us about their poverty, backwardness and suffering at the hands of the higher authorities. Yet very quickly the group was made to understand that they had overstepped the boundaries of the acceptable. Suddenly, the police started inquiring after our research permit and temporary aliens' registration and we were told not to engage in any further research activities until these matters had been sorted out. Much frantic activity ensued, particularly on the part of our Beijing hosts at CIAD, to obtain clearance for our research from the Ministry of Agriculture and Hebei province. When these matters were looked into, the long-festering issue of appropriate payment for the various services rendered by county and township resurfaced. The upshot of all these developments was that CIAD had to send one of its directors down to pay off the county and township, pack our belongings and hurry us back to Beijing before the local authorities could find further pretexts for harassment and extortion.

Personally, I found myself in an ambiguous position. As the only Westerner who spoke Chinese, I was privy to at least some of the discussions taking place between the many Chinese parties involved, and in fact often sympathised with (at least some of) them rather than with the group of students, who seemed utterly out of place in China.

Clearly, in this context I could not hope to do much fieldwork myself, although I did interview or hold conversations with many cadres and farmers, which have enabled me to reconstruct much of the politicking around our project. In addition, I acted as interpreter during some of the interviews by group members and co-designed the group's household survey. This experience provides a very clear illustration of an interesting methodology that I think many anthropologists employ, but often seem insufficiently aware of. This I call the *thermometer effect*, which in Raoyang amounted to a more deliberate and self-conscious application of the lessons learned in Beijing in 1988 and 1989.

In the natural sciences, the act of experimentally measuring a given variable often leads to a certain degree of distortion, as measuring itself is an activity that usually invades and thus changes the environment that is being tested. The prototype of this is measuring the temperature of a liquid by sticking a thermometer in it. Since the temperature of the thermometer is always slightly different from that of the liquid, taking this measure must change the temperature of the liquid, thus distorting the outcome. In the natural sciences this is usually considered an undesirable side-effect that should be minimised (for instance by using a very small thermometer and a very large quantity of liquid); I would argue, however, that in the social sciences we can actually use the same effect to our advantage. As the case of Raoyang clearly reveals, all sorts of interesting insights into local politics and the local political economy can be gleaned from the ripples on a previously smooth surface caused by the insertion of a profoundly alien element, namely the fieldworker(s), into local society.

The methodological point of the thermometer effect in anthropology is thus *not*, as in the natural sciences, how one accurately measures something. What I want to highlight here is that the thermometer effect is a powerful methodological tool and an often overlooked additional argument for first-hand fieldwork by outsiders. The fieldworker's own presence and fumbles create extraordinary events (social dramas) in their own right. The methodological implications of the thermometer effect are thus rather similar to those of the total event discussed above in the context of my fieldwork in Beijing in 1989. Events generated by the thermometer effect should not be ignored or relegated to a methodological appendix, but ought to be an integral part of the ethnography.

The Raoyang experience also illustrates something else. As I have pointed out in the preceding sections, much of the success of a fieldwork project hinges on one's ability accurately to gauge what expectations relevant others entertain, what discourses these expectations are rooted in, and, following from this, how then to cater for these expectations. The ICRA project in Raoyang shows what happens if researchers do not manage to do all of these things. The group and myself were parachuted into a situation of which we had no previous knowledge. The practical aspects of the research had been negotiated and arranged by other people than us (ICRA and CIAD in particular), who in the process had nurtured expectations of the research that were totally unfounded. Lastly, the group and myself had virtually no power to renegotiate the terms and conditions of the research, as all relevant decisions after our arrival were made by CIAD and their counterparts in Raoyang county and Hengshui prefecture.[9]

Serendipitous careers

Work in Raoyang was thus full of serendipitous and not so serendipitous events, and I fully agree with Evans-Pritchard in his comment that anthropologists should

> beware of a joint team of research. Meyer Fortes told me that when he was in such a team he spent much of his time and energy in trying to explain to other members of the team the significance of their observations, and when I became a member of a team for study in Kenya I was the only member of it who turned up and did anything (Evans-Pritchard 1973: 9).

Yet even adversity can yield results and participation in joint research teams, while producing much agony and frustration, by no means 'can only lead to waste of time and energy' (ibid.). Joint projects can be serendipitous also in a broader sense. After having written up my dissertation, I had for some time thought of working on rural China to complement my earlier research in a Chinese city, but had not yet resolved which issues I should work on, let alone started making practical arrangements. The invitation to participate in the ICRA team therefore provided a most welcome occasion (albeit not entirely serendipitous, as one of my colleagues, who knew about my budding interest, had put them in touch with me) to spend a relatively long period of time in a Chinese village without the commitments that come with a formal research project of one's own.

In Raoyang, I learned a great deal about rural China (and particularly the state-society nexus), that I have been able to bring to bear on my current fieldwork in Chinese villages. Just as importantly, being a participant observer of the team's fumbles reinforced several basic but crucial rules about fieldwork in China: the importance of solid relations with the local authorities which goes well beyond enabling initial entry; the need for a clear understanding of local expectations and perceptions, making sure that one can either cater for them or cut them to more realistic proportions; and, most revealingly, potentially how much better anthropological research methods fit a rural than an urban setting. In Beijing five years earlier, it ultimately took an extraordinary event before I felt I was getting close to the textbook involvement and empathy that anthropologists are supposed to achieve. In Beiliuman, the involvement in daily life that comes by simply living in a village – despite all the problems we encountered – made me feel that being an anthropologist was, after all, possible for a normal human being under normal circumstances.

A blend of conscious career planning and serendipity brought me to Raoyang and prepared me for the work on rural China that I am currently engaged in (more about this below). I suspect that many anthropologists share this experience. Writing up the initial fieldwork poses questions of an implicit or explicit comparative nature that cannot be answered by investigating one culture or one community alone. Toying with these questions, the anthropologist begins to consider a new fieldwork project somewhere else where the similarities and differences with the earlier site will hopefully shed light on these issues. Yet the actual selection of new sites, or even the design of the project, often hinges on the serendipity of contract research, consultancy, appointment to nonacademic positions, or study tours. Far from trying to dissociate ourselves from the real world beyond the safety of the walls surrounding academia, we should allow it to shape the direction that our careers, and the discipline as a whole, takes. We may even end up in places we did not know existed.

I first began working on the Chinese in the Netherlands in the early 1980s as an undergraduate student in Amsterdam. With only rudimentary Chinese language skills and virtually no funding, fieldwork in China seemed an unrealistic proposition. I decided that my first direct encounter with Chinese culture had better take place close to home. This youthful choice has come back to haunt me on several occasions. In 1987, having just arrived at the Sinological Institute in Leiden as a junior researcher, I had little choice but to accept a government contract for an investigation into the social position of the Dutch Chinese. At the time, I considered this project the price I had to pay for being left alone after submission of the mandatory report. Yet, while becoming, over time, an authority on Chinese in the Netherlands (and by extension, the Chinese in Europe), simply because there was hardly anybody else working in this field, I gradually began to realise the potential of this doubly marginal subject (marginal to Chinese studies and marginal to the study of immigrants in Europe). In the 1990s, China became a regional power and a serious candidate for superpower status. Its economy opened up further to the international market, and quickly began to make its impact felt, first in East and Southeast Asia and later in North America, Australasia and, yes, Europe.

Journalists, economists and political scientists and other modern China specialists, never shy to latch on to new trends, began talking about a 'Greater China' in which the overseas Chinese (particularly those in Southeast Asia) were identified as key players. Suddenly, the humble Chinese restaurant workers in Europe were no longer isolated strangers in a strange land, but the bridgeheads of the aggressive expansion of the Chinese economy into one of the core areas of the capitalist world system.

It is, of course, easy to be flippant about the opportunistic shifts and changes of academic fashion; nonetheless, some real and important analytical issues are at stake here. First, a greater integration of overseas Chinese communities into the Chinese internationalising economy is no doubt taking place (although Europe, it must be admitted, is hardly at the forefront of this development) and China specialists, including myself, can no longer afford to consider the overseas Chinese an issue tangential to changes taking place in China. Quite unexpectedly then, my long-term involvement in the Chinese in Europe seems to have given me a headstart in a burgeoning subfield directly related to my core interests.

Second, my current fieldwork in rural China focuses on the multistranded connections of villages with the world beyond, and migration is an obvious and important aspect of this. The Chinese in Europe, again emerging as serendipitously relevant, provide me with an understanding of the process of migration when viewed from the receiving end. What is more, Chinese international and internal migration are in some cases even ethnographically connected. As it turns out, certain groups of migrants in Europe and in many Chinese cities are drawn from the same area (although not, as far as we know, from the same villages), inviting comparisons and generalisations that a predesigned research plan, no matter how carefully thought through, would probably not have yielded.

Serendipity and control

When Clifford Geertz, then a wholly inexperienced graduate student from Harvard, arrived at Jogjakarta, Indonesia, together with the five other members (all graduate students as well) of his research team, he encountered a situation somewhat different from what he had expected:

> The plan was that we would go up to a mountainous area north of Jogjakarta where there was an old Dutch resort hotel, now unoccupied. Under the general surveillance of the [Indonesian] professors ... we would summon people in from the countryside round and about – or, more exactly, local officials, who would know who was appropriate, would summon them for us. Working from a prepared schedule of topics, we would interview these people in groups (so they could correct one another, and come to a consensual view) about this or that matter. Then we would prepare a report and leave ... It would be hard to conceive an image of social research more entirely opposed to our notions ... than this extraordinary reincarnation of the pith-helmet procedures of colonial ethnology (Geertz 1995: 105).

This experience is an – almost farcically – extreme example of the situation that many anthropologists encounter when they enter a field-site for the first time. Until this point, I have spoken of serendipity as something that comes naturally, indeed unavoidably, its exploitation merely requiring an open mind and lots of time. Although this may seem an almost tautological point, in fact it is not. After a long period of negotiations and compromises (longer even than my enforced inactivity in Beijing thirty years later), Geertz and his team-mates chose a solution that was as radical as the arrangements were unworkable: '[W]e decided to cut the knot in the Gordian way. Four of us ... piled into the chauffeured automobile Ford had provided the project and, asking nobody's leave, headed east, looking for a new site' (ibid.: 107).

Geertz found, as I am finding in my current fieldwork project, that it may be necessary actively *to create* the conditions to encounter the unexpected, and when it happens, to pursue it. Anthropology, in other words, requires a methodology (or at any rate a strategy) to invite serendipity in, as much as positivist research requires a methodology to keep it out. It would be futile – and fundamentally misguided – to try to devise a procedure to do this as each project poses its own methodological challenges. Here I can merely outline how I am trying to solve the concrete and immediate problems that I find myself confronted with in my current project.

I am fortunate enough to work together with local researchers of a wholly different calibre than Geertz's Indonesian professors. Yet some of the same problems pertain, often through the fault of nobody in particular. The project is designed to be both comparative and collaborative. It is comparative, because it entails fieldwork at three different rural sites throughout China; it is collaborative, because I do not carry out all of the fieldwork myself, but work with two Chinese sociologists. Both are very good friends and co-workers of my former student and main contact at the Institute of Sociology at the Chinese Academy of Social Sciences; he, too, is actively involved in the fieldwork arrangements.

During a discussion in 1992, I floated the idea that it would be refreshing to set up a project in which Chinese and Western researchers would participate on a basis of equality, rather than the Chinese being either used by a Western researcher simply to gain access to the field, or else as cheap labour to collect data for a project entirely designed by the Westerner. My suggestion met with much enthusiasm as both researchers had worked on several projects for Westerners and never felt they were taken quite seriously as researchers themselves.

After we obtained some start-up funding, we spent ten days at each of two field-sites in the summer of 1996 to explore the possibility of working there on a more systematic basis. Briefly stated, the project intends, as I put it in a grant application, to

> examine local level social, economic and political change in [three] sites over a period of five years. Together, localism on the basis of the welding together of entrepreneurship and political power, and a proliferation of regional, national and even transnational linkages between individuals, groups and localities are at the heart of China's unfolding modernity. This project is an exploratory anthropological study that will investigate the complementary processes of social fragmentation and integration from the bottom up, and yield fresh insights into the opposite yet complementary processes of China's simultaneous regionalization and globalization....

Despite the inflated rhetoric that comes with grant applications (it could actually be a lot worse; here at least I felt I could get away with inserting the word 'exploratory'), the point is, I hope, clear. Over the last couple of years, we have worked at a project design that, we hope, creates enough opportunity for the unexpected to happen. By casting our net very wide (there is little that is not included in our list of topics), being in two very different places, and returning there frequently over a long period of time, we try to keep the project as open-ended and exploratory as possible.

Yet the explicitly comparative nature of the project also requires a fair degree of control, which undoubtedly will preclude at least some of the serendipitous discoveries we would otherwise make. The sites are carefully chosen in such a way that they reveal some of the variety throughout China of local responses to market and administrative reform. At each site (county) we concentrate on an affluent, industrial village, but, for comparative purposes, we also carry out a more super-ficial reconnaissance of a poorly industrialised village in the immediate vicinity. We return to the same villages several times, both in order to tease out longer-term processes and to be able to make comparisons over time. And, crucially, the same people do the fieldwork in each site.

Yet I do appreciate that this project runs the acute risk of not achieving the freshness of traditional 'lone ranger' anthropological fieldwork. First, collaborative fieldwork, I have found, requires a considerable amount of planning, coordination and compromise: over schedules, activities, preferences, or ideas of what social research entails. With this, a very real risk exists of losing anthropology's most precious asset: the use of accidents that I have come to appreciate so much during my earlier fieldwork experiences.

Earlier, I explained that working with researchers at the Chinese Academy of Social Sciences means living in a fish bowl. Other (particularly less senior, or more Chinese) researchers have done and continue to do long-term fieldwork in China. Yet my status as a collaborator on a project of the Academy precludes fieldwork of more than ten days at the time. Being in the field for only such a short period of time, one can be presented only to observe (*guancha*), visit (*fangwen*) or inspect (*kaocha*), all established and respectable bureaucratic activities in China. Beyond that, fieldwork is classified as investigation (*diaocha*) or even research (*yanjiu, diaocha yanjiu*), both of which entail a much higher level of information gathering and independence of the visitor, activities which the Academy has explicitly been forbidden to facilitate for foreigners. Nowadays, one is rarely seen as a spy, unless one is unlucky enough to encounter one of China's many military or state secrets, but that does not mean that one is free to do what one wants for as long as one wants to do it. In short, going to the field for a longer period of time is at present impossible for me. Instead, I try to go to the field-sites for shorter periods of time but more frequently, while my collaborators stay on after my departure. While this is less than ideal on several counts, I hope that it sufficiently emulates long-term fieldwork to yield at least some serendipitous results.

Whereas there is undoubtedly an inclination in China to treat foreign researchers with especially great suspicion, this is merely an amplification of the way that nosy outsiders are generally received. As I explained earlier, bureaucratic powerholders carefully and routinely hoard information to assert their power and interests in the bureaucratic system. Dealing with outsiders is considered 'propaganda work' (that is, the presentation of the official truth), no matter whether the outsiders in question are Western anthropologists, Chinese sociologists, Japanese businessmen, higher-level bureaucrats, or inspection delegations from other localities. While working with my Chinese collaborators I frequently noted that they, coming from the Centre in Beijing, were treated as high officials. They were struggling, like all non-local researchers, to gain access to research sites and reliable data. As Chinese, they undoubtedly had an advantage, but it was one merely of degree.

Serendipity, comparison and culture

This brief discussion of my current fieldwork project in rural China brings me to the issue of comparison and generalisation, an issue as elusive as it is central for anthropology. Anthropological fieldworkers pursue comparison in a variety of ways. Comparison can be a strategy behind one fieldwork project, for instance studying a community and their radically different neighbours, or one group of people in radically different settings. Comparison, as we have seen, can also be a strategy behind the selection of new fieldwork sites and the progress of an academic career. Few anthropologists would claim that such fieldwork and career strategies were fully planned in advance, and even fewer, I guess, would insist that this ought have been done.

This brings us back to the beginning of this chapter. Anthropological analysis – including comparative analysis – amounts to the systematic exploration of serendipitous events, disjunctions as much as co-occurrences. This will not lead to the discovery of natural laws, or even systematic correlations, but it does help us uncover the culturally specific, actor-centred logic through which culture, an endless stream of continually changing possibilities, is, and indeed has to be, transformed. Serendipity and anthropology are inextricably linked, because culture *itself* is an unending serendipitous process. Culture-in-the-making cannot be reduced to a limited set of logically connected statements that parade as truth, and the anthropologist's attempts at understanding (rather than explaining) it are actually just one such process. In other words, 'theory' does not exist outside and above 'practice' (Herzfeld 1987: 203–4).

This actor-centred anthropology of knowledge is different from postmodern anthropology which maintains that we cannot study anything beyond our own dialogue with 'the other'. Culture is not solely in the eye of the beholder, and studying cultural knowledge-in-the-making is a way to put the initiative back into the hands of the people we study. The pursuit of anthropological knowledge is possible and even necessary. In Parkin's phrase, what is at stake in constructing anthropological knowledge is 'how to represent continuity in the diversity we call cultures' (Parkin 1987: 67).[10]

Thinking through the question of serendipity in anthropology and culture thus leads to the conclusion that ours is a generalising and exploratory vocation, and part of the larger endeavour to develop a nonpositivist science. Methodologically, serendipity is vital to us as a strategy of ethnographic discovery, a guiding principle for the design of research projects and a compass for charting our careers. Epistemologically, serendipity in culture and anthropology entails that the pursuit of knowledge does not lead to the discovery of a finite truth, but will help us understand how we and others make sense of, and simultaneously create, the reality we live in.

NOTES

1. The ideas presented in this chapter were presented in roughly their current shape in September 1998 at the panel on *Fieldwork: the value of serendipity*, at the fifth biennial conference of the European Association of Social Anthropologists in Frankfurt. I am grateful for the many helpful suggestions I received during this event.
2. For a brief but illuminating overview of the origin and growth of modern China studies in the US, see Madsen 1995, chapter 1.
3. This is not the place to discuss in detail the diverse meanings that have been heaped upon anthropology in the various corners of the academic world in China, and I have to refer the reader to a paper that I recently completed on this subject (Pieke 1998a).
4. I had been in China before (1982–3) as an exchange student and had done fieldwork on the Chinese in the Netherlands (1981 and 1987). The remainder of this section has been excerpted from an earlier article in which I specifically discuss the issue of how I dealt with the unexpected during my 1988–9 field research (Pieke 1995).
5. My studying Chinese society and culture through the prism of a total event is clearly indebted to analysis of social dramas of Victor Turner (1996 [1957]) or the (extended) case studies of other scholars of the Manchester School, such as Gluckman or Epstein. Yet as David Parkin (personal communication, 1998) points out, the Mancunians analysed crisis situations from a privileged outsider's point of view, while my own approach is influenced by more recent postmodernist and poststructuralist thinking and takes a position which is neither fully insider nor outsider.
6. For an account of my research findings in Raoyang, see Pieke 1998b.
7. ICRA was set up and funded by the Dutch Ministry for Development Aid as a training centre for mainly Third World agricultural development workers.
8. The head of that institute had been a student at ICRA several years earlier and was very keen to maintain and deepen this relationship.
9. This experience has made me a lot more sympathetic to the plight of joint-venture investors or workers on development projects in China and elsewhere. At the same time, it has also made me more critical of the viability of such ventures and projects that seem to be bogged down by many of the same constraints of parachute reconnaissance that we were facing in Raoyang.

10. Yet it would be fair to say that without the postmodern critique of structuralist and symbolist approaches, poststructuralism, theories of practice and the anthropology of knowledge would probably never have gained the prominence that they now enjoy. The postmodernists' critique of anthropology has forced us squarely to face the issue of how far our theories had travelled from the lived-in reality of the cultures that we study. What can, and should, be rejected, however, is the denial of epistemology that radical postmodernism has advocated: there is a reality out there, we do have ways to understand it that go beyond our own preoccupations, and the development of anthropological knowledge continues to be as much informed by ethnographic facts (convenient or inconvenient) as by our own assumptions.

Chapter 7

FIELDWORK AND REFLEXIVITY:

THOUGHTS FROM THE ANTHROPOLOGY OF JAPAN

Roger Goodman

What used to be considered the relatively simple act of doing fieldwork in other societies has increasingly been seen as complicated and politicised. Attention has become focused on the role of the researcher almost as much as the researched. One approach that has come particularly under attack for neglecting the presence of the fieldworker has been the concern with 'scientistic' cultural translation at the centre of which, according to Talal Asad (1986: 142), lies the Oxford tradition of Evans-Pritchard, Lienhardt and Beattie. This chapter sets out to review, very briefly, some of the debates about reflexivity in the anthropological process; to examine how these have affected the anthropology of Japan; and to propose that Japan provides a good case for the argument that the necessity for reflexivity does not get in the way of cultural translation, at least as conceived by those Asad attacks, but may actually be central to it.[1]

Anthropologists have long been self-conscious about the experience of fieldwork, but explicitly analysing or incorporating this experience is relatively recent. Since the 1960s, however, each decade has brought its fresh conveyor of what has been essentially the same message to all social scientists, a message which anthropologists have taken to heart more closely than colleagues in many other disciplines because in anthropology the anthropologist is so directly the research tool. The message is very simple: all research reflects, at some level, the assumptions and prejudices of the researcher. The question becomes how best to conceive this truth.

Anthropologists have been told that they need to examine almost every aspect of their personal background to see how it affects the study they have undertaken.[2] Age, gender, sexuality, ethnicity, class have all come under the reflexive spotlight, so that, at times, ethnography has come to be as much a study of the anthropologist, their textual constructions and their native societies as a study of the societies they set out to examine.[3] This type of confessional anthropology seems to have taken hold much more firmly in the US than in Europe, perhaps because of the greater acceptance of being in therapy in the former. I still find it very hard to admit in print to some of the really stupid mistakes which I have made, and offence which I have caused, in the course of fieldwork, though I would accept that I have probably learnt more from the fall-out of these than from almost anything else. My confessions have always been of a much lower level of personal culpability, indeed made to look almost heroic (see Goodman, 1990a), and I am constantly reminded of the sociologist John Lofland's quote of almost thirty years ago that 'What goes into "how the study was done" are typically the second worst things that happened' (1971: 132).

I believe, however, that to reduce the experience of fieldwork simply to the personal feelings of a single anthropologist at a particular place and point in time is to miss badly the real point of what goes on in the interaction between anthropologist and host society. It is not simply that, if they so desire, anthropologists can find ways around the inevitable effects that they have on the societies they study and those which the societies reciprocally have on them, but that such interactions are the very stuff of the anthropological project, providing as they do important information on the way that societies (both that of the anthropologist and the society they study) operate, think about themselves and change. We should embrace, incorporate and 'translate' the effect of these interactions rather than try to avoid them.

The reflexive anthropologist

The so-called 'reflexive turn' in anthropology has had a powerful effect on the discipline from which few have been immune.[4] Since the late 1970s, some anthropologists would appear to have us abandon the whole operation of 'objectively' analysing other societies, since we can never hope to understand all the component factors (Ortner [1984: 143] lists Rabinow, 1977, Riesman, 1977, Crapanzano, 1980). Others would have us write everything down so that the reader can have something against which to judge the quality of the final monograph (see Okely and Callaway, 1992). Others still have argued that the reflexive school of anthropology is little better than 'navel-gazing' and its self-indulgence must be resisted for the sake of a more objective, Durkheimian approach to the study of other societies. The discipline, as a whole, finds itself endlessly caught on the horns of the dilemma as to whether the researcher creates social reality or records it. When this debate takes place on a theoretical plane it appears dry and unhelpful. When, however, as Fardon suggests (1990), it is carried out in the context of the study of a particular society, it can take on an interesting vibrancy which both illuminates the role of the researcher and tells us something about the society being studied.

The anthropology of Japan has certainly not been immune to the 'crisis in anthropology' and at times, indeed, has been in the vanguard of confronting it. In the late 1980s, for example, a group of anthropologists of Japan took part in an experimental meeting to test the effect of national background. Harumi Befu and Josef Kreiner (1992) invited ten anthropologists from ten different countries to discuss what they felt was the significance of being a member of that particular society in the way that they approached Japan. At the same time, Japanese anthropologists and historians representing each of the ten countries were asked to present their view on the significance of the background of each foreign anthropologist in the study of Japan.

In my own paper at this meeting (Goodman 1992a), I chose to take an historical perspective to show how the way in which Japan has been studied by British scholars has reflected, among other things, the relative position of the two nations in the world. Throughout the Victorian and Edwardian period, Japan was just another source of curiosities for the British public who looked down on this global funfair from their imperial height. For the academic, it was a further source of ethnological and ethnographic material to be used in grandiose world theories, behind which lay the same assumption of British superiority. Almost exactly a hundred years later, however, as Japanese economic growth in the 1980s seemed to dominate the world, the main thrust of the literature on Japan in Britain was to use Japan to berate the British for lagging behind in fields such as industrial relations, law and order, education and social welfare (see Goodman 1992b, White and Goodman, 1998 for overviews of this literature) in the manner that thinkers in the Enlightenment period invoked Far Eastern examples indirectly to castigate their own countrymen (see Roberts 1989). The new economic strength of Japan meant a dramatic and sudden growth in Japanese studies and a boom in the anthropology of Japan.

In the 1980s the anthropology of Japan came up with a series of imaginative responses to questions raised by the demands of reflexivity. These were perhaps stimulated by the fact, as we shall see, that

Japan is itself such a self-reflexive society. Some anthropologists drew on the fact that Japan is a literate society (possibly the most literate society in the world) with a long and honourable tradition of letters – the world's first 'novel', *The tale of Genji*, was written by a Japanese woman, Murasaki Shikibu, in the eleventh century – in order to try and translate Japanese society into terms comprehensible to the West that did not do ethnographic violence to the society itself. Ben-Ari, for example, has written an extended review of three ethnographies – Lisa Dalby's *Geisha*, Brian Moeran's *Okubo diary*, and Oliver Statler's *Japanese pilgrimage*, all published in 1985 – which 'make explicit attempts at utilising certain aesthetic forms taken from Japan's traditions in order to construct their ethnographic accounts' (Ben-Ari 1990: 142).

Moeran's *Okubo diary* is a particularly potent use of indigenous literary forms and writing styles to plot the trajectory of an individual anthropologist in rural Japan whose initial enthusiasm and delight in the country gradually turns to disillusionment and sorrow at the thought that he will never be accepted in the community: while others in the community might tacitly agree with his feelings of anger against the authorities (for allowing the accident that befell his son), in the end his insistence on seeking restitution for the incident means they turn a deaf ear to his pleas for support.[5] Masayuki Matthews Hamabata (1990) and Dorinne Kondo (1990) also draw on their personal experiences – of being Japanese-Americans – in order to explore issues of identity and class in contemporary Japanese society. While we learn a great deal about the authors, we also at the same time learn much about Japanese society and its reception of those who are both members (Japanese) and not members (Americans).

Another noticeable feature of the anthropology of Japan is that a large number of research projects have been built around personal circumstances. The one advantage for anthropologists in being themselves the research tool is that they can build their research around such situations. David Plath, one of the *éminences grises* of the field, in reviewing Ben-Ari's book *Body projects in Japanese childcare* (1997) comments on this tendency approvingly: 'Watching his sons in a Japanese pre-school, Ben-Ari the scholar was alerted to cultural differences in the magic [of growing up]. So Ben-Ari the ethnographer, invoking the law of academic hot pursuit, forthwith became a volunteer aide in that pre-school so he could study body-projects more directly' (Plath 1998: 868). Much the same could be said for Rodney Clark's book on Japanese banks (1979); Joy Hendry's account of day nurseries (1986); Gail Benjamin's work on Japanese schools (1997); or Brian McVeigh's monograph on Japanese Junior Colleges (1997), to name only a few.

There is no doubt, therefore, as Befu and Kreiner (1992) conclude, that features of individual background do affect the way that Japan has been approached and interpreted. Fieldwork is agglutinative and as we change so our views of society become increasingly complex.[6] There is no doubt that a measure of reflexivity is necessary in all ethical anthropological practice. The study of reflexivity, however, is not limited simply to a study of ourselves as we interact, in the process of fieldwork, with other societies. As anthropologists, we need to reflect not only on what happens to us as we interact with another society (and what this tells us about that society) but also what happens to that society as it interacts with us (and again what this tells us). In this manner we can produce a genuinely reflexive anthropology. This is an idea I would like to explore with reference to an apparent contradiction which has long puzzled me about the way that Japanese society appears to deal with the ideas that foreigners, here limited to Westerners,[7] express about Japanese society. I introduce the idea with two vignettes of a kind familiar to any anthropologist who has undertaken research in Japan.

Vignette 1: March 1985, Tsukuba
It is the last day (officially) of my fieldwork on returnee schoolchildren (*kikokushijo*). There has been a party to celebrate the end of the school year and to say goodbye to all the staff who are leaving. I have made my farewells and asked all the staff who have not returned the questionnaires that I asked them to fill in for me, to do so within the next couple of days. Among the others to be leaving is Azuma, who turned out to be an important figure in my final monograph (see Goodman 1990b: 120–3). He is one of the best-known teachers in Japan and many speeches have been made acknowledging the debt owed him: one teacher says he would have given up without his help; another breaks down in tears while trying to express his thanks.

On the bus back to the school. We have all eaten well and drunk plenty. Drink, as everyone present knows, allows one to talk about one's real feelings, freed from normal social constraints.[8] Azuma is sitting in the next-to-back row. Behind him sits Hope, a part-time English teacher and the wife of Martin, an American who arrived six months earlier, his first time in Japan, to teach English at the school. Hope is the daughter of a Christian missionary and was born in Japan and lived there until the age of fifteen in Kagoshima Prefecture, the southernmost part of Kyushu island. Kagoshima has a very distinctive dialect – often said to have developed as a means of identifying spies of the shogunate during the Tokugawa period who could not manage it – and Hope is often talked about by a proud school Principal as 'our American English teacher who can even talk *Kagoshima-ben*' (Kagoshima dialect). Although she went to America for her high school and university education, Hope has spent most of the rest of her life in Japan, where her parents still live.

I sit alongside Martin and Hope and next to Kojima, Head of the English Department, and one of my best informants.[9] Soon an unpleasant situation develops as Azuma begins insulting the foreigners sitting behind him. None of us will ever be able to understand Japan; Hope, he says, may, having grown up in Japan, be able to understand Japanese words (*kotoba dake oboete iru*) but never their real meaning. Hope, who feels that her whole identity is tied up with having grown up in Japan, starts crying and Martin starts shouting at Azuma to stop talking or apologise, neither of which he does, but instead accuses the pair of them them of being typical Americans who scorn (*keibetsu suru*) Japan. Only when the journey finishes, and Martin and Hope leave, does he calm down. He had just been testing, he says, if Faith really understood Japan after all these years: he had been making illogical statements, and if she had responded in an equally illogical manner, then it would have shown that she did; her insistence that she did understand (*rikai dekiru*) Japan simply showed that she did not. It was clear, he argues, that while she knew things (*shite ita*) about Japanese society, she did not understand it (*rikai dekimasen deshita*).

The next day, Azuma sends apologies to Martin and Hope via an intermediary and invites them to go for a drink with them. They decline and he leaves the school a couple of days later.

While perhaps it is less common now than at the date of this vignette, for reasons which I will explain later, every Westerner has been told in Japan that they cannot and will never be able to understand the Japanese. I use the example of Hope, above, only because she was unusual in being a young white American female who had lived so long in Japan and was completely bilingual. My field notes from the same period contain several examples expressing my frustration at, instead of receiving an explanation, being told that I would not be able to understand (a policy decision, a cultural belief) because I was not Japanese.

Roy Andrew Miller (1982) has explored this concept of cultural exclusivity in the context of the use of the Japanese language.[10] He proposes a Law of Inverse Returns: the better one is at Japanese, the less praise one receives for it, which he describes in terms of Japanese feeling that their linguistic territory is being invaded. Miller explicitly relates this linguistic defensiveness to race. Japanese Americans are expected to be able to learn Japanese because they share Japanese blood; those without Japanese blood will never be able to learn it.

Many commentators (see Dale 1986, Mouer and Sugimoto 1986) have suggested that this same equation applies to foreigners understanding Japanese society in general. Japan is unusual, according to such authors, in the explicitness of its sense of ethnic identity: Japaneseness = Japanese 'blood' plus Japanese cultural skills plus Japanese language ability. To be lacking in any one of these is to be less than fully Japanese. 'Blood' is the key variable since the other skills may be acquired whereas 'blood' is a given. But the idea of exclusivity that lies behind this equation also goes one stage further in Japan. The thinking runs that Japanese society cannot be understood except in its own terms and since it is a society where feeling and emotion are given higher status than logic and principle, it is impossible for anyone socialised into Western logical ways of thinking to be able fully to understand why things are done in the way they are and people think the way they do.[11]

Vignette 2: June 1998, Osaka
My sponsor at the National Museum of Ethnology, where I am a visiting professor for a year, gets a phone call from a journalist from the *Asahi Shinbun*, one of Japan's four daily newspapers with a daily circulation of around 14 million copies. He has never met nor heard of this journalist who asks him if there is a foreign anthropologist at the Museum who can speak Japanese. He puts him in touch with me. The journalist explains that he would like me to accompany him to an election meeting taking place the following Saturday and get my thoughts on Japanese hustings in comparison with the election system in the UK. I point out (in the hope of escaping the commitment) that I am not a political scientist, nor an expert on Japanese politics, nor even politically active or particularly knowledgeable about politics in my own country. Indeed, when the journalist comes to discuss the details of our trip a couple of days later, it is clear that his rapid encyclopaedia reading about the British political system makes him at least as knowledgeable about its outlines as I am. He insists however that he wants an anthropologist and that I will do fine.

I am chauffeur-driven to the meeting, arrive early, am interviewed about who I am and what I have studied in Japan (none of which we had discussed before), listen to three hours of election platform speeches, and then have a debrief interview in the car during the forty-five minutes it takes to get back to my apartment. He apologises that he has not been able to give me a meal and tells me that he will ring if there is anything he needs to check before the article is published on Monday morning.

He doesn't ring, and on the Monday the article appears with three headings in diminishing size: (i) *SHITSUMON.IKEN DENAI ENZETSUKAI* ['Hustings without questions or opinions']; (ii) *GUTAITEKINA SEISAKU DE GIMON WA* ['But what is the basic policy?']; (iii) *98 Saninsen: Eikokujin Roger Goodman-san (38) to aruku* ['1998 Upper House Elections: In the company of Roger Goodman, from England, age 38']. The article concentrates on my surprise that, in the middle of a recession, there was no discussion of political or economic policy, only a request for support at the upcoming election, and my comparison with some British hustings where candidates from different parties sat on the same platform and took questions without notice from the audience. In the next few days, many people I meet tell me that they have seen the article, including the man from the other side of Osaka from whom I am buying a second-hand car. A couple of them tell me that they agree with what I have said.

The episode left me flattered and confused in roughly equal measure, but it was by no means a unique experience. Indeed, I have found the amount of my own work on Japan that is translated into Japanese surprising (Goodman 1992c, 1994, 1999). Such translation is a costly and time-consuming process – I am not confident enough to translate away from my own language and hence the time and cost is not mine – and yet it is clear that some people in Japan think that there is a market for and interest in the ideas of a Westerner about Japanese society even, contra Miller's theory of inverse returns and linguistic territory, a Westerner who can handle Japanese, both written and spoken, to some extent.

The reflexive society

The apparently contradictory status that the Westerner[12] has in Japan is brilliantly captured in Alan Booth's account, published as *The roads to Sata* (1985), of his walk along the length of Japan during which he was both asked almost daily for his views on Japanese society and told that he could not understand it because he was not Japanese. Booth's response to this aggravation, as he saw it, was to develop an inimitable genre of misleading and ironic responses to these enquiries. For an anthropologist, however, it is interesting to explore in more depth the ambiguity of the role of the Westerner in Japan.

Like the stranger in any society, the stranger in Japan is both dangerous and lucky, to be avoided and to be embraced.[13] How they are interpreted depends not so much on the stranger per se as on the circumstances in which they operate. This is a common theme also in Japanese folk beliefs. Yoshida Teigo, for example, has shown how the stranger in Japanese folk beliefs can be ascribed a negative or positive value depending on different circumstances – 'potentially dangerous in ordinary contexts, when there is a release from calamity or unusual good fortune, strangers may be credited for having brought about the happy turn of events' (Yoshida 1981: 96). Similarly, Emiko Ohnuki-Tierney has proposed that the status of some of Japan's minority groups has been interpreted very differently at different periods of Japanese history: 'There is massive historical/ethnographic evidence to support the approach that the structurally marginal member of a class, be it a person, a being, an object; may be assigned the positive role/power of mediation, the negative meaning of pollution and taboo, or the role of the trickster/clown' (1984b: 305).

Westerners in Japan play a similar role to the stranger and the minority group in the way in which they are incorporated into Japan's debates about its own nature and this explains to some extent the apparent contradiction between the two ethnographic vignettes given above. The reflexive mode has a long history in Japanese society. Tanaka (1995) demonstrates how until the end of the nineteenth century Japan's Other was provided by China, since when it has been provided by the West. This change was a conscious political choice, best demonstrated by Fukuzawa Yūkichi's famous '*Datsu-A ron*', a call in the 1870s for Japan to turn its back on Asia and face the West (see Sakamoto, 1997).

Japan's fascination with the West has not wavered over the past 120 years. The role of the West and the Westerner in this process has essentially been that of providing an alternative model to Japanese society, a model against which the society can differentiate itself since, as many commentators have pointed out,[14] the great tendency of Japanese society over the past century has been to develop its own sense of uniqueness. At times, this sense of uniqueness has been accompanied by a sense of superiority, at times by one of inferiority, in relation to the West.

It is interesting in this context to note, for example, that the same values have been given both negative and positive evaluations at different times in recent history. In the immediate postwar period, so-called Japanese values (often discussed at that period in terms of a Japanese version of Confucianism) were perceived to be a feudal legacy which Japan would need to overthrow in order for its economy to begin developing. Such values were felt to overemphasise the status quo and hold back the dynamic qualities of younger, more creative, individualistic, nonconformist entrepreneurs. It was accepted that there was a connection between such values and Japan's weak economy.

As the economic strength of Japan began to overshadow that of Europe in the 1970s and the 1980s and Japan looked set to become the centre of world economic power by the turn of the century, so the commonly-held perceptions and interpretations of the relationship between such 'feudal' or 'Confucian' values and economic growth were reevaluated (see Morishima 1982). Those values which had been perceived to be a negative heritage were suddenly given a positive value in a genre of literature called *Nihonjinron* (literally Theories of Japaneseness). This genre was explicitly comparative but limited comparison to that between Japan and the West. There were virtually no comparative references to other Asian nations with whom Japan clearly shares much closer cultural and historical ties. 'Japanese' values of exclusivity, homogeneity, conformity, mutual dependence, group-orientation and harmony were given increasingly high status while opposite values ascribed to the West of openness, heterogeneity, individuality and reliance on principle (all of which had thirty years earlier in Japan been seen as the values needed for economic growth) were now used to explain the decline of Western societies and evaluated negatively. As I have described (Goodman, forthcoming) in the case of Japanese views of the Western welfare state, what could be described in the 1960s as 'Positive Occidentalism' (à la Carrier 1995) became negative Occidentalism in the 1980s, as so-called Western values which underpinned the Western welfare state (itself, of course, not actually a homogeneous model) were evaluated increasingly negatively. Yet just ten years later, as Japan went into recession in the late 1990s, and America and Western Europe remained in a period of relative economic growth, the process appeared to be reversing again.

There may, therefore, be some significance in the dates of the two vignettes above. In the 1980s the power of the Westerner was comparatively muted as the country's economy took off and Japan was on the very brink of becoming the world's leading economic superpower. In the late 1990s, as Japan plunged deeper into its worst ever postwar recession, there was a powerful sense of breast-beating and disillusionment with the way the society was going, in particular with its political process, and hence the voice of the Westerner was considerably empowered.

The role of the Westerner, however, is not just explained in terms of Japan's relative economic and political strength vis-à-vis the West. In my field notes I find counter-examples where the Westerner was given voice at times of great self-confidence in Japanese society, and muted at times of great anxiety. This is not surprising, since evaluations within a society are never homogenous but always presuppose the existence of an alternative discourse, however minor it may be. In the case of Japan for the past hundred years, not only has something called the West (*seiyō*) been a mirror to Japan, but it has also been the site of what Parkin calls its 'internal cultural debates' (1978). One way of characterising all major debates in the nation about its contemporary institutions – educational, social welfare, legal, economic and political – is whether Japan should develop along its own 'traditional' path, or whether it should follow a Western path.

Here lies another part of the explanation for the treatment of Western voices in Japanese society. On the one hand, they can be drawn upon to illustrate ways of doing things which Japan needs to learn in order to become 'Westernised' and thereby 'modern'. There is a well-known process in Japan, found in many different arenas, called *gaiatsu*, literally 'external pressure', whereby interest groups in Japan find it more effective to call upon an outside voice to promote change within society rather than to rely on their own power (see Schoppa 1997). Many Westerners have found their 'basic' comments on Japanese society being used in this way.[15] On the other hand, those who argue that Japan should pursue its own path of modernisation can oppose such views by arguing that the views of the Westerner should be ignored since he or she cannot understand how and why things are done in the particular way that they are in Japan.[16]

The ambiguity of the status of Western voices in Japanese society means that the society is in a position to listen to such voices, but not be dictated to by them, and this indeed is how the process of the development of Japanese society has taken place ever since the Meiji Restoration of 1868. Japanese leaders in all fields have shown a consistent propensity to look at, listen to, and evaluate Western modes of thought and operation and then select those elements which they think can best and most easily be added to and complement existing Japanese practices and institutions. Even critical junctures in modern Japanese history such as the Meiji Restoration, defeat at the end of the Second World War, the oil shocks in the 1970s that left a resource-scarce Japan vulnerable to every turn in the world market, have not led to any form of revolution in the social system. Instead, Japanese social development has been marked by a pragmatic adoption of Western ideas and their adaptation and incorporation into already extant Japanese practices.

The reflexive anthropologist and the reflexive society

No anthropologist of Japan can avoid becoming part of Japanese reflexive debates. But to suggest that this should get in the way of our research or that we are 'contaminating' our fieldwork data or that we should turn the focus of our attention on ourselves and our own societies to compensate for this involvement is to lose sight of the whole point of the ethnographic enterprise. Anthropology is, among many other things, the study of reflexive debates within other societies. While some societies may be more reflexive and more dynamic than others (a matter on which more comparative research is clearly needed), no societies are static and nonreflexive.[17] All societies must debate at some level what type of society they are and should be. To be a society is to engage in such debates and to be an anthropologist is to plug in to and record them.

Little of what is written above will surprise anthropologists of Japan, but it may be of interest to anthropologists of other societies since, for various reasons, it may be easier to observe the reflexive process in Japan than elsewhere. In part this is because of the literary culture in Japan that includes the large *Nihonjinron* genre referred to above. Several scholars have tried to measure the extent to which *Nihonjinron* ideas have permeated Japanese society (see Mouer and Sugimoto 1986; Yoshino 1992; Befu 1992) and there is little doubt that they serve the interest of certain sectors of the society, such as businessmen, more than they do others. There is little doubt also, however, that they have penetrated deep into the society as a whole. Many works in the genre are simultaneously available in academic form, in popular form (*keimōsho*) and in newspaper articles, and anthropologists working in Japan consistently come across these ideas as explanations in the course of their research.[18]

Moreover, it is important to note that a large amount of research that has been carried out by anthropologists in Japan has been conducted inside well-defined institutional walls (such as companies, schools, welfare institutions, clubs) which allow them to attend meetings and observe discussions about the institution and its development, discussions which often illustrate the underlying assumptions of the institution.[19] There are a number of reasons why this approach to fieldwork is so common in Japan. Japan is an expensive country to live in for most foreign researchers and many need to earn money while doing research.[20] In Japanese society, also, individuals are expected to have defined roles and an academic who is not based in a university, such as an anthropologist doing fieldwork, can create confusion over classification.[21] But, perhaps most importantly, the learning process in Japan is based much more on participation than observation. Training and education from primary school to companies is through what Singleton (1998) calls 'learning in doing' rather than through listening: hence it may be that a level of participation in local life is not only better tolerated but indeed more often expected in Japan than in some other societies. The anthropologist has one other research advantage in undertaking their work in an institutional setting. All institutions in Japan are characterised by divisions into groups (see Nakane Chie, 1970, for the classic account of this process). These groups are self-referential and exclusive. In many cases, however, as an ambiguous and temporary outsider, the anthropologist is able to avoid total identification with any particular group and hence is free to move between them and to perceive the field setting from a variety of different angles.[22] Indeed, many an anthropologist has found that this ambiguity has made them the recipient of confidences that would not otherwise be easily shared.

There is one other area that the anthropologist of Japan finds it hard to avoid, but which is ignored in the anthropology of many other societies, and that is the role of the Japanese academy where social institutions are discussed and analysed. In the course of my study of children's homes in Japan, I attended a great variety of different research groups: groups that specialised in the study of fostering and adoption; the child welfare law; child abuse; children's rights; and reform of children's homes. Some of these groups were official, others were unofficial, but they all added an extra layer of reflection on the Japanese situation and, as a Westerner (almost always the only Westerner) attending such meetings, I was pulled into these debates and discussions too and, as mentioned above, without doubt affected them at the same time as I tried to record them.

The anthropologist of Japan, therefore, must examine several levels of self-consciousness in the course of their work. In the society they study they must treat this self-awareness at the fieldwork site itself, in the study groups that think through the issues of the fieldwork site, and in the literature not only about the fieldwork site but more generally about the nature of Japanese society. In the society from which they come, they must reflect about themselves, their discipline and their motivations for the project in hand. Ultimately, however, it is the effect of one version of self-contemplation on the other (the society on the anthropologist, and the anthropologist on the society) that leads to the final ethnography. What we produce may no longer look like the classic monograph of the type produced by our forebears, but that does not negate their encouragement to us to attempt to understand how other societies operate and to translate that understanding into terms comprehensible to members of our own society.

NOTES

1. The subject matter of this paper requires me to include a considerable amount of personal intellectual history, mostly in the form of footnotes to support my main argument. As such, it offers a perfect occasion for me to acknowledge my intellectual debt to my teachers, but since many of these are co-authors in this volume I will forbear doing so individually. I would like, however, to acknowledge Dr Thomas Ernst who was forced to listen to an early version of the paper as we walked to and fro from the National Museum of Ethnology in Osaka, where we were both based on sabbatical in 1998, and of course the Museum itself which had invited me.

2. Recall, for example, David Pocock: 'The observations of the sociologist, no less than the myths of the primitives he studies, are determined by his own society, by his own class, by his own intellectual environment' (1971: 84). In the course of writing this paper, I have increasingly become aware that my own tendency to analyse Japanese society in terms of class rather than cultural determinants is almost certainly in part the result of my coming from a British environment (where class is still seen to play such a major role) and the fact that my own educational experiences included almost every type of school within that system (which perhaps made me unusually sensitive to the significance of class in British society).

3. While, as will be seen, I believe this was generally a positive development, it did lead to some bizarre results where anthropologists tried to incorporate even the most unpleasant of experiences into their research in the belief that there is no such thing as bad data. Alison Shaw lampoons this genre in her review of Kulick and Willson's *Taboo, sex, identity and erotic subjectivity in anthropological fieldwork* (1995), where she writes: 'Next time a man won't take "No" for an answer, try asking, 'What was the locus of our radical miscommunication that made it impossible for him to hear my disinterest and impossible for me to get out of his interpretative framework?' (Shaw 1996: 273).

4. For an overview of some of these views in British anthropology in the late 1980s, see Ingold 1996, especially on the debate of 1989, 'The concept of society is theoretically obsolete' (55–98).

5. Moeran provides an unusually frank deconstruction of this text in Fardon's volume on *Localizing Strategies* (1990). I have also tried to deconstruct my own monograph. In Goodman, 1990a, I try to show how, as a single anthropologist, I managed to

produce a series of different accounts about the role of returnee schoolchildren (*kikokushijo*) on return from fieldwork, and how each reflected (subconsciously) my adherence to a different model – functionalist, Marxist, structuralist – of the relation between society and the individual.

6. For me the biggest effect has not been so much gender, class or nationality, though these are clearly important (see note 2 above), but life course. Each time I have spent a year in Japan doing research it has been at a different stage of my life: first as a single graduate student; next as an expectant father; then as a family man with a child at school and a child at full-time nursery. Each time I have been incorporated into a different sector of the local community relevant to my age and position and have seen a different aspect of Japan. Each time, my view has obviously been modified considerably by this different perspective. My view of the role of teachers in Japanese society (see Goodman 1989) is now much modified by having been a parent with a schoolchild in the country. My view of the concept of the child and childhood in society is similarly modified by the (vicarious) experience of giving birth in Japan and then having a child in nursery.

7. I write the word Westerner here with a capital letter to emphasise the amorphous, homogenous sense in which it is discussed in debates in Japan as if all 'western' societies shared the same values and perceptions. For a fuller discussion of different categories of foreigner, see Matsunaga (this volume).

8. See Moeran (1998); Befu (1974).

9. While he was certainly insightful, it was often difficult to get Kojima to sit still long enough to finish his thoughts. One day he was halfway through his analysis of a recent argument in the staff room, when he announced he needed to catch the next train to Tokyo. Desperate not to miss the end of the story (which turned out to be crucial in my final thesis), I told him I would come with him. On arrival in Tokyo ninety minutes later, I caught the next train back to Tsukuba. This was a story that I discovered was still being recounted with hilarity several years later when I returned to the school!

10. A theme that Martin himself was to go on to explore in some of his publications on comparative linguistics, possibly inspired by the incident cited above!

11. The Oxford-trained anthropologist, Nobuhiro Nagashima, offers an early version of this argument in his paper 'A reversed world: or is it?' (1973) where he suggests that in Japan the emphasis is on the receiver of the message to understand it, rather than the sender, while in Western societies it is the other way around. This sensitivity to context and the other's way of thinking (*omoiyari*) is highly valued in Japanese society and spelling things out can be considered rude if it implies that the other person is not sensitive enough to pick up the code or message being sent.

12. In what follows, the word Westerner should probably be mentally glossed with the word White, since the role that Black people from Western societies play in Japan's reflexive debates is quite different to that of White people (see Russell 1991).

13. Tsuda (1998: 337–8) writes that: 'A dual symbolic understanding of the foreign outside ... has been historically documented by numerous researchers in such diverse societies as the Fiji Islands, India, the Americas, and the ancient Western world.'

14. The best summary of this process is Peter Dale's *The myth of Japanese uniqueness* (1986).

15. In my own case, I have found my work (Goodman 1990b) on the special system for returnees being cited by those who feel that such children have excessive advantages in the society, and also a brief article I wrote comparing the situation of Japanese and British Children's Homes (Goodman 1996) being cited in a parliamentary committee debate about the need to ban institutional abuse in Japanese children's homes (*yōgoshisetsu*). In both cases, my work drew very heavily from Japanese sources which could have been cited just as easily in these debates.

16. As Norgren (1998: 76) points out in the context of her examination of debates about the Eugenic Protection Law, *gaiatsu* is a fairly blunt tool: 'Small, politically weak groups can use it effectively to turn attention to an issue, but when it comes to penetrating the decision-making process, *gaiatsu* is no substitute for the membership, resources, and established political connections that larger groups have.'

17. I have yet to meet a doctoral research student who did not comment on return from fieldwork that they were exceptionally lucky to be studying a society at exactly the time of crucial debates about what sort of a society it should be.

18. I have argued elsewhere (Goodman 1994) that *Nihonjinron* accounts do as much to legitimate or even create social values in Japanese society as they do to explain them.

19. My own two main pieces of fieldwork have been in a school for children who have returned from living overseas (Goodman 1990b) and in a Home for children whose parents cannot look after them (Goodman 2000). Whilst I was interested in the children themselves, in both cases the main focus of my research became the attitudes and ideas of the staff of the institution whose meetings I was able to attend. Byron K. Marshall sums up the strength of this approach well when he writes: 'One of the swiftest entrées to understanding any modern society is through listening to political discourse about education. Power struggles and ideological controversies about how to socialize and enculturate youths are at the heart of the processes by which a society is continually recreated, affording ... some of the most audible records of those processes over time' (1995: 1).

20. My doctoral work on returnee children was determined to some degree by the impossibility of living off an ESRC grant (as then calculated) in Japan and the need to find somewhere I could work and live while researching.

21. My original research in a school for returnee children almost foundered on this role confusion: I was refused a research visa on the basis that I would not be in a university, and a teaching visa on the basis that I would not be teaching enough hours to qualify as a full-time teacher. In the end, I had to go to the Ministry of Justice, extract my original application from a file, leave the country and start the whole process over again, having increased my teaching hours sufficiently to qualify for a teaching visa.

22. This is what sociologists calls the 'Rashomon Factor' (after the classic Kurosawa film which depicts four different views of the same incident), one of the very few Japanese concepts to have entered the social scientific vocabulary.

Chapter 8

RECOLLECTIONS OF LIFE CRISIS:

DISTANCING THE PERSONAL

Louella Matsunaga

Introduction

This chapter is a reflection on my experience as an anthropologist who has married into the society about which I teach and write, and on some of the difficulties presented by this dual involvement, both professional and personal, particularly looking back on moments of life crisis. To an extent, the account given below is very personal in that it takes as its focus a miscarriage I had while living in Tokyo in 1991, the subsequent difficulties I experienced in obtaining medical care, and the various interpretations of this event by myself and others, at the time and since. It is also in some respects highly culture-specific, as it relates to my shifting position within Japanese society as a foreign wife in the early 1990s, when the category of 'foreigner' was becoming publicly emphasised as a social problem.

There are also links with wider anthropological concerns: most centrally, can personal experience illuminate anthropological analysis, or is there a danger of too subjective a distortion? How can the personal be effectively integrated with wider issues in anthropological writing?[1] Attempts to use one's own life as source material also raise the issue of memory. How reliable are our own recollections of our past? To what extent do we construct idealised narratives of past events which illuminate more of our own concerns than of the social setting within which they unfold?[2] There is also the problem of placing events within a temporal frame: how can short-term crises, whether personal or social, be situated within a broader, long-term view of the societies we study?

Marrying in: the anthropologist as bride

I first went to Japan as an English teacher in 1983, and worked in a language school in Tokyo. Shortly after arriving in Tokyo I met my husband, Hidetaka, who had moved there to work as a graphic designer. Over the next three years I met his family in Kyushu, in western Japan, and my father also came over from England to visit my future in-laws. At the end of 1985 my mother became seriously ill, and I returned to England. Hidetaka also moved to England where he enrolled at an art college. A couple of years later we married, and I embarked on a Ph.D. at London University. In 1990 we moved back to Japan with our first child. This was my first visit to my in-laws since our marriage, which they had not been able to attend, and I found that my status was quite transformed. Previously I had been a guest, treated with great courtesy but also a degree of distance. I was now a new wife and daughter-in-law, a member of the Matsunaga household: I had married in. My position as a married-in member of a Japanese household has to a great extent framed my subsequent experience in the country.

However, it would be naive to claim any special authority to speak about Japan on this basis. Marilyn Strathern has pointed out that anthropology 'at home' can be an infinitely receding idea (1987). Distance and belonging are relative: it is quite possible, and indeed common, to do fieldwork in one's own country but in a context which is unfamiliar and socially distant.[3] Similarly, for those of us with affinal links our local knowledge is likely to be uneven, and our fieldwork anyway may have a different focus from the circles in which our in-laws move.[4]

Marrying in can also in some ways restrict social access, and thus fieldwork. An incoming bride may operate within a more limited circle, and have a lower status than that of the visiting anthropologist – as Tamara Kohn points out in her comparison of the anthropologist and the incoming bride among the Yakha in eastern Nepal:

> The roles and positions of power held by the two are different – the anthropologist is led out and about to meet leaders and shamans, attend ceremonies, teach English to students and interview a huge range of people.... In a sense, the bride who works together with her new family day in and day out is locked into the very centre of human life, while the busy anthropologist who delights in sampling more variety over a relatively short time-span is kept dancing on the periphery of the experience (Kohn 1994: 19–20).

What Kohn to some extent glosses over or romanticises here are the constraints placed on the bride, and consequently on her perspective. For the would-be anthropologist who is also a bride, her dual role may be frustrating. This seems to have been the case for Pettigrew during her fieldwork among landowning Sikhs in the Punjab, where she found her research constrained both by the factional affiliation of her in-laws, which restricted her access to the opposing faction, and also by the conventions observed by her family regarding the seclusion of women (1981).

On the other hand, at least in societies where the bride enters her husband's family on marriage, the anthropologist-bride's position in her new family may offer some advantages. In Japan, the important kinship unit is the *ie*, or household, which must be perpetuated over time. The preferred successor to the *ie* is the eldest son, although there is a great deal of flexibility in the system, allowing alternatives such as younger son succession, or succession by a daughter's husband, who is then adopted into the *ie*. In any event, in every generation one successor should remain in the *ie*, while his or her siblings leave. That successor's spouse also joins the *ie*, and from that time their loyalty to their new *ie* should take precedence over their loyalty to their natal *ie*.[5] In most cases, this incoming spouse is a bride, referred to as the household's *yome*, and her first task, at least where the new couple live with the husband's parents,[6] is to learn the ways of her new household – a position analogous to that of an apprentice. In this sense, the roles of bride and anthropologist are complementary – as Jenkins observes, 'fieldwork, like indigenous life, is characterized by a series of apprenticeships' (Jenkins 1994: 442).

The particular apprenticeship undergone by the new bride of a household heir offers to an anthropologist a great opportunity to learn about some aspects of Japanese society, most obviously those concerning relations within the household, the responsibilities of the *yome* in terms of care of the household and its members, and the socialisation of the next generation. There is a marked gender asymmetry here, as even in the (much rarer) cases where the husband enters his wife's household on marriage, gender roles in Japan mean that he would not take on equivalent responsibilities, or be expected to learn the same sorts of skills. The opportunities presented by the position of *yome* are, however, accompanied by considerable stresses, as is well documented in Japanese literature and film, and it is a position which many Japanese women consider undesirable, so that where a choice exists a second son may be seen as a better marriage prospect than an elder son.

My husband's position as eldest son of his household thus had considerable implications for my own role. However, it is also important to bear in mind that not all Japanese households are alike, and experience within a particular household will be affected by a number of factors including socio-economic standing, property held by the household, and current household composition. In our case, my husband had been born into the household of a younger son in Kyushu in south-western Japan. His father died when the children were still young, leaving the family in severe poverty. There were thus no issues of household property to inherit, and there was only one generation of ancestors (my father-in-law) to be cared for – other ancestors were cared for by the main branch of the family. The main issues of concern were to care for my husband's widowed mother, and to run the household and care for the children according to the norms laid down by my mother-in-law. Ritual and religious duties of the household, primarily the care of the household Buddhist altar where my father-in-law's spirit is enshrined, were undertaken by my mother-in-law. The pressures of being a *yome* in such a household are undoubtedly far less than those in more well-to-do households, as I have had the opportunity to observe by comparing my own situation with that of my husband's younger sister, who is married to the eldest son of a prosperous property-owning household in Kyushu. In particular, the pressure for me to provide a male successor to the household has been much less marked than that experienced by my sister-in-law. If asked, my husband would simply say, 'What is there to succeed to?' The household's situation has also contributed to my own acceptability as daughter-in-law: when my husband informed his mother he wanted to marry a foreigner his mother reportedly replied, 'Just as well, no Japanese girl would have you.'

My experience of married life in Japan was also affected by the fact that my husband took up a job in Tokyo – a six-hour bullet train ride away from Kyushu, where my mother-in-law continued to live. At first my daughter and I moved in temporarily with her and other relatives. After some months, my husband found us somewhere to live in Tokyo; we moved there, and I embarked on 'fieldwork'. We then saw my mother-in-law only for brief periods when she came to stay. However, it was understood that eventually we would all live together as a single household, with discussions about exactly how and when this was to be achieved surfacing periodically, but remaining unresolved.

Partly reflecting these shifting, fluid, patterns of residence, I found that my identity and the spheres in which I was able to operate in Japan were also variable and shifting. My identity as bride or *yome* was most stressed within my new household, especially during those periods when we were living with my mother-in-law. During these periods she would organise the day-to-day running of the household, while my task was to learn the ways of the household, and how to bring up my daughter, Maya, in the approved way. While the influence of my mother-in-law was sporadic and mostly indirect, at times of crisis our relationship again took centre stage, as described in the account of my miscarriage below.

My doctoral fieldwork occupied a different sphere of my life. I took a job as a part-time employee in a chain store in suburban Tokyo where I was investigating competing representations of the company, employment relations, and the importance of gender in the workplace. My husband had selected the neighbourhood and a suitable apartment while I was still living with my mother-in-law in Kyushu. Initially we knew absolutely no one in the area. I gradually established my own network of friends: local Japanese housewives, a few foreign wives (mainly American, but also including one British woman), and one particularly close friend of Burmese-Japanese origin. All my friends had children, and it was mainly through my daughter and her various informal play groups that I was able to make local connections, eventually securing an introduction to the store where I did my fieldwork. Friendship networks then intersected with fieldwork mainly when my friends came into the store where I worked to do their shopping.[7]

In our local area of Tokyo, then, I had a range of identities. For the mothers of my daughter's friends and others associated with the day-care centre I was Maya's mother. For some of the Japanese mothers I was also an English teacher – as the children became older and began to talk I agreed to teach their children simple English words and games in weekly get-togethers. I shared concerns with other foreign wives about bringing up our children as bilingual. For other women in our apartment building I was a neighbour, and fellow member of the building's shopping club. In the local chain store, I was a part-time employee and local housewife, while at the same time known to be attached to Tokyo University doing research. And generally wandering around the area, I gradually became a known and familiar face: one of an increasing number of local foreigners who were also long-term residents. In all of this, although my foreignness was a constant element of my identity, I did not experience my foreign status in terms of exclusion. Although the Japanese word for foreigner is *gaijin*, meaning outside person, and it is tempting to regard foreigners in Japan as the quintessential outsiders, in my situation being foreign, and more specifically being white and identified as a native English speaker, was in many ways a path to inclusion.

Teaching English to children of Japanese mothers was an easy means to enter and sustain a friendship group, while my visible difference made me easily identifiable as a foreign wife, and I was often approached by other foreign wives in public places with offers of help and friendship. My dual status of anthropologist/researcher and bride on the whole worked to my advantage, as I was readily able to gain access to a wide range of groups, and the constraints that I did experience – for example, being unable to participate in certain company activities owing to my family commitments and perceptions of appropriate behaviour for a wife and mother – seemed not unduly burdensome, as I felt they were richly compensated for by my access to other areas of Japanese life.

It is important to note, however, that my experience was that of a relatively privileged type of foreigner, as well as being married into a Japanese family. The category of foreigner in Japan in the early 1990s did not appear by any means monolithic. Many foreigners were in Japan on a short-term basis to work or to study. Of those in Japan to work, important distinctions were drawn between the legal workers, who often had high prestige occupations such as teaching, and the illegals. Among the illegals there was a further division, generally on gender lines, between those employed in the sex industry (women) and those employed in the undesirable jobs described in Japanese as three K – *kitanai, kitsui, kiken* – often glossed in English as three D – dirty, difficult and dangerous.[8] This division also tended to have ethnic overtones: many of the illegal male workers in the three-K jobs were from South or West Asia, notably Pakistan, Bangladesh, and Iran (there were also East Asian illegals in these jobs, but they tended to be relatively 'invisible'), while many of the illegal female sex workers were from Thailand or the Philippines. The association widely made between illegal, 'dirty' work and these ethnic groups contributed to the formation of widespread and very negative popular images of Southeast Asian women and South or West Asian men in Japan at that time.

Alongside the considerable numbers of foreigners in Japan for work or study, relatively few were there simply because of marriage. Foreign couples tended to be affluent, self-sufficient and in the country on a short-term basis. Foreign wives married to Japanese, in contrast, lived in a way which did not differ markedly from all-Japanese couples. Contacts between these two types of foreign wife were, in my experience, fairly limited. In the discussion which follows I am concerned with the latter category, and use the term 'foreign wives' to refer to those married into Japanese families. In 1990, the majority among foreign wives in Japan were in fact the Koreans, often themselves brought up in Japan (I do not discuss them further here). After the Koreans, the next largest group was from the United States, and then an increasing number of Chinese and Southeast Asian nationalities, as well as a few Europeans.[9]

Although there were negative stereotypes of foreign women, and Southeast Asian foreign wives in particular may well have suffered from this, efforts were made by many foreign wives to avoid being seen as in any way a problematic category.[10] Indeed a priority for many was fitting in to Japanese society, particularly in the context of child rearing, and how to ensure that our children would be accepted as full members of Japanese society while maintaining a knowledge of their mother's language and whatever was identified as the mother's 'culture'. On the whole, then, we did not see ourselves as a distinct group, but rather as individuals each with our own links to Japanese society, although for some the (largely English-speaking, and American-dominated) Foreign Wives Association in Japan did also become an important social and friendship focus.

For most of us our foreignness was experienced as problematic only in certain situations, often those where we had to deal with institutions, such as the immigration authorities or the local city offices where all foreign residents had to register and have their fingerprints taken. The other situation in which many of us found our foreignness emphasised was in first interactions with strangers, who had no way of conceptually situating us within Japanese society as part of, say, a Japanese household or other institution. As has been widely noted by commentators on Japanese society, although a number of minority groups, for example Koreans, Ainu, Okinawans, and *burakumin*,[11] have long existed in Japan, there is a strong ideology in Japan of a homogeneous society,[12] where intermarriage of Japanese with other non-Japanese groups is discouraged.[13] When I was working in the chain store, and thus had a clear identity and institutional affiliation as a part-time shop assistant, no one showed any surprise.[14] But the idea of the married-in foreigner is still unusual, and people may be curious when they see us with our children. However, numbers of such marriages have been increasing, and the term 'international marriage' *(kokusai kekkon)* has recently gained wide currency. It is against this background that the disputes and conflicting interpretations of my miscarriage and treatment at a Japanese hospital should be placed.

Pregnancy and miscarriage: a personal account

In trying to set boundaries to this experience, the beginning, for me, lies in the hospitalisation for pneumonia of my daughter Maya, by then aged two. One night I decided I had to take her to the nearest 24-hour accident and emergency department, located at the Red Cross Hospital in the west of Tokyo, a short taxi ride from where we lived. I was told she had a chest infection, and to give her antibiotics and return the next day. When we returned she was diagnosed as having pneumonia, and hospitalised as an emergency. My husband was in Hawaii on a business trip, and, despite some confusions over the paperwork, I too entered the hospital in order to help care for her.

There followed ten extremely difficult days. Maya was on an antibiotic drip for the first few days, and I could not leave her side. When my husband returned he suggested bringing my mother-in-law up from Kyushu to help. I refused, feeling that we should try to cope with this crisis ourselves, as a couple. My only relief was therefore through my network of women friends, both Japanese and foreign, who took it in turns to give me a break. They would also sometimes bring me food – an American friend brought a wonderful spaghetti bolognese and red wine, which cheered me up considerably. Finally Maya was discharged, and we returned home.

It was some time before I realised that my general state of distress during this hospital drama was partly due to the fact that I was once again pregnant. I consulted with friends, and decided to book myself in for antenatal care at a small local clinic which some of my Japanese friends had used in the past, rather than one of the larger hospitals. The local clinic only operated an office-hours service, so I asked what I should do if I needed attention out of hours. The doctor said I should simply go to the Red Cross Hospital. A few weeks later the pregnancy did indeed run into difficulties. It was a Sunday, the local clinic was closed, and so my husband called a taxi. My recollection of what follows is necessarily fragmentary, but reflects at least the impression which events made on me at the time.

Arriving in the accident and emergency department we explained the problem, and were told to wait. There was only one obstetrician on duty for the whole hospital. We wandered off to find some coffee but a nurse dashed up and called us back, ushering me straight into a consulting room while my husband was asked to wait outside. I apologised for keeping the doctor waiting and slumped into a seat opposite him, my legs crossed, elbows on the table.

The doctor, a youngish man, looked very annoyed. Why had I come to the hospital in the first place, since I was not receiving antenatal care there? I had 'no connection' *(kankei nai)* with the Red Cross Hospital. I tried to explain. Barely placated, the doctor announced that I might be putting the hospital staff at risk – 'You are bleeding after all, and you may have AIDS for all we know.' Shocked, I had to admit that I had never been tested. He informed me that all pregnant women attending the hospital had to be tested beforehand, and so they could not admit me. With obvious reluctance, he eventually agreed to examine me, but only after my answering a set of questions.

The questioning only seemed to make things worse. He demanded: 'How long have you been married?' I was so taken aback, that I had to ask him to repeat the question – out of surprise and confusion, rather than not having understood what he said. Irritated, he then asked me a question in which I failed to identify the key word, although I did understand it related to my husband. After repeating it a few times in Japanese, the doctor yelled in English, 'Syphilis!' I retorted that if he wanted to know about my husband's health he'd better ask him directly. However, he refused to bring my husband into the room. The doctor finally examined me, and conducted a scan, which seemed to have a sobering effect on him. Far from admitting me for treatment, however, he dismissed me and said I should visit my own obstetrician in the morning.

The following morning I duly returned to the clinic where I was registered, only to be told that I ought to be in a large hospital, such as the Red Cross Hospital. This I vetoed. The doctor agreed to try ringing another place nearby – Sakura Machi, a smaller, Roman Catholic hospital – and I was eventually seen by the doctors there. It was not possible to do anything about the miscarriage, which took its course, but I was able to receive the medical care which, by that time, I needed, complications having set in. On leaving Sakura Machi hospital some days later I found that my husband had contacted his mother, who had come up from Kyushu to stay with us and look after me and Maya.

There ensued a period of rest and reflection. The doctor at Sakura Machi had instructed me to rest at home, and my mother-in-law would not allow me out, even to the local shops. She took over all aspects of shopping, housework and child care, while I sat, watched television, read, and thought about what had happened. I became very close to my mother-in-law during this time, as she talked to me about her own experiences of pregnancy and pregnancy loss, and how she saw what had happened to me. Her interpretation of events was apparently simple: the miscarriage was a consequence of Maya's hospitalisation. In her words, I had saved one child and lost the other. It only occurred to me much later that there may have been an implicit criticism here: had I been willing to take my husband's advice and bring her to Tokyo during Maya's illness, I would not have exhausted myself as much as I did – she would have been there to help me. By refusing, and insisting on handling the situation 'as a couple', I had gone against the ethos of the Japanese household, and excluded my mother-in-law from the role which was properly hers. In that sense, the miscarriage could be viewed as a consequence of my failure to observe Japanese household norms. This particular interpretation of events was never made explicit, but it was made clear to me that my mother-in-law was hurt because we had not called on her to help earlier.

If my mother-in-law's interpretation of events was perhaps not entirely transparent to me at the time, my husband's reaction was even harder for me to understand. Although he was very supportive of my criticisms of the hospital and complaints about my treatment, he tended to make light of the miscarriage itself, cracking jokes and saying that he didn't think this kind of thing affected men as much as it did women. At the time, this appeared to me to be insensitive, but with

the passage of time, and having in the interim seen how other pregnancy losses were responded to within our family, another interpretation seems possible. While I think that my husband's response in part
reflects Japanese social norms regarding the expression of emotion by
men in front of women (seen as a weakness, especially in Kyushu,
renowned within Japan for the stress placed locally on gender differences), it also reflects a desire to play down the loss of pregnancy, and
to make light of it, out of concern for the pressures placed on me. That
is, there is in many Japanese households a strong pressure for a *yome*
who has not yet done so to produce a son. In these circumstances,
pregnancy loss could be seen as failure, and could place the woman
concerned in a very difficult position within the household. Against
this background, to make light of pregnancy loss could be seen as an
attempt to reassure.

There were also other aspects of my husband's interpretation of
events which were not voiced at the time, and only became apparent
during a third pregnancy some time later, when he expressed concerns
that I was visiting a local temple which had a *Jizo* statue[15] dedicated to
mizuko, literally water children, the term for unborn foetuses which die
through miscarriage or abortion, and stillborn children.[16] The statue
was close to a Buddhist temple in pleasant grounds near us, and I used
to take my daughter there to introduce her to Buddhism and the
Japanese tradition of prayer in a general sort of way (we also used to
stop and pray at Shinto shrines). According to my husband's later
comments, however, it was very unlucky to pray at such a statue during pregnancy, as the foetus currently being carried could also become
a *mizuko* as a result. He also pointed out that I had regularly prayed at
this statue during the pregnancy which I lost. Generally, in the third
pregnancy, my husband took much greater care than before to ensure
that I observed various ritual precautions, and also visited a shrine
specialising in safe childbirth. So it would seem that there are possible
explanations for the miscarriage in ritual terms which I largely
ignored at the time.

My reaction at the time was focused in quite another direction, and
was dominated by a growing sense of anger and resentment over the
fact that I had initially been refused medical treatment. I interpreted
this refusal as a response to my status as a foreign woman in Japan,
and the widespread association in Japan at that time of foreigners, and
especially foreign women, with AIDS.

When AIDS was first written about in the Japanese press in the early
1980s, the media linked the new disease principally with haemophiliacs and with male homosexuals. For both of these categories a link was
drawn with contamination from abroad – for haemophiliacs via contaminated blood products, and for homosexual men via their travels

abroad, particularly to the United States. Foreigners resident in Japan were not at first particularly highlighted as a potential source of infection. However, by the late 1980s this was changing. Non-Japanese men found themselves increasingly barred from the massage parlours and other venues associated with the sex industry (Valentine 1990, Bornoff 1991), while in the media there were three highly publicised cases in 1987 involving women who had contracted AIDS. Each story served to illustrate a particular category of perceived risk: 'the first was a foreign woman and a prostitute; the other was a prostitute who had had relations with foreigners, and the third woman had been involved with a haemophiliac' (Miller 1994: 65). Foreign women and prostitutes, with the two categories often appearing as merged, were thus by the late 1980s becoming identified by the Japanese media as being the main potential sources of HIV infection.

Public anxiety about AIDS, encouraged by sensational media coverage, increased in the early 1990s. In 1991 the number of new reported cases of AIDS in Japan had more than doubled from the previous year, reaching a total of 238, of whom 105 (the largest single group) were foreign women (Japan Almanac 1999). Although I, like most of the housewives I knew, had never thought such concerns relevant to me – after all, this concerned those other foreign women from whom we considered ourselves so different – I thought it likely that the doctor who had first seen me was responding to me primarily as a foreigner, and therefore, by the logic of the time, an AIDS risk. This, I thought, raised serious issues of discrimination against foreigners as well as anyone attending hospital who might be HIV-positive, and should be pursued.

In this somewhat crusading frame of mind, I expressed these views to my family and friends, both Japanese and non-Japanese, and found them extremely supportive. All agreed that the treatment I had received was appalling. One Japanese friend offered to introduce me to a lawyer in order to sue the hospital but, in the end, my husband and I decided to simply lodge a formal complaint with the hospital about my treatment, and a meeting was arranged for us, to be attended by the doctor concerned, his head of department and a senior manager.

The meeting was not very satisfactory. I had expected an apology, but did not receive one, or even an acknowledgement that their approach in this case might have left something to be desired. It was, however, interesting in some respects. The young doctor who had given me such a hard time began by justifying himself with reference to my inappropriate behaviour, in keeping him waiting and in my rude way of crossing my legs and slumping on the table. He had previously worked in prisons, and had felt threatened by the way I sat with my elbows on the table, which could have been a prelude to a physical attack (which as a fairly small person I could scarcely believe). The questions he had asked me were simply standard hospital questions. It was hospital practice to screen all pregnant women for HIV and syphilis. Any other interpretation of his remarks on my behalf reflected my inadequate command of the Japanese language. He explained that my husband had not been allowed to be present during all of this in order to preserve patient confidentiality. My suggestions that a Japanese woman in the same situation would not have been treated in the same way were flatly denied.

Shortly after this meeting, exhausted and depressed, I left Japan, and returned to England to write up my Ph.D. It felt at the time like a definitive departure – although in fact I returned to live in Japan some six months later. A second child was born there, and after a further year, my husband and I moved back to England with the children.[17]

Interpretations

For me at the time the experience of the miscarriage was, in addition to being devastating on a personal level, a sharp reminder of my foreign status – I seemed to have been abruptly pushed back into the category of outsider to which I thought, having married into a Japanese household, I no longer belonged. As such, it represents an episode of disillusionment, a realisation of failure in a naive quest to join another society, which probably has common elements with the experiences of many other anthropologists. It is in this sense reminiscent of Brian Moeran's account of personal crisis during fieldwork in Japan, when his son was seriously injured in an accident at the local school (Moeran 1985). Following the accident, in the light of a number of events which combined to make him feel he could not make his home there, Moeran decided to leave the country. Quest for belonging, personal crisis, disillusionment, departure: these are common elements to both narratives.

In my case this crisis was compounded by an abrupt loss of confidence in my own ability to understand or interpret what had happened, even where I was so centrally involved. In retrospect it seems to me that language was a powerful tool in the hospital doctors' construction of their own version of events. As a foreign woman living in Japan I was sometimes expected to cope without help: my Japanese was deemed adequate, for example, for the purposes of excluding my husband from the consultation with the doctor. On the other hand, my own accounts of events were always suspect, and subject to the interpretation – 'She didn't really understand what was going on – her Japanese is not good enough.' Even my body language was criticised as contributing to the failure in communication.

Some of what was going on here seems, however, in a longer-term perspective, far from specific to Japan. An imbalance in power and authority between doctor and patient characterises medical institutions throughout the world. The use of cultural or linguistic difference as a disempowering device is again a fairly widespread phenomenon. On the other hand, the denial of one's ability to understand Japanese language and/or social interactions has a particular resonance for those of us with a long-standing involvement with the country. As Goodman (this volume) and others have noted, the idea that foreigners cannot understand Japan is pervasive. Rather, understanding in some sorts of *Nihonjinron* (theories of Japaneseness) is linked to ethnic identity, and is thus beyond the reach of anyone not born Japanese.

There is much, then, in this experience which tends to pull me into an explanation of what happened in terms of the strong distinctions drawn in Japan between foreigner and Japanese. There is certainly no shortage of anthropological theory to support this interpretation. The special status of the foreigner as outsider has been widely written on, for example by Ohnuki-Tierney, who remarks that 'in the past calamities and epidemics were believed to come from outside, and often to be brought by strangers and foreigners'. She goes on to describe beliefs recorded in premodern Japan concerning potentially dangerous gods *(marebito)* which would visit the village from outside. This ambiguous view of the outside, as a source of both benefit and danger, she argues, persists in contemporary Japanese attitudes towards foreigners – at least, those European or American foreigners to whom the label *gaijin* is applied (Ohnuki-Tierney 1984a: 33–34). Building on Mary Douglas's theories of dirt and pollution, Ohnuki-Tierney contrasts the dual status of these 'clear' outsiders, with that of people located on the margins, neither Westerners *(gaijin)* nor Japanese, a category in which she includes non-Japanese Asians and overseas Japanese and also some categories of *burakumin,* a former outcaste group within Japanese society. Valentine has further explored marginality in Japan, seeking to identify which groups might be seen as most marginal, and what notions of marginality can tell us about the Japanese mainstream (1990). He suggests that the idea of marginality, particularly marginality as threatening, is closely linked with the dominant discourse in Japan which stresses ethnic, cultural and social homogeneity.[18] Among the categories of person Valentine discusses as marginal are those who are seen as in some sense impure, often because they are suffering from some sort of disease or physical or mental disorder. This links with a pervasive association made between physical and moral purity. In this category Valentine includes the mentally ill, the disabled, and victims of environmental pollution and of the atomic bomb. Also, and of particular interest in the context of my discussion, he includes those who are known to be HIV-positive, noting that 'these suffer the added stigma of the perception of AIDS as affecting marginal groups and as a foreign disease' (Valentine 1990: 41).

Taken together, Ohnuki-Tierney's and Valentine's accounts offer a temptingly elegant analysis of the position of foreigners in contemporary Japan, and of the discrimination which they often encounter. The view of 'the foreigner' as being an inherently problematic category in Japan draws further support from folk models of Japanese society (the *Nihonjinron*) which stress Japan's centuries of isolation under the *sakoku* (closed-country) policy. Could my experience of being refused hospital treatment be seen as one example of this discomfort in dealing with foreigners, and in particular with the marginally foreign? On one level, perhaps yes. A general point can be made about the ways in which foreigners and minorities may be seen as in some way dangerous, and linked in popular ideas of the origins and spread of illness. This, of course, is hardly unique to Japan – one of the common features of the perception of AIDS throughout Western Europe and North America too appears to be the way in which it has been linked in the media and elsewhere with groups perceived as marginal, different or foreign.[19] But in another sense, to explain this event in these terms places the interpretation at such a general level as to be trivial, and obscures much of the specific detail.

One point to be noted is the historical context. Miller (1994) argues that although there have been resident foreigners in Japan throughout this century, the construction of foreigners as a particular category of risk, and the association of AIDS with foreigners and more particularly foreign women in the early 1990s, is the product of a particular set of historical and economic circumstances. Specifically, the rising rate of HIV infection happened to coincide with a growing media focus on the 'problem' of increasing numbers of illegal (male) foreign workers in the construction industry. The concerns voiced by the media about these male foreign illegals echo those voiced about the female foreign workers in the sex industry, portrayed as threatening the domestic sphere through the spread of disease. It might be added that the growing social stigma attached to these groups of foreigners in early 1990s Japan as sources of crime or of infection served to legitimate discrimination against them, and the implementation of measures such as deportation or withholding of public services such as health care. In this way, constructing foreigners as a category of risk may have acted as a form of social control.

Miller's insistence on the importance of placing events like the AIDS scare in Japan in historical perspective is useful, and helps in contextualising the remarks directed at me by the hospital doctor. However, taken as a whole, the events recounted above reveal a much more complex situation than can be encapsulated by any explanation dealing with foreigners, or even, more narrowly, foreign women, as a unitary category. This is not a case of a simple opposition between foreigner/outsider and Japanese/insider, as neither category is itself homogeneous or constant. Throughout the events described I relied heavily on Japanese friends and family, none of whom appeared to see my foreignness as problematic, or as constituting a danger to themselves. To depict myself as a victim, universally discriminated against, viewed as a polluting, dangerous outsider in Japan would clearly be a travesty. Indeed the immediate effect of my exclusion by the hospital was a withdrawal into the inner world of my Japanese household and the care of my mother-in-law.

The emphasis on establishing connections and context in Japan may also help to illuminate the question with which the Red Cross Hospital doctor began our meeting, asking how long I had been married. In the light of my deeply held beliefs regarding universal access to medical care as a right regardless of individual background this question seemed irrelevant and offensive. However, from the point of view of the Japanese medical system one of the first matters to be settled when treating a patient is their family situation – I discovered when my children were at different times admitted to hospital in Japan that one of the basic pieces of information requested on the hospital admissions form is the position of the child within the family – eldest daughter, second daughter and so on.

It would seem then that to interpret my experience in terms of discrimination against foreigners is to emphasise only one particular aspect of that experience. And while that was the aspect which struck me most forcibly at the time, to give undue weight to it may reveal as much about my own feelings of vulnerability in Japan as it does about Japanese society itself. It is also noteworthy that my preoccupations were not necessarily those of other members of my family. The concerns of my mother-in-law and husband centred around minimising the impact of the miscarriage on me, and on ensuring that I was better prepared for a future successful pregnancy. Part of this entailed making explicit prohibitions on certain behaviour in pregnancy of which I had previously been unaware – such as visiting the *mizuko Jizo* at the local temple. This was also the approach taken by the doctor at Sakura Machi, to whom I returned for antenatal care in my subsequent pregnancy. He explained that Europeans were prone to taking risks during pregnancy by engaging in activities such as cycling, owing to their past as nomadic herdsmen, when it was a useful adaptation to allow only babies who could withstand such treatment to survive. However, the Japanese, as rice-growing people, were naturally more cautious, and never rode bicycles in pregnancy. He advised me to behave more like a Japanese woman in order to ensure the success of this pregnancy. Although I am sceptical of this dichotomy, which seems to owe a great deal to popular *Nihonjinron* works,[20] and which provoked howls of laughter from some of my Japanese friends, it does serve to illustrate that dichotomies of Western versus Japanese are not always invoked in Japan as evidence of an unbridgeable divide, but often enough as examples of the sorts of behaviour we are expected to learn, and those we are expected to avoid, as long term-residents, and in some sense members, of Japanese society.

Conclusion

To return to the question posed at the beginning of this chapter: what, if anything, does all this tell us about using our own personal experiences and life crises as anthropological material? One issue that has become very clear to me in the process of writing and rewriting this account is the difficulty of 'distancing the personal' in an effort to analyse any event in which one is so closely involved. This is for a number of reasons. Firstly, the emotions evoked by life crises such as this make it impossible to attempt to analyse them at the time, and undoubtedly affect our memories of these events when we try to reconstruct them later. All such narratives are therefore personal and partial. Details relating to our own interpretations of events are vividly recalled, while retrieving other aspects, other perspectives, is a struggle.

Secondly, in events where we play a central role, our knowledge is partisan. It is not possible to write an objective account, giving equal weight to all players. In a situation of confrontation and antagonism, the perspectives of others involved in the confrontation can only be guessed at. Explanations offered will never be neutral, but will always be informed by the possible consequences of offering such an explanation. As Jenkins remarks, regarding cattle markets in the South of France,

> as far as the participants are concerned, there is no such thing as objective, uninvolved knowledge. There is no place for an 'objective observer': there is no neutral position or neutral knowledge, and no place for someone who will say what has gone on. Either the actor is on the peasant's side or else on the dealer's, in either case, he does not articulate what he knows (Jenkins 1994: 443).

On the other hand, although writing of one's own experience as actor inevitably gives a partial account, no anthropologist is uninvolved with the society he or she studies. In this sense the partiality of knowledge is a given, and, as Jenkins argues, to oppose anthropologist to actor is in any case artificial. Furthermore, situations of crisis are sometimes revealing in unexpected ways, and one's own life crises tend to be more accessible than those of others. Such crises may, for example, force into the open conflicts which in everyday life simmer beneath the surface. So, in my case, the miscarriage revealed, amongst other things, a conflict between my mother-in-law and myself regarding the composition of our household and the relationships within it. By insisting on dealing with my daughter's illness independently, and refusing to ask for my mother-in-law's help, I effectively shut her out. The subsequent miscarriage gave her the opportunity to redress this situation, and to express her feelings about my actions.

Viewed in this way, the significant drama involved in the miscarriage can be seen as one involving the household, its continuation, and the relationships of those within it. Childbearing is at the heart of a bride's relationship with her new household in Japan, as in many other societies. And pregnancy loss at least potentially throws that relationship into question, especially where the bride has yet to bear a son. In addition, as I discovered subsequently, the dead child may be seen as having an effect on the remaining members of the household, especially surviving children, or future pregnancies. In addition to beliefs concerning the inadvisability of praying to *mizuko Jizo* during pregnancy, a veritable industry of religious services aimed at dead foetuses has grown up in Japan. These are often backed up by pamphlets explaining that, for example, behavioural problems in surviving children can be explained by the intervention of the *mizuko*, jealous of the attention surviving children enjoy from their parents, while the *mizuko* itself is condemned to limbo.

Interpretations of one's own experience thus tend to shift over time, as the immediate concerns of the moment give way to a more long-term view. At the time, my experience of miscarriage in Japan seemed an extreme example of attitudes towards foreigners during the AIDS scare. But with the passage of time other layers in the ways in which this event was responded to by the various people concerned become evident. And although aspects of the way in which the hospital doctor responded to me may have been conditioned by his perception of me as a foreigner and the equation of foreignness with risk, it seems with hindsight that for the other members of my household this was a domestic crisis, involving their *yome*, where foreignness was only an issue in so far as I, as a foreigner, needed to have the obvious made explicit.

Finally, in terms of the anthropology of Japan, one conclusion to be drawn from this experience is that although the construction of foreigner and Japanese as opposed categories has provided one of the more compelling motifs running through the literature, both popular and academic, foreignness is a complex and shifting category, and dichotomies are unhelpful. This is perhaps especially so in a context where marriages between Japanese and non-Japanese are increasing rapidly, and there is a growing number of long-term foreign residents in Japan, many of whom are wives, daughters-in-law and mothers, actively engaged in the care of members of their household and the socialisation of the next generation. The experience of such foreign residents cannot easily be summarised by oppositional categories. Rather, we all have a range of attributes which may be given different emphases in different contexts: foreigner, *yome*, mother, company employee and so on. The category of foreigner in Japan is neither uniform nor fixed.

NOTES

1. See, for example, Rabinow 1977, Okely & Callaway 1992, Srinivas 1996.
2. See Spencer 1992 for a discussion of this issue related to his own fieldwork experience.
3. One of the interesting features of this noted by several anthropologists is the necessity of creating a new identity for themselves through use of dress and language for the purposes of fieldwork (Mascarenhas-Keyes 1987; Okely 1987), and the dissonance and sense of 'double vision' (Okely 1987) induced by adopting this identity in close geographical proximity to places where the fieldworker is known under quite another guise.
4. As Narayan (1998) has argued regarding the dichotomy between 'native' and 'non-native' anthropologist, there is often in practice no hard and fast divide between anthropologists who marry into the field and those who do not in terms of their closeness to those among whom they research.
5. A contemporary example of this concerns the care of elderly parents: when both the parents of the wife and those of the husband need care, the parents of the *ie* to which the couple belong should come first. In practice this does not always happen, but it remains a powerful ideal (Hendry 1981).
6. It should be noted, however, that an increasing number of newly married couples form a new residential unit, giving the *yome* much greater independence.
7. I explore the roles of various categories of employees in more detail in my doctoral thesis (Matsunaga 1995; cf. Hendry 1992).
8. Dirty, exhausting and dangerous might be a more accurate translation, but lacks the alliterative appeal of the three-D version. Many foreigners were employed in these jobs as a response to the labour shortage in Japan from the late 1980s, although their numbers have decreased with Japan's economic downturn.
9. This position has since changed: in 1996 the Philippines led the list of foreign wives, with numbers of Thai and Chinese brides also continuing to show an increase (Japan Almanac 1999).
10. This reflects a more general tendency in cross-cultural marriage to resist the classification of such marriages as problematic (Breger and Hill 1998).
11. Ainu and Okinawans are the indigenous populations of the northernmost island of Hokkaido, and the southern Ryukyu Islands respectively. The origin of the *buraku-min* is complex, but this group can broadly be described as a former outcaste group, whose legally separate status was abolished in the Meiji period, but who have continued to be widely discriminated against. For more on these and other minority groups see Weiner 1997.

12. See, for example, Yoshino 1992.
13. In extreme cases, there may even be a reluctance to accept that a 'real' Japanese man would marry a foreigner, as illustrated by the following experience. At the time of my marriage I was working for a Japanese bank in London. On announcing my forthcoming marriage I was asked about my husband, and particular interest was shown in my statement that he was Japanese. One of the senior (Japanese) managers asked where in Japan my husband came from, and on learning it was Kyushu commented, 'Oh he must be of Korean descent then, as Kyushu's so near Korea. If he were really Japanese he wouldn't marry a foreigner.'
14. As Valentine (1990) argues, regarding attitudes towards minorities, the importance of small group membership in Japan may mean that individuals are, for much of the time, insulated. Awareness of discrimination thus tends to be fragmented and focused on events in the public sphere in which the individual is no longer cushioned by his or her support group.
15. Jizo is a Bodhisattva associated with travellers and children. Jizo statues are commonly erected in Japan for *mizuko*, children who die before or shortly after birth, and have in this context a dual symbolism, representing both the *mizuko* and the compassionate Bodhisattva who is believed to help them escape from the limbo to which their early death consigns them (LaFleur 1992).
16. See LaFleur 1992 for a full account of beliefs and practices relating to the *mizuko*.
17. This move was forced on us by the declining health of our younger child, despite the best efforts of doctors at the same Red Cross Hospital with which we had had the dispute described here.
18. There is an abundance of literature on the social exclusion of Koreans and *burakumin* in Japan, which extends to employment, education and intermarriage with other Japanese. See for example Lee and DeVos (1984) or Weiner (1997).
19. See, for example, Farmer (1992), on 'the geography of blame'.
20. A similar explanation of the origin of differences between the Japanese and Westerners is advanced in Ben Dasan's *The Japanese and the Jews* (1972), one of the most popular publications in the *Nihonjinron* genre.

Chapter 9

VIEWS OF JAIN HISTORY

Marcus Banks

Introduction

As Richard Burghart, amongst others, has pointed out (1990), one of
the issues that any anthropologist of South Asia must deal with is that
sections of South Asian society have self-consciously and overtly constructed accounts of themselves. For the student of contemporary Jain
society this is especially true, for not only have the Jains sought to
define and understand themselves over the past two and a half millennia, through textual and visual representation, and through political
and religious action, they have sought to do so in the acute self-knowl-
edge that they are a minority within Hindu India (or Mughal India, or
British India, or secular India).

Over the past fifteen years or so of intermittent study of the Jains, I
have come gradually to the conclusion that one of the most profitable
ways to engage sociologically with the Jains is by a consideration of
their movements through time and space, and that 'viewing' this
movement can only be properly effected by an understanding of the
location of the viewer. Thus in this chapter I aim to demonstrate how
my own view of the study of Jain society has changed over the years,
and in particular to present two such views in detail. By doing so I
hope I am placing myself in a better position to understand the ways in
which contemporary Jains view themselves.[1]

When I began to learn about the Jains and Jainism in the early
1980s, first through reading and subsequently through fieldwork, I
found myself encountering two rather different discourses. The first,
the product of a Jain intellectual and organisational revival that took

place in India in the early years of this century,[2] was manifest most explicitly in a series of books published by Jain and non-Jain authors.[3] These works sought to define Jainism as a world religion, akin to Islam or Catholicism, and are best exemplified by the voluminous writings of the lawyer C.R. Jain (for example, his *The key of knowledge* 1919).[4] C.R. Jain and others – including their Western counterparts such as the Orientalists Buhler, Jacobi and Schubring[5] – were educated men, writing in English or other European languages for an educated audience. Their presentation of Jainism relied on a process of intellectual disembedding, isolating a set of ahistorical, atemporal doctrines and revealing a form of Jainism without the Jains, as it were. Later Jain apologists, most notably P.S. Jaini (1979), gave greater attention to the historical development of Jainism and sketched out some basic sociology, but in the early 1980s there was only one significant work on the sociology of the Jains – V.A. Sangave's 1959 *Jaina community* (republished 1980). Though relying heavily on earlier secondary literature, the book nonetheless covered previously unmentioned topics such as caste among the Jains.

When I began fieldwork – first in Leicester in the British Midlands, and then subsequently in Jamnagar, Gujarat State – I consequently knew a great deal about Jainism, but next to nothing about the Jains. I did not regard this as a significant problem – indeed, for a doctoral student in social anthropology it was an ideal position to be in: to produce the ethnography that explored whatever gap might exist between doctrine and practice.[6] I therefore expected to find the second discourse – the discourse of Jainism as lived experience (see Banks 1989). This discourse was nuanced in accordance with straightforward sociological categories of age, gender and so forth, as well as in accordance with individuals' personal experience and personal history. It was to some extent also a discourse of the Jains without Jainism – at least in the disembedded sense of the Western Orientalists – in so far as many (but not all) of my informants understood their Jainism not in terms of doctrine and belief, but in terms of marriage practice, caste and sub-caste based ownership of temples and other religious properties, dietary observances and the like.

For me, this discourse was also filtered through an entirely different literature, one we could call the 'two cultures' paradigm of migration studies, after Watson's influential edited collection *Between two cultures* (1977). In as much as I thought about the Jains and movement at all at this time, it was to reconstruct the history of the Jains' movement through western India and on overseas. This is how I first presented the material (for example, Banks 1992, and particularly Banks 1994). The categories of both 'Jainism' and 'the Jains' remained relatively unproblematic for me (but see the 'Conclusions' to Banks 1992).

Later on, as a result of more fieldwork (in Leicester, but particularly in India) I came to realise – as every fieldworking anthropologist must – the inverse relationship that exists between the increasing breadth and depth of ethnographic experience and ability to maintain an adequate representation of the whole. That is, the closer one moves in to concentrate on the fine-grained detail of people's life experience, the less certainty one has of the contours of the overall picture. This was particularly apparent when I made my third or fourth visit to Jamnagar to produce a documentary film with some of my informants.[7]

Although I was keeping field notes and conducting my own ethnographic enquiries to some extent independently of the film, I became acutely conscious both during the filming and especially afterwards when editing, of the differences that exist between conventional notetaking and recording interaction on film and audiotape. I subsequently explored some of these differences (see Banks 1988a, 1990) and this article continues that exploration.

Below, I give brief accounts of two very different 'views' of Jain movements through time and space – one as it were from the outside, the other from the inside. More substantively, the issue I address in this paper is one of seeing a single family's history against the backdrop of the history of an entire society stretching over many centuries, even millennia. Neither view is intended to supersede the other, although I think I encountered them in the common order for an anthropologist – a synoptic 'big picture' account to meet the requirements of a doctoral dissertation or first major publication, followed by a concentration on problematic fine detail. I would, however, suggest that the two remain in tension throughout an anthropologist's fieldworking career.

The problem is as much representational as conceptual. Conceptually, it seems fairly straightforward to link the fine detail of everyday life experience to the broader sweep of historical events. The specific details of one family's life and migratory history are either exemplary of the broader trend, or they are not. If they are exemplary, then they stand in synecdochal relationship to the broader trend – one of the many parts that make up the whole. If they are not exemplary, then it is not particularly difficult either to modify the general model of the broader whole to accommodate the specific case, or to dismiss the specific case as exceptional, aberrant, a statistically insignificant anomaly. From some more formalist perspectives in the social sciences neither of these two courses of action – acceptance as typifying case, or rejection as an anomalous one – is particularly hard to accomplish. However, from a more phenomenological perspective neither is satisfactory. Both strategies are reductionist, both subvert or suffocate the agency of individuals in favour of the apparently inexorable tide of history.

So I have sought instead for some other way to reconcile what I have loosely called the 'big picture' – the sweep of Jain migrations over centuries and continents – with what I will equally loosely call the 'close up' – the more chronologically and spatially limited ethnographic detail of one family that I have gathered over the years.

Figures 7 and 8 are visual emblems of these two bodies of data.[8] The first is a frame-still, taken from the film referred to above, which appears to document a moment of conversation, messily snatched between the shoulders of passers-by. The content, however, is less important in this context than the fact it represents one of those fleeting moments of ethnographic experience – the observation of and perhaps participation in a daily activity, one that may be repeated many times with minor variations, all similar but all unique. It is a simultaneous strength and weakness of film as a medium of record and representation that it captures such moments of specificity, while at once freezing them, granting them a spurious importance by isolating them from the stream of events and from similar moments within which they were embedded. The second image is very different, a second-order visual inscription, not taken from life but distilling in visual form several different bodies of data relating to Gujarati Jain migration. It excises the apparently superfluous (where, for example, is the rest of the African continent?) and presents instead a picture that is at once grand and overarching, and at the same time reductionist and unsatisfactory.

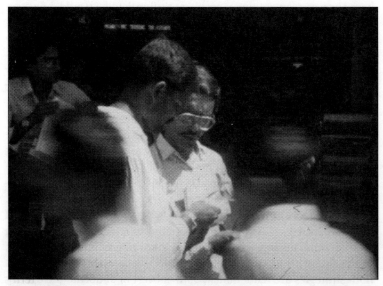

Figure 7 *A moment of conversation (from* Raju and his friends)

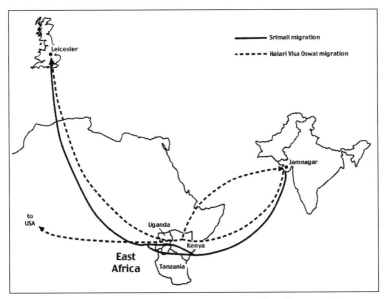

Figure 8 *A synoptic representation of Jain migrations (based on map 6.2 in Banks 1994)*

An overview of Jain migratory history

In common with a variety of other groups in India and elsewhere the Jain laity are known as a mercantile group, entrepreneurs and traders. Such as it is, the sociology of the Jains has dwelt in some detail on the apparent paradox of the laity's relentless pursuit and extravagant display of wealth and the world-rejecting asceticism and anti-materialism of their religion's core tenets.[9] For my purposes, however, the relevant aspect of their socio-economic position in Indian society (precolonially, colonially and postcolonially) is its apparent concomitant mobility. In seeking new markets and new opportunities the Jains have moved across India and overseas over the course of at least the past six centuries.

My ethnographic focus in Jamnagar in the 1980s lay with three particular sub-sections of two Gujarati Jain castes: two sub-sections of the Oswal caste – the Halari Visa Oswals and the Jamnagari Visa Oswals; and one sub-section of the Srimali caste – the Jamnagar Visa Srimalis. It was from this vantage point that I looked back in time. In India the castes are more or less territorially limited and are largely endogamous groups. That is, there are several groups of people calling themselves Oswal (for example) throughout contemporary Gujarat and Rajasthan, but each group will have one or more descriptive terms (possibly territorial) prefixing the name Oswal, will not exchange marriage partners with other Oswal groups and may deny that there is any link or common origin which unites all Oswal groups. The three castes are all almost exclusively Jain, and have marked their movement across four continents by constructing temples as they have gone. There is undoubtedly a link between their Jainism and their movement, though it is not causative in my opinion, any more than is the link between their Jainism and their occupation presumed by early scholars such as Jacobi and Weber. What it is probably fair to say is that their distinctive faith (but not too distinctive) has probably served at times as a boundary reinforcing mechanism to protect trade flows and markets, in a manner akin to Cohen's Hausa traders (1969).

From various sources, including contemporary interviews, it is possible to see five main phases of long-distance migration for these groups and their ancestors, summarised in Table 1. During the course of these migrations, particular territorial links and marriage strategies appear to have caused increasing differentiation between the groups, reifying the castes' separate identities even further (Banks 1994: 140–2).

An origin in Rajasthan seems probable for these castes, not in the sense of some autochthonous homeland, but in the sense that Jain castes known as Srimali and Oswal came into being there, both names being place names in Rajasthan. The date of the move out from Rajasthan, together with the motivation for it, is unclear. It is unlikely that an entire bloc of people uprooted themselves and moved south to the Gujarat region. Rather, the evidence of the Mawaris – another regional Rajasthani Jain caste who have spread throughout India – would seem to indicate that outposts of caste members were established progressively further away from the original Rajasthani centre. As these came to dominate local trade and operate independently of the 'home' group, and as they became large enough to maintain endogamy, so relations with the ancestral group would have withered.

Table 1: *Synopsis of Jain migrations (based on Table 6.3 in Banks 1994)*

Migration	Date	Cause
Rajasthan to Kaccha	?	?
Kaccha to Jamnagar	16th cent.	'invitation'
Jamnagar to Bombay	19th cent.	entrepreneurial expansion
Jamnagar to East Africa	19th/20th cent.	entrepreneurial expansion/ entrepreneurial entrée
East Africa to UK	mid-20th cent.	forced/political
East Africa to N America	mid-20th cent.	forced/political/ entrepreneurial expansion

Note: *the migrations from Jamnagar to Bombay and from Jamnagar to East Africa are partial alternatives, taken by different groups.*

The move from the arid desert region of Kaccha, between contemporary Rajasthan and the Saurashtran peninsula of Gujarat, is better documented and has both an identifiable date and a clear motivation. Although the area has long been settled, the important kingdoms of Saurashtra at the time of British domination were all of relatively recent establishment. Important among them was Jamnagar state, established in 1540 CE by Jam Raval, a member of a Kacchi ruling family who fled across the Gulf of Kaccha following a power struggle. Accounts differ of the motivation of the Srimali and Oswal Jains who came after him from Kaccha to establish trade in his newly founded city. Some see them as opportunistically fleeing the disruption left in the wake of Jam Raval's failed struggle for succession. Others, including their contemporary descendants, claim that they were 'invited' by Jam Raval. The latter version is perhaps more convincing, and more in accord with other similar accounts.[10]

At this point differentiations became more marked; the Srimalis settled initially in Jamnagar and then later in the smaller bazaar towns of the region. Some even become involved in agricultural activities, both as producers but also more commonly as traders and money-lenders to farmers in the area. Some Oswals settled in Jamnagar too, becoming the Jamnagar Visa Oswals, while others began to develop agriculture in the rural hinterland, known as Halar, from which they take their (sub) caste name. Over the next three and a half centuries there were no major migrations involving the three groups, although other groups of Jains in the region continued to move, some becoming involved in the Indian Ocean trade. During this period, however, the Jamnagar Jains continued to reify both their religious and caste identities and to fragment into smaller sectarian groups, establishing separate and rival temples and so forth.

The next set of movements come at the end of the nineteenth century. A combination of commonly identified push and pull factors contribute towards a movement of the Jamnagar Visa Oswals towards Bombay (the premiere west-coast port of the British), and of the Halari Visa Oswals and the Jamnagar Visa Srimalis to the British colonies and protectorates of East Africa and the Gulf. Commonly identified push factors include a major drought in the Saurashtra region at the end of the nineteenth century, and the British demand for skilled clerical labour and mercantile development in Africa.

The mid twentieth-century story of Indian postcolonial emigration from East Africa to the UK and then on to the USA is a largely familiar one, and I shall not rehearse it here (see Banks 1992: chapter 5), save to note that some – including some Jamnagar Jains – returned to India in the 1960s and 1970s rather than moving on to the UK and beyond.

What I will note is that as the twentieth century passes the account of migrations I have just given becomes less a collective one – a synthesis of work conducted by others (and a little by myself) – and more an account that I have constructed from the memories and stories of those I worked with in India and the UK. The passages of time experienced by the Jains as a collectivity, by the individual Jains of Jamnagar, and by myself begin to converge. I also experience increasing difficulty as I try to place the recollections of my informants within an appropriately broad perspective. No one I talked to spontaneously mentioned the Saurashtran drought as a precipitating factor, or indeed really discussed the move from Jamnagar to Africa or from Africa to the UK in collective terms. Most, however, mentioned the movement of kin and articulated their own narratives within these terms – 'my brother called me to Kampala', 'I went to Kenya with my husband', 'After my father returned to India to marry he went back and I was born there'. From the homogenising perspective of the 'big picture', a perceptual shift becomes apparent, a shift to a multiplicity of accounts that could contain sequences of events linked by specific and local causal logic, but which could also consist simply of fragmentary references to places, names, and movements in the course of vignette-like memories.

Close up views of Jain migrations

I wish to turn now from this broad-brush sweeping view of the movements of thousands of people across centuries and continents, to consider instead the movements of a handful of people over a few decades within a relatively small region. This is a close-up view, a concentration on fine detail. It is also an insider's view, not because I the ethnographer am in any sense an insider, but because I am able to rely on the statements and actions of my informants to form the basis of the account.

Although some Jains settled in Jamnagar shortly after its founding in 1540, many others settled in the rural hinterland; in the 1980s there were actually slightly more Jains in the small towns and villages of the region – Jamnagar District – than in the city itself (Banks 1992: 45–46). Over the last century, prompted in part by the development of the city under the progressive ruler Jam Ranjitsinhji (r. 1907–33), and in part by the drought and famine of the 1890s, some families began to migrate from the hinterland into the city. One such was the Mehta family, Jamnagar Visa Srimalis and the principal subjects of the documentary film mentioned above.[11]

During the course of filming Raju and Kailash, the adult sons of two Mehta brothers, took my camera operator and myself by car to the village of Beraja, some 30 km from Jamnagar, to visit their ancestral home. The day before the trip we had been filming at a distant relative's wedding and the events had led to a discussion of the ways in which a new bride was incorporated into her husband's family: 'When some-one in our family gets married they must come here for *darshan* on the same day if possible, or on the next day if the marriage is out of town. In our marriage rite, when we get married, they tie [special lengths of cloth] into a knot joining the bride and groom. To untie the knot we must come here, if it's the marriage of a son from our family.' *Darshan* normally refers to the worshipper 'taking sight' of – and being seen by – a deity in a temple and is a basic component of Hindu and Jain ritual practice. Here at Beraja, the *darshan* was of the *kuldev*, the family's ancestral deity. By seeing – and being seen by – the *kuldev*, the bride is accepted as a member of her husband's family.[12] Although both Raju and Kailash were single at the time, veneration of the *kuldev* can be performed at any time (often at times of stress or trouble, or at the new year), and they wanted us to film them performing *darshan* and mak-ing some offerings.

The *kuldev*, in this family and in others I know of, both is and is not identified with a specific ancestor. When pressed, various members of the family on both this and other occasions, identified either Raju's paternal great-grandfather Bhimjibhai or Bhimjibhai's father as the *kuldev*. But on other occasions, the *kuldev* was seen simply as a distant ancestor, or as an unnamed deity associated with the family in some way. Physically, the *kuldev* is manifest in the world as an amorphous lump – perhaps of stone – about 30 cm tall, smeared with layers of ver-milion paste and housed in a small wall-cupboard in the Beraja house (see Figure 9).

Figure 9 *Making an offering to the* kuldev *(from Raju and his friends)*

The ritual that Raju and Kailash performed was brief, consisting of an offering of light and an offering of coconut. The coconut flesh, after being placed in the shrine briefly, was later distributed to children in the village and the remainder brought back to Jamnagar for other members of the family to share. In the film Kailash is seen and heard explaining confidently to the camera what is going on; later he and Raju become a little less certain, until Raju finally comments in exasperation, 'These things! This is the first time I've come here by myself.' Their uncertainty is perhaps typical of younger men in such ritual contexts, performing actions of which they are the instigators but not the authors (Humphrey and Laidlaw 1994), and reflecting the partial, sometimes piecemeal knowledge that is typical of some insiders' views of their context.

After the offerings, Raju and Kailash told me what they knew of the family's migration from Beraja to Jamnagar. At some time in the early 1930s their grandfather Natubhai gave up on farming in Beraja and with his two sons came to Jamnagar to open a shop, leaving his wife in Beraja with their daughter. His wife died shortly afterwards and Natubhai married her sister, Samratben, and had three sons. Natubhai died in 1945, and his wife and sons came to Jamnagar, leaving the Beraja house in the care of a distant relative, whose son lives there today. The five brothers married and lived together until 1970, when they demolished the family home and divided the joint estate. Raju's father took over the shop as sole owner, another business was divided between two other sons, and the remaining two inherited the land on which the Jamnagar house stood, on which they subsequently rebuilt. The house at Beraja retains a symbolic significance for all of them, however, as the ancestral home and location of the *kuldev* shrine.

Raju and Kailash's narrative was sketchy, and lacking a great deal of detail. They seemed conscious of this, particularly given the importance they felt that an accurate account of family history had for the film we were making. After we had returned from Beraja we went to the home of Manilal, the youngest of Samratben's sons. His house is the normal meeting place for all the family: partly because at that time it was the largest, but mainly because it is where Samratben herself, then in her eighties, lived. We began filming again and, without prompting, Raju and Kailash began to ask their grandmother about the time when she was a young bride in Beraja, her husband away in Jamnagar. 'So who lived with you at Beraja?' asks Raju. 'Only my father-in-law, Bhimjibhai.' 'And what did he do?' 'He was farming. But then there was famine for two or three years, and he and Darbar [Bhimji's deceased wife's brother] couldn't do anything.'

The conversation continued, listing various relatives and how they had made their way in the world. At the time I was struck, and con-

tinue to be, by how flat Samratben's narrative was. It lacked highlights, with few details to bring any kind of story alive but rather a
dogged insistence on names, places and kin relationships (see the
Appendix for a partial transcript of the conversation).[13] Her responses
to Raju's and Kailash's questions served to establish a series of events,
movements of named individuals through space and certain actions
they performed there. For example, leaving Beraja for 'abroad' and disappearing from contact and sight:

'Why don't we have as close a relationship with Balachandbhai as we do
with these people?'
'They aren't here. They went abroad.'
[lines 9–12];

A conflict between education, self-employment and wage labour:

'Did they – all the brothers – sit at the shop?'
'Bapuji said 'Shop! Shop! What do you mean? Do business with these five
rupees?' [i.e. there's not enough business at the shop to employ them all.]
'So two brothers started working [for someone else]?'
'All three brothers. They called [Ramnik from Songhad, where he was at
school] – oh, how they had all studied. Every year they passed [their exam-
inations] well! But [Dharamjibhai] called them here and they took jobs for
five rupees salary each.'
'So all three started working, and the other two brothers [Dharamjibhai
and Chotalal] sat at the shop – yes?'
[lines 23–27];

A death at a railway station:

'[Natubhai] went to Rajkot. Shamjikaka [Natubhai's brother] died at
Rajkot station.'
[line 51];

And also, the marking of women as non-actors:

'In between [Natubhai and the third son] there was an aunt.'
'So there were five other brothers after her. Ok.'
'One aunt.'
'One aunt. Only one aunt. Only one sister.'
[lines 46–50].

But in the narrative there was no particular continuity to these
events, and a marked absence of cause-effect relationships: people just
do things, with little indication of motivation, little sense of 'because of
this ... that happened'. This could, of course, be no more than an arte-

fact of the circumstances: bored responses to questions, an old woman's idiosyncrasies, the retelling of stories well known. But the flatness, the lack of causal linearity in the narrative, and – critically – the decentred viewpoint with kin terms being used which are relative to neither speaker nor hearer [for example, Appendix, lines 7, 17, 20, 32, 36, 45, 50] could also be seen as an insider's view of a web or network of events, where the perspectival viewpoint makes sense only to the speaker and a few very intimate hearers. Indeed, Samratben's opening remark, about the famine making farming difficult when she was a young bride [line 4], and later a brief comment (in response to a direct question) about the date when the family moved to Jamnagar [line 14, see also line 38], are the only points that can be linked to any wider flow of events.

Although the family's move from Beraja to Jamnagar was completed half a century ago, Jamnagar should not be considered the final stopping point. In the early 1980s Raju's two elder brothers relocated to Bombay, in common with many Gujaratis over the past century, in search of wider business opportunities. Successful in the housing and construction businesses there by the early 1990s, they began to finance a range of business ventures back in Jamnagar, overseen by Raju and his younger brother. At the time of making the film I had assumed that the whole family would eventually relocate to Bombay, replicating the move from Beraja two generations earlier.

In another conversation, however, Raju and his father revealed that they had mixed and differing opinions on this migration. Raju's father clearly had no intention of ever moving to Bombay ('Too noisy. Why should I want to go?'), and while Raju acknowledged that Bombay is the place to be in order to get on, he was ambivalent about going himself. He could see the bigger picture, take a more objective overview of the situation ('Bombay is better than Jamnagar because you can run any kind of business easily ... Jamnagar's a small place – if a business is established right from the start then it's all right. Otherwise for those who don't already have a business it's better to go to Bombay'). But on the other hand, the close relationships with kin and friends in Jamnagar (the main subject matter of our film) reinforced a sentimental attachment to Jamnagar ('Do you like Jamnagar?', 'It's a good place for business and to live. I have lots of friends here because I've lived here from childhood and at every stage of my life I've made more friends'). While undoubtedly younger and more articulate than his grandmother, Raju could present an account of his generation's movements through time and space that took account of two views – a normative overview of what could be, and a subjective insider's view of what might be.

At present, the family in Jamnagar can be seen as a satellite held in orbit by the *kuldev* and the ancestral home in the village of Beraja.

Some individuals have broken free, pulled by stronger forces of the Jains' migratory history, but they risk being flung into outer space, beyond knowledge, like the relatives in Samratben's narrative who went to East Africa and the UK. But as time passes, as Raju's elder brothers' children marry and establish further households in Bombay, Raju's father's strength of attachment to Jamnagar would seem to make him a prime candidate for becoming the next ancestor to be associated with the *kuldev*, and in future its shrine may be relocated to a new 'ancestral home' in Jamnagar.

Conclusions

It is inevitable that the passage of time, and the intersecting movements of ethnographer and ethnographic subjects, should lead to shifts in perspective and understanding. As outlined above, my own understanding of Jainism, the Jains and Jain migrations has passed through several phases. An initial, pre-fieldwork, view was of a disembedded religious tradition being manifest in a variety of places and events through the last two and a half millennia of Indian history. After early fieldwork I could see that this religious tradition had local and temporally specific contours, affected in part by the Jains' migration from the Jamnagar region through to the British Midlands. It was also evident that the project of coming to a socially- and historically-located understanding of this religious tradition could only be accomplished once a clear understanding had been reached of who 'the Jains' actually were (but see Carrithers 1990, Cort 1990). With more fieldwork, and more historical research, the certainty of fixed groups undertaking this and earlier migrations was thrown into doubt (Banks 1994: 131–3), but from a distance, the 'big picture' still retained some analytical validity. In trying to view some of those involved through the close-up scrutiny of a camera lens, however, the big picture seemed to dissolve, leaving a series of fragments, partial accounts and partial understandings, that could only be resolved by adopting a different perspective.

The process of constructing a film from the raw film footage is similar to the process whereby a written ethnography is constructed from field notes, but the limitations are more acute – material cannot so easily be synthesised or generalised from the particular to form a bigger picture (Banks 1990: 17). Nonetheless, most ethnographic films aim for some kind of narrative coherence and reflect – literally, given the evident physical positioning of the camera – a particular viewpoint.[14] My inability to cut the footage of Samratben's account of the Mehta family history into the final film (see note 13) was partly due to the fact that hers was an insider's view presented to others presumed to share the same perspective but which did not conform to what I hope was my intimate but nonetheless outsider's view.[15]

I should stress again, however, that quite apart from the question of scale my attempt above to present Jain migratory movement as seen from the inside, is not intended to supersede my earlier 'big picture' viewpoint. It is perhaps a truism that from the ethnographer's viewpoint the passage of time, and continued fieldwork involvement with friends and informants, leads to a sense of greater, not lesser complexity. What once seemed relatively clear and straightforward looks increasingly complex as one gets closer, and like Borges's famous map, it seems at times as though the only adequate representation would have to be a life-sized descriptive replica, perfect in every detail. I have chosen instead to follow some of the insights arising from visual anthropology and ethnographic film practice. The camera, as mentioned above, is inevitably positioned, allowing a greater insight into the perspective from which the view is taken; the passage of time allows more and more viewpoints to be considered, close up as well as distant.

APPENDIX

Note: the film transcript below has been edited down for the purpose of this paper and contains no indications of camera movement, etc.; edited-out sections are marked [...]. My own editorial comments are also marked with square brackets; kin terms, with Raju as ego, are also in square brackets.

[R =Raju; S = Samratben, Raju and Kailash's fathers' mother; FBW = daughter-in-law to S; K = Kailash]

l. no.

1 R: So who lived with you at Beraja?

2 S: Only my father-in-law [FFF], Bhimjibhai.

3 R: And what did he do there?

4 S: He was farming. Then there was famine for two or three years. He and Darbar [FFMB] couldn't do anything. Our *mamaji* [FMMB]...

5 FBW: Harjivan ... what was his name?

6 S: Harjivan Sundarji. There was Pragjibhai, then Kevalchand Vagjibhai, and Balachandbhai's grandfather, all three were brothers [all members of S's natal family].

7 FBW: Then Balachandbhai's grandfather... Balachandbhai isn't our *mamaji* is he? [*mamaji*=MB; unclear who 'our' refers to here]

8 S: No, he's *mamaji's* grandson. Bhagvanji is his father.

9 FBW: Then why don't we have as close a relationship with Bal-achandbhai as we do with these people?

10 S: Which people?

11 FBW: This Balachandbhai and the others.

12 S: They aren't here. They went abroad.

13 K: Grandmother, what year did we come to Jamnagar?

14 S: Here? About fifty-five years ago [c. 1930; S was born c. 1900]

15 K: Fifty-five years.
      [...]

16 S: Chaganbhai and Ramchand were at the shop [in Jamnagar].

17 K: So what did the other three brothers do? [referring to his own father and two brothers, all sons of S]

18 S: They were at school. They were very small. Two studied at Beraja and one at Songhad.

19 K: And were you at Beraja or here?

20 S: I lived at Beraja, but when Bapuji ['father' – her elder step-son] started a shop here, I came here.

21 K: So you came here, leaving the three brothers at Beraja.

22 S: No, two came with me to Jamnagar and one was [away at school] in Songhad.

23 K: One was at Songhad, two were here. Ok. Then what? Did they all sit at the shop?

24 S: Then Bapuji said 'Shop! Shop! What do you mean? Do business with these five rupees?' [i.e. there's not enough business at the shop to employ them all].

25 K: So that means these two brothers started working [for someone else]?

26 S: All three brothers. They called him [Ramnik, from Songhad where he was at school] – oh, how they had all studied! Every year they passed [their examinations] well. But [Dharamjibhai] called them here and they took jobs for five rupees salary each.

27 K: So all three started working, and the other two brothers [Dharamjibhai and Chotalal] sat at the shop – yes?

28 FBW: Ask her how many of her sons got married.

29 K: So all of you were living together?

30 S: All of us. At that time, many years ago.

31 K: Didn't you feel that the house where you all lived was too small?

32 S: But who were we? No so many. Just me and the two 'uncles' [i.e. her step-sons, Dharamjibhai and Chotalal]

33 K: No, after everyone else came.

34 S: They were all that were here then.

35 K: I'm talking about the time after we came. We [i.e. the rest of the brothers] came here, all married. Then what ...? Here, you didn't say ... Where did you move to?

36 S: Then 'father' [Dharamjibhai? not K's father Amrit] separated [set up an independent household]...

37 K: 'Father' separated ...

38 S: ... and we came to Pagala Shesi from Agarbathivalla's house. There we lived for three years. Then we left and came here to Vaju Kandoi's dela where we lived for twelve months in Manubhai Raval's house. We came to this house in V.S. 2002 [1946].

39 FBW: After coming to the house Bachukaka [Ramnik, Kirit's father] got married.

40 R: Where was I born? In this house? [i.e. the house that previously stood on this site]

41 FBW: In this house.

42 R: Were we all [his siblings] born here?

43 FBW: Everyone except Manubhai [R's elder brother], I think.

44 S: No, at this place. No, I brought Manubhai here when he was one year old.
           [...]

45 K: [Bhimjibhai – FFF] had seven sons, yes? Which number was our father [FF in fact], Natubhai Bhimji?

46 S: The second. In between [Natubhai and the third son] there was an aunt.

47 K: So there were five other brothers after her. OK.

48 FBW: One aunt.

49 K: One aunt. Only one aunt. Only one sister.

50 FBW: Just as we have only one aunt [i.e. her husband and four brothers, plus one sister], so they have only one.
           [...]

51 S: [Natubhai, her husband] went to Rajkot. Shamji-kaka [Natubhai's brother] died at Rajkot station. Bhavan-ada [younger brother of Natubhai] died at Jamnagar.

52 K: The eldest, Bhavan-ada, died in Jamnagar, and after that [Natubhai-]ada died at Beraja. Is that correct?

53 FBW: He died outside Rampa [a village].

54 S: No, he died at Beraja.

55 K: And who next?

56 S: Then Shamji-ada; but before that Devchand-kaka died. Jadavji-kaka died at Rajkot. He died first of all.

57 K: And then?

58 S: Liladharkaka died at Mombasa.

59 K: Mombasa.

60 FBW: When Liladhar-kaka went to Mombasa, Kanti-kaka [L's son] was not even born

61 S: He was in the womb.

NOTES

1. I am grateful to several of my informants and friends in Jamnagar for comments on an earlier draft of this paper, as well as for their comments and feedback on earlier publications and a documentary film. For my own part, this continued if sporadic dialogue over the years has proved the major intellectual benefit of sustained field engagement rather than, for example, the mere accumulation of more and more field data. The various field trips that allowed this dialogue were the result of funding from a variety of bodies including the SSRC and ESRC (Social Science Research Council, later Economic and Social Research Council), the Universities of Oxford and Cambridge, the British Academy and the Royal Anthropological Institute, to all of which I am indebted.

2. Space does not permit a presentation of this, but see in particular Banks 1997 and forthcoming. This revival sought to counteract a perceived 'decline' in Jainism throughout India, but especially in the south. One facet of the 'decline' was the collapse of certain religious offices, such as the guardianship of certain sacred sites, and certain categories of ordained professional religious; another facet was the rise in Jains registering as 'Hindu' in the decennial censuses. See Carrithers 1990, Sangave 1991, Dundas 1992: chapter 9.

3. See Banks 1986 and Dundas 1992: 6–10; Cort 1986, 1990 and 1997 together provide an exhaustive view of more recent sociological scholarship.

4. This kind of literature is still produced – see J. Jain 1975, for example.

5. See Buhler 1903, Jacobi 1914, Schubring 1935.

6. This was the time for such things – see for example Gombrich 1971 and Southwold 1983 on Sri Lankan Buddhism.

7. The film was produced while I was an RAI/Leverhulme Fellow at the National Film and Television School (Banks 1988b) and was accompanied by a written guide (Banks 1988c). It is not, in fact, explicitly about the Jains or Jainism at all, but is rather an exploration of love and friendship. However, the protagonist and his family were Jains and it was through a consideration of the embeddedness of their Jain practice and identity in trade, in migration and in kinship, that I began to consider Jainism independently of the intellectually disembedded discourse of doctrine discussed above (see Banks forthcoming). The relationship between a series of publications produced over a fieldworking career is an aspect of the nature of long-term ethnographic fieldwork which space precludes me from exploring here.

8. Figure 8 is reproduction of Map 6.2 in Banks 1994.

9. Amongst the many good publications that have emerged in recent years on the anthropology of the Jains, this particular issue of wealth and renunciation is dealt with extensively by Laidlaw (1995).

10. See, for example, Richard Fox on the relationship between merchants and rulers in the market town of 'Tezibazar' in Uttar Pradesh (1969). Harold Spodek also notes that in Saurashtra in particular (the region of Gujarat state within which Jamnagar is located) rulers attracted elite groups such as Jain merchants to their capitals, these groups gaining their power through the control of capital and human resources, not land, and for whom their urban location should be seen as 'a base of operation', not 'home' (1974: 450).

11. This is not a pseudonym, nor are any of the personal names mentioned below. The use of film in ethnographic research generally precludes the anonymity in ethnographic reporting that some anthropologists call for. On the other hand, the inevitability of personal identification brings about – in my experience at least – a far closer collaboration between ethnographer and subjects. While not strictly necessary, the element of mutual trust in this collaboration is undoubtedly strengthened by fieldwork ties stretching over several years. The corpus of films on the Mursi of Ethiopia, made by the British television company Granada in their 'Disappearing World' series in collaboration with David Turton is an outstanding example of this. Like some other visual anthropologists, I am sceptical of the value of 'hit and run' ethnographic films made by film crews and/or anthropologists who have had little or no previous contact with the subjects of the film.

12. *Kuldev* worship is actually a Hindu rite, and by no means exclusive to Jains. Not all families have a *kuldev*, at least today, though I know of British couples who have travelled from the UK some time after marriage, to visit kin in India but also to venerate the husband's *kuldev*.

13. It is a source of some embarrassment to me that this sequence was not included in the final cut of the film, given Raju and Kailash's interest in presenting the family's history. Part of the problem was technical – poor light, shooting indoors at night. But the real problem in terms of constructing a filmic narrative was the very flatness and disjointedness of Samratben's account, leading me to believe that viewers beyond the immediate family circle would be able to make little sense of it. Before abandoning it, I spent a considerable amount of time cutting and re-cutting the relevant material, trying to identify a viewpoint that would give coherence and conform to the narrative viewpoint of the rest of the film. In some senses, this section of my presentation can be seen as a further recut.

14. Subversions of both narrative and viewpoint, similar to the 'experimental ethnography' of the 1980s, with its attempts at multivocality and a decentring of authorial authority, are by definition a recognition of coherent single narrative and single viewpoint as normative.

15. In the film, brief snatches of voice-over commentary from myself, which tie my perceptions to the action, are intended to act as a key narrative structuring device.

Chapter 10

THE ETHNOMUSICOLOGIST IN THE WILDERNESS

Hélène La Rue

The practice of doing fieldwork is considered central to becoming an ethnomusicologist. Although scholars of the subject struggle to define what it is they do and why, and although the subject has been described as being woven from such polytheoretical fabric that there is little continuity in matter or approach, the single unifying element is a common understanding that it takes fieldwork, specifically work in a country other than one's own, to make an ethnomusicologist. Bruno Nettl in *The study of ethnomusicology: twenty-nine issues and processes* (1983) sets out the four aspects of the 'ethnomusicologist's credo' in which he states categorically that 'Fieldwork is an indispensable method', particularly 'intensive work with small numbers of individual informers' (Nettl 1983: 9).

More recently, Timothy Rice developed Nettl's position further to say that the ethnomusicologist must travel to the field, which is that 'place where we outsiders must go to encounter these insiders and their culture, and explain to other outsiders the relationship between music and culture posited by our theories'. Rice continues: 'according to this credo, sometime during or after fieldwork one becomes an ethnomusicologist' (1997: 105). This contrasts with the earlier practice in which an anthropologist or ethnographer collected material – instruments, photos and recordings – as part of their own fieldwork, and brought it back to museums and archives where specialised musicians studied and interpreted material deposited in their care.

A background to the subject

Ethnomusicology is a sufficiently young subject that it is still considered by some practitioners not to have come of age (Myers 1992: 11). Much conference time is spent discussing what the term means. Although a new academic discipline, ethnomusicology in fact has its roots in the long history of contacts between different groups of people. Interest in the musics of other traditions has always existed and from quite an early date European travellers describe musical events and even exchanges of musical entertainments. It is generally considered that it was the invention of the recording machine in 1877 that facilitated the scientific and academic development of the subject, enabling music to be recorded and then transcribed from these recordings which in turn enabled exact repetition. This exact repetition is never possible in live performance, as no musician is capable of playing a piece in exactly the same way twice. The invention of a machine which was so admirably suited to laboratory work enabled the music to be studied within the new ideals of 'scientific' rigour. As well as having the machine which facilitated transcription and analysis there was a parallel development of ideas, namely Alexander Ellis's invention of the cents system by which pitch could be measured accurately. This invention resulted in a greater interest in the comparative measurement of the musical pitches used world-wide than in the actual music and its performance.[1]

The ability to record music opened up new possibilities. In fact the invention of the wax phonograph machine enabled anyone, not only the trained musician, to record and collect music. Precious time in the field could be concentrated on the making of recordings. These could then be sent to central archives in which other highly specialised scholars could do the analysis and prepare transcriptions for publication. In Europe the first of these archives were founded in Vienna in 1900, closely followed by the Berlin Programmarchiv in 1902. These were staffed by psychologists and acousticians who processed the recordings as they arrived but did not themselves collect. This division of labour between scholars who worked in the field and the scholars in museums and archives was considered to be an admirable method as the immediate need was to record all the world's musics before the inevitable process of change took place. As the musics, pitches and scales were compared one with another the subject was given the name Comparative Musicology.

Parallel with this research, which claimed to be based on new scientific principles, was the collecting carried out by composers and musicians of classical music inspired by the late nineteenth-century Nationalist movement. This stimulated the collection of indigenous traditions including folksong and instrumental music. The collectors' main interest was in the music's performance and the notes themselves. Music was objectified and collected as though a finite number of musics existed and the most pure of these existed in a form unchanged from earliest times. In this we can detect a fundamental similarity of thinking between the composers who collected in their own countries, and the comparative musicologists who worked elsewhere. However, the purpose of the musicians' collection was different; rather than examining the music for ideas of comparison between one country's music and another's, their end was to collect music which could be presented as distinct national forms.

Bélar Vikár, Béla Bartók, Cecil Sharp and Percy Grainger were among those who collected European folk music. They considered themselves to be different from the comparative musicologists as they were primarily musicians who worked within their own cultural traditions. The recording machine was not always used. Collectors such as Cecil Sharp relied on transcribing songs directly from the singers. The usual result was the production of new musics in the classical genre based on the material they had collected. This group and their descendants have always been regarded as less scientific and systematic than the comparative musicologists, partly because they were working in their own countries, and partly because many of them added instrumental accompaniment and harmony, as well as often remodelling the music they collected in a contemporary classical style. The products of their research could then be concert forms of national expression or folksongs arranged for the drawing-room and music party.

In the mid-twentieth century Comparative Musicology grew in popularity as a subject of study but it was expanding its interests away from the earlier concentration on pitch. The subject was given a new name when Jaap Kunst coined the word 'ethnomusicology' in 1950, arguing that the subject was no more 'comparative' than any other. The subject was further diversified with the development of two theoretical camps, reflecting whether the exponents had an anthropological or musicological background.[2] It was the musicologist Charles Seeger who first highlighted the inadequacy of talking about music. In his paper, 'Systematic musicology: viewpoints, orientations, and methods,' he explored the problems of using words to describe a nonverbal mode of communication, as well as the difficulty inherent in understanding musical forms other than those from one's own tradition (Seeger 1951: 240–8). As a result of his questions, 'bi-musicality' (a word developed from bi-linguality) was held to be necessary for a real appreciation and study of other musics. From this it was a short step to travel from the analysis of the musics themselves to the processes of music creation and performance.[3]

However, the need to record music and performance remained as a guiding star, this perception of need being reinforced by the more recent work in other fields: 'In 1973, at the International Congress of Anthropological and Ethnological Sciences, held in Chicago, a special conference on visual anthropology adopted a resolution on the urgency of adequately filming the existing varieties of cultural diversity and adaptation on the planet, and, for gathering and preserving existing footage for the benefits of researchers, future generations, and indigens alike' (Feld 1976: 207). This quotation has a curiously nineteenth-century flavour rather at odds with mainstream anthropology.

The subject became increasingly popular with the greater public interest in world musical traditions through the 1970s and 1980s. As a result, there was an increasing number of festivals of 'world music' in these decades which enabled artists from many different traditions to make international tours. These world music festivals can be seen as the natural and final development of nineteenth-century ideas of music collecting as represented in the World Exhibitions.[4] It was in the 1980s when the combination of easy travel as well as generous sponsorship led to an explosion of such events, that any idea of finding traditions untouched and unchanged by foreign influence finally became untenable, though the various cross-over styles retain the idea of distinctive musical genres.

It was not so long ago still considered possible to collect and observe the playing of music and instruments so completely that the resulting evidence could form a basis for the representation of the 'culture as a whole' in another context such as the museum or festival (Dournon 1996: 37). A plethora of method and techniques were used in the collecting process, exploiting skills derived from musicology, anthropology and the social sciences. This led to the criticism that ethnomusicology was a derivative subject, lacking any unity of theory and method, even to a crisis of agreement about ethnomusicology's identity. The situation can be said to have continued from that time up to now, topics such as 'what is ethnomusicology' and 'whither ethnomusicology' still occupying many conference hours.

Various theories have been held by practitioners of the subject; the vital need to preserve traditions before they disappear, that music can be preserved when made into a recording; that music is (to quote Rice) a 'sound fact' which must 'be interpreted and compared, at least by ethnomusicologists using ordinary language description and Western musical notation' (Rice 1997: 102); and that music is a form of activity created within a coherent cultural system. Added to this has been the belief, commonly held since the 1970s, that the traditional exponent of the musical form, the insider, stands opposed to the fieldworker who always remains an outsider.

The only constant has been an agreement as to the necessity of field-work. The need for fieldwork is the main element of continuity between two main theoretical camps: the first holds that the ethnomusicologist should participate in the music being studied by becoming proficient in playing it, while the second claims the ethnomusicologist should remain a nonparticipant observer on the grounds that learning any aspect of playing the music would be a distraction and a dissipation of energy. In both, fieldwork is considered indispensable. Being in the field is the only way in which to observe the music practised within its own tradition and milieu.

My special 'field'

I have never been able to 'do' fieldwork in the accepted sense of the term. At the time when I was a research student, my particular subject (musical instruments in England 1200–1900) was hardly considered ethnomusicological at all. From the perspective of Nettl's credo I can be criticised in that I never moved out from my familiar world for any length of time to work with the unfamiliar 'other'. However, now that fieldwork research by those from within the culture studied has earned respectability if not the blessing of fashion, my early work, with its approach to the place of instruments within an English music cultural context can be acknowledged as ethnomusicology. But I would like to claim a new 'field', one in which I have worked for more than twenty years. In making this claim I find myself contradicting Mantle Hood when he writes: 'The "field" is not a group of musicians and dancers from India on a tour of the United States' (1982: 206). I believe it may be.

Since the start of my doctoral research in 1974 I have been employed, in one capacity or another, in the Pitt Rivers Museum, Oxford. Here I have been concerned with the care and interpretation of other people's fieldwork collections of musics and music objects. In this I have been concerned with a 'double other': the music of others collected by others. As for many curators, short periods of research 'in the field' have been carried out, not as an extension of my own research, but principally as the result of the wish to 'fill in gaps' in the Pitt Rivers Collection. The material I have collected is aimed not only at filling these lacunae but at being well enough documented to provide material for informative exhibitions designed for the general public. A part of my job, too, has been the arrangement of Oxford events given by musicians visiting the United Kingdom as part of the 'world music' circuit. Here I am closely involved with the arrangements of their local concert programme as well as the accompanying public events which always include school programmes. In the course of this work I have had the opportunity to work closely with, and to observe, musicians from a wide geographical range of traditions. In one sense all this work has had aspects of the fieldwork experience which are reminiscent of the 'real thing'. The one difference being that I have never had an extended time in which to learn an instrument or a form of song, let alone to get 'under the skin' of one particular musical culture.[5]

I must disagree with Mantle Hood and his statement that I have quoted above. However, my field is not the musicians and their tour but the museum environment itself and my experience working in it over a long passage of time, in my case twenty-five years, which enables me to reflect on my observations and make them useful. No longer is 'collecting' the music performed an issue, for it is a rare musician who does not come with a case full of tapes to sell. Those recordings they will have made in studios not differing at all from any found in this country. However, the problem of trying to capture a complete record of the event is not solved by buying a disc. Trying to capture the complete record depends upon a process of translation, not only of the musicians' speech, thus understanding their conceptualisation of the music, but of the music itself.[6] So here I have the problem twice over. With the need to make recordings obviated, however, I can at least concentrate on my observation of the musicians and on their own adaptation of performance to the unfamiliar environment both here and in other centres, as well as to the consideration of the reception of their performance by their many audiences.

The observing ethnomusicologist

Ethnomusicologists can be said to be the most naturally participant of all observers. Musicians have always shared and exchanged musical ideas and there is nothing more easily acceptable than someone who comes to study music, or more particularly folksong. That songs must be collected and studied before they are forgotten is a deeply held theory now to be found world-wide as part of feelings of nationalism and cultural identity. This was brought home to me while I was on a collecting visit in Gueichow Province in China in 1989. My hope was to find out about Miao musical instruments and if possible see them in use and meet some of their makers. It was not long before I realised that whatever I had come to do, there was another agenda driven by the people I met, both my scholar companions and the Miao themselves, who assumed I had come to collect songs.[7] The sessions were driven by the singers themselves, who seemed always to be fighting against the limitations of time to sing for me everything that they knew.

In one instance I was travelling in a packed train with my colleagues from the University of Guiyang. A lady stopped and asked what I was doing there. When I told her I was working on music she moved my colleagues out of the way, sat down opposite me, told me to get my tape recorder out and proceeded to sing, undaunted by the train's canned music, teasing comments from the other passengers and general hubbub. Pausing for breath she introduced herself as Ei Zhi-Zhong from Gan Ba Sao, a village in Fu Qiuan County; she told me that she was the best singer from her village and it was most important for me to collect as many of her songs as I could. Ei Zhi-Zhong was still singing as the train arrived at my station and I had difficulty getting my equipment together in time to get out. I felt an immediate sense of recognition when reading Mervyn McClean's writings in 'Preserving world musics' in which he tells us of his work in New Zealand in the 1950s: 'The old people had no great interest in advancing the cause of scholarly research. Their motives were simple, personal and direct. They saw themselves as the repositories of a sung tradition which was precious and already rare' (McClean 1983: 33). As a result of this experience he became caught up in the movement to record, preserve and teach Maori chant in Maori communities.

Ei Zhi-Zhong showed me the general assumptions of the singers in China that I met; I was there to record folk song and there was so little time to collect it that no moment was to be wasted. My academic colleagues were also most keen that I should collect, but they were insistent that these 'primitive' musics should be improved. In the long train journeys from one region to another we would argue over this matter. I have often wondered whether my arguments changed their ideas in any way.

That an ethnomusicologist can influence or change a tradition, or its perception, for better or worse is well established. Jaap Kunst, working in Java, was responsible for the popularisation of the gamelan in the West. He not only wrote a major work on the tradition (1994) but on his return to Amsterdam collected gamelans for exhibition at the Tropical Institute. In their turn these exhibitions encouraged and facilitated the manufacture of other gamelans which are still to be seen and heard in Dutch institutions. He became such an accepted authority that his books are even used in Java itself by indigenous Javanese musicians to explain the music to visiting Westerners. More recently the work of Lucy Duran, who worked in Cuba and Mali, has stimulated a popularity of these 'world music' styles well beyond any academic field – to the point where the instruments are familiar sounds in the popular music world.[8] As a result the visiting ethnomusicological curator making contact with indigenous musicians may now raise expectations of fame and fortune.

The museum as observation tower

When working organising a museum event in contrast to the 'normal' fieldwork experience, I always belong and the musician is in the position of outsider. However, within their performance dynamic they are in their own world. Part of the performance itself becomes the adaptation to the new location and the adjustment of the musical performance to a new, perhaps less informed audience. Here we come back once again to the problem of describing these processes. Gilbert Lewis sums it up in a nonmusical case: 'One of the reasons for the difficulty anyone faces in trying to put the meaning of a rite (or a poem or a painting for that matter) into discursive language, or into other words, stems from the inward-pointing aspects of its meaning and the particularity of the media used; it underlies the heresy of paraphrase' (Lewis 1990: 144). To that we have to add the more general problems of putting music into words.[9]

My experiences working with the Langas and Manganiyars from Rajasthan on their visits to the United Kingdom provide some illustrations of how they adapted to the Museum and school as locations, and how they made use of me in their performance. I have worked with these groups more than once but the most intensive period was in the summer of 1986 when they visited Oxford and London. On this occasion they spent a day visiting local schools as well as spending a weekend giving concerts in the Balfour Building of the Pitt Rivers Museum. I then worked with them holding public workshops for a Commonwealth Music Village in Holland Park, London. Before their first afternoon performance in the museum I asked whether I could record them. They agreed enthusiastically. The following evening they told me, through their interpreter, that if I wished they would be very happy for me to record them again. Overnight I copied the tapes of both performances and gave them the copy in the morning. That next day they said I was welcome to record them again. I did so, thinking that it was because they were interested in having the record of their performance as well as being able to listen to it and assess it – which they certainly did.

I followed them to London where they performed in far more formal venues. The Commonwealth Institute hosted a concert using the staging in the exhibition area. The Institute has galleries above and below the musicians, who performed on a central circular stage. Manohar Lalas, their interpreter, himself a museum curator, asked me whether I would record the concert for them. Knowing that the National Sound Archive would be coming, I explained that there would be a far better recording than any I could make. They insisted that they wanted me to do it too. So there I sat, just below the concert platform's rim close to the recording machine (I must explain that my microphone had only a short lead to the machine so I could not retreat into anonymity in the audience and always had to sit quite close to the musicians). Later an evening on a Thames pleasure boat was arranged (Figure 10a). The Langas and Manganiyars were to be the entertainers and once again I was fetched to make my recording. It was only then that I realised why they were so keen to have me there. It was not the recording but my presence they wanted.

Over the short weeks of getting to know them and their music I could not but help reacting to the unexpected variations and turns they made with the set programme. At times I found it difficult not to laugh from the sheer fun of the musical games they were playing. Of course, at home the audience did not sit respectfully ten yards away in anonymous darkness, they sat in front reacting to the music which in turn reacted to them. The performance becomes constantly variable, as a result of the audience reactions. Not having this response must have been very strange to the musicians, so discovering someone who could not help the expressions on her face they made good use of her. Being positioned by the musicians so as to be a point of reference, I became a tool which was used to recreate certain aspects of their performance tradition.

Figure 10a *An evening on the Thames*

On another occasion I had visiting group of musicians to stay with me. Once again I was working with people away from their home and traditional performance milieu. As I wished to make them feel as much at ease as possible I ensured that all of the house was theirs and that they had all they needed to make themselves comfortable. I pointed out where my room and private part of the house was and then left them to it. As a result of their process of making themselves at home I was to learn far more and far more quickly about the musicians' preparation for performance, daily meditation and prayer as well as music practise than I would have done had I been working in their own country. There I would have had to establish links before being able to live in such close contact. The very different use of space and time was brought home to me all the more vividly because it was happening in my own house.

As a curator I have a role in these musical happenings, both in preparing them, working with the musicians, and in the times afterwards when I am able to observe the response and reception of the events by their audiences. The musicians come here and see an audience that they want to keep; often they see a museum curator as a person in a position to keep their music in mind. The Langas and Manganiyars themselves commented about my responsibility to them and their music near the end of their visit to London, when they stopped me escaping from a group photograph. They explained that to them I was an important person. As a result of several years of drought the traditional musicians' role had been lost and the village families had now all moved away from their farms and were living in shanty towns around large cities in the state. There was no longer the money to pay for the traditional musical performances at weddings and festivals.

The musicians regarded this with resignation and the strong feeling that the changes would never be reversed, but they were certain that their music was a cultural richness of which they were proud. They had been very interested to work with the smaller school audiences and in the intimate events at the Balfour Building. They had had the chance to observe a museum, to study its displays and to see how music could be taught through the institution. They wished they could always work with institutions in this way as they felt that it was vital for them to be remembered. They stressed this point. They did not wish to be known merely as people suffering from want and possible famine, but as a proud people with a rich, and enjoyable, musical tradition. They regretted the fact that, lacking English, they could not themselves talk to the audiences for whom they played. But they told me that in my country, through their music that I had collected and armed with all I had learnt about it whilst listening to them, I could continue to teach people about them long after they had gone home.

Not only did they see their performance itself as reinforcing their cultural tradition through its repetition in performance world-wide but they saw the collecting of it, together with teaching about it, as a way of being remembered. Not only being remembered but being respected and admired through their skills as musicians. Additionally, although the music recordings I now have were not made in a conventional fieldwork situation, I have been able to observe another context, that of performance itself through which the musicians created a context of their own.

The Oxfordshire Festivals of Traditional Music

The period through which we were able to host groups of musicians in Oxford was comparatively short. These events were the inspiration of the late Robert Atkins, in 1987 the Arts Director of the Commonwealth Institute, London. He envisioned a series of Arts Festivals which would explore different areas of the Commonwealth primarily through music and dance. Linking with organisations such as Extra European Arts, he arranged for groups of musicians to come to England where they would perform at the Commonwealth Institute, the Edinburgh Festival, the Festival of the South Bank in London and also in Oxford. Such events are costly and they were only made possible with the help of a combination of funders. Oxford was the least financially viable of the whole series. As a result of the fact that most of our funding came through local Arts Bodies and Educational Trusts, the performances themselves were held not only at the Museum but in schools and community centres. My input was to prepare beforehand those who were to host and hear the musicians and then to be with the groups during their visits to Oxfordshire.

Through the three years of the Festival (1987–9) we hosted groups from India, (Rajasthan, Madhya Pradesh), Papua New Guinea and New Zealand, and lastly West Africa (Cameroon, Nigeria, Senegal; see Figure 10b). The first year was the most experimental. This was the first time that I had linked with an area outside Oxford City itself: through the help of the Cherwell Arts Officer, Pauline Scott-Garrett, we were able to link with various schools in Banbury, an area with a much larger population of Asian families than Oxford. The Festival developed from events at which the parents formed the audience in the school to their active participation through the months which preceded the visit and a final performance which involved the whole community such as the Banbury Carnival.

I was well aware of the dangers of events such as these. They can all too easily end up as self-indulgent tokenism: a flamboyant and extrav-

Figure 10b *The Senegambian* balafon *in Bletchingdon*

agant nod in the direction of the need to introduce children to multi-
cultural studies through a study of the arts, without taking it any further. Reflecting after the first occasion, the Arts Director and I decided
that we had got it wrong. Apart from the more intimate events at the
Balfour Building site of the Pitt Rivers Museum we had held big events
in Banbury aiming to get as large audiences as possible. Neither of the
groups that we took was suited to this approach and as a result it
became far more of a brief spectacle than an event which could have
been woven into the life of the schoolchildren through a longer period.
This would require better preparation and input from me; working
closely with their teachers beforehand, I needed to know exactly who
would be coming.

The following year we tried a different formula. Once again there
were two groups, one of Highlanders from Papua New Guinea (Huli
men and Melpa women) and a Maori concert party from New Zealand.
Some months before, it was decided to take each group to a different
venue, the Maoris to Queensway School in Banbury and the Papuans
to Bletchingdon Primary School. In both of these schools I went to

work with the teachers shortly after Christmas. Having discussed with them our method of approach, I then went to both schools and spent a day with the children. In the course of the following months some of the children also visited the Pitt Rivers Museum.

This time we tried exchange, so the children would host the visitors. Through these months I tried to lay a foundation for the big weekend in June when the children would actually meet the musicians and themselves show them around their school. I found the reaction of the children in Bletchingdon School most interesting. Bletchingdon is a village north of Oxford. The first time I went to talk to the children I asked whether anyone knew where Papua was and what it was like there. I got the response that they did not know, but that it must be hot, dry, of a brown sandy colour all over and that probably everyone was starving! When I showed the first slide that I had brought – of two children standing on a hill with the rainforest stretching out behind them – there was a gasp of delight. They had never realised there were places like that. When I showed them a picture of a Huli man, face painted, wearing wig and feathers, I got the predictable response of laughter; but then I introduced the thought that, in fact, we all look rather odd, dressed up for special occasions – had any of them seen the Lord Mayor of Oxford in full regalia. The laughter was just as loud.

The preparations for the coming visit were then taken over by the teachers, with constant phone calls, questions about details concerning Papua, traditions there and the possible diet of the visitors, as the school parents' association was to give them lunch. Owing to the complications of bringing groups like this to Europe and the various uncertainties of preparation, we did not know exactly where the visitors were to come from, and more important what kind of food they would enjoy, until very near the day.

On the day a blackboard went up outside the school, 'Parents and friends are invited to join us this afternoon for a performance by the musicians and dancers from Papua New Guinea to start at 2.00 p.m. It will last for about an hour. Bring a chair and sunshade if you want to be comfortable. Come earlier if you want to see the preparations.' It takes some hours to prepare for SingSing. Some of the children were prepared for performance and others played an active part in helping the Papuans and their schoolfriends to dress and paint their faces. This point of the event I found very difficult to document. The preparations themselves, as much as a rehearsal, are important to observe, but how can one watch a happening on this scale? Should I follow one child or get some measure of the whole group? How was I to assess the effect of this event on the children, let alone their parents? For the afternoon I was overwhelmed by the sheer number of 'events' that were happening around me, as well as the central performance.

Observing the musicians and their performances over the next two days in the Balfour Building I saw different forces at work. In the schools both the Maoris and the Papuans worked with the children, much as parents would do and as naturally and seemingly 'at home'. In the museum they were working primarily as entertainers. For the Maoris this was obviously no problem; although they all had other careers back home, they were also an extremely professional 'concert party' with years of experience. For the Papuans, on the other hand, this alien 'performance' of what at home would be a village celebration was not congenial.

During the weekend there was one event which served to make a change between the Saturday performance and that of the Sunday. On the Saturday evening as we ate together I realised that there was something troubling the Papuans. I finally got to the bottom of it. The Papuans wanted to go to church on Sunday and the English guide who had come from London with them had told them that, as they were staying in an Oxford college, they could attend the college chapel. It took a little while before I could ascertain why this would not do: they did not want to make things difficult, they said, but the chapel would not be correct, for they were Roman Catholics and they wished to go to Mass. I suggested that if they wished I could take anyone who wanted to go to Mass the following day to Blackfriars.

The next morning I found a little group already waiting. By the time everyone had turned up it was a substantial number of members of both the Papuan and the Maori groups. Once there, a member of the congregation summed up the situation quickly and the leader of the Papuan group and one of the Maori women were immediately given the task of taking up the offerings, a job they both did often at home. Of course the sudden influx of a Maori concert party in particular, all of whom knew the hymns, could hardly go unnoticed! Afterwards at coffee another member of the congregation came up to a group of Huli men and started talking in Pidgin. The lively conversations that followed led to an invitation to their concert on the one hand and an invitation to the pub afterwards on the other. The concert that night was quite different from the one the previous day. This time there were friendly faces in the audience.

It was the last of the three festivals which was to have the most intensive period of preparation and from which I was to have the greatest feedback. Once again with Banbury School, I began working with the staff and children about six months before. This time we knew a great deal about the visiting group who came from Jos in Nigeria. Not only was it possible to know about the group itself in advance, but we were also fortunate in that a previous Pitt Rivers director had worked in the area and his widow, Catherine Fagg, still living in

Oxford, was able to help enormously by supplying more background not only from her own memory but from books of traditional stories directly from that region.

Queensway Primary was the key school to be involved, but this project was also to incorporate two other schools, one a sixth form college and the other for children with special needs. Not only did they learn about the music but they focused on festival, dance and masks, producing giant processional puppets and costumes portraying the characters from the Anansi spider story. The musicians' visit then became a pivot between the earlier preparation and the later performance of the story by the children and the use in Banbury Carnival of the puppets and masks. So now the visit was not only a climax of one set of preparations but also an eagerly awaited chance to learn skills which were then to be used in another performance (Figures 11a, b).

One of the most frustrating aspects of my work is that I am rarely able to observe the effect upon audiences of the events or exhibitions which I organise. This whole series of events offered me a very special insight into a community response. This is because the Banbury project (as in a smaller way was the case in Bletchingdon with the

Figure 11a *Dancing with the Jos musicians, Queensway School*

Figure 11b *Exchanging addresses*

Papuans' visit) involved staff, students and their parents and ulti-mately, through the Carnival, the wider community. In both places I had the chance over three years of special events to work with the same groups of people experiencing different musicians, just as I often have the chance to meet the same musicians visiting England over sev-eral years. In passing may I say that some of the children who laughed at their first sight of a Huli man in festive wig are still writing to their Papuan friends.

Music observed

As I review the three years of performances I realise that I was able to witness a number of different dynamics. Many of the groups, such as the Langas and Manganiyars, the Maori Concert Party and the groups from Western Africa, were organised groups who saw what they were doing in terms of performance event just as any Western musician would. The Papuans, on the other hand, were offering us the possibil-ity of experiencing a musical event which took place within their community and which was not primarily an event designed to be observed only. Comparing their concerts over the weekend with the school SingSing showed this difference. Within the school they most clearly enjoyed working with the children who were their hosts and guides, and the event was a shared experience. The school visit was the first time in their whole stay in Europe that they had had a chance to meet people in such a relaxed and informal way, and they told me that how much they missed their children back home. At the weekend concerts, after a day spent preparing, once the concert began the audiences reverted to Western 'concert mode' and sat watching the dancing. There was actually a difference between the Saturday and the Sunday event as by that time they had had a chance to meet people in Oxford who came to watch.

Working as I do, I find that the aspects of both the musicians' performance and their manipulation of an alien environment, and also of the audiences' reception of the music, are thrown starkly into focus. I am aware of the fact that the performances I witness are more than just the sound of the notes that I record on my machine.[10] Not only would it never be possible to record all of the performance, but I must add to this the reaction to and reception of the performance by the audience and how their response shapes the musicians' own. How may this differ from the response they might receive in a performance environment in which the audience is familiar with the music?

The music is only one element: staged performances such as those of the Langas and Manganiyars have so many variables that there can be no 'ur-text'. The gestures of communication between the musicians, as well as between the musicians and the audience, just as much as the notes played are part of the performance in that they shape and change its dynamic and even the notes themselves. Each performance in a different place is once again different, the musicians making use of acoustic and environment. This would surely have also been the case in performances in Rajasthan.

In the case of the Papuans' performance, they themselves changed the atmosphere by making contact with their audience and inviting them to take part (as in the school) or getting them to come to the concert (as at Blackfriars). In all these cases there was more to be learnt about the performance than just watching the evening events. Watching the teaching session beforehand formed a rare opportunity to see how the performer communicated the salient features of the performance to inexperienced beginners. However, even though these sessions were planned and by then I had worked for some time with both the musicians and the children, there was still that element of the unexpected. So many things happened at the same time. Most of the groups would begin a teaching session working as a group, but soon

they would split the children into as many groups as there were performers. Then they would teach the rhythms, the movements and the
dance steps. All at once the problem of watching one group and the
interrelated reactions was fragmented into as many as fifteen groups
and a kaleidoscope of performance, reception, reaction and interaction. Although I have sound recordings, video footage and photos of
the last events, they can only represent and remind me of that day as
nearly as a line drawing can of the reality of Niagara Falls.

There was not only the problem of trying to watch one performance, trying to take photographs or film whilst also trying to ensure
that nothing was missed that could be informative later. There were
two events happening concurrently; one in Banbury, the other in
Bletchingdon, so even if I managed to get help to film the other event I
still always had to work on my own at one of the sites and then move
with all the speed of a rescue archaeologist in order also to experience
the second site and so relate my own experience to the records
acquired later. And yet somehow this amounts to a total event of the
kind ethnographers claim to record.[11]

Here we have the nub of a problem. What is the result that I hope to
get from my work with musicians when the material I am dealing with
is so ephemeral and unrepeatable? How can I live up to the Rajasthanis' vision of the curator being somehow their representative? – particularly when I must acknowledge that recreating this type of
performance in a museum context is impossible, and no words can do
justice to the events. As Seeger points out, describing a musical performance which itself exists within its own period of time and is performed in a particular way can only be done using words which
themselves exist within their own time and with their own rhythms.
'The careful student will keep ever in mind the fact that he is employ-
ing one art utilizing a highly selective set of tonal and temporal materials (speech) to deal with another utilizing a somewhat different but
no less highly selective set (music)' (Seeger 1951: 242).

It is all too easy to forget the difficulties of this situation. Within the
Western European tradition of classical music we are trained to think
that notated music is the most sophisticated and to forget that no notation is ever sufficient of itself. The classic example which demonstrates
the shortcomings of notation is jazz, which is impossible to interpret
from the written text alone but must be realised through the medium of
performance-example: a teacher, together with experience of the style
and sound of jazz, is the only way in which those elements which are
impossible to notate can be incorporated into the performance. We also
find it easy to forget the complexities of musical performance more generally because most of our experience now comes second-hand –
through the medium of recordings, in the main sound recordings on CD

or cassette, where any visible aspect is absent. Increasingly too, the ritual of going to a concert has become one in which musician and audience are segregated and even eye-contact is now discouraged by concert hall design.[12] Now, too, all the audience appreciation in the world will only rarely draw forth an encore at the most formal of concerts.

One sees how easy it is to forget the spatial element of performance and the numbers of different levels of interaction: between performer and performer; between performer and audience; between audience members and even the response between audience and performer which can lead to that unique performance of the individual piece. Nowadays we are so used to listening to our CDs, with their digitally enhanced and corrected performances, that we forget that in live music each performance is unrepeatable.[13] There are even those who will not go to a concert of a loved work because they cannot bear to hear mistakes nor cope with an unfamiliar interpretation of the score. There are so many layers of preconceptions which surround the performance of music, that most ephemeral of all the arts, that it is no wonder that observing musical performance, and 'collecting' it is not straightforward and neither is interpreting it and presenting it after the performance in another performance space, that of the museum itself.

Music and the museum

Music only exists during its performance. Because that performance is necessarily within its own time and space, any verbal analysis, description or explanation will immediately add another layer of experience, that of the commentator, upon the performance itself. This is a further problem when it comes to 'labelling' music within a museum context. Can we present it merely as a sound-object among the three-dimensional music objects, as an illustration of those three-dimensional objects or as a reasoned exhibit in its own right? The last option carries with it its own problems. Such an exhibit demands time and patience of the museum visitor and has to be followed in a logical sequence. A museum visitor does not expect to sit down to listen to long musical examples, and there are practical difficulties when the visitor leaves halfway through an example and the next visitor joins the experience in the middle of the exhibition.[14]

Once again this raises a number of other questions: how has my work, over the last twenty and more years as a museum curator, shaped my 'fieldwork' experience. How does my position as a curator in a museum of the University of Oxford shape the material I am able to record and the contacts I am able to make? What continuities can I have through my work when I am constantly working with musicians from different traditions and the tradition of my own field of study is to follow just one? Now that my work itself has been given the added dimension of more contact with the European classical music world, how will this enrich or change my experiences?

Now perhaps I am coming full circle because I have the opportunity to watch European musicians train, teach, rehearse and perform. As curator of the Bate Collection in the Music Faculty I not only lecture on ethnomusicology and the history of the instruments in the Collection, but I also have visits from musicians who come to study the collection or to work in the Music Faculty with the students. Now, by walking to the other side of the front door, I can watch performers, quartets and orchestras as well as jazz bands rehearse. I can see exactly those aspects of the musical world that make visiting musicians so interesting and which in concert are rigorously excluded.

In the Music Faculty the students have the chance to hear the Allegri Quartet rehearse as well as perform as, for a week of each term, they are the quartet 'in residence'. They have been coming to Oxford for many years; in fact they were coming whilst I was a doctoral student. It is interesting that, although they rehearse with the door to the Hall open, there are very few who wander in or out to listen to the rehearsals, although that is the very reason for their residency at the Faculty. I myself have felt quite shy about doing so for my whole training when hearing classical music is to wait until the end of a movement before walking in as quietly and unobtrusively as possible. However, I often do wander in and sit to listen for a few moments. One or other of the musicians will look up at the end of a phrase and smile in welcome and may well often include me by referring to a previous conversation we have had as they break to discuss a point of technique or style.

Once a year the quartet incorporates student players to form an octet. As they work with the students it is often remarked how the musicians glance at each other and at them and the watchful looks are answered by smiles as the musical phrases are answered by the students. The exchange of glances is accompanied by an exchange of incorporation of interpretive style as the students increasingly learn as they play the interpretation of phrases. However, once in the concert venue, although this eye-contact is maintained between the musicians, there is a studied avoidance of eye contact with the audience. How very different from the Langas and Manganiyars!

To recapitulate, I know that through my shared experiences with the musicians I have met through my work I have acquired responsibilities. So far I have not worked with anyone who did not ask me to include their tradition in the museum at some point. In fact, contrary to the usual preconceptions that we should perhaps be returning our objects to the countries of origin, I have only ever been asked to visit and collect more so that the representation can be more complete. This was certainly the case with the Rajasthanis, who have asked me to visit them so that they could help me make a fine collection 'before it is too late'.

My responsibility is to share my memories and my enjoyment of the musics I have heard, to make use of the images and recordings in such a way that they might give pleasure to the museum visitor and perhaps, through the medium of that pleasure, ensure that the music and thence musician is not forgotten. I suspect that for the musicians themselves it does not matter how I use the material, as long as it is done with sensitivity. The important thing is that their music is there, within the context of the museum exhibition which chronicles the world's musicianship and instruments. For them one of the central points is to be heard, if possible to be seen, in a museum that is a part of an Institution of which they had all heard, the University of Oxford.

Here I come to that other issue: how does my position as a curator in a museum of the University shape the material I am able to record and the contacts I am able to make? Certainly Oxford is known wherever I have gone, and whoever has come to the Museum has been very aware of the fact that they are coming to an institution which is famous. When Dembo Konteh and Kausu Kouyaté, the kora players, visited Oxford to give a concert in 1985, I took them to see the Holywell Music Room so that they could check the balance of the acoustics and do some practice before their concert.[15] As they walked in I could see that they did not look very impressed with the old building. I explained that this was the first public Music Room in Europe, built in 1748, and that it was the hall where Handel and Haydn had performed when they visited Oxford. Their reaction was to bend to touch the staging lovingly, unpack their koras and sit at once to sing a praise song.

This brings me back to the museum. Over the twenty-five years I have been at the Pitt Rivers, and particularly since 1995 when I was appointed curator of the Bate Collection and of the musical collections in the Pitt Rivers Museum, I have had special opportunities to work with musicians and performers from all parts of the world. My 'field' is indeed here. It is unique, as no other post has quite the layers of responsibilities of university teaching and work with schools as well as with the public. Nor are there many other collections world-wide which cover such a broad geographical area, most being limited to the European tradition or to ethnology. Within my work I have both the responsibility of curation and description of the musical objects I collect. Here too I am at a fixed point which is visited by public and artist and it is important to have someone here to observe the encounters.

As well as an observer I also must be a mediator, or rather a conduit, between one tradition and another. This is not so necessary between the musicians themselves from different traditions – in the main they are only too keen to learn and exchange musical ideas and will communicate without the need for any common language other than their musics. But the two groups I must mediate between are the musicians and the museum-visiting public. Whereas in popularist terms music is the universal language, it still needs interpretation to get beyond the superficial presentation of the three-dimensional objects in a museum case and the music used as illustrative examples of them.

Music is powerful and evocative. It takes time to speak for itself, however, and listening to a piece in full can never be hurried. Although the Museum takes its name from the idea that it should be home to the Muses, it is the muse Euterpe, music's muse, who finds her place there the least comfortable. This muse needs the conviviality of human interaction. It is in this environment, both working within it and collecting for it, that I have found my field and here, just as in any live musical performance, I have to observe the musicians' lead to represent them as they would wish and the visitors' reactions to understand what it is they need explained. Through the museum gallery I must learn how to build a bridge between the two. Perhaps it is as a music curator that I can most richly understand the resonances of the phrase 'music when soft voices die vibrates in the memory'.

NOTES

1. The two earliest publications of this new field, which appeared in 1885, highlight the areas of greatest interest to this emerging discipline (Adler 1885, Ellis 1885).

2. The anthropological school was led by Alan Merriam and the musicologists by Mantle Hood; this history is summarised in Myers 1993: 7.

3. The musician has another level of 'translation' with which to contend, in addition to the multifaceted problems of talking about an observed performance, understanding those who talk about their own performance and giving due weight to the language through which the associated concepts are communicated. This is explored by Ardener 1971: ix-cii and Hymes 1971: 47–93.

4. These festivals carry on the traditions of the nineteenth-century World Fairs. For an analysis of the problems of regional ethnography see Dresch 1992: 17–36.

5. For a description of the acquisition of musical skill and a consequent deeper knowledge of the tradition from which it came, together with an analysis of the reception of these skills see Rice 1997: 101–20.

6. The problems of the analysis of events are discussed in Ardener 1989: 86–104.

7. It did not surprise me that it was song which would form the centre of their attention. Songs have a double resonance, in having both text and music. However, it has often intrigued me that I never had to open a session by being called upon to sing an English song. According to many accounts the best way to encourage the singing of songs is to start off by singing oneself.

8. It is a rare CD recording that does not acknowledge Duran's help in its production: see Toumani Diabate, Kaira, HNCD 1338, Yasimika, Jali Musa Jawara HNCD 1355, and Soubindoor, Jali Musa Jawara, WCD 008.

9. It is not a problem that belongs merely to the ethnomusicologist. The tensions involved in talking about performance are commonplace in the ballet world; Wulff 1998: 104–20. The layers of description of events in media reportage not only explain but add layers of interpretation; see Pink 1998: 121–40.

10. For the problems of talking about music, see Becker 1995: 349–64.

11. See Wulff 1998 for an example of the different modes of description.

12. 'The modern concert hall is built on the assumption that a musical performance is a system of one-way communication, from composer to listener through the medium of the performers' (Small 1998: 26).

13. The Economist review of 'Great pianists of the 20th Century' comments upon this: 'A generation raised on the glossy perfection of records will not tolerate mistakes, no matter how engrossing the overall performance may be' (*Economist* 1999: 101).

14. In this the museum visit itself fits firmly into a tradition in which performance always has a beginning, middle and end. For a description of the Wayang and its contrasting practice see Becker 1995: 23–70.

15. The kora is a stringed instrument, technically described as a harp-lute, found in Senegal, the Gambia and Mali.

Chapter 11

TRYING TO GET THERE:

APPROACHES TO INDONESIA

R.H. Barnes

Any formula for the writing of ethnography spells sterility
P. Kaberry in *Man and culture,* 1957

Evans-Pritchard once wrote, 'Anyone can produce a new fact; the thing is to produce a new idea' (1973: 3). He also said, 'One is burdened for the rest of one's life with what one has recorded, imprisoned in the prison one has built for oneself' (ibid.: 12). Evans-Pritchard's problem was that he felt that he would never be able to publish all of his notes in his lifetime, which was true. 'I have had much, too much, field-experience, and I have long ago discovered that the decisive battle is not fought in the field but in the study afterwards' (ibid.: 3). My own experience, I am afraid, has been the opposite. I have been able to do far less field research than I desired, and I am quite uncertain that I will ever again be able to carry out an extended period of intensive research in the field, but I am now at that point in my career where the attempt to do so must be my first priority.

When I found that the year of sabbatical leave which I took in 1993–4 was approaching, I had to decide whether to spend it by extending the research in Lamalera, which had begun with a brief visit in 1970 and continued with longer trips in 1979 and 1982, or to write up the already extensive notes which had accumulated by then. Being afraid that if I did more fieldwork there, I would never publish more than a few articles from it, I decided that it was more responsible to spend the year writing the book which appeared in 1996. That book proved to be considerably longer than the publisher and most readers wanted.

The climate for the kind of research I want to undertake has deteriorated dramatically on almost all fronts. Setting aside facetious popular books mocking serious field research, and others suggesting that it may even be immoral, the policies of the research funding bodies in Britain have turned decisively against empirical research in anthropology carried out in poor and remote parts of the world like eastern Indonesia. It remains to be seen whether it will prove possible to find funding for a new project in the Flores Timur and Alor regencies lasting as long as two years. It also remains to be proven that it would be possible to get leave from the University to be away for that period, although that may be less unlikely. Then there is the difficulty of getting research permission from the Indonesian authorities, which is absolutely indispensable for research lasting for more than a few weeks. I have done so three times in my life. In the first case, due to the assistance of the Mayor of Braunschweig, Germany, it came after the delay of only a few months. In the second two cases, it came at the last minute after a delay of nearly two years at a moment when, air tickets booked and paid for, it appeared that I would have to cancel the trip and to return grants in full. A financial intervention in Jakarta by Professor James Fox righted the situation in the third case, while that service was provided in the second case by representatives of the World Wildlife Fund for whom I was doing the research. The problem lies not with the Indonesian Institute of Sciences, who are courteous and cooperative, but with the fact that such applications have to be vetted by the Internal Security Service (*Bakin*) who can be extremely slow. Added doubt derives from the present economic turmoil in Indonesia and the accompanying political uncertainty as well as the continuing social unrest.

My D.Phil. research in Kédang lasted nineteen months, from October 1969 to June 1971, with a brief break in which I visited Lamalera and travelled on Flores. My research in Lamalera amounts to somewhat over nine months accumulated from visits of varying length in 1970, 1979, 1982, 1987 and 1995. My wife, Ruth Barnes, and I spent two months in each of the summers of 1995 and 1996 tracing the steps of the museum ethnographer Ernst Vatter, who with his wife Hanna Vatter travelled widely in the area in 1928 and 1929, collecting information for his book *Ata Kiwan* (1932). We were able to visit for the first time many places we had previously heard of on our visits to Flores, Adonara, Solor, Pantar and Alor, greatly expanding my firsthand understanding of the general region and increasing my awareness of the questions that might be asked of it, as well as seeing old friends and making new ones. From these trips, I would like to draw the material for a new research project on the economic interconnections, both in the past and in the present, within the region (defined as the East Flores and Alor regencies, although of course the economic ties reach far away to Java, Sulewesi, Malaysia, Sarawak, Tewau, Kalimantan, the Moluccas, New Guinea, Timor, and Australia). I do not want to do yet another village study, so that I would have to expect a good deal of travel, but I would hope to establish a base, probably on Adonara. Perhaps also worth mentioning as not entirely irrelevant is three weeks spent visiting various Aboriginal peoples of Taiwan with David Faure in September 1997, since Taiwan is the original homeland of the Austronesian language family which includes Bahasa Indonesia, Lamaholot and Kédang.

Evans-Pritchard's description of preparation and practice of fieldwork at Oxford was in part true when I arrived as a student in 1966. The first year was spent taking the Diploma in Anthropology, later renamed as a Master's degree. I was required to take the Diploma course, even though I had a B.A. in anthropology when I arrived. Whether that was good for me or not, we would not be allowed to impose this requirement today on anyone with a straight undergraduate degree in social anthropology from a British university, and only do so in cases where there are doubts about the extent and relevance of a student's anthropological training in a foreign university. Often they are best advised to take the Master's level course nevertheless, and it is quite usual for them to want to and even insist on doing so. So I have spent pleasant years having weekly anthropological conversations with people who are already perfectly adequately trained, but actually want to know what my opinions are. The next stage was to survey the available literature on the potential field site in a B.Litt. thesis of between fifty and a hundred thousand words written in a year or so. This requirement has been whittled down to the M.Phil. thesis or the assessment paper of about thirty thousand words. Finally the student was expected to spend at least two years in the field. Evans-Pritchard spoke enticingly of a break for a period after the first year to order one's notes. In fact, as he acknowledged, this pattern was rarely possible (Evans-Pritchard 1951: 76, 1973: 10). Recently, funding authorities have put so much pressure on the universities to reduce the amount of time students spend on their doctorates that it has become virtually impossible for them to stay more than a few months in the field, to the great loss of the profession and of the students themselves.

The reason that this loss is so serious is that in order to do good ethnography you often need to learn languages, which if they are not recorded or are poorly recorded you cannot do in the brief time now available, and therefore you can do no worthwhile work. Among the reasons Evans-Pritchard gave for learning languages is that, 'to understand a people's thought one has to think in their symbols. Also, in

learning the language one learns the culture and the social system'
(Evans-Pritchard 1951: 79). 'The most difficult task in anthropological fieldwork is to determine the meaning of a few key words, upon an
understanding of which the success of the whole investigation
depends' (ibid.: 80). Of course, there are anthropologists who do not
bother to learn even the national language and who hire anthropologically trained assistants to collect the information for them. Those
who use this method are best advised to acknowledge that the ethnography is not their own. The result is that the ethnography they publish
is no more competent than are the assistants and that is something on
which it is difficult to get an independent check. It is also difficult to
'get away from servants and regular informants from time to time, and
meet people who do not know you' who might be able to give you a different assessment of your knowledge of the culture and, if you had
acquired any, of your language skills (Evans-Pritchard 1973: 12).

My own D.Phil. followed the sequence outlined by Evans-Pritchard,
except for the absence of an extended break. I wrote a B.Litt. thesis on
the available literature on the peoples speaking the Lamaholot language, most of it in German or Dutch, which I had to learn to read.
There was a grammar of Lamaholot in German (Arndt 1937), but no
dictionary, as there still is not. The principal authorities were Ernst
Vatter and the mission anthropologist Paul Arndt. Both of these men
spent their time in the Lamaholot area travelling widely (the opposite
of my subsequent experience until 1995) collecting comparable information in many different places, but staying only briefly in any one
place. The result was that in my B.Litt. I could not go into any depth on
a particular topic, but instead I was able to trace the considerable variation there is on any given theme within this language area. So I
started with a knowledge of variety, rather than of an integrated func-
tional whole. Anyway, I already knew that 'Malinowski's thesis that
cultures are functionally integrated is no more true, empirically speaking, than Hitler's thesis that Germans are the master race' (Leach
1957: 124). Although there were many more openly avowed func-
tionalists around when I started my undergraduate education in
anthropology than there are now, they never persuaded me, any more
than did the behaviourists, in their insistence that we should avoid all
vocabulary that implied that people can think.

Having prepared myself for field research in the Lamaholot area, I
went just one language area too far to the east and ended up in
Kédang. I had had the opportunity to seek the advice of the missionary
Willem van Leur, then on leave in Holland. He told me that I should go
to Kédang because the people were very nice there, which they are.
There was almost no information at all available about Kédang, which
is regarded as odd and apart even in the local region. No matter how

much of an idiot I was, there seemed a good chance that I would discover something new, which I think in general I did. It was even reported by one authority, erroneously, that their language belonged to the Papuan family. I did not know what I would find there; certainly there was no indication that they would have a social structure relevant to the analytic concerns of my supervisor, although there was such evidence for the Lamaholot. The language then was also completely unrecorded. I arrived in Indonesia unable to speak Bahasa Indonesia, the national language, and arrived in Kédang with a command of only a few words of Bahasa Indonesia and unable to speak Kédang. I had to learn Bahasa Indonesia, not only to cope with the authorities and to travel, but as the sole possible way into Kédang.

Because I wanted to study the traditional religion, rather than the Catholicism of the majority, I was kindly placed by the village head of Leuwayang up the mountain in the old village, where my daily companions were mostly much older than I and many of them, including my host, monolingual. Had it not been for a wonderful friend, Molan Bala, who had a smattering of Bahasa Indonesia, I do not know how I should have acquired such Kédang as I did. Certainly the Indonesian I learned from him in the process did not pass muster when, at the end of the first year, I travelled in what by then looked to me the much more cosmopolitan Flores. So I worked harder on that. At least there were grammars and dictionaries. But somehow I had learned a good deal about the culture in that first year, which I consolidated in the second. At one time I thought I could speak Kédang, although there were those who had their doubts and my active range was limited. My active command of the language has since lapsed, but my passive command has expanded. You might wonder how that could be, given that I have made only brief visits to Kédang since I left in 1971 and there is nowhere else you can speak the language. The answer is that first of all, Ursula Samely conducted research for her Frankfurt Ph.D. in Leuwayang and published the results as a grammar of the Kédang language, which clarified speech patterns I understood, but was unable to account for in grammatical terms. The second reason is that after I compiled all of my Kédang vocabulary and correlated it with hers, she took the results to Kédang, and later Jakarta, and worked through it with Guru A. Sio Amuntoda, who, except for a Muslim teacher who worked in Kalikur briefly, was the first school teacher in Kédang, and M. Suda Apelabi, who was the village head of Leuwayang when I was there first. They have carefully annotated and added to our material, and we have been correcting our records and corresponding with them about questions which arise in that process. We have now brought what will be a joint dictionary to a very advanced stage. The three weeks I recently spent in Kédang in 1998 helped revive both my active and passive command of the language.

Recently, I have been testing the dictionary by translating into Indonesian stories and other linguistic material collected in Kédang in 1947 by the missionary Karl van Trier and passed on to Samely after his death. I was told that he had done work on the Kédang language by Guru Sio and others when I arrived in Kédang, but apart from a brief vocabulary he had left there, I had no access to it. I corresponded with him from the field (he was then on Java), but he replied with a polite note telling me that what he had was of no real value. Of course, it was for him to decide whether he wanted to share his unpublished work with a complete stranger, but I now see that I would have been deeply indebted to him had he decided otherwise, for he had established for himself a fairly complete record of standard vocabulary, and moving around on patrol in 1947 he was able to record a far more extensive range of texts than I was able to manage, isolated and stationary up in the mountain in 1969–71. He also worked out the phonemic pattern (there are four different *e*'s and two versions of all the other vowels) and spelled the language with fair accuracy, which is as good as anyone else including my Kédang friends have until recently been able to do. If the question of intellectual property rights can be suitably sorted out, it may prove useful to arrange to have this material published sometime. The consolation for not having had access to van Trier's material when I was in the field is that it can now provide an independent confirmation of the information we have collected, which it does to a very considerable extent.

In 1987, while making a television film in Lamalera, I listened as the Bishop of Larantuka, during the ordination of a local man as a priest, praised two of my friends for their pioneering work in education. When two people who have done you the courtesy of helping you and who started out modestly become admired and regarded with affection in the wider local region, I suppose it is well to say so and to express gratitude for their help – with language, stories and wonderful jokes in Guru Sio's case and with local history in the case of Guru A. Bumi Liliweri. By the same token, Om Suda not only took a very naive and helpless young couple (my wife was with me) in hand and did an outstanding job in making understandable to the village why we were there and in keeping us safe and, at the same time, relatively harmless, when even he could not be expected to fully understand this totally novel attention being given his people, but he showed me a level of administrative skill in running the village government that I have seldom seen matched in academic departments.

Our friends in Leuwayang invited Samely and myself to return in July 1998 to study a revived harvest ritual now conducted by the community as a whole on an ecumenical basis. When my wife and I were there for a few days in August 1996, we found that the distance between Kédang and the main town Lewoleba, which used to take us two days by foot, could be covered in three and a half hours by truck. A black-topped road runs from Lewoleba all the way to Wairiang on the east coast of Kédang via the south side of the mountain. The Dutch-constructed road along the north had not yet been black-topped, and I was astonished to realise when we were (slowly) driving over it that I recognised every stone in it from the days when I walked over it on my way to market. By 1998 this stretch of road, still not black-topped, had been widened in two constricted places, so that vehicles could use it without obstruction. As a result there were five locally owned minibuses (*bemo*) in Leuwayang providing daily passenger service to the port of Balaurin and to the administrative and commercial centre of Lewoleba.

My trips to Lamalera have always been too brief to permit much in the way of acquisition of active knowledge of Lamaholot. The absence of a dictionary has also been a hindrance. However, Gregorius Keraf's grammar of the language as it is spoken in Lamalera has been a big help (Keraf 1978). I have compiled for my own use a series of Lamaholot vocabularies from Keraf's grammars, the works of Arndt and other sources. So there is hope that if I do further field research I will be able greatly to improve my knowledge of Lamaholot. At any event, when I have time to work on it, I am already improving my passive knowledge. Karl-Heinz Kohl has made available an extensive vocabulary collected by him in Belogili, East Flores, which the linguist Karl-Heinz Pampus is using as the basis for his work on an eventual dictionary of the East Flores dialect of Lamaholot. There are other sources as well, including work by local linguists. Among them are the accession notes made by Ernst Vatter on his extensive ethnographic collection, brought together for the Frankfurt Ethnographic Museum. Ruth Barnes has recently completed a catalogue of this collection (in press); so these notes are now available as an electronic database. One of the facts that Arndt's work in particular demonstrates is that there is very great variation in speech practice from place to place within the Lamaholot region, even though the dialects remain mutually intelligible, a situation confirmed by Keraf.

No ethnography can be complete. This is a matter of principle, because life does not stop just because the ethnographer leaves the field. Evans-Pritchard acknowledged the shortness of his field experience among the Nuer and clearly stated that his sociology was inadequate (1940: 14). Malinowski even went to the extent of cataloguing all those weaknesses and shortcomings he thought he could find in his fieldwork notes, including those obvious everyday things that he forgot to write down (1935, vol 2: Appendix II 'Confessions of Ignorance and Failures'). Whether anyone ever pays attention to these concessions to

the inevitable and obvious is another matter. It is certainly the case
that there is more important ethnography to be done in Kédang and in
Lamalera. As a matter of principle there always will be so long as they
are inhabited, no matter how much and how good the existing ethnography may be. It is also true that the interests and personality of the
individual anthropologist will have a lot to do with what comes out of
his or her research. Evans-Pritchard discussed this matter cogently:

> Since in anthropological fieldwork much must depend, as I think we would
> all admit, on the person who conducts it, it may well be asked whether the
> same results would have been obtained had another person made a partic-
> ular investigation. This is a very difficult question. My own answer would
> be, and I think that the evidence we have on the matter shows it to be a cor-
> rect one, that the bare record of fact would be much the same, though
> there would, of course, be some individual differences even at the level of
> perception.... But while I think that different social anthropologists who
> studied the same people would record much the same facts in their note-
> books, I believe that they would write different kinds of books. Within the
> limits imposed by their discipline and the culture under investigation
> anthropologists are guided in choice of themes, in selection and arrange-
> ment of facts to illustrate them, and in judgement of what is and what is
> not significant, by their different interests, reflecting differences of person-
> ality, of education, of social status, of political views, of religious convic-
> tions, and so forth.... The personality of an anthropologist cannot be
> eliminated from his work any more than the personality of an historian
> can be eliminated from his (Evans-Pritchard 1951: 83–84).

He also commented that, 'To some extent at any rate, people who
belong to different cultures would notice different facts and perceive
them in a different way.' He then stated that the facts recorded in our
notebooks are not social facts but ethnographic facts, by which I think
he means that the selection and interpretation that produces them are
shaped by the culture of the ethnographer (ibid.: 85).

I have always agreed with these views and see no reason to change
my mind. In fact, we can regard this situation as a good thing. It would
be terrible if an ethnographer could simply 'do' a people and move on
with no further need for revision, amplification or change of perspective. All ethnography, including the best, should be read as provisional
and as probably containing a certain amount of error. After all, it is
possible that even the people you get your information from may occasionally make a mistake. I am not a particularly reliable informant
about my own culture, although I suppose I could be of some use to an
anthropologist who took care to talk to others too. However, the work
on the Kédang dictionary gives me confidence that apart from the
occasional vulgar error, my description of Kédang life is not greatly
deviant from the actual situation. I think that ethnography should be

read critically, as the historian would read documents (a position I share with Mauss; see Barnes 1984: 18). My experience in using the works of Vatter and Arndt in the field is that they were generally pretty good at the things they did, but that they left out an awful lot. You do not often catch them in an error of fact, although that occasionally happens, but no great harm is done if you can correct the record.

It was with a critical spirit that I investigated two great early classics on Omaha social organisation. By critical spirit, I do not mean lack of appreciation or sympathy. It should be remembered that most of the early ethnographers at the Bureau of American Ethnology wanted to spend as much time in the field as they could, but for political reasons were harnessed to Washington and the Handbook of American Indians project (Hinsley 1981: 156–7). J. Owen Dorsey worked with the Ponca and the Omaha in their own languages. He presents a model of intensive field research in the medium of the local language often ignored in the British literature on the origin of modern field methods. It was his misfortune that he died young, before he could complete publication of his research. Perhaps it was also a misfortune to his reputation that John Wesley Powell insisted on writing L.H. Morgan's sociological theories into his monographs (for background, see Barnes 1990).

There are various implied criticisms of Dorsey in Fletcher and La Flesche's later monograph on the Omaha. Elsewhere they even claim that his numerous inaccuracies arose from his 'lack of a clear understanding of the Omaha language which he persistently used while carrying on his inquiries' and to 'his inability to distinguish between information honestly given him by serious-minded persons and misleading information given in jest by mischief-loving individuals'. In other words, he should have used English alone and listened only to some approved Omaha, in which case for both reasons he would have been captive of a specific Franco-Omaha faction within the tribe. Far from silencing the native voice, Dorsey published many vernacular texts with interlinear translations, and he carefully recorded the divergent views of his informants (Barnes 1984: 18–20). In fact it was the extent to which real Omaha personalities come through the published literature and documentation on the Omaha that attracted me to look at them again in the hope of answering certain analytical questions posed by Lévi-Strauss. I think I did manage to answer them and the answer turned on the personalities of certain Omaha and the personal relations among them. In any case, there must be some reason that so many Omaha asked Dorsey to write letters for them to their friends and relatives *in Omaha*. I am sure that anyone who wished to continue Dorsey's unfinished project to publish an Omaha dictionary would find things to correct, but I do not see how they could fail to be indebted to him. In general, I found an encouraging degree of mutual confirmation in these rival publications, and it is usually possible to decide why such discrepancies as may be found occur. In other words, for those who are willing to make the effort, the ¬ecord for the Omaha at least is more transparent than some fashions in anthropology would admit was possible.

I do not think that it is right to say that an anthropologist should not generalise about institutions and collective representations. For example, the Kédang have patrilineal descent groups and practise a form of asymmetric marriage alliance. The history of anthropological thought on both these issues is highly relevant to understanding their life. The same is true in most Lamaholot areas. Within these generalisations, the ways in which both institutions are put into practice vary enormously. In addition, in eastern Adonara descent groups seem to disappear. In the extreme west of the Lamaholot-speaking area, descent seems to be traced matrilineally, although we need ethnographic investigation to confirm this situation. Nor do I think that you cannot compare. Here is a comparison: the patrilineal descent groups and marriage institutions of the Omaha and Kédang are so different that they have little in common (see Barnes 1974, 1984).

To my regret, there is virtually no documentation on Kédang history; so there is little that one can say about it. My information came almost exclusively from intensive field research, although Guru Bumi did give me a copy of the oral history that he wrote down. Recently Ursula Samely has passed on to me an account of Kédang history written by the Rian Baraq (ruler) of Kédang some decades ago, which might someday be worked on (Sarabiti 1938). It contains the unexpected claim that Lamalera owes the Rian Baraq tribute in the form of a whale. If so, this would be news to Lango Fujo clan (lord of the land of Lamalera) and the Raja of Larantuka (to whom they owed allegiance). I did no field research among the Omaha, and my work was exclusively based on published work and on documents which had to be critically assessed in the fashion of historians. In fact, to judge by reviews, or their absence, it seems to have been more enthusiastically received by historians than anthropologists, who have generally ignored it. Lamalera is situated somewhere in between these extremes. I have done a certain amount of research there, and there is a certain amount of documentation on Lamalera and even more on regional history. In fact Lamalera history, in this sense, goes back further than that of the Omaha – to the early part of the seventeenth century – while the first mention of the Omaha comes in 1673–4. But there is virtually no further information on Lamalera until late in the nineteenth century, while Omaha history is fairly rich from the end of the eighteenth century. These circumstances have done much more to shape the three very different contributions to ethnography I have written, than my own biases.

According to Evans-Pritchard, 'An anthropologist has failed unless, when he says goodbye to the natives, there is on both sides the sorrow of parting' (1951: 79). There are funny, if sad, stories of Elsie Clews Parsons and Franz Boas being thrown out by their hostess at Laguna Pueblo. Parsons had told the woman that Parsons' friends were foolish, and the woman interpreted that to mean that she was foolish (Hare 1985: 150). Not everything goes well in the field. Anthropologists make mistakes, breach standards of decorum, and can be both moody and demanding. They can be very awkward to have around sometimes. Nevertheless, the people I have lived with have almost always politely and firmly put me back on course when I have gone wrong – indeed, some of my most embarrassing mistakes have been the most revealing incidents in the field from the point of view of research discoveries. I suppose that people can survive without my being around, but I have found many friends happy to see me and anxious to talk on my returns; and I have benefited from much spontaneous kindness. My wife and I were childless when we left Kédang in 1971, causing much concern. When we returned to Lembata in 1979, we took our daughter and infant son to Kédang and up the mountain to show them that we were capable. The children were greatly appreciated. It was certainly the first time that the people had seen blond, blue-eyed children; and they would never stop touching their hair. Because our son was only five months old at the beginning of that trip, we took a basket of sufficient size and shape with us to serve as a bed and as a carrier as we moved around. When the motorboat pulled up in the breakers at the beach in Lamalera, and we had to hand our goods down to the men ferrying people ashore in small, unstable sampans, I had to warn the man I was handing this basket to that my son was in it so that he should be careful. That comment caused general surprise and wonderment, which he reminded me of when in 1995 we brought our fully-grown children back to the village. The women, Maria Korohama, Katarina Sefai Keraf and Maria Belikolong, who had cared for the children on two trips, keeping them fed, well and protected from the spirits, could not believe that they had become so big. Petrus Hidang and his wife Mama Tore were pleased once again to be able to be photographed with them. Because they have lived on the island, a legend has grown up that they were born there, and they are widely referred to by the names Ina Lembata and Jan Lembata (Lembata is the name of the island). Though essentially a Dutch name, Jan is a commonplace Christian name in the region and Ina has the characteristic that it is a common word meaning mother which is used as a given village name for women, factors which link them even more closely with the locality. However, they regret that my children have lost the small Indonesian vocabulary they once possessed, and the children were missed everywhere in 1996 and 1998 when they did not accompany us.

Anthropologists and their families do not last long as legends. Of course I have met a lot of people recently who had never heard of me. That did not stop them from being courteous to me and my family. In 1996 it was still possible to find people who remembered Ernst Vatter and his wife sixty-seven years after they left the area. Vatter was remembered as being extremely hard-working, while a descendant of a former Kakang (district head) of Pamakayo, Solor, remembers Hanna Vatter, whom he met when he was a small boy, with affection. He told us how he helped her after she fell on the beach in front of Pamakayo while taking one of the pictures included in *Ata Kiwan*. Others whom we met remember stories their parents had told them about the Vatter visit. But this is a story which should be told by my wife (Ruth Barnes in press).

I have been asked how I did my research in the field. The answer is probably the one that most ethnographers would give. I listened to people, especially when they were telling me something they thought was important, and I occasionally asked for clarification. Whenever something special was happening, I tried to be on hand. About some matters, genealogies for example or economic data, I asked directed questions. But most of my information came in piecemeal in what were essentially casual conversations. The pieces eventually fell into patterns.

The return to Kédang in 1998 after nearly thirty years was a remarkable experience. We witnessed two ceremonies which did not take place during our first trip. One was an annual village 'birthday' which was an innovation of the 1980s and which has developed into a public display of traditional songs, dances and crafts, quite suitable for tourists, although apart from ourselves none were present. A frequently reiterated theme during these performances was that of restoring and revivifying local culture. The other was a revived harvest ceremony and recitation of the genealogies of the clans, which extended over three days in the site of the 'old village' high up the mountain. This ceremony was reintroduced in the 1970s and at first was (so I am told) a fairly perfunctory affair conducted by a single priest. The ceremony now takes up the energies of three men and various assistants, as well as elders of all the clans, and lasts for three exhausting days and nights. In many respects, this ceremony in its present form is an innovation too, although it is deemed to be traditional and certainly expresses traditional Kédang culture. While modern trappings such as video recorders and electric generators have become part of the environment, themes which were important to record in 1969–71 are still as important today. Clans, marriage alliance and bridewealth, for example, are still prominent in conversations and daily affairs. In 1998 I was frequently reminded that certain things (house rafters, betel nut sections and *sirih* peppers offered to guests et cetera) must be odd in number, while certain ritual actions must be done four times. I have given a good deal of attention to this opposition between odd and even numbers in my writings on Kédang. Although I had never seen the ceremony before, I knew what to make of the fact that Ledo Kewa danced four times around the new temple (*huna hale werun*) that was being consecrated with a sacrifice before beheading a goat with a single blow. I did not have to be told that the direction in which he danced around it corresponded to the rule *wana pan* or 'travel to the right' which is also exemplified by the way the wood from which it was constructed was oriented. I also understood that the man who grabbed the goat carcass and ran with it around the building smearing blood on the bases of each of the house posts was also travelling to the right. The chants recounting the mythical or cosmological aspects of the genealogies had to be repeated four times, which considerably lengthened the process. Some things do not change.

Given the highly unusual circumstances Indonesia found itself in during 1997 and 1998, some comment about how they affected people in Kédang, and indeed the region in general, should perhaps be made. The circumstances were the collapse of the Indonesian economy and a sharp decline in value of the national currency, the fall of the government as a consequence, and independently the disruption to normal weather patterns due to the El Niño effect. In some areas, particularly along the coasts, crops failed completely as the rains stopped just before they bore fruit. This effect was selective, and most areas had good harvests. The extreme east and the south of Kédang experienced the loss of crops, but villages around Leuwayang on the north coast had no such trouble. However, because the rains continued unusually long into the period of the normal dry season, people were afraid that the rains would be disrupted in the coming rainy season. Because these were rural communities providing their own food, and because many people grew some cash crops destined for the export market, they were somewhat insulated from the worst effects of the collapse of the national economy and the rupiah. Still, many manufactured goods had become prohibitively expensive. The change of government had brought with it nationally a much less repressive political climate, and people were talking about national and local politics with an openness that I had never experienced before. They were generally very well informed too, because they regularly listened to the Indonesian language broadcasts of foreign news services. Despite the misfortunes, Leuwayang was plainly more prosperous than when I first went there. After we were through in Kédang, I had the good fortune of spending an intense week of travel in East Timor, organised for me by my former student Father Filomeno Abel, SJ and his friends. This was my first trip to East Timor and an opportunity to witness at first hand the consequences of the political and diplomatic position in which the country currently finds itself.

The events that have led on from my decision to go to Kédang in 1969 and subsequently to work in Lamalera have meant that various other people have been influenced to some extent or another by the resulting publications, as of course have I by those of my predecessors. The first book to appear from the work in Lamalera was my wife's account of Lamalera textiles (Ruth Barnes 1989). Stefan Dietrich's account of colonialism and missions on Flores (Dietrich 1989) made use of my work in Kédang, while his Habilitationsschrift (1997) on the town of Larantuka has paid me the compliment of frequent reference to my work on Lamalera. Ursula Samely went to Kédang to study the grammar expressly because there existed an ethnography, while the language was unstudied. Penny Graham's studies in Lewotala, Flores, follow on from some work I published on Wailolong and her own Oxford M.Phil. thesis (Graham 1985, 1987, 1991). I have twice been visited in Oxford by the explorer Tim Severin, who was planning work in Lamalera, and others with research plans have contacted me from time to time, including quite recently. I have even had a small impact on zoology (Rudolph, Smeenk and Leatherwood 1997). The reason I bother to mention these facts is to show that their work and mine is not conducted in a situation of individual scholarly isolation, with no means of test or confirmation. The question whether ethnographic reports are arbitrary and beyond testing can be answered in these cases. They can and are being checked. So far no reason has appeared to panic. We seem to be seeing the same sorts of thing, within the range of empirical variation that exists in the area. The ethnographic record is accordingly much richer than it was when I was writing my B.Litt. thesis. That richness makes it that much easier to specify what the lacunae are. They are many. A great deal of work needs to be done, and no doubt will be. Certainly Lamalera is going to be studied and studied again over and over. Soon anyone who wishes to know will be told whether what I have had to say about the place holds up. Of course this expanding range of scholarship will make it that much easier for me to shift my focus from a village to a regional level; for I can benefit at least as much from the others as they may from me.

Chapter 12

THE FIELD AND THE DESK:

CHOICES AND LINKAGES

N.J. Allen

> Malinowskian fieldwork ... soon became the defining feature of social anthropology – though officially, at least, all investigators still aspired to contribute to a cross-cultural, comparative enterprise
>
> A. Kuper, 1997

An earlier draft of this paper was entitled 'The case against fieldwork', but that was ambiguous, grandiose and misleading. Ambiguous since it left open whether the paper would support the case against fieldwork or oppose it; grandiose in that it implied a claim to represent or oppose all those who have in some way or other raised objections to this research method; misleading in so far as it implied that I had made a special study of such objections.

In fact I am not against fieldwork as such. There is a place for it in anthropology and a very important place. What I am against is exaggerating that place, fetishing fieldwork, and turning it into the defining essence of the discipline. I am worried that this may be happening, and that if it does, it will damage the discipline by leading to a shrinkage of our proper intellectual ambitions. It is these ambitions that are the real point of the essay. If I am against the view that all anthropologists should always be contemplating past or future fieldwork, it is because I *favour* a pluralism in the practice of the discipline such that leaving fieldwork on one side remains a respectable option for those of us who choose it.

We all know nowadays that a writer's authority cannot be taken for granted. What qualifications do I have for writing about not doing fieldwork? For my D.Phil., around 1970, I did twenty months' fieldwork in the east of Nepal; then, when the opportunity of a sabbatical first presented itself, I did nine or ten months in 1981–3 in the Western Himalayas. But since I have done none for the last fifteen years, and have no plans to resume, perhaps my qualifications are adequate.[1] If the reader understands these facts as an 'admission', as something for which I am or ought to be apologising, then I have something definite to argue against. I should like to practise a discipline where they were understood as expressing simply one choice of method among others, a choice to be evaluated by its results.

A proportion of professional anthropologists are put off fieldwork not so much by the domestic disruption and general hassle it involves as by illness or other unpleasant or dangerous experiences. I have been lucky. My Nepalese fieldwork was very traditional, as I wanted it to be. I did it alone, my future wife, Sheila, only visiting me for six weeks. It involved learning what was essentially an unwritten 'tribal' Tibeto-Burman language, of which I published the first serious grammar. In the language I was able to record a whole corpus of mythology which, certainly at the time, seemed on the point of disappearing. I lived in a peasant household, surrounded by the beauties of the Himalayas. Thirty years later, it is easy to romanticise one's youth, and I should not gloss over the loneliness, anxieties and occasional tensions (I sometimes made the mistake of lending money). But overall it was a thoroughly rewarding experience for which I feel privileged and grateful. It has provided the basis for a dozen of my fifty or so articles, and may yet serve for other publications.

The Western Himalayan fieldwork in the early 1980s was a marvellous experience for a young family, and I cannot forget our first sight of the village of Bari in Kinnaur, to which the headman had so kindly invited us.[2] Situated around eight thousand feet, an hour's walk above the road, it lay amid apricot blossoms beneath extensive tracts of intact forest that extended up to the 'Alpine' meadows above twelve thousand feet (see Frontispiece). I have to admit (and here I *am* apologetic) that this fieldwork bore rather little direct fruit in terms of publication, useful though it has been for teaching and in other ways. But if the work was broken off before it reached a point with which I could be satisfied, it was not because the fieldwork itself was disagreeable.

Nor do I have any deep-lying moral or epistemological worries about fieldwork as such. As regards morality, I am thinking here of those, anthropologically informed or not, who see fieldwork as an exploitation of the personal kindness of informants or as an intrusion into their individual or collective privacy. For some politically sensitive critics the whole enterprise of ethnography reeks of neocolonialism. Communities everywhere, they will say, have the right to develop their own self-image and present themselves to outsiders as they see fit. Hence it is simply wrong for outsiders, on the basis of brief visits and primarily for the benefit of their own careers, to arrogate this right, and to represent the community according to some currently fashionable theory – and then to publicise the resulting image.

In the late 1990s such objections cannot be treated as negligible, but their force should not be overrated. They represent reasonable worries, but they can be broken down into discrete issues to which there are partial answers. If I did not think this, it would be hypocritical to continue in a career where it is often one's job to help or encourage students who are contemplating fieldwork. I do this happily, trusting and hoping that fieldwork, properly conducted, is a morally justifiable activity, as well as a recommendable career move for those with academic ambitions. As for my own ethnographic contributions, which are largely in the areas of language, myth and ritual, I suppose they scarcely raise interesting problems of this kind.[3]

In these postmodern times there may be some extreme epistemological relativists who think that fieldwork is theoretically impossible because the world of the other is simply inaccessible to the understanding of outsiders. This view is scarcely worth taking seriously, the best argument against it being the relativity of otherness. There is no cut-off point where otherness begins or ends. From the point of view of a male middle-class Oxfordian, if a Nepalese villager lives in an impenetrably alien world, what about a Sicilian or Orkney or Oxfordshire villager, or a middle-class neighbour in Oxford? The series ends in ego (or ego's consciousness), and the extreme relativist must become a total solipsist.

Choices

Thus, if I have done no fieldwork for fifteen years, it is not because I do not enjoy or approve of the activity, but rather a matter of priorities. Rightly or wrongly, I think I can contribute more to the discipline and to human understanding in other ways. It is a personal choice, and others will choose differently. But in order to weigh priorities, one needs an aim, which in this case implies a definition of social anthropology. I take it that our aim is to come to terms intellectually with the whole range of socio-cultural forms about which we can know. The definition may need some glossing.

Firstly, who exactly is attempting to achieve this aim? It is of course a collective undertaking by the discipline as a whole, and the individual researcher can do no more than try to contribute here and there within the field.

What is the point of the phrase 'come to terms with something intellectually'? Although encyclopaedic knowledge is by no means to be despised, the highest aim of a discipline cannot be to maximise the number of known facts within its remit, but rather to know what to make of them. The verbs 'understand' and 'explain' seem to me to stand a little too close to the facts. Quite often a discipline needs to operate at a more abstract level, for instance by considering how one could go about understanding or explaining if one chose to, or by identifying domains of knowledge that must provisionally be left to other disciplines or sub-disciplines. Sometimes one needs not so much to understand the facts as to understand what sorts of question have been asked of them and with what success. What concepts or models have proved helpful? How can facts from one area of global space-time be compared with those from another?

The expression 'socio-cultural form' is similarly intended to be somewhat abstract and thereby to avoid unwanted connotations of 'society' and 'culture' – both of which can be taken inappropriately as referring to entities that are essentially bounded and denumerable (as in 'how many cultures are present on this island?'). The expression covers the phenomena that fell within the domain of the *Année sociologique*, but simply to refer to 'social facts' might unnecessarily alienate those who, whether by prejudice or after reflection, consider themselves anti-Durkheimian.

The reference to the 'whole range' of knowable forms is meant to cover a number of different dimensions. Clearly it is intended to refer to variation in demographic scale, ranging from groups measured in tens and hundreds to contemporary global society. It refers to technological complexity from hunters and gatherers onwards, and to the temporal scale from the lower palaeolithic onwards. Less obviously perhaps, it refers to the range of rubrics such as religion, politics, economics, art, medicine, folklore and language.

There is nothing novel in this definition, but I wonder how many colleagues in practice think of the discipline in this way, and how often they do so. It seems to me that an alternative definition, much narrower, and more implicit than explicit, is gaining ground. Is not social anthropology often presented as the discipline whose practitioners conduct fieldwork and theorise about doing so? But to make fieldwork the defining feature of the discipline is to impoverish it in several ways. We risk committing ourselves to a definition that is unsustainable, and we risk losing touch with longer-term history – not to mention losing to other disciplines part of the audience who would otherwise turn to us.

There was a time when fieldwork was essentially the monopoly of anthropologists. Others, such as missionaries, administrators and travellers, sometimes studied and wrote about 'the customs of the natives', but it was only anthropologists who made it the central aim of their trips and were paid to do so. That time is long past. Fieldwork is now undertaken by a whole host of disciplines: sociologists, political scientists, students of religion, economists, geographers, linguists, not to mention oral historians, ethnoarchaeologists, and agriculturalists.[4] Among academics, anthropology has long ago lost its monopoly on the method, and it cannot hope to regain it.

But the problem goes deeper. It is not only academics who write about socio-cultural forms in different parts of the world. Virtually wherever the anthropologist goes, there will be a sprinkling, thick or thin, of local university graduates who were brought up in the area and know it well. Increasingly, their numbers will include writers (journalists, novelists, autobiographers and so on). They would not claim to 'do fieldwork', but they can draw on their own experience, relate it to what others have written, and produce their own accounts. Very possibly they have done a module or two of anthropology as undergraduates.

It used to be thought, and some no doubt still think, that anthropologists write better ethnography than locals, partly because they bring to bear the objectivity of outsiders, partly because they draw on the experience of previous generations of ethnographers and their explicit reflections on methods and pitfalls, partly because they are more sophisticated theoretically. But I wonder how confident we can be of such superiority, and how long it will endure. It seems to me that our claims to excellence are somewhat fragile, and may prove ever harder to substantiate. The advantages of the locals include easy long-term access to the field and native knowledge of the language; and objectivity is a matter of degree.

But this potential source of competition is not my real point. Given that anyone can live in a place, keep their eyes open, and ask questions about what seems interesting, the point is why anthropologists should even think they are special. The answer is that they bring to the field an anthropological education lacking in the non-anthropologist. No doubt the education includes formal instruction in 'fieldwork methods', but the main part of it, certainly at present, consists in exposure to thought addressing the aims of the discipline. It is this body of thought that gives the discipline its specificity, not the fieldwork itself. Useful though it is in the education of an anthropologist, fieldwork is too widespread a method and too imprecise a notion to give us an enduring identity.

As for history, most modern fieldworkers (though not all) will be interested in seeing the society they study not only synchronically as a more or less coherent world of ideas, but also as immersed in and growing from the processes of history. They are glad to draw on older ethnography, on oral history, on local archives or published historical work. But in so far as their main concern is to make something of their field notes, it is usually relatively recent history that will be relevant – say the last couple of centuries or less. History measured in millennia, let alone tens or hundreds of millennia, will seldom intrude. Palaeoanthropology is left to the biological anthropologists and the archaeologists, and the intermediate spans to the historians, if anyone. I return to this last point below in connection with the study of India and the Indo-Europeans.

But if we take seriously the definition offered above, or the coverage of the Royal Anthropological Institute, or the example of figures such as Mauss or Kroeber, this deeper historical perspective is very much part of the discipline. Socio-cultural forms from the past are as much our business as those of the present. It may sometimes be felt that whereas small-scale history is fine for anthropologists, world history is somehow contaminated by the ethnocentrism and errors of the Victorian evolutionists. But we are dealing with a continuum. The series leading from local history to national and continental histories does not cross some crucial threshold when it takes the next step to world history. Moreover, no one objects to world histories of population or technology, and if we as anthropologists do not tackle the world-historical questions about more centrally sociological phenomena, there are plenty of other disciplines that will be happy to cater to the public's curiosity, without being able to draw on relevant insights.

It is not only a matter of selling books. As a potential recruit to anthropology in the 1960s I was attracted partly because the subject would enable me to undertake exotic fieldwork, but partly too because it seemed to offer an environment in which, if I were lucky enough to have any ambitious theoretical ideas, I would be well placed to pursue them. Those were heady days when Lévi-Strauss talked of 'the structure of the human mind' (1970), but I suppose some students today have a similar combination of motives, whether or not they avow them, and they need to be encouraged.

It would be ridiculous to posit a sharp divide between micro and macro undertakings, between fieldwork as local, specialist and narrow, and theory as reaching out to broader and more exciting questions. Except perhaps for some applied anthropology, which has its own value system, and for the minority who aim to strike a purely literary and humanistic note, most fieldworkers try to make their field notes relate to some wider theoretical issue, and they may succeed. But the question then arises whether this combination is the most efficient way of pursuing the theoretical issues. The answer will depend on the issue in question. It is not obvious that all big anthropological questions will respond to fieldwork, either by one individual or by a group contributing to a collective volume. Certainly it is not obvious that fieldwork is the only way to tackle them, while it *is* obvious that fieldwork is extremely time-consuming. It is for the professional to choose how best to allocate their time, given the aims of the discipline and their own aptitudes and interests.

Linkages

In what follows I attempt an account of how one anthropologist, no longer a fieldworker, has tried to build on ethnography in addressing two large-scale questions. I wish I had as much published work to look back on as Mauss had at a similar age, when he composed the intellectual self-portrait that presumably helped him gain admission to the Collège de France, and whose translation I have recently been revising (Mauss 1998). But my aim is again not apologetic. It is to argue that, in this particular case, further fieldwork would not have been the best way to use expensive academic time.

In writing my pre-fieldwork B.Litt. thesis, responding to the interests of my supervisor Rodney Needham, I devoted a chapter to comparing a dozen kinship terminologies reported from along the Himalayas. Most of them belonged to the Tibeto-Burman language family, and of these some, such as Byansi, were of symmetrical prescriptive type. In other words, they showed the same semantic structure as the Dravidian terminologies of South India, and for the same reason – namely, that they expressed a rule prescribing marriage with the classificatory bilateral cross-cousin. As I eventually realised, close comparison between these terminologies and others of the same language family showed that symmetrical prescriptive was the basic type from which the others had diverged, and therefore the one that was probably present in the proto-language. Sometimes the divergence showed the influence of Indo-Aryan speaking neighbours, who lacked positive marriage rules and the corresponding semantics, and whose loan-words could be recognised as they infiltrated the old structure; but sometimes, as in Tibetan, the change was presumably endogenous. In any case, before the Indo-European speakers drove a wedge between the Himalayas and the rest of the subcontinent, Tibeto-Burman and Dravidian speakers apparently formed a vast geographical continuum using this one particular type of terminology.[5]

My own fieldwork contributed rather little data to this direction of interest. While trekking, both on a mountaineering expedition in Lahul and thereafter during the fieldwork proper, I took advantage of opportunities that arose to collect lists of kinship terms in various Tibeto-Burman languages. This was not done in the thorough manner recommended by Rivers (impractical while travelling), but simply by stringing together terms for primary relatives (as in 'What is your word for the husband of the sister of the father?'). Nonetheless, it was a useful exercise for thinking about prescriptive systems (the affinal equations of parent's sibling terms are in fact particularly important for the typological shifts that interested me). As it happened, the terminology of the Thulung Rai themselves had been so influenced by loan words from Nepali (an Indo-European language) that it was hard to collect clear information bearing on what it might once have been, and I did not long persist.[6] On the other hand, the fact that they, like several related peoples, claimed to descend from four proto-clans, set me thinking about fourfold social structures in general, and this indirectly fed into my interest in changes in kinship systems (as well as in origin myths).

Across the world, it seemed, there was evidence of symmetrical prescriptive terminologies changing to other types, but much less evidence, and less convincing, of changes in the opposite direction. So if terminologies such as Byansi did not derive from any attested type, how did they originate? Presumably from something typologically simpler. But numerous theorists, Mauss, Hocart and Granet among them, had emphasised how often one finds the assimilation of alternate generations, terminological equations being one mode of assimilation. Now the simplest symmetrical prescriptive terminologies have in the central three genealogical levels four terms per level, that is, two male-female pairs of terms. But if a terminology consistently equates alternate levels, it only needs to recognise two of them, one for even-numbered levels, one for odd. And if each level has only two pairs of terms, overall the terminology needs only four such pairs. Finally, if each male-female pair of terms is replaced by a single term, we have the ultimate 'rock bottom' four-term terminology.

If such a terminology is applied to the whole of society (as terminologies often are), it has interesting effects. Firstly, it generates an implicit four-section system in the Australian sense, bringing us back to quadripartite social structures. Secondly, it implies the impossibility of marriage (and potentially of sex) with all primary relatives or their classificatory equivalents, thereby relating to theories of incest. Thirdly, the whole structure rests neatly on two types of exchange: *within* generations, on the 'horizontal' exchange of siblings (I avoid sex-biased language), and *between* generations, on the 'vertical' exchange of children. In sum it seems to provide what is logically and anthropologically the simplest possible way to combine egocentric and sociocentric ways of ordering human relationships – though to grasp all the implications and possible variants may demand a certain effort (Allen 1998c). This approach reopens questions that L.H. Morgan asked in 1871 but answered wrongly, proposing as he did a starting point in primitive promiscuity and a Hawaiian or generational type of terminology. More recent writers have improved on Morgan, but none seems to me to hit all the nails on the head.

From a world-historical point of view one might want to move either backwards or forwards from this quadripartite or tetradic model. Looking back, one wonders how, simple though it may be, such a comprehensive organisational scheme could come into existence, there being nothing at all like it among nonhuman primates. Perhaps the origin lies in the splitting of the group *for other purposes* on those occasions of tribal effervescence to which Durkheim (following Mauss) called our attention (Allen 1998a). Perhaps too, child exchange was not just an abstract principle linking generation moieties, but also an event, realised at initiation, much as 'the exchange of women' is realised at weddings. These reflections – unabashedly speculative – were intended partly as an answer to the scientistically phrased speculations of biological anthropologists, who ignore some of the relevant ethnographic facts.

Looking forward, the tetradic model sketched above offers a starting point for thinking about kinship systems on a global historical scale. Questions arise about the rupture of the various types of equation present in the starting point and their replacement by various types of discrimination (of cognates from affines, lineals from collaterals, and so on); and equally, about the overruling of discriminations present in the starting point and their replacement by new types of equation (notably generational, Crow-Omaha and cognatic). In parallel with the changes in vocabulary one can envisage changing rules of marriage and recruitment, and changing sociocentric structures.

In spite of a common suspicion, it is not the case that verbal equations are somehow less real than marriage gifts, spread out for all to see. Naturally, working at this level of generality, one must abstract away from much of the richness of fieldwork material, from local ethnophysiological interpretations, from complications and anomalies, from the predictable gaps between models and reality, from individual agency and manipulation. Of course too, like any other theory, the claim that all attested kinship systems descend from realisations of tetradic models needs to be tested, and I have suggested some possible methods (Allen 1989). Until such testing proves the theory wrong, I would suggest that sceptics might propose and argue for alternatives. Or was Morgan's question somehow meaningless, or beyond the scope of human enquiry?

Fieldwork lies behind this sort of enquiry in obvious senses. Someone had to collect both the terminologies, without which typologies could not have been constructed and comparative work could not have started, and the evidence on assimilation of alternate genealogical levels (not, as it happens, a salient feature among Tibeto-Burmans). Potentially too, new or old fieldwork could invalidate the theory, for instance if unambiguous evidence were found of a society in the process of endogenously inventing a symmetrical prescriptive terminology, having previously had one of asymmetrical or nonprescriptive type. However, the propounder of a theory may not be the best person to attempt its invalidation, and I have not looked hard for such evidence. As for attempts to confirm it, or rather to assemble further evidence that fits it, in the first instance I suppose this could be done most economically in the library, no doubt close to a computer, not in the field. But there is no reason why it should not guide ethnographic enquiry, directing attention to types of equation and discrimination, and helping to avoid the straitjacket of synchrony.

About the same time as I became interested in the global history of kinship systems I also began studying Indo-European comparative mythology. Before visiting Nepal I had given little attention to myth, but the Thulung themselves regarded it as the core or essence of their traditional culture, and since I was making an effort at the language and was in general oriented towards 'salvage ethnography', it provided an obvious focus. The society had been deeply involved in processes of Hinduisation for at least two centuries (Allen 1997), and although no doubt at one time the myths served as a charter for everyday life or reflected its underlying ideological structures, such connections would have been very difficult to demonstrate in 1970. My thesis therefore concentrated on comparing Thulung myths with those of neighbouring and culturally related peoples. I had been encouraged to read Dumézil's *Mitra-Varuna* during my initial taught course in anthropology, but had found it extremely difficult to grasp. However, now that I was working on comparative mythology, I began buying Dumézil's works in the hope that their approach could be adapted to Tibeto-Burman material. My first thought was that since Himalayan groups tended to refer to four proto-clans, any pervasive ideological structures would probably be fourfold and not, as Dumézil argued for the Indo-European world, triadic.

When I left Durham, after nearly four years teaching in the Department of Anthropology, and returned to Oxford to a position specifically linked with South Asia and having a tradition of interest in Hinduism, I gradually came to see two things. One was the tremendous scope that existed for comparative work applying to Hinduism the language-family framework with which I had been experimenting in the Tibeto-Burman world and which Dumézil had used to found the new comparative mythology of the Indo-Europeans. It was an undertaking such as could only be attempted by someone with reasonable security, who could think in terms of decades of work. It was necessary to acquire a minimum of Sanskrit, revive my schoolboy Latin and Greek (dormant for a quarter century), and try to come to terms not only with the fifteen or twenty substantial volumes of the mature Dumézil but also with a considerable body of secondary literature – not to mention the primary literature, so far as was practical.[7] This was in addition to gaining some feel for mainstream Indian culture generally, both the conventionally anthropological present and recent past, and the conventionally Indological deeper past.

If I persisted in what might have seemed an excessively ambitious undertaking, it was because of the second thing that I saw, or thought I saw – namely that, both for the Hindus in particular and the Indo-Europeans in general, Dumézil's schema was too constricted. In conducting his comparative work, Dumézil again and again found manifestations of an abstract ranked triadic schema. Instantiated by the priests, warriors and producers of Hindu social ideology, the elements of the schema had come to be called the first, second and third function. But I was soon convinced that (as had been first suggested by two Celticists) the schema needed to be enlarged, so as to include at least a fourth function. Thereafter it took nearly a decade of hesitation before I accepted that it needed to be enlarged at both ends. The fourth function was made up of two half-functions, one at the top of the hierarchy, often transcendent, one at the bottom, present but somehow excluded. In the Indian case, to put it simply, the half-functions were represented by the king and by the serfs or outsiders. Many similar five-element structures can be found, provided one looks for them; and Dumézil's triadic structures can often be interpreted as historical or analytical reductions of the full pattern.

Logically, an attempt to situate Hinduism within the Indo-European framework and the exploration of three- or five-element structures in Hinduism could be quite separate undertakings, but in practice they have intertwined. The reason lies in the primitive form of classification that must have existed among the proto-Indo-European speakers and that left its mark on the cultures that derived from theirs. I am alluding, of course, to the 1903 essay by Durkheim and Mauss.

This essay has not always been well understood (Allen 1994). One must distinguish two dimensions of classification (quite apart from any hierarchical organisation by levels of inclusiveness). On the one hand, members of society may be classified into one or other of a set of clans, the visual world may be classified under a set of colours, days may be classified under seasons, space under cardinal points, and so on. On the other hand, members of one clan may be classified together with a particular colour, season, cardinal point, etc., perhaps under a totemic animal. If the first dimension of classification is envisaged as horizontal, the second will be vertical. But however we choose to

describe them, it is intuitively clear that the two dimensions of classification are different. Horizontally, the culture is taking objectively similar things and introducing distinctions and assimilations (which may
or may not seem to us arbitrary or surprising); but vertically it is taking dissimilar things and introducing associations that seem to us
unreal (imaginary, symbolic or metaphorical). In general, the scientific
world-view devalues the vertical dimension present in a primitive form
of classification. But this dimension was crucial to the ideology of the
early Indo-European speakers, and in interpreting an individual god,
hero, talisman, event or whatever as representing a particular function, this is what the analyst is recovering.[8]

Thus, although most of the material studied by Indo-European
comparativists is traditionally regarded as the property of philologists,
what it exemplifies is the standard anthropological phenomenon of
classification. In fact, not all the material comes from ancient texts.
Apart from the pseudo-history of early Rome, the Greek, Sanskrit and
Old Irish epic traditions, Arthurian romance and Buddhist hagiogra-
phy, I have been particularly interested in Nuristan, the area of northeast Afghanistan that retained its pagan Indo-Iranian polytheism until
forcible Islamisation in 1896. Most of the ethnography on the old religion naturally comes from the nineteenth century, but although valuable salvage work continued thereafter, and one very useful narrative
was collected as late as 1956 (Allen in press), it is unlikely that fieldwork with contemporary Nuristanis would relate to Indo-European
comparativism. Possibly their geographical and cultural neighbours,
the Kalash Kafirs of Pakistan, who are still pagan, may have retained
traces of archaic structures, but at present I remain doubtful.

In any case, from an analyst's point of view, what is the difference
between narratives tape-recorded around the hearth of a smoky
Nepalese hut and narratives written by native participants in an oral
tradition a couple of thousand years ago? The ethnographer can know
more about the narrators, the audience and the whole performative
context, and may benefit from native commentary, even perhaps from
hesitations on the tape. But the problems posed by the narratives
themselves are not different in kind, and for this I soon turned to
Dumézil. His most substantial work on India is his analysis of the great
Sanskrit epic, the *Mahâbhârata*, a text whose significance for understanding classical Hinduism was well emphasised by Madeleine
Biardeau (for example, 1981).[9] The epic is an excellent source for char-
acteristically Indo-European five-element structures, but the most surprising fact to emerge is that considerable stretches of its story are
cognate with parts of Homer's *Odyssey*. The similarities are so many
and so precise that, although only five papers on this have come out so
far, there is little room for doubt. The only reasonable explanation is

that the two epics go back to a common origin from which they diverged in the course of separate oral transmission.

The relationship between the two epics would not have struck me if I had not been on the lookout for five-element structures, and to that extent the finding grew from an interest in classification. However, since the classification in question concerned types of marriage (dowry, capture, brideprice, etc. – see Allen 1996), another factor was probably a descriptive fieldwork-based article I had written on Thulung weddings. In any case, the comparison also derives from fieldwork in a deeper sense. Though it is scarcely the sort of thing one says in grant applications, part of the point of doing fieldwork is to consolidate a personal and affective involvement in a region or topic. Would I ever have become fascinated by narratives if the Thulung themselves had not given me a sense of their importance?

One wonders whether, conversely, comparative work on these ancient texts can feed back into accounts given by fieldworkers. I can glimpse a number of ways in which the ancient ideological heritage is still relevant (not only to narratives), and there must be many that I have not seen. By way of examples, let us consider some features of the contemporary Hindu world. An ethnographer wishing to describe and analyse the social problems associated with dowry might well wonder why this form of marriage is so highly valued. Part of the answer comes, and can only come, from the comparativist: the valuation of dowry weddings goes back more than five millennia[10] and reflects the ranking of the first function. Again, although it is well known that yoga has a history reaching back before classical Hinduism into the Vedic period, the phenomenon takes on new aspects when linked with the quasi-shamanic journeys of Arjuna and Odysseus (Allen 1998b), which themselves are reminiscent of many a Himalayan shamanic ritual. Thirdly, lives have been lost in recent communal conflicts over the birthplace of Râma, and great efforts continue to be made to mine the epics for facts about a battle at Kurukshetra (not to mention Troy). But such historicist readings of the epics seem to the comparativist totally ill-founded. Although the method is a form of historiography, what it offers is a history of ideas and stories, not of real punctate events. Even if such events have left marks here and there in the story, they can practically never be distinguished from the nonhistorical events. Of course one could describe contemporary claims about the past without holding a view on their historical plausibility, but would that really be satisfying?

More generally, though the precedents hardly suggest that all historians will welcome its help, language-family based comparativism does offer a method, complementary to archaeology and linguistics, of pushing back the historical record into periods before the first documents. Thus a traditionally nonliterate group such as the Nuristanis, whose past would have seemed to a functionalist ethnographer almost totally inaccessible, can be given at least some fragments of a cultural history. Moreover, in literate societies, the method can demonstrate the existence of channels of cultural transmission that bypass the written record. Such channels existed both in Greece and India. For instance, late classical sources tell us that, after returning to Penelope, Odysseus became a horse. Although the tradition is totally ignored by all the sources BC, comparison shows that some such link between hero and horse goes back to the ancestral narrative. Much that is in the *Mahâbhârata* similarly bypassed the Vedas.

Although this chapter has concentrated on the Indo-European speakers, comparison based on language families is only one form of what used to be called 'the comparative method'. But it is a specific way of investigating social phenomena, contrasting with ahistorical types of comparison, functionalist or structuralist, and complementary to the potentially historical evolutionist and diffusionist approaches. As with any method its usefulness will have limits, but hopefully, as happened in linguistics, application to the Indo-European world will aid application elsewhere. One instance could be the Austronesian world, where comparativism is quite active and where so many of the sources derive from fieldworkers (or travellers and others). Of course one cannot assume that all proto-languages were spoken by people who demonstrably used a primitive form of classification – how typical the Indo-Europeans were in that respect remains an open question.

These large issues, then, are not altogether remote from fieldwork, and in any case it makes sense that an anthropologist should tackle them. Within the British academic division of labour, who is better placed to do so? Would I really have been better employed writing ethnography about that apricot-blossomed mountain village? I dislike the label 'armchair anthropologist' both because it implies lack of effort and because it is inaccurate – most of the time one is at desk or table. But we need to keep open a place for such non-fieldworkers, making it clear to students and wider public alike that the discipline can accommodate not only the emulators of a Malinowski but also those whose interests, background and aptitudes direct them rather towards Mauss.

NOTES

1. I do not count as fieldwork the three month-long trips I have made since 1987 to various parts of the subcontinent (also to Kenya and Australia). These family holidays, mostly undertaken at my own expense (though they involved some academic contacts and many visits to museums and antiquities), lie on the uneasy continuum between fieldwork and tourism, but closer to the latter.

2. I had hoped to go to northeast India, but the prevailing political conditions made that impracticable. While staying in Delhi in the winter of 1980–1 I tried, but failed, to obtain permission to go a little further north in Kinnaur, to the Baspa valley.

3. Since so much of the work was linguistic – training my ear for Thulung phonemic differences, collecting paradigms and vocabulary, transcribing and glossing tape recordings, I worked a lot with a few youngish educated Nepali-Thulung bilingual assistants, who were paid on an hourly rate, explicitly based on the earnings of a primary school teacher.

4. The word may even be used by pure textualists. A classicist entitles a chapter 'Poetic Fieldwork', defining it for his purposes as the attempt 'to work out the mental and social structures of the *Iliad* by accumulating and comparing the evidence from within the poem' (Taplin 1992: 48).

5. Austro-Asiatic speakers probably participated in the continuum. Bibliographical references are kept to a minimum here. For a list of my own papers, updated annually, see http://www.rsl.ox.ac.uk/isca/njapub.html .

6. I had chosen to study the Thulung Rai partly because a comparative linguist (Robert Shafer) had once characterised it as particularly archaic within the East Himalayish branch of Tibeto-Burman.

7. The exercise of tackling an unwritten language for fieldwork reinforced a long-standing interest in language and made it easier to come to grips with philological approaches.

8. Whether any comparable form of classification can be found in the Tibeto-Burman world remains unclear.

9. Incidentally, Biardeau provides a good example of anthropology's loss of any monopoly over fieldwork. A Sanskritist by training, she has done a lot of fieldwork in and around Indian temples and is a well-recognised figure in the social anthropology of South Asia.

10. The common origin of the two epics probably goes back to the period of the proto-language, and although the subject is notoriously controversial, 3500 BC would be a middle-of-the-road estimate.

FIELDWORK UNFOLDING

David Parkin

Casting around for a new methodological perspective on fieldwork in anthropology seems doomed to failure. In the vast and increasing corpus of literature on the subject, it is difficult to find questions that have not been raised. It is in the answers given that there is still debate, such as on the issue of fieldworkers seeming to straddle their own and others' generations over time and perhaps also of successively working in different areas. A sad fact of inequalities in human longevity between rich and poor countries is the astonishment of people in the latter on seeing yet again, after many years, the fieldworker whom their parents and even late grandparents knew in their youth, still evidently fit and apparently youthful, while they seem themselves to be rapidly ageing. The equal studying the equal as a more recent feature of fieldwork in, say, Europe, or as a feature of 'anthropology at home' (Jackson 1987; Okely 1996), has yet to have its impact on images of repeated fieldwork over time. Time spent in the field by any one individual, however, is often thought of in relative terms: it is counted less in years and more through observations on events in the passage of time and in personal changes and capacities mutually reported by fieldworker and members of the society.

A methodological archetype is still, in fact, of problems confronting the young fieldworker more than the maturing returnee. The jokes caricaturing older supervisors advising doctoral students about to enter the field to take quinine but not women are the male-oriented ironic reversals of an otherwise strict insistence on empirically scientific rather than humanistic enquiry characteristic of the post-Malinowskian era of fieldwork, and inextricably part of the analytical quest for natural laws and systematically interconnected social facts (Crick 1982: 16; Evans-Pritchard 1973). The jokes are now in poor taste, eclipsed by serious analytical attempts to understand sexuality and identity in the field (Kulick and Willson 1995), while social anthropology itself has, since Evans-Pritchard's famous denunciation in 1950, inclined towards the humanities and away from natural science (Evans-Pritchard 1962 [1950]). But disciplinary distinctiveness has remained, partly because competing university subjects and departments perpetuate boundaries and partly because no new hybrid subject, including media and cultural studies, has emerged which does better what anthropology has done. A notion of disciplinary form is further aided and abetted by funding councils' expectation that all social scientists, including sceptical anthropologists, demonstrate methodological rigour in research training. This has ensured that the manner in which anthropologists write fieldwork proposals are not allowed to move too far away from a format of rules, guidelines, stages and timetables, which few can in reality observe, nor indeed should, given the inductive nature of the work. A more modern scenario might now be for the supervisor to advise the student when they are in the field not to heed too much the obligatorily formulaic presentation contained in the research proposal successfully submitted for funding. But we are not supposed to admit this.

This formulaic emphasis has not, however, been imposed on methods of writing culture. Writing is, after all, pressed into the domain of literature rather than social science and the funding councils are loathe to trespass there. The discussion by anthropologists in the 1980s of the poetics and politics of representation (e.g. Clifford and Marcus 1986; Marcus and Fischer 1986), itself emanating from literary theory and an earlier critical anthropology (for example, Scholte 1971, 1972, 1978), marked not so much an apprehension or hesitancy in the subject as a post-Marxist attempt to redress the power inequalities believed since the 1960s to pervade relationships between observers and subjects (Asad 1973; Parkin 1982). Here, there was almost a celebration of writing styles unbound by home-based theories, nationalities and personalities, and dialogically created: the message was that ethnographers should not pretend that their writings had truth value but that they might convey humanistically what, in good faith, they could seek to portray, captured vividly in Clifford's report of the Native American telling the fieldworker that, while he might not be able to provide the truth, he could at least tell the fieldworker what he knew.

Imagine us applying a similar celebratory edict of rule-lessness to fieldwork. It would be that the anthropologist should simply immerse themself in the field, not framing their observations in any systematic way, nor linking them to existing theory, but absorbing experience without specific reference to prior anthropological knowledge as might a novelist who had never, or hardly ever, read another's novel. In fact, even bows in the direction of experiential ethnography never went this far. Writing may be allowed free flow and play, but fieldwork is apparently always likely to be hedged about by rule-governed expectations, however much altered or disregarded in practice. Both are often spoken of as ethnography.

There is both a merging and a confusion in the relationship of terms describing what anthropologists do. 'Ethnography' is commonly taken to include the physical and mental acts making up fieldwork together with the writing up of the data resulting from it. 'Fieldwork' is here an implicit element of ethnography, the implication being that while the latter is by definition an act of writing, it can only be on the basis of collected facts. The well-known introduction to ethnography by Hammersley and Atkinson (1995 but originally 1983), neither of them apparently an anthropologist, illustrates this merging, for there is little reference to the idea of extended fieldwork over at least a year, conducted in the local language, as a *sine qua non* of ethnography. We may contrast this with Barnes's detailed description in this volume of the importance of language learning and long-term fieldwork, and of his own meticulous attempts to do both. Epistemologically, Hammersley's and Atkinson's conflation of ethnography with fieldwork, with the latter minimally tucked into the former, might be justified by the view that, as anthropologists come to understand that which they observe and hear about in the field, they are likely already to be framing what they will write, so the observing, hearing and written interpretations are in fact inseparable. Experientially, however, there is much in fieldwork that escapes this trajectory: not everything that happens in the field fits the emerging paradigm. As Crick put it at about the same time (1982), fieldwork and ethnography are in fact two very different kinds of activity. Perhaps following Gupta and Ferguson's focus on fieldwork as a concept (1997), Marcus seems to accept this in his later work when he actually separates the conduct of fieldwork from the published ethnographies resulting from such fieldwork, while recognising what he calls the 'research imaginary' as the total set of influences which shape both fieldwork proposals and their written issue.

Part of this touches on the subject of this book, namely the straddling of fieldwork site(s) and periods, of space and time, within the career of a single field anthropologist, captured in the notion of multi-sited ethnography and the dilemmas of being caught between first and second projects pulling in different directions (Marcus 1998: 10–11, 239–40). But there is a major difference which Marcus unwittingly acknowledges. It has been an oft-remarked but undocumented impression (which with time might or might not have been demonstrated) that British and, to a lesser extent, some British-influenced European anthropologists tend to return to the same generally African or Asian society and/or socio-cultural region over a number of years. In the United States the tendency is for the first field project to take place 'in a traditional culture area abroad', and for the second to involve 'work in one's own society, that is, the US', a distinction that Marcus observes appears to apply at least to his own cohort (Marcus 1998: 250, fn. 4). This is a significant observation which may partly explain some divergent tendencies between anthropology in the US and Europe, until recently.[1]

While speculative, the difference is interesting for its indication of contrasting influences. With its indigenous peoples and successive waves of settlers from other parts of the world, America is thought of as quintessentially culturally heterogeneous. It already incorporates the Other, while Europe has preserved for longer the myth of homogeneity, seeking its Other outside Europe, often in colonised territories divided for administrative purposes into unambiguously demarcated 'tribes' and 'peoples', the distinctiveness of each lasting until present time. The result is British (and also French, Belgian, Portuguese, German and Dutch) investment in a single region and language and the development of theoretical concepts having provenance in such regions (Fardon 1990), by contrast with American global rather than intensive regional comparison (which in turn lends itself to more generalised theorising). Abstracted from this comparison between American and European tendencies, the contrast perhaps partakes of what Stocking (1987: xvi) calls a tension within anthropology between the generalist (global) approach which tries to subsume human variation under single laws and the particularistic (regional) which seeks to excavate and lay bare the 'secrets' of individual human phenomena.

In the present volume, the difference between long-term intra-regional and staccato global fieldwork has relevance for what is meant by multi-sitedness over time: to work in Sudan for some years and to return there after an interval in neighbouring Ethiopia, as did James, or between the Luo, Giriama and Swahili of western, eastern and coastal Kenya as did Parkin, affects the projects and their investigation quite differently from the study of, say, a transnational community 'simultaneously' investigating the spatially separate groups making up the diaspora. The first is to move slowly within a region and compare cultural variations of local themes; the second is to coordinate observation of distantly linked peoples with, at the same time, an overview of their understanding and practice of commonality in the face of globalising pressures. Banks's approach is rooted in the tradition of the former (long-term study of a single or cognate peoples) and yet captures something of the multi-sited diaspora approach in his image of worldwide Jains of South Asian origin moving over the generations in some kind of concomitant or relational pattern and of himself as observer also moving, both through his career and between Jain settlements and events in India and Britain. This image of the moving observing the moving, one within a single life and the other over many, both draws on and gives substance to Banks's distinctive theoretical development in the direction of visual anthropology as a sub-field of the discipline (Banks and Morphy 1997). The field is a 'moving target', according to James, who characterises her own fieldwork experience as 'rather like trying to capture shifting scenery from a series of moving escalators'. To this visual metaphor she adds the sheer importance in her fieldwork of listening, which presupposes long-term attentiveness made salient through sensitive knowledge of the language. Passive as well as active, anthropologists are thus re-workers as well as products of theory through their own personal reflection on fieldwork experience.

There are here two senses of 'the moving' in fieldwork. First is that conveyed by the metaphor of moving-escalator/shifting-scenes. This captures well the interaction of two sources of change: that of the anthropologist's own situation, theoretical interests and perceptions; and that of the history and ethno-history of the people(s) being studied. Second, it is also commonly the case that a particular and unique event is taken, by both the anthropologist and the people, to be of such significance during a single period of fieldwork that it becomes subject to changing interpretations over the years on the part of the fieldworker. This is the unchanging object of enquiry evoking alterations in one's analytical view of it, as its social significance is gradually unpacked and as one moves through a consideration of different facets of the one event.

One is here reminded of Gluckman's early methodological advice to start fieldwork analysis from observation of a single event or set of related events and work, so to speak, outwards from it, unravelling the relevant structural principles in doing so. The classic examples of this approach, which is certainly foremost a question of fieldwork judgement more than of abstracted theory, are Gluckman's description of a bridge being built in Zululand (1958 [1940]), Epstein's focus on the boycott by African urban workers of European-owned butchers' shops in what is now Zambia (1958), Mitchell's analysis of the Central African Kalela dance (1956), and the more methodologically explicit uses of such notions as social drama, micro-history and network, by which works of the Manchester School were known.

Pieke's unpacking of the Tian'anmen Square massacre of political demonstrators in Beijing in 1989 as a critical event is discussed in the context of his own fieldwork trajectory, which is more of the moving-escalator/shifting-scenes kind, since the event is then placed in the recent history of changing political fortunes in China and of Pieke's repeated visits. By contrast, holding its background relatively constant, O'Hanlon contemplated for over a decade his view of several hours of warfare among the Wahgi people of the Papua New Guinea Highlands, a phenomenon rarely documented in published form by those who have actually witnessed it. It was one of the last battles among Wahgi fought with traditional bows, arrows, spears and axes, subsequent ones often carried out largely through the use of firearms, dynamite and grenades.

O'Hanlon describes how compelling the event was for him, taking him away from his main field-site, and yet difficult to write about, partly through the contradictory responses it aroused in him. First, the battle had in a sense a pre-history attached to it, by virtue of the various verbal accounts of warfare given O'Hanlon by Wahgi, who would speak a lot about the subject except on magic and ritual which, unlike the Mae Enga, they regard as helping the outcome of war and therefore as secret information. Second, however, O'Hanlon saw discrepancies between these accounts and what he observed at this particular battle. But, while the battle itself was not actually ethnographically informative, he came to realise that the ambivalence of Wahgi in talking to him about warfare generally reflected their sense of cultural distinctiveness: wars are times of betrayals and secrets which cannot be communicated to outsiders; yet, through their recurrence over the generations, they provide the self-perpetuating lines of constituent Wahgi groups which can be talked about.

Goodman comments on a similar kind of ambivalence experienced in his fieldwork in Japan, where, as a 'Westerner', he could be summoned as external commentator but not regarded as cultural confidant, for the stranger is both dangerous and a potential source of good fortune. Such circumstances do not perhaps favour the technique of learning through patient listening proposed by James for the Sudan. Instead, Goodman found that he could only learn through doing. Listening is evidently of varying cross-cultural usefulness. From ambivalence we move to what Dresch calls the 'uncomfortable' realisation among ethnographers that some field areas may be more difficult to study than others. Similar variations are sometimes alluded to in such broad contrasts as 'hot', 'cold', open or closed societies, but not always addressed in the theory and methodology of pre-fieldwork preparation for a particular society.

It is perhaps obvious, and certainly clear from the above, that the mutually reinforcing influences of pre-fieldwork training, the conduct of fieldwork and the writing up and publication of results form a composite whole and can be distinguished from each other only arbitrarily.

On the other hand, fieldwork is also made by the local conditions under which it is conducted and so is by no means a slavish reflection of factors external to itself. It contains within itself some degree of perceptual and conceptual autonomy made distinctive and yet changing through the individual fieldworker's on-going experience of remembering and forgetting events and conditions, and sometimes exploring these with informants. Working over time and sometimes in different areas, or working within local ideas of change over time and space, produce within the single fieldworker a career history which, while personalised, also informs the ethnographic and theoretical exchanges among anthropologists and so makes up the subject.

This sense of personalised field experience and its commitment to field notes as the makings of anthropology is discussed in Sanjek (1990). A particular value of a number of the book's contributions, especially by Sanjek himself, is their focus on the sometimes rapidly widening gap, so to speak, between field experience and its written expression. For example, personal familiarity with the raw event is taken up by theory, as when the field notes, while themselves unchanged, constantly undergo new 'headnotes' as the fieldworker back from the field comes under the sway of other influences (Sanjek 1990: 93–94). Or, field notes may be accidentally burned or lost, sometimes prompting a long period of reconstruction for writing up, with the reduced data couched in more general ideas than might otherwise have been the case (ibid.: 34–41). Of course, taken over many years and sometimes in different field areas, such gaps are a recurring characteristic: the anthropologist witnesses and perhaps participates in a ritual and hastens to write it down, trying to separate the attempt at a faithful rendering from digression on its import for the wider aim of filling out a broader picture, doing so many times over in different places and for different events. Multi-sitedness over time and space is then partly a prolongation of memorised writings re-collected at later dates and sometimes for different intellectual purposes than those originally expressed (cf. Meneley 1998).

Far from clarifying the fieldworker's view of their field(s), the process may deepen the subtleties and hence widen the range of interpretations. Each new interpretation becomes less definite. The closer we get to our field through prolonged involvement, the more fuzzy the categories by which we know it, while the more distant the clearer, as instanced in the inevitably increasing cases of short-term anthropological fieldwork on development projects of the Rapid Rural Appraisal kind. But the two projects aim for different results: the long-term view raises questions about the tangled skein we call humanity in culture, while the short-term suggests answers to specific practical problems. There need be no conflict provided we remember the distinction between objectives.

Nevertheless, it is both a truism and evident from the cases in this volume that an anthropologist's subject matter and objectives alter through protracted and repeated fieldwork in the same or contrasting socio-cultural formations. Uncertainty about facts within the 'same' society over time, which had once been thought to be beyond question, become reinterpreted as due either to intrinsic or to peoples' interpretive indeterminacy. One way out of this is for the fieldworker to work in a quite contrasting society, to wipe the previously fuzzy slate clean and start afresh among new people. A different kind of problem can arise. The new society reacts quite differently to the fieldworker from the first. Comparing the two reactions it becomes clear that the fieldworker's identity simply cannot escape an indigenously determined category. So, how much do fieldworkers represent such indigenous categories and how much are they captured by them?

Rivière provides a clear case. The Amazonian Trio Indians of the Surinam/Brazilian frontier were studied in the 1960s and, while never isolated from outside contacts, retained a self-contained view of the world. Seeing Rivière alone, without possessions, nonauthoritarian, a non-Christian living in a Trio family and woefully inexpert in local practical skills and language, they identified him as having been cast out by his own community and, while initially suspected of being a sorcerer, in due course as a person evidently of no significant substance who should therefore be taught the civilising ways of the Trio. This evidently succeeded since, on Rivière's return to the Trio fifteen years later, by now well versed in the genealogies, customs and beliefs he had collected, he was sought out as a cultural expert. Over time he had progressed from ignoramus to sage but all within the confines of the Trio world-view.

Contrast this with the perception of him by ranchers in what was at first a remote and backward area of northern Brazil, whom he had been visiting over much the same period. Although cut off from the rest of Brazil, residents of the small cowtown where Rivière stayed knew about it from radio, magazines and occasional visits to the outside. They concluded that other Brazilians regarded them as uneducated and stupid rural hicks, by contrast with the educated Rivière of assumed superior status, who was never really able to enter into this frontiersman society as had been possible among the Trio Indians who regarded themselves as superior and able to be receptive.

Not dissimilarly, Parkin's reception among the non-Muslim Giriama of Kenya was made easier through learning by apprenticeship, with the result that twenty-five years after initial fieldwork, he was approached as an expert on customary knowledge, including genealogies. Among the Muslim Swahili of the East African coast and islands, however, only long absorption in, preferably, a Middle Eastern centre of Islamic learning would have conferred similar status, despite in both cases linguistic fluency and long, repeated residence. More dramatically, it was Pieke's experience of the People's Movement in 1989 in Beijing's Tian'anmen Square that persuaded him how what he calls a total event can even force its study on the fieldworker: 'During the movement, I felt thus that I had no option but to study it.'

Following on from Rivière's conclusion, a society not only collaborates in the production of a particular type of ethnographic writing, it also shapes the possible movements through fieldwork which, at best, can only be negotiated by the fieldworker. The cultural as a determining factor in how the fieldworker acts, perceives and goes about collecting data is evident in Dresch's analysis of the role of the 'secretive' in the minutiae of Middle Eastern everyday life, by contrast with the openness and obviousness of so-called major political issues. This situation, echoed also among Muslim Swahili, reverses what we might ordinarily think to be the case in Euro-America. Here it is state politics which are supposed to be shrouded in secrecy and protected at high cost and risk to those illicitly daring to discover them, while the domestic, mundane and quotidian are supposed to be of no importance and so accessible to anyone. It is probably not only in Middle Eastern/Islamic societies that, for example, historical backgrounds containing the information needed for arranging appropriate marriages on the basis of lineal or other purity make the domestic necessarily opaque and reduce wider political matters to foregone conclusions. It is likely to some degree to apply to other societies where the political emanates from generationally repeated marriages between kin or habitual allies. In the case of China, Pieke argues, the treatment of 'everyday life as a secret' is a feature of government officials reluctant to divulge the reality of continued failures and yet wishing to perpetuate the ideology of communism and their positions. The result for the fieldworker is not only one of cultural translation but of deciding whether purported secret knowledge inspires awe but is otherwise an empty claim or does indeed mask information hidden from others, and whether it is ethically proper to know which of these is the case.

The question of ethics in fieldwork is a kind of pivot articulating how much of a culture shapes fieldwork and how much the fieldworker has purchase over the representation of culture. Rivière, Dresch, Pieke and Parkin examine how they were socially defined by their respective field-sites, the paradox emerging that while fieldworkers may try to fit a people to a theory, the people themselves fit fieldworkers to their own socio-cultural understandings. Thus, all fieldworkers in due course identify rules of behaviour which they ought to follow but may sometimes choose not to. Changing perceptions of the ethical are sometimes like changing theoretical fashions, indeed are part of them. Protests against female circumcision might once have been regarded as cultural interference, but are now inscribed in post-fieldwork debates on the subject, if not actually directed at the people among whom the fieldworker lived. In the late 1990s, fieldworkers were slow to respond anthropologically to popular and media-led Western criticism of the use of child labour in various forms of production throughout the world, major capitalist and local-level, despite the wide range of possible cases, from goat-herding to sweatshop manufacturing. In development studies judgements of appropriate advice and action have often altered, as the anthropology of ethical issues spreads its net in unanticipated directions.

The two chapters by Matsunaga and Goodman touch on a widely reported and seemingly pronounced feature of Japanese society, namely the tendency to believe in and express a unique Japanese mode of thinking and acting (*Nihonjinron*), from which foreigners are likely always to be excluded despite residence in Japan and fluency in the language from birth. It is a kind of cultural eugenics, possibly derived from biological eugenics, and apparently found in other parts of East Asia (Dikötter 1998), and culturally presented through such dichotomies as pure/impure and insider/outsider. Both authors provide examples of how, despite the many kindnesses expressed and acknowledgement of their Japanese linguistic and cultural competence developed over many years living and working in Japan (in one case of having married into the society), they are at various crucial points treated or celebrated as irreversibly outsiders.

Of course, writ small, this is the case with any society whose members concur in their definitional characteristics, although the East Asian cases are marked by special vocabulary supporting a consistently applied ideology (Koreans resident over a number of generations and speaking only Japanese may still not claim full Japanese citizenship; note also that claims of descent through blood, though not necessarily language competence, entitle German citizenship). Is this an ethical issue on which anthropologists should report? It is certainly an experience gleaned from their own long familiarity with the field in the face of which it is evident that they cannot remain emotionally nor perhaps in other ways neutral, as is particularly evident in Matsunaga's account. The culture shapes the fieldworker's responses but also sows the seeds of their rebellion as outside observer.

An implication here is that anthropology may be moving away from the most recent ethical paradigm of fieldworker-informant relations. The great achievement of first the Marxist (Asad 1973) and then the post-Marxist/postmodernist and feminist critiques of ethnographic representation was to try to sensitise anthropologists to the inequalities and iniquities of fieldwork-based studies and convert them to a sense of accountability to the societies in which they worked and to the idea that informants should be more equal partners in the construction of ethnography. The researcher as advocate thus trod a thin line between acting as a communication conduit for the researched and imposing a view on them, sometimes claiming that one's own background, for example as women, especially qualified one to understand the needs of the oppressed (Wolf 1996: 28–31). The claim therefore addressed home as well as indigenous injustices. The widening gap between rich and poor world regions will continue to provide a niche for such dual advocacy. Yet, alongside the sometimes effective but sometimes ineffectually pious declarations of egalitarian intent, run murmurings of a different kind. As fieldwork is increasingly undertaken in Europe, North America, Japan and among the world's elites, it dares to challenge the cultural presuppositions of other peoples.

This challenge is increasingly extending to other societies, and not just those of the wealthy first world, which harbour patterns of behaviour judged to be unacceptable to the liberal democratic middle class which anthropologists generally belong to. To the examples of female circumcision and child labour may be added those of domestic violence, religious and political persecution, ideological brainwashing et cetera, all no doubt highly contestable conditions along a continuum of cross-cultural variability (Nordstrom and Robben 1995: 4–7), and yet singled out through their contestability for protest or complaint alongside, if not obliquely within, the traditional ethnographic monograph.

Moreover, the passage of time alters the perception of oppression or wrong-doing from the fieldworker's perspective. James first shared the anti-mission, anti-authoritarian sentiments of the Uduk of the Sudan but later, as the civil war worsened, found the Uduk confronted by the Sudanese government and its repressive use of Islam and herself more in sympathy with the missions.

A good example of a kind of personal revolution in thinking is evident in Pieke's chapter on the effect on him of the changes in China from before and after the 1989 uprising in Beijing, in which he became intellectually involved, even having at some stage to write under a pseudonym. Just as Banks juxtaposes his essentialised big picture of Jains in the world against the disconnected and fragmentary understandings sometimes held by members of the global community of each other, so Pieke contrasts his own understandings of China before and after 1989. He first worked on the assumption that he would study 'ordinary' adaptations within a wider social and cultural order, but later realised that he was dealing with the extraordinary construction of a newly pieced-together order challenging the old one. This was a process of personal understanding that came to him not through structured analysis but through the dislocated accidents and events of 'serendipity'. Making scientific discoveries by accident is a long-reported feature (Newton 1992) and shares in the creativity of intuition (Bergson 1975). However, the indeterminacy implied in recognising serendipity's methodological role in fieldwork is still often unwelcome in the social sciences, despite its being an inevitable aspect of inductive understanding (Parkin 1982: xvii–xxv). Following Pieke, it can be claimed that intensive linguistic, ethnographic and regional preparation and alert, round-the-clock participative observation and patient listening, are in fact the conditions for serendipitous discovery, not obstacles to it.

Thus, critical judgement on the part of the fieldworker arising unexpectedly from the accidents of their fieldwork experience appears increasingly to characterise anthropology. It is the result of fieldwork experience and not theory, but is informed by the latter's ethical reflexivity. Blaming external causes of cultural malaise and destruction is what more and more anthropologists do, as with tourism. But, as mentioned above, their criticism does nowadays sometimes shade into questioning practices internal to the society or produced by an interaction between inside and outside. This may well emanate from the more dialogical nature of fieldwork that has been propounded. After all, urging fieldwork to become discussion between equals allows for argument as well. The development goes hand in hand with restitution claims to ethnographic knowledge in addition to objects on the part of the people studied. Is the dialogue increasingly becoming confrontational? Having moved during the last generation from its initially positivistic activity as 'objectively neutral observation' to what is now familiarly called reflexive ethnography (Davies 1999; Goodman this volume), we may ask whether fieldworkers have in some cases already moved in the direction of becoming cultural *agents provocateurs*, by not only reporting on society but promoting attitudes within it. Has, for some fieldworkers, the representational crisis metamorphosed into one of direct action advocacy? Or, as Ahmed and Shore ask (1995: 15), does the crisis of relevance rather than of representation now threaten the discipline?

In fact, fieldworkers still need to try to understand the categories by which peoples represent themselves and are represented before deciding on their relevance to whatever is deemed, by whomever, to be an ethical problem. Nor was there ever a crisis. Looking back, it looks more like a period of significant methodological stocktaking, which seems unlikely to divert many fieldworkers from continuing to share the traditional assumptions of history and historiography in not overtly seeking change but in continuing to seek the socio-cultural understandings making up the further possibilities of what it is to be human, both now and in the past. To repeat, it is the assumptions of history that are important here, not the fact that history's primary sources are generally written. It is this point that informs Evans-Pritchard's distant claim, drawing on Collingwood, that anthropology is a kind of history. What are the implications for the discipline, however, if anthropology turned more and more from long-term fieldwork conducted in the local language to the analysis of documented socio-cultural data? Barnes describes his reading and re-analysis of published work on Native American Omaha social organisation, which was, however, sandwiched between his field-based Indonesian accounts. Allen has, however, turned exclusively to the analysis of published and archival work. He does not regard this as a retreat from field to textual data so much as a division of labour within the profession allowing for a special kind of contribution to anthropology. How else, he asks, can the occasional scholar embark on large, comparative projects which draw on extensive literary and archival holdings? As in his own study of common themes in Greek and Indian mythology, the work requires expertise in anthropological theory but, he argues, is unlikely to profit from yet more fieldwork on a particular society. Indeed, like long-term fieldwork, such textualist interpretations may require deep linguistic knowledge and cultural sensitivity acquired over many years. The understanding of society drawn from texts may, he intimates, be helped by the raw personal experience of earlier fieldwork, but it is not essential. His point is that fieldwork is not the defining essence of anthropology, for it does not advance the discipline's intellectual ambitions. Fieldwork may sometimes be discussed and thought of apart from theory and ethics but is, in the end, epistemologically subsumed within them, the texts of which therefore provide the comparative frameworks. Of course, anthropologists have always at different points in the subject's development felt able to work from documents, and the obligatory sense of fieldwork as a necessary form of apprenticeship has perhaps grown particularly strong only since the Second World War. Anthropologists may be able to remain healthily divided on this issue. They may be less happily divided on the questions concerning advocacy and restitution.

As regards restitution, possibly some of the greatest future tensions in anthropology will be expressed in and over ethnographic museums, as a result of the competing claims concerning ownership of collected objects in them and arguments over whether they are exhibited in a manner acceptable to the various branches of humanity involved. Many such objects no longer have the use value for which their makers intended them, and in some cases the historical commentaries which have been attached to them by museum curators are no longer regarded as accurate or legitimate. Thus contested, objects have sometimes instead assumed iconic power as indicators of newly found ethnic identities. La Rue's work as an ethnomusicologist is unusual in that the objects within her realm of interest, musical instruments collected from Asia and Africa, can in fact be played. In practice, rare and delicate ones may not be, but the idea of their playing potential is evident through the visits of indigenous musicians from Africa and Asia, whose performances constitute a kind of middle way, originating in areas from which objects were traditionally taken but now communicating directly with the generation of those collectors' children. For La Rue, the field is in fact the visiting musicians on tour, and one which, moreover, does not incur restitution claims.

There is here a more general possibility. Between remaining firmly in the museum to which they were once taken by collectors or being re-appropriated by indigenous peoples, objects may move, so to speak, between museum and people, either on peripatetic display or through use. Similarly, the performances studied and descriptions made by anthropologists on the basis of fieldwork are potentially subject to ownership claims by the people who have offered them through conversation and demonstration. Dialogical anthropology implies that those to whom fieldworkers talk should be acknowledged as part authors in the description. Sometimes they actually appear as individual co-authors in publications. This does not translate, however, into a group being written about being able to become legal owners of the anthropologist's field notes and ethnographic accounts: artefacts may sometimes be reclaimed but not, it seems, indigenous knowledge. Even successfully pursued legal charges of defamation provide not ownership but compensation.

This discourse is, of course, premised on the idea of a sharp distinction between predatory metropolitan and sometimes formerly colonial interests and the dispossessed. This dichotomous view of the world is clearly based on historical reality, notwithstanding that major and minor lines of demarcation between plunderer and plundered have inevitably shifted over time. Nowadays fixed ideas of the self/other kind have at a scholarly if not popular level given way to more nuanced gradations of otherness, although the ease with which the global map of 'Northern' rich and 'Southern' poor can broadly be drawn should not be forgotten. Alongside such overarching distinctions of advantage and disadvantage, the fieldworker also becomes immersed in more subtle ranges of otherness, as closeness to informants reveals hierarchies of power and privilege which, while invisible to the outsider, are important to the local people themselves. As Allen puts it, there is no cut-off point at which otherness begins or ends: the very dynamic of the concept is its relativity and its application to particular situations of judgement, prejudice and action. Davies notes that this is because any society is in some way heterogeneous and so generates a multiplicity of social boundaries, sometimes nesting and sometimes cross-cutting (Davies 1999: 34).

We are all in some sense other, a common theme in early phenomenological writings. While, then, it is right to avoid fixing and essentialising ideas of self and other, they can hardly be jettisoned as dimensions of humanity. Indeed, it is the situational and historical tensions and balance between perceptions of self and other that remain distinctive objects of anthropological study. This is sometimes expressed as the 'pick and mix' approach to social organisation and human conduct, and may be accompanied by the celebration of notions of creolisation over and above firmly demarcated cultural pluralism. Moreover, one of the ways anthropology differs from other disciplines is in its focus not just on the otherness in all humanity but also on what may be called its exotic presentation. By this latter I refer to the fact that both within and between societies some actions, objects and personalities are rendered as defying conventional definition and as made up of special, often alluring, qualities not shared by the majority. Idols, icons and fetishes come and go and so this is a waxing and waning process, much nowadays produced by the media. That anthropology may then wish to demystify such exoticisation is not to deny its effect on people in the first place. However, given the relativity inherent in such concepts, their changing nature and their captivating influence, it is not easy in fieldwork to assess the socio-cultural significance of boundaries between what peoples themselves say is familiar and strange. It may be anthropology's biggest empirical challenge to generalisations about the effects of so-called globalisation.

NOTE

1. Here I can only speculate, but the difference may be on the point of dissolving. European scholars have since the late 1980s become more interested in the study of diasporas and transnational communities rather than remaining focused on particular regions (e.g. Vertovec 1999), and of working 'at home' in Europe. Some African and Asian anthropologists study other as well as their own societies and so converge with the above.

BIBLIOGRAPHY

Abbreviations:

JASO: Journal of the Anthropological Society of Oxford
JRAI: Journal of the Royal Anthropological Institute (incorporating Man)

Abu-Lughod, L. 1986. *Veiled sentiments: honor and poetry in a bedouin society.*
    Berkeley, CA: University of California Press.
———— 1989. Zones of theory in the anthropology of the Arab World.
    Annual review of anthropology 18: 267–306.
———— 1993. *Writing women's worlds: bedouin stories.* Berkeley, CA:
    University of California Press.
Adler, G. 1885. Umfang, Methode und Ziel der Musikwissenschaft. *Vmw,* I.
Ahmed, A.S. and Shore, C. (eds) 1995. *The future of anthropology: its relevance
    to the contemporary world.* London: Athlone.
Allen, N.J. 1989. The evolution of kinship terminologies. *Lingua* 77: 173–85.
———— 1994. Primitive classification: the argument and its validity. In *Debating
    Durkheim* W.S.F. Pickering and H. Martins (eds). London: Routledge.
———— 1996. The hero's five relationships: a proto-Indo-European story. In
    Myth and myth-making, J. Leslie (ed.). London: Curzon.
———— 1997. Hinduization: the experience of the Thulung Rai. In
    *Nationalism and ethnicity in a Hindu kingdom: the politics of culture in
    contemporary Nepal,* D. Gellner, J. Pfaff-Czarnecka and D. Whelpton (eds).
    Amsterdam: Harwood.
———— 1998a. Effervescence and the origins of human society. In *On
    Durkheim's elementary forms of religious life,* N.J. Allen, W.S.F. Pickering
    and W. Watts-Miller (eds). London: Routledge.
———— 1998b. The Indo-European prehistory of yoga. *International journal of
    Hindu studies* 2: 1–20.
———— 1998c. The prehistory of Dravidian-type terminologies. In
    Transformations of kinship, M. Godelier, T. Trautmann, and F. Tjon Sie Fat
    (eds). Washington: Smithsonian Institute.

————— in press. Imra, pentads and catastrophes. In *Georges Dumézil (1898–1986): dix ans après: témoignages, bilan, perspectives,* J.H. Michel and C. Sterckx (eds). Brussels: Institut des Hautes Etudes de Belgique.

Ardener, E.W. 1970. Witchcraft, economics and the continuity of belief. In *Witchcraft confessions and accusations,* M. Douglas (ed.). ASA Monograph 9. London: Tavistock.

————— 1971. Introductory essay. In *Social anthropology and language,* E.W. Ardener (ed.). ASA Monograph 10. London: Tavistock.

————— 1989 *The voice of prophecy: and other essays,* M. Chapman (ed.). Oxford: Blackwell.

Armbrust, W. 1996. *Mass culture and modernism in Egypt.* Cambridge: Cambridge University Press.

Arndt, P. 1937. *Grammatik der Solor-Sprache.* Ende, Flores: Arnoldus Drukkerij.

ASA (Association of Social Anthropologists of the Commonwealth). 1987. *Ethical guidelines for good practice.*

Asad, T. (ed.) 1973. *Anthropology and the colonial encounter.* London: Ithaca Press.

————— 1986. The concept of cultural translation in British social anthropology. In *Writing culture: the poetics and politics of ethnography,* J. Clifford and G. Marcus (eds). Berkeley, CA: University of California Press.

Auden, W.H. 1976. The unknown citizen [March 1939]. In *Collected poems, 1907–1973,* E. Mendelson (ed.). London: Faber & Faber, 253.

Banks, M. and Morphy, H. (eds) 1997. *Rethinking visual anthropology.* New Haven, London: Yale University Press.

Banks, M. 1986. Defining division: an historical overview of Jain social organisation. *Modern Asian studies* 20: 447–60.

————— 1988a. Forty-minute fieldwork. *JASO* 19: 251–63.

————— 1988b. *Raju and his friends.* Beaconsfield, UK: NFTS/RAI.

————— 1988c. *Reading Raju: a study guide to the film 'Raju and his friends'.* London, Oxford: Royal Anthropological Institute and ISCA, University of Oxford.

————— 1989. The narrative of lived experience: some Jains of India and England (photographic essay). *Critique of anthropology* 9: 65–76.

————— 1990. The seductive veracity of ethnographic film. *Society for Visual Anthropology Review* 6: 16–21.

————— 1992. *Organizing Jainism in India and England.* Oxford: Clarendon Press.

————— 1994. Why move? Regional and long distance migrations of Gujarati Jains. In *Migration: the Asian experience,* J. Brown and R. Foot (eds). London: Macmillan in association with St Antony's College, Oxford.

————— 1997. Representing the bodies of the Jains. In *Rethinking visual anthropology,* M. Banks and H. Morphy (ed.). London, New Haven: Yale University Press.

————— (forthcoming). Indian Jainism as social practice at the end of the twentieth century. In *Jainism and early Buddhism in the Indian cultural context: essays in honour of Professor P.S. Jaini,* O. Qvarnström (ed.). Lund: University of Lund Press.

Barley, N. 1983. *The innocent anthropologist: notes from a mud hut.* Harmondsworth: Penguin.

Barnes, R.H. 1974. *Kédang: a study of the collective thought of an Eastern Indonesian people.* Oxford: Clarendon Press.

—— 1984. *Two Crows denies it: a history of controversy in Omaha sociology.* Lincoln, NB: University of Nebraska Press.

—— 1988. Ethnography as a career: second thoughts on second fieldwork in Indonesia. *JASO* 19: 241–50.

—— 1990. A legacy of misperception and invention: the Omaha Indians in anthropology. In *The invented Indian: cultural fictions and government policies*, J.A. Clifton (ed.). New Brunswick, NJ and London: Transaction Publishers.

—— 1996. *Sea hunters of Indonesia: fishers and weavers of Lamalera.* Oxford: Clarendon Press.

Barnes, Ruth. 1989. *The Ikat textiles of Lamalera: a study of an Eastern Indonesian weaving tradition.* Leiden: Brill.

—— in press. *Gegenwart der Vergangenheit: Die Ernst-Vatter-Sammlung im Museum für Völkerkund, Frankfurt.*

Basso, K. 1988. 'Speaking with names': language and landscape among the Western Apache. *Cultural Anthropology* 3: 99–130.

Baumann, G. 1988. Village fieldwork overseas versus urban research at home: textbook dichotomies in the light of second fieldwork. *JASO* 19: 225–32.

Bayart, J.-F. 1993 [1989]. *The state in Africa: the politics of the belly.* London: Longman.

Beattie, J.H.M. 1964. *Other cultures: aims, achievements and methods in social anthropology.* London and New York: Cohen & West.

Becker, 1995. *Beyond translation: essays toward a modern philology.* Michigan: University Press.

Bédoucha, G. 1997. Review of Mundy 1995. *L'Homme* 144: 153–236.

Beeman, W.O. 1986. *Language, status and power in Iran.* Bloomington, IN: Indiana University Press.

Befu, H. and Kreiner, J. (eds) 1992. *Othernesses of Japan: historical and cultural influences on Japanese studies in ten countries.* Philipp-Franz-von-Siebold-Stiftung Deutsches Institut für Japanstudien, Monographien 1. Iudicum Verlag, München.

Befu, H. 1974. An ethnography of dinner entertainment in Japan. *Arctic anthropology* XI (supplement): 196–203.

—— 1992. Symbols of nationalism and Nihonjinron. In *Ideology and practice in modern Japan*, R. Goodman and K. Refsing (eds). Routledge: London.

Beidelman, T.O. 1966. Swazi royal ritual. *Africa* 36: 373–405.

—— (ed.) 1971. *The translation of culture: essays to E.E. Evans-Pritchard.* London: Tavistock.

Ben Dasan, I. 1972. *The Japanese and the Jews.* New York: Weatherhill.

Ben-Ari, E. 1990. Many voices, partial worlds: on some conventions and innovations in the ethnographic portrayal of Japan. In *Unwrapping Japan: society and culture in anthropological perspective*, E. Ben-Ari, B. Moeran and J. Valentine (eds). Manchester: Manchester University Press.

———— 1997. *Body projects in Japanese childcare: culture, organisation and emotions in a pre-school.* Richmond, Surrey: Curzon Press.

Ben-Ari, E., Moeran, B. and J. Valentine (eds) 1990. *Unwrapping Japan: society and culture in anthropological perspective.* Manchester: Manchester University Press.

Benjamin, G.R. 1997. *Japanese lessons: a year in a Japanese school through the eyes of an American anthropologist.* New York: University Press.

Bergson, H. 1975 [1946]. *The creative mind.* Totowa, NJ: Littlefield, Adam and Co.

Berndt, R. 1964. Warfare in the New Guinea Highlands. *American anthropologist* 66: 183–203.

Béteille, A. 1996. Indian anthropology. In *Encyclopaedia of social and cultural anthropology,* A. Barnard and J. Spencer (eds). London: Routledge.

Biardeau, M. 1981. *L'Hindouisme: anthropologie d'une civilisation.* Paris: Flammarion.

Bloch, M.E.F. 1998. *How we think they think: anthropological approaches to cognition, memory, and literacy.* Boulder, CO and Oxford: Westview Press.

Booth, A. 1985. *The roads to Sata.* New York and London: Weatherhill.

Born, G. 1995. *Rationalizing culture: IRCAM, Boulez, and the institutionalization of the musical avant-garde.* Berkeley and London: University of California Press.

Bornoff, N. 1991. *Pink Samurai: the pursuit and politics of sex in Japan.* London: Grafton.

Borofsky, R. 1987. *Making history: Pukapukan and anthropological constructions of knowledge.* Cambridge: Cambridge University Press.

Bourdieu, P. 1977 [1972]. *Outline of a theory of practice.* Cambridge: Cambridge University Press.

Brandjes, P., Chemjong, P.B., Mulatu, E., Sidhu, J.S., Yongolo, C., Zhang, G. and Zhou, X. 1994. *Vegetable boom and the question of sustainability in Raoyang county, North China.* Wageningen: International Centre for Development Oriented Research in Africulture (ICRA).

Brantley, C. 1981. *The Giriama and colonial resistance in Kenya, 1800–1920.* Berkeley, CA: University of California Press.

Breger, R. and Hill, R. (eds) 1998. *Cross cultural marriage: identity and choice.* Oxford: Berg.

Bruce, R.G. 1992. The study of law and order in Papua New Guinea: social deviance and identity among the Kuma-Kondika of the South Wahgi. Ph.D. thesis, Cambridge University.

Buhler, J.G. 1903 [1887]. *On the Indian sect of the Jainas.* London: Luzac & Co.

Burckhardt, J.L. 1830. *Notes on the Bedouins and Wahabys.* London: Colburn & Bentley.

Burghart, R. 1990. Ethnographers and their local counterparts in India. In *Localizing strategies: regional traditions of ethnographic writing,* R. Fardon (ed.). Edinburgh: Scottish Academic Press.

Burke, J. 1989. Becoming an 'inside-outsider'. *JASO* 20: 219–27.

Burton, J. 1984. Axe makers of the Wahgi. Ph.D thesis, Australian National University.

———— 1990. Tribal fighting: the scandal of inaction. *Catalyst* 20: 226–44.

Carlin, E. 1998. Speech community formation: a sociolinguistic profile of the Trio of Suriname. *Nieuwe West-Indische Gids* 72: 4–42.

Carrier, J.C. 1995. *Occidentalism: images of the West*. Oxford: Clarendon Press.

——— (ed.) 1992. Introduction. In *History and tradition in Melanesian anthropology*. Berkeley, CA: University of California Press.

Carrithers, M. 1990. Jainism and Buddhism as enduring historical streams. *JASO* 21: 141–63.

Champion, A. (ed. J. Middleton) 1967. *The Agiryama of Kenya*. London: Royal Anthropological Institute Memorandum No. 25.

Clark, R. 1979. *The Japanese company*. New Haven, London: Yale University Press.

Clifford, J. and Marcus, G.E. (eds) 1986. *Writing culture: the poetics and politics of ethnography*. Berkeley CA: University of California Press.

Clifford, J. 1986. Introduction. In *Writing culture: the poetics and politics of ethnography*, J. Clifford and G. E. Marcus (eds). Berkeley: University of California Press.

Cohen, A. 1969. *Custom and politics in urban Africa: a study of Hausa migrants in Yoruba towns*. London: Routledge and Kegan Paul.

Collingwood, R.G. 1932. *Roman Britain*. Oxford: Clarendon Press.

——— 1970 [1939]. *An autobiography*. Oxford: Clarendon Press.

——— 1993 [1946]. *The idea of history*. Oxford: Clarendon Press.

Connolly, B. and Anderson, R. 1992. *Black Harvest* (film). Arundel Productions, Australia.

Cort, J. 1986. Recent descriptive accounts of the contemporary Jainas: a review essay. *Man in India* 66: 180–87.

——— 1990. Models of and for the study of the Jains. *Method and theory in the study of religion* 2: 42–71.

——— 1997. Recent fieldwork studies of the contemporary Jains. *Religious studies review* 23: 103–11.

Crapanzano, V. 1980. *Tuhami: portrait of a Moroccan*. Chicago, IL: Chicago University Press.

Crick, M. 1982. Anthropological field research, meaning creation and knowledge construction. In *Semantic anthropology*, D. Parkin (ed.). ASA Monograph 22. London: Academic Press.

Dalby, L. 1985. *Geisha*. New York: Vintage.

Dale, P. 1986. *The myth of Japanese uniqueness*. London, Sydney and Oxford: Croom Helm and the Nissan Institute.

Davies, C.A. 1999. *Reflexive ethnography: a guide to researching selves and others*. ASA Research Methods in Anthropology. London: Routledge.

Davis, J. 1987. *Libyan politics: tribe and revolution. an account of the Zuwaya and their government*. London: I.B. Tauris.

de Waal, A. 1997. *Famine crimes: politics and the disaster relief industry in Africa*. Oxford: James Currey.

Dietrich, S. 1989. *Kolonialismus und Mission auf Flores (ca. 1900–1942)*. Hohenschäftlarn: Renner.

——— 1997. *Kota Rénya, 'Die Stadt der Königin': Religion, Identität und Wandel in einer ostindonesischen Kleinstadt*. Stuttgart (Habilitationsschrift, Universität München).

Dikötter, F. 1998. *Imperfect conceptions: medical knowledge, birth defects and eugenics in China.* London: Hurst.

Donham, D. L. and James, W. (eds) 1986. *The southern marches of imperial Ethiopia: essays in social anthropology and history,* Cambridge: Cambridge University Press.

Donham, D.L. 1999. *Marxist modern: an ethnographic history of the Ethiopian revolution.* Berkeley, Los Angeles and Oxford: University of California Press & James Currey.

Doughty, C.M. 1988 [1936]. *Travels in Arabia deserta.* 2 vols. London: Jonathan Cape.

Douglas, M. 1966. *Purity and danger.* London: Routledge & Kegan Paul.

Dournon, G. 1996 [1981]. *Guide pour la collecte des musiques et instruments traditionnels,* 2nd edn. Paris: Editions Unesco.

Dresch, P. 1981. The several peaces of Yemeni tribes. *JASO* 12: 73–86.

——— 1986. The significance of the course events take in segmentary systems. *American ethnologist* 13: 309–24.

——— 1989. *Tribes, government, and history in Yemen.* Oxford: Clarendon Press.

——— 1992. Ethnography and general theory or people versus humankind. Review article based on Fardon (ed.) 1990, *JASO* 23: 17–36.

Dumont, L. 1970 [1966]. *Homo hierarchicus.* Chicago, IL: Chicago University Press.

——— 1972. Une science en devenir. *L'Arc* 48: 8–21.

Dundas, P. 1992. *The Jains.* London: Routledge.

Durkheim, E. and Mauss, M. 1963 [1903]. *Primitive classification,* trans. R. Needham. London: Cohen and West.

Economist. 1999. The keys of the kingdom. 27 February 1999, 101–2.

Ellis, A.J. 1885. On the musical scales of various nations. *Journal of the Society of Arts* 33: 485–527.

Epstein, A.L. 1958. *Politics in an urban African community.* Rhodes-Livingstone Institute. Manchester: Manchester University Press.

Evans-Pritchard, E. E. 1937. Witchcraft, oracles, and magic among the Azande. Oxford: Clarendon Press.

——— 1940. *The Nuer: a description of the modes of livelihood and political institutions of a Nilotic people.* Oxford: Clarendon Press.

——— 1949. *The Sanusi of Cyrenaica.* Oxford: Clarendon Press.

——— 1951. Fieldwork and the empirical tradition. In *Social anthropology.* London: Allen & Unwin.

——— 1962 [1950]. Social anthropology: past and present. In *Essays in social anthropology.* London: Faber & Faber.

——— 1965. Luo tribes and clans [1949]; Marriage customs of the Luo of Kenya [1950]. In *The position of women in primitive society.* London: Faber & Faber.

——— 1973. Some reminiscences and reflections on fieldwork. *JASO* 4: 1–12.

Farage, N. 1991. *As muralhas dos sertões. Os povos indígenas no rio Branco e a colonização.* Rio de Janeiro: Paz e Terra.

Fardon, R. (ed.) 1990. *Localizing strategies: regional traditions of ethnographic writing.* Edinburgh and Washington: Scottish Academic Press & Smithsonian Institution Press.

Farmer, P. 1992. *AIDS and accusation: Haiti and the geography of blame*. Berkeley, CA: University of California Press.

Fawaz, L. 1997. Review of Gilsenan 1997. *Middle East studies association bulletin*, 31: 78–9.

Feld, S. 1976. Ethnomusicology and visual communication. *Ethnomusicology* 20: 293–325.

Fiumara, G.C. 1990. *The other side of language: a philosophy of listening*. London: Routledge.

Foucault, M. 1972 [1969]. *The archaeology of knowledge*, trans. A.M. Sheridan. London: Tavistock.

——— 1980. *Michel Foucault: power/knowledge: selected interviews and other writings 1972–1977*, C. Gordon (ed.). Brighton: Harvester Press.

Fox, J. 1971. Sister's child as plant. In *Rethinking kinship and marriage*, R. Needham (ed.). London: Tavistock.

Fox, R.G. 1969. *From zamindar to ballot box: community change in a North Indian market town*. Ithaca, NY: Cornell University Press.

Frake, C.O. 1996. Pleasant places, past times, and sheltered identity in rural East Anglia. In *Senses of place*, S. Feld and K. Basso (eds). Santa Fe, NM: School of American Research Press.

Pratt, M.L. 1986. Fieldwork in common places. In *Writing culture: the poetics and politics of ethnography*, J. Clifford and G.E. Marcus (eds). Berkeley, CA: University of California Press.

Frikel, P. 1971. *Dez anos de aculturação Tiriyó: 1960–70*. Museu Paraense Emilio Goeldi, Publicações avulsas 16.

Geertz, C. 1973. *The interpretation of cultures*. New York: Basic Books.

——— 1995. *After the fact: two countries, four decades, one anthropologist*. Cambridge, MA: Harvard University Press.

Gell, A. 1995. The language of the forest. In *The anthropology of landscape*, E. Hirsch and M. O'Hanlon (eds). Oxford: Oxford University Press.

Geschiere, P. 1997 [1995]. *The modernity of witchcraft: politics and the occult in postcolonial Africa*. Charlottesville and London, University of Virginia Press.

Ghosh, A. 1992. *In an antique land*. Harmondsworth: Granta/Penguin.

Gillin, J. 1936. *The Barama River Caribs of British Guiana*. Papers of the Peabody Museum of American Archaeology and Ethnology, Harvard University 14.

Gilsenan, M. 1990. Very like a camel: the appearance of an anthropologist's Middle East. In *Localising strategies: regional traditions of ethnographic writing*, R. Fardon (ed.). Edinburgh and Washington: Scottish Academic Press & Smithsonian Institution Press.

——— 1997. *Lords of the Lebanese marches: violence and narrative in an Arab society*. London: I.B. Tauris.

Gluckman, M.G. 1958 [1940]. *Analysis of a social situation in modern Zululand*. The Rhodes-Livingstone Papers 28. Manchester: Manchester University Press.

Goffman, E. 1971 [1961]. *Asylums*. Harmondsworth: Penguin.

Goldman, I. 1963. *The Cubeo: Indians of the Northwest Amazon*. Illinois Studies in Anthropology 2. Urbana, IL: University of Illinois Press.

Gombrich, R.F. 1971. *Precept and practice: traditional Buddhism in the rural highlands of Ceylon.* Oxford: Oxford University Press.

Good, K. 1979. The formation of the peasantry. In *Development and dependency: the political economy of Papua New Guinea*, A. Amarshi, K. Good and R. Mortimer (eds). Oxford: Oxford University Press.

Goodman, R. 1989. Japanese education: a model to emulate? *The Pacific review* 2: 24–37.

—— 1990a. Deconstructing an anthropological text: a 'moving' account of returnee schoolchildren in contemporary Japan. In *Unwrapping Japan: society and culture in anthropological perspective*, E. Ben-Ari, B. Moeran and J. Valentine (eds). Manchester: Manchester University Press.

—— 1990b. *Japan's 'international youth': the emergence of a new class of schoolchildren.* Oxford: Oxford University Press (reprinted in Clarendon Paperbacks, 1993).

—— 1992a. From colonialism to Thatcherism: influences in the approach of British anthropologists to the study of Japan. In Befu and Kreiner (eds), *Othernesses of Japan: historical and cultural influences on Japanese studies in ten countries.* Philipp-Franz-von-Siebold-Stiftung Deutsches Institut für Japanstudien, Monographien 1. Iudicum Verlag, München.

—— 1992b. Japan: pupil turned teacher? In *Lessons of cross-national comparison in education*, D. Phillips (ed.). Oxford Studies in Comparative Education, Volume 1. Triangle Books: Oxford.

—— 1992c. *Kikokushijo: Atarashii Tokkensô no Shutsugen* (translation by Nagashima Nobuhiro and Shimizu Satomi of Goodman 1990b). Tokyo: Iwanami Shoten.

—— 1994. *Kikokushijo no Kenkyû: Shakai Kagakuteki na Kenkyû no Hensen to Mondaiten* (Kikokushijo research: shifting paradigms and the problem of social scientific research) trans. N. Shigehiro. *Jidô Shinrigaku no Shinpo (Annual review of Japanese child psychology)*, 33, (Kaneko Shobô): 325–52.

—— 1996. On introducing the UN Convention of the Rights of the Child into Japan. In *Case studies on human rights in Japan*, R. Goodman and I. Neary (eds). Japan Library (Curzon Press).

—— 1999. *Nihon no Yôgoshisetsu to Eikoku no Children's Homes: Hikaku Shakai Jinruigakuteki Bunseki ni Mukete* (Japanese Yôgoshisetsu, British Children's Homes: towards a comparative social anthropological analysis) trans. Yui Kiyomitsu and Sasaki Junko. *Shakaigaku Zasshi (Sociological review)*, 16: 1–19, Kobe University.

—— 2000. *Children of the Japanese State: the changing role of child protection institutions in contemporary Japan.* Oxford: Oxford University Press.

—— Forthcoming. Images of the Japanese welfare state. In *Japan outside Japan*, H. Befu and S. Guichard-Anguis (eds). London: Routledge.

Gosden, C. 1994. *Social being and time.* Oxford: Blackwell.

—— 1999. *Anthropology and archaeology: a changing relationship.* London: Routledge.

Graham, P. 1985. Issues in social structure in Eastern Indonesia. M.Phil. thesis, University of Oxford.

—— 1987. East Flores revisited: a note on asymmetric alliance in Leloba and Wailolong, Indonesia. *Sociologus* 37: 40–59.

——— 1991. To follow the blood: the path of life in a domain of Eastern
Flores, Indonesia. Ph. D. thesis, The Australian National University,
Canberra.

Granet, M. 1973. Right and left in China. Trans R. Needham. In *Right and
left: essays on dual symbolic classification,* R. Needham (ed.). Chicago, IL:
Chicago University Press.

Grossman, L. 1982. Beer drinking and subsistence production in a Highland
village. In *Through a glass darkly: beer and modernization in Papua New
Guinea,* M. Marshall (ed.). Monograph 18, Institute of Applied Social and
Economic Research: Port Moresby, Papua New Guinea.

Gupta, A. and Ferguson J. (eds) 1997. *Anthropological locations: boundaries
and grounds of a field science.* Berkeley, CA: University of California Press.

Hamabata, M.M. 1990. *Crested kimono: power and love in the Japanese business
family.* Ithaca, NY: Cornell University Press.

Hammersley, M. and Atkinson, P. 1995 [1983]. *Ethnography: principles in
practice.* London: Tavistock.

Hann, C. and Dunn, E. (eds) 1996. *Civil society: challenging Western models.*
London: Routledge.

Hannerz, U. 1992. *Cultural complexity: studies in the social organization of
meaning.* New York: Columbia University Press.

Hare, P.H. 1985. *A woman's quest for science: portrait of anthropologist Elsie
Clews Parsons.* Buffalo, NY: Prometheus Books.

Harris, C. 1997. Struggling with Shangri-La: a Tibetan artist in exile. In
Constructing Tibetan culture, F. Korom (ed.). St. Hyacinthe, Canada: World
Heritage Press.

——— 1999. *In the image of Tibet: Tibetan visual culture after 1959.* London:
Reaktion Books.

Harris, M. 1964. *The nature of cultural things.* New York: Random House.

Harrison, S. 1993. *The mask of war: violence, ritual and the self in Melanesia.*
Manchester: Manchester University Press.

Hastrup, K. and Hervik, P. (eds) 1994. *Social experience and anthropological
knowledge.* London: Routledge.

Hemming, J. 1994. Indians, cattle and settlers: the growth of Roraima. In
The forest frontier: settlement and change in Brazilian Roraima, P.A. Furley
(ed). London and New York: Routledge.

Hendry, J. 1981. *Marriage in changing Japan.* London: Croom Helm.

——— 1986. *Becoming Japanese: the world of the pre-school child.* Manchester:
Manchester University Press.

——— 1992. The paradox of friendship in the field. In *Anthropology and
Autobiography,* J. Okely and H. Callaway (eds). ASA Monograph No. 29.
London: Routledge.

——— 1995. *Understanding Japanese society,* 2nd edn. London: Routledge.

Herzfeld, M. 1987. *Anthropology through the looking-glass: critical ethnography
in the margins of Europe.* Cambridge: Cambridge University Press.

Hinsley, C.M. 1981. *Savages and scientists: the Smithsonian Institution and the
development of American anthropology, 1846–1910.* Washington, D.C.:
Smithsonian Institution Press.

Hood, M. 1982. *The ethnomusicologist.* Ohio: Kent State University Press.

Humphrey, C. and Laidlaw, J. 1994. *The archetypal actions of ritual: a theory of ritual illustrated by the Jain rite of worship.* Oxford: Clarendon Press.

Hymes, D. 1971. Sociolinguistics and the ethnography of speaking. In *Social anthropology and language,* E.W. Ardener (ed.). ASA Monograph 10. London: Tavistock.

Ingold, T. (ed.) 1996. *Key debates in anthropology.* London and New York: Routledge.

Ingold, T. 1980. *Hunters, pastoralists and ranchers: reindeer economies and their transformations.* Cambridge: Cambridge University Press.

Jackall, R. 1988. *Moral mazes: the world of corporate managers.* New York and Oxford: Oxford University Press.

Jackson, A. (ed) 1987. *Anthropology at home.* ASA Monograph 25. London and New York: Tavistock.

Jacobi, H. 1914. Jainism. In *Encyclopaedia of religion and ethics* [Vol. 7], J. Hastings (ed.). Edinburgh: T. & T. Clark.

Jain, C.R. 1919. *The key of knowledge.* Arrah: Central Jaina Publishing House.

Jain, J. 1975. *Religion and culture of the Jains.* Delhi: Bharatiya Jnanpith.

Jaini, J.L. 1916. *Outlines of Jainism.* Cambridge: Cambridge University Press.

Jaini, P.S. 1979. *The Jaina path of purification.* Berkeley, CA: University of California Press.

James, W. and Johnson, D.H. (eds) 1988. *Vernacular Christianity: essays on the anthropology of religion presented to Godfrey Lienhardt.* Oxford and New York: JASO & Lilian Barber Press.

James, W. and Allen, N.J. (eds) 1998. *Marcel Mauss: a centenary tribute.* Oxford: Berghahn.

James, W. 1970. Are 'primitives' necessary? *JASO* 1: 82–3.

——— 1973a. The anthropologist as reluctant imperialist. In *Anthropology and the colonial encounter,* T. Asad (ed.). London: Ithaca Press.

——— 1973b. Illusions of freedom: a comment on Barth's individuals. *JASO* 4: 155–67.

——— 1979. *'Kwanim Pa: the making of the Uduk people. An ethnographic study of survival in the Sudan-Ethiopian borderlands.* Oxford: Clarendon Press.

——— 1986. Lifelines: sister-exchange marriage among the Gumuz. In *The southern marches of imperial Ethiopia:: essays in social anthropology and history,* D.L. Donham and W. James (eds). Cambridge: Cambridge University Press.

——— 1988. *The listening ebony: moral knowledge, religion and power among the Uduk of Sudan.* Oxford: Clarendon Press. (Reissued in paperback with new preface, 1999.)

——— (ed.) 1995. *The pursuit of certainty: religious and cultural formulations.* London: Routledge.

——— 1996. Uduk resettlement: dreams and realities. In *In search of cool ground: war, flight and homecoming in Northeast Africa,* T. Allen (ed.). London and Trenton, NJ: James Currey/Africa World Press.

——— 1997. The names of fear: memory, history and the ethnography of feeling among Uduk refugees. *JRAI* (N.S.) 3: 115–31.

———— 1998. 'One of us': Marcel Mauss and 'English' anthropology. In *Marcel Mauss: a centenary tribute*, W. James and N.J. Allen (eds). New York and Oxford: Berghahn.

James, W., Baumann, G. and Johnson, D.H. (eds) 1996. *Juan Maria Schuver's travels in North East Africa, 1880–1883*. London: The Hakluyt Society.

Japan Almanac 1999. Tokyo: Asahi Shinbunsha.

JASO (Journal of the Anthropological Society of Oxford). 1988. Vol. 19, Special issue on 'Second fieldwork'.

Jedrej, C. 1995. *Ingessana. The religious institutions of a people of the Sudan-Ethiopia borderland*. Leiden: Brill.

Jenkins, T. 1994. Fieldwork and the perception of everyday life. *Man* 29: 433–55.

———— 1999. *Religion in English everyday life: an ethnographic approach*. Oxford and New York: Berghahn.

Josephides, L. and Schiltz, M. 1982. Beer and other luxuries: abstinence in village and plantation by Sugu Kewas. In *Through a glass darkly: beer and modernization in Papua New Guinea*, M. Marshall (ed.). Monograph 18, Institute of Applied Social and Economic Research: Port Moresby, Papua New Guinea.

Just, R. 1995. Cultural certainties and private doubts. In *The pursuit of certainty: religious and cultural formulations*, W. James (ed.). London and New York: Routledge.

———— Forthcoming. *A Greek island cosmos: kinship and community in Meganisi*. World Anthropology series. Oxford and Santa Fe, NM: James Currey & School of American Research.

Kapferer, B. 1990. From the periphery to the centre: ethnography and the critique of ethnography in Sri Lanka. In *Localizing strategies: regional traditions of ethnographic writing*, R. Fardon (ed.). Edinburgh and Washington: Scottish Academic Press & Smithsonian Institution Press.

Keesing R. and Jolly, M. 1992. Epilogue. In *History and tradition in Melanesian anthropology*, J.C. Carrier (ed.). Berkeley, CA: University of California Press.

Kenya Human Rights Commission. 1997. *Kayas of deprivation, kayas of blood: violence, ethnicity and the state in coastal Kenya*. Nairobi.

Keraf, G. 1978. *Morfologi Dialek Lamalera*. Ende-Flores, Indonesia: Arnoldus.

Knauft, B.M. 1990. Melanesian warfare: a theoretical history. *Oceania* 60: 250–311.

Koch, K.F. 1974. *War and peace in Jalemo: the management of conflict in Highland New Guinea*. Cambridge, MA: Harvard University Press.

Koelewijn, C. and Rivière, P.G. 1987. *The oral literature of the Trio Indians of Surinam*. Koninklijk Institut voor Taal-, Land- en Volkenkunde, Caribbean Series No 6. Dordrecht and Providence, RI: Foris Publications.

Kohn, T. 1994. Incomers and fieldworkers: a comparative study of social experience. In *Social experience and anthropological knowledge*, K. Hastrup and P. Hervik (eds). London: Routledge.

Kondo, D. 1990. *Crafting selves: power, gender and discourses of identity in a Japanese workplace*. Chicago and London: University of Chicago Press.

Kornai, J. nos. 1980. *The economics of shortage*. Amsterdam: North Holland Press.

Kulick, D. and Willson, M. (eds) 1995. *Taboo, sex, identity and erotic subjectivity in anthropological fieldwork.* London and New York: Routledge.

Kunst, J. 1994. *Indonesian music and dance, traditional music and its interaction with the West.* Amsterdam: Royal Tropical Institute.

Kuper, A. 1997. Review of H. Vermeulen and A. Roldán (eds) *Fieldwork and footnotes. Journal of the history of the behavioral sciences* 33: 268–9.

LaFleur, W. 1992. *Liquid life: abortion and Buddhism in Japan.* Princeton: Princeton University Press.

Laidlaw, J. 1995. *Riches and renunciation.* Oxford: Clarendon Press.

Leach, E.R. 1957. The epistemological background to Malinowsk's empiricism. In *Man and culture: an evaluation of the work of Bronislaw Malinowski,* R. Firth (ed.). London: Routledge and Kegan Paul.

――― 1958. Magical hair. *JRAI* 88: 147–64.

――― 1961. *Rethinking anthropology.* London: Athlone Press.

Lee, C. and DeVos, G. 1984. *Koreans in Japan: ethnic conflict and accommodation.* Berkeley, CA: University of California Press.

Lévi-Strauss, C. 1961 [1955]. *A world on the wane,* (trans. of *Tristes tropiques* by J. Russell). London: Hutchinson.

――― 1969 [1958]. *Structural anthropology,* I. London: Allen Lane.

――― 1977 [1973]. *Structural anthropology,* II, trans. M. Layton. London: Allen Lane.

――― 1970 [1964]. *The raw and the cooked: introduction to a science of mythology,* I, trans. J. and D. Weightman. London: Jonathan Cape.

Lewis, G. 1990. *Day of shining red.* Cambridge: Cambridge University Press.

Lienhardt, P.A. 1975. The interpretation of rumour. In *Studies in social anthropology: essays in memory of E.E. Evans-Pritchard by his former Oxford colleagues,* J.H.M. Beattie and R.G. Lienhardt (eds). Oxford: Clarendon Press.

Lienhardt, R.G. 1961. *Divinity and experience: the religion of the Dinka.* Oxford: Clarendon Press.

――― 1964. *Social anthropology.* London: Oxford University Press.

Lofland, J. 1971. *Analyzing social settings: a guide to qualitative observation and analysis.* Belmont, CA: Wadsworth.

Lyon, P.J. (ed.) 1974. *Native South Americans. ethnology of the least known continent.* Boston: Little, Brown and Co.

MacClancy, J. 1996. Fieldwork styles: Bohannan, Barley, and Gardner. In *Popularizing anthropology,* J. MacClancy and C. McDonaugh (eds). London and New York: Routledge.

MacDougal, D. 1997. The visual in anthropology. In *Rethinking visual anthropology,* M. Banks and H. Morphy (eds). New Haven, CT: Yale University Press.

Madsen, R. 1995. *China and the American dream: a moral inquiry.* Berkeley, CA: University of California Press.

Malinowski, B. 1922. *Argonauts of the Western Pacific. An account of native enterprise and adventure in the archipelagoes of Melanesian New Guinea.* London: Routledge and Kegal Paul.

――― 1927. *The sexual life of savages in north-western Melanesia.* London: Routledge and Kegan Paul.

———— 1935. *Coral gardens and their magic: a study of the methods of tilling the soil and of agriculture rites in the Trobriand Islands*, 2 vols. London: Allen & Unwin.

Maranh, T. 1993. Recollections of fieldwork conversations, or authorial difficulties in anthropological writing. In *Responsibility and evidence in oral discourse*, J.H. Hill and J.T. Irvine (eds). Cambridge and New York: Cambridge University Press.

Marcus, G. and Fischer, M. (eds) 1986. *Anthropology as cultural critique*. Chicago, IL: Chicago University Press.

Marcus, G. 1998. *Ethnography through thick and thin*. Princeton, NJ: Princeton University Press.

Marshall, B.K. 1995. *Learning to be modern: Japanese political discourse on education*. Boulder, CO: Westview Press.

Martin, D. 1980. *Wilderness of mirrors*. New York: Harper and Row.

Mascarenhas-Keyes, S. 1987. The native anthropologist: constraints and strategies in research. In *Anthropology at home*, A. Jackson (ed.). ASA monograph No. 25. London: Tavistock.

Massad, J. 1997. Review of Shryock 1997. *Journal of Palestine studies* 27: 103–6.

Matsunaga, L. 1995. Working in a chain store: a case study of a Japanese company. Ph.D thesis, London University.

Maugham, R. 1947. *Nomad*. London: Chapman and Hall.

Mauss, M. 1998. An intellectual self-portrait. In *Marcel Mauss: a centennial tribute*, W. James and N.J. Allen (eds). Oxford: Berghahn.

Maybury-Lewis, D. 1967. *Akwê-Shavante society*. Oxford: Clarendon Press.

Mboya, P. Chief. 1938. *Luo kitgi gi timbegi*. Nairobi: East African Standard.

McClean, M. 1983. Preserving world musics: perspectives from New Zealand and Oceania. *Studies in Music* 17: 23–37.

McVeigh, B. 1997. *Life in a Japanese women's college: learning to be ladylike*. Nissan/Routledge Japanese Studies Series. London: Routledge.

Meggitt, M.J. 1977. *Blood is their argument: warfare among the Mae-Enga tribesmen of the New Guinea Highlands*. Palo Alto, CA: Mayfield Publishing Company.

Mell, M.Y. 1987. *Wahgi: the handbook of the Western Highlands Province and its government: celebrating ten years of provincial government*. Port Moresby: Mell Productions.

Melman, B. 1995. *Women's orients: English women and the Middle East 1718–1918*. London: Macmillan.

Meneley, A. 1998. Analogies and resonances in the process of ethnographic understanding. *Ethnos* 63: 202–26.

Merlan, F. and Rumsey, A. 1991. *Ku Waru: language and segmentary politics in the Western Nebilyer Valley, Papua New Guinea*. Cambridge: Cambridge University Press.

Miller, E. 1994. A borderless age: AIDS, gender and power in contemporary Japan. Ph.D. thesis, Harvard University.

Miller, R.A. 1982. *Japan's modern myth: the language and beyond*. New York and Tokyo: Weatherhill.

Mitchell, J.C. 1956. *The Kalela dance*. Rhodes-Livingstone Paper No. 27. Manchester: Manchester University Press.

Moeran, B. 1985. *Okubo Diary: portrait of a Japanese village*. Stanford: University Press. Republished as *A Far Valley* 1997. Tokyo: Kodansha International.

———— 1990. Beating about the brush: An example of ethnographic writing from Japan. In *Localizing strategies: regional traditions of ethnographic writing*, R. Fardon (ed.). Edinburgh and Washington: Scottish Academic Press & Smithsonian Institution Press.

—— 1998. One over the seven: sake drinking in a Japanese pottery community. In *Interpreting Japanese society*, 2nd edn. J. Hendry (ed.). London: Routledge.

Morishima, M. 1982. *Why has Japan 'succeeded'?: Western technology and Japanese ethos*. Cambridge: Cambridge University Press.

Mouer, R.E. and Sugimoto, Y. 1986. *Images of Japanese society: a study in the structure of social reality*. London: Routledge and Kegan Paul.

Muke, J.D. 1993. The Wahgi Opo Kumbo: an account of warfare in the central Highlands of New Guinea. Ph.D thesis, Cambridge University.

Mundy, M. 1995. *Domestic government: kinship, community and polity in North Yemen*. London and New York: I.B. Tauris.

Myers, H. (ed.) 1992. *The New Groves handbooks in music: Ethnomusicology, an introduction*. London: Macmillan.

———— (ed.) 1993. *The New Groves handbooks in music: Ethnomusicology, historical and regional studies*. London: Macmillan.

Nagashima, N. 1973. A reversed world: or is it? The Japanese way of communication and their attitudes towards alien cultures, in *Modes of thought: essays on thinking in Western and non-Western societies*, R. Horton and R. Finnegan (eds). London: Faber & Faber.

Nakane, C. 1970. *Japanese society*. Harmondsworth: Penguin.

Narayan, K. 1998. How 'native' is a native anthropologist? in *Anthropological journeys: reflections on fieldwork*, M. Thapan (ed.). London: Sangam Books.

Needham, R. 1960. The left hand of the Mugwe: an analytical note on the structure of Meru symbolism. *Africa* 30: 20–33.

———— 1962. *Structure and sentiment*. Chicago, IL: Chicago University Press.

———— (ed.) 1971. *Rethinking kinship and marriage*. London: Tavistock.

———— (ed.) 1973. *Right and left: essays on dual symbolic classification*. Chicago, IL: Chicago University Press.

———— 1975. Polythetic classification: convergence and consequences. *Man* (N.S.) 10: 349–69.

Nettl, B. 1983. *The study of ethnomusicology: twenty-nine issues and processes*. Urbana, IL: University of Illinois Press.

Newton, D.E. 1992. *James Watson and Francis Crick: discovery of the double helix and beyond*. New York: Facts on File.

Ngala, R. 1949. *Nchi na desturi za Wagiriama*. Nairobi: Eagle Press.

Nordstrom, C. and Robben, A.C.G.M. (eds) 1995. *Fieldwork under fire: contemporary studies of violence and survival*. Berkeley, CA: University of California Press.

Norgren, T. 1998. Abortion before birth control: the interest group politics behind postwar Japanese reproduction policy. *Journal of Japanese studies* 24: 59–94.

O'Hanlon, M.D.P. 1989. *Reading the skin: adornment, display and society among the Wahgi.* London: British Museum Publications.

———— 1993. *Paradise: portraying the New Guinea Highlands.* London: British Museum Press.

———— 1995. Modernity and the 'graphicalization' of meaning: New Guinea Highland shield design in historical perspective. *JRAI* (N.S.) 1: 469–93.

Ohnuki-Tierney, E. 1984a. *Illness and culture in contemporary Japan: an anthropological view.* Cambridge: Cambridge University Press.

———— 1984b. Monkey performance: a multiple structure of meaning and reflexivity in Japanese culture, in *Text, play and story: the construction and reconstruction of self and society,* E. Bruner (ed.). Seattle: American Ethnological Society.

Okazaki, A. 1997. Open shadow: dreams, histories and selves in a borderland village in Sudan. Ph.D. thesis, SOAS, London University.

Okely, J. 1987. Fieldwork up the M1: policy and political aspects. In *Anthropology at home,* A. Jackson (ed.). ASA Monograph No. 25. London: Tavistock.

———— 1996. *Own or other cultures.* London: Routledge.

Okely, J. and Callaway, H. (eds) 1992. *Anthropology and autobiography.* ASA Monograph No. 29. London: Routledge.

Olivier de Sardan, J-P. 1992. Occultism and the ethnographic 'I': the exoticisation of magic from Durkheim to 'postmodern' anrthropology. *Critique of anthropology* 12: 5–25.

Ortner, S.B. 1984. Theory in anthropology since the sixties. *Comparative studies in society and history,* 16: 126–66.

Ottenberg, S. 1990. Thirty years of fieldnotes: changing relationships to the text. In *Fieldnotes: the makings of anthropology,* R. Sanjek (ed.). Ithaca and London: Cornell University Press.

Parkin, D. 1969. *Neighbours and nationals in an African city ward.* London: Routledge and Kegan Paul.

———— 1972. *Palms, wine and witnesses: public spirit and private gain in an African farming community.* San Francisco, CA: Chandler.

———— 1978. *The cultural definition of political response: lineal destiny among the Luo of Kenya.* London: Academic Press.

———— (ed.) 1982. *Semantic anthropology.* London: Academic Press.

———— 1985. Being and selfhood among intermediary Swahili. In *Swahili language and society,* J. Maw and D. Parkin (eds). Beitraege zur Afrikanistik. Band 25. University of Vienna: Afro-Pub.

———— 1987. Comparison as the search for continuity. In *Comparative anthropology,* L. Holy (ed.). Oxford: Blackwell.

———— 1991. *Sacred void: spatial images of work and ritual among the Giriama of Kenya.* Cambridge: Cambridge University Press.

———— 1995. Blank banners and Islamic consciousness in Zanzibar. In *Questions of consciousness,* A.P. Cohen and N. Rapport (eds). ASA Monograph No. 33. London and New York: Routledge.

Peers, L. 1994. *The Ojibwa in western Canada, 1780–1870.* Winnipeg and St. Paul: University of Manitoba Press (Native History Series) and Minnesota Historical Society Press.

———— 1999. 'Playing ourselves': First Nations/Native American
    interpreters at living history sites. *The Public Historian* 21: 39–59.
Pettigrew, J. 1981. Reminiscences of fieldwork among the Sikhs. In *Doing
    Feminist Research*, H. Roberts (ed.). London: Routledge and Kegan Paul.
Pfaff, W. 1999. This international economic crisis was unnecessary.
    International Herald Tribune, 1 March 1999.
Pieke, F.N. 1987. Social science fieldwork in the PRC: implications of the
    Mosher affair. *China Information* 1: 32–7.
———— 1995. Accidental anthropology: witnessing the 1989 Chinese
    people's movement. In *Fieldwork under fire: contemporary studies of
    violence and survival*, C. Nordstrom and A.C.G.M. Robben (eds). Berkeley,
    CA: University of California Press.
———— 1998a. The place of anthropology in the People's Republic of China.
    Lecture given in the series 'The 21st century: cultural awareness and
    cross-cultural dialogue' organised for the Centenary celebration of
    Peking University, Beijing, 15–28 June 1998.
———— 1998b. Networks, groups, and the state in the 'private' rural
    economy of Raoyang county, Hebei province. In *Cooperative and
    collective in China's rural development: between state and private interests*,
    E.B. Vermeer, F.N. Pieke and W.L.Chong (eds). Armonk, NY: M.E.
    Sharpe.
Pink, S. 1998. From ritual sacrifice to media commodity: anthropological
    and media constructions of the Spanish bullfight and the rise of women
    performers. In *Ritual, performance, media*, F. Hughes-Freeland (ed.). ASA
    Monographs No. 35. London: Routledge.
Pitt-Rivers, J. 1977. *The fate of Schechem*. Cambridge: Cambridge University
    Press.
Plath, D. 1998. Review of E. Ben-Ari, 1997, *Body projects in Japanese
    childcare: culture, organisation and emotions in a pre-school* (Richmond,
    Surrey: Curzon Press). *The Journal of Asian studies*, 57: 868–9.
Pocock, D.F. 1971 [1961]. *Social Anthropology*. London: Sheed and Ward.
———— 1988. Persons, texts, and morality (Marett Memorial Lecture,
    Oxford). *International journal of moral and social studies* 3: 203–17.
———— 1994. The idea of a personal anthropology (paper originally given in
    1973). *Journal for the anthropological study of human movement* 8:11–42.
Podolefsky, A. 1984. Contemporary warfare in the New Guinea Highlands.
    Ethnology 23: 73–87.
Poewe, K. 1996. Writing culture and writing fieldwork: the proliferation of
    experimental and experiential ethnographies. *Ethnos* 61: 177–206.
Pospisil, L. 1963. *The Kapauku Papuans*. New York: Holt, Rinehart and
    Winston.
Prins, A.H.J. 1952. *The coastal tribes of the North-Eastern Bantu (Pokomo,
    Nyika, Teita)*. London: International African Institute.
Raban, J. 1979. *Arabia through the looking glass*. London: Collins.
Rabinow, P. 1977. *Reflections on fieldwork in Morocco*. London and Berkeley,
    CA: Quantum Books & University of California Press.
Rapp, R. 1999. *Testing women, testing the fetus: the social impact of
    amniocentesis in America*. London and New York: Routledge.

Reay, M.O. 1982. Lawlessness in the Papua New Guinea Highlands. In *Melanesia beyond diversity*, vol. 2, R.H. May and H. Nelson (eds). Canberra: Australian National University Press.

———— 1987. The magico-religious foundations of New Guinea Highlands warfare. In *Sorcerer and witch in Melanesia*, M.Stephen (ed.). New Brunswick, NJ: Rutgers University Press.

Rice, T. 1997. Toward a mediation of field methods and field experience in ethnomusicology. In *Shadows in the field*, G. Barz and T. Cooley (eds). Oxford: Oxford University Press.

Riesman, P. 1977. *Freedom in Fulani social life: an introspective ethnography*. Chicago, IL: Chicago University Press.

Rivière, P.G. 1966. A policy for the Trio Indians of Surinam. *Nieuwe West-Indische Gids* 45: 95–120.

———— 1969. *Marriage among the Trio*. Oxford: Clarendon Press.

———— 1972. *The forgotten frontier: ranchers of north Brazil*. New York: Holt, Rinehart and Winston.

———— 1981a. A report on the Trio Indians of Surinam. *Nieuwe West-Indische Gids* 55: 1–38.

———— 1981b. The wages of sin is death: some aspects of evangelisation among the Trio Indians. *JASO* 12: 1–13.

———— n.d. Pepper and salt: Amerindian and Brazilian relations in North Brazil. Unpublished paper.

Roberts, J.A.G. 1989. Not the least deserving: the philosophies and the religions of Japan. *Monumenta Nipponica* 44: 151–69.

Rosaldo, R. 1986. From the door of his tent: the fieldworker and the inquisitor. In *Writing culture: the poetics and politics of ethnography*, J. Clifford and G. Marcus (eds). Berkeley, CA: University of California Press.

Rudolph, P., Smeenk, C. and Leatherwood, S. 1997. *Preliminary checklist of cetacea in the Indonesian archipelago and adjacent waters* (Zoologische Verhandelingen 312). Leiden: Nationaal Natuurhistorisch Museum.

Russell, J.G. 1991. Race and reflexivity: the black other in contemporary Japanese society. *Cultural anthropology* 6: 3–25.

Said, E. 1978. *Orientalism*. London and Henley: Routledge and Kegan Paul.

Sakamoto, R. 1997. Imagining Japan: national identity and the representation of the other in early Meiji discourse. Ph.D. thesis, University of Essex.

Sangave, V.A. 1980 [1959]. *Jaina community: a social survey*. Bombay: Popular Book Depot.

———— 1991. Reform movements among Jains in modern India. In *The assembly of listeners: Jains in society*, M. Carrithers and C. Humphrey (eds). Cambridge: Cambridge University Press.

Sanjek, R. (ed.) 1990. *Fieldnotes: the makings of anthropology*. Ithaca, NY: Cornell University Press.

Sarabiti, A.S. 1938. Culikan Sejarah Peperangan Kedang. Handwritten manuscript with R.H. Barnes, unpublished.

Scholte, B. 1971. Discontents in anthropology. *Social research*. 38: 777–807.

———— 1972. Toward a reflexive and critical anthropology. In *Reinventing anthropology*, D. Hymes (ed.). New York: Pantheon.

———— 1978. Critical anthropology since its reinvention. *Anthropology and humanism quarterly* 3: 4–17.

Schoppa, L. 1997. *Bargaining with Japan: what American pressure can and cannot do.* New York: Columbia University Press.

Schubring, W. 1935. *Die Lehre der Jainas.* Berlin: W. de Gruyter.

Seeger, C. 1951. Systematic musicology: viewpoints, orientations, and methods. *Journal of the American Musicological Society* 4: 240–48.

Shaw, A. 1996. Review of Kulick, D. and Willson, M. (eds) 1995, *Taboo, sex, identity and erotic subjectivity in anthropological fieldwork* (London and New York: Routledge). *JASO* 27: 272–3.

Shore, C. 1993. Inventing the 'People's Europe': critical perspectives on European Community cultural policy. *Man* 28: 779–800.

Shryock, A. 1997. *Nationalism and the genealogical imagination: oral history and textual authority in tribal Jordan.* Berkeley, CA: University of California Press.

Singleton, J. 1998. *Learning in likely places: varieties of apprenticeship in Japan.* Cambridge: Cambridge University Press.

Small, C. 1998. *Musicking: the meanings of performing and listening.* Hanover, NH and London: University Press of New England & Wesleyan University Press.

Southall, A.W. and Gutkind, P.C.W. 1957. *Townsmen in the making.* East African Studies No. 9. Kampala: East African Institute of Social Research.

Southall, A.W. 1952. *Lineage formation among the Luo.* IAI Memorandum 26. London: Oxford University Press.

———— 1953. *Alur society: a study in processes and types of domination.* Cambridge: Heffer.

Southwold, M. 1983. *Buddhism in life: the anthropological study of religion and the Sinhalese practice of Buddhism.* Manchester: Manchester University Press.

Spear, T.T. 1978. *The Kaya complex: a history of the Mijikenda peoples of the Kenya coast to 1900.* Nairobi: Kenya Literature Bureau.

Spencer, P. 1992. Automythologies and the reconstruction of ageing. In *Anthropology and autobiography*, J. Okely and H. Callaway (eds). ASA Monograph No. 29. London: Routledge.

Sperber, D. 1974. *Rethinking symbolism.* Cambridge: Cambridge University Press.

Spodek, H. 1974. Rulers, merchants and other groups in the city-states of Saurashtra, India, around 1800. *Comparative studies in society and history* 16: 448–70.

Srinivas, M.N. 1996. Indian anthropologists and the study of Indian culture. *Economic and political weekly* 31: 656–7.

Statler, O. 1985. *Japanese pilgrimage.* London: Picador.

Steiner, F. 1954a. Notes on comparative economics. *British journal of sociology* 5: 118–29.

———— 1954b. Enslavement and the early Hebrew lineage system: an explanation of Genesis, xlvii. 29–31, xlviii. 1–16. *Man* 102: 73–5.

———— 1954c. Chagga truth: a note on Gutmann's account of the Chagga concept of truth in *Das Recht der Dschagga. Africa* 24: 364–9.

———— 1956. *Taboo*. London: Cohen & West.

Stocking, G.W. 1987. *Victorian anthropology*. New York: The Free Press.

Strathern, A.J. 1977. Contemporary warfare in the New Guinea Highlands — revival or breakdown? *Yagl-ambu* 4: 135–46.

Strathern, M. 1987. The limits of auto-anthropology. In *Anthropology at home*, A. Jackson (ed.). ASA Monograph No. 25. London: Tavistock.

Tanaka, S. 1995. *Japan's Orient: rendering pasts in history*. Berkeley, CA: University of California Press.

Taplin, O. 1992. *Homeric soundings: the shaping of the Iliad*. Oxford: Clarendon Press.

Thapan, M. (ed.) 1998. *Anthropological journeys: reflections on fieldwork*. London: Sangam Books.

Tidrick, K. 1989. *Heart-beguiling Araby: the English romance with Arabia*. London: I.B. Tauris.

Tonkin, E., McDonald, M. and Chapman, M. (eds) 1989. *History and ethnicity*. ASA Monographs 27. London and New York: Routledge.

Trilling, L. 1955. *The liberal imagination: essays on literature and society*. London: Secker & Warburg.

Tsuda, T. 1998. The stigma of ethnic difference: the structure of prejudice and 'discrimination' toward Japan's new immigrant minority. *Journal of Japanese studies* 24: 317–60.

Turner, V.W. 1996[1957]. *Schism and continuity in an African society*. Oxford: Berg.

Valentine, J. 1990. On the borderlines: the significance of marginality in Japanese society. In *Unwrapping Japan*, E. Ben-Ari, B. Moeran and J. Valentine (eds). Manchester: Manchester University Press.

van Maanen, J. 1988. *Tales of the field: on writing ethnography*. Chicago, IL: Chicago University Press.

Vatter, E. 1932. *Ata Kiwan: unbekante Bergvölker im tropischem Holland*. Leipzig: Bibliographisches Institut.

Verrier, A. 1983. *Through the looking glass: British foreign policy in an age of illusions*. London: Jonathan Cape.

Vertovec, S. 1999. Conceiving and researching transnationalism. *Ethnic and racial studies* 22: 447–62.

Vial, L.G. 1942. They fight for fun. *Walkabout* 9: 5–9.

Viveiros de Castro, E. 1992. O mármore e a murta: sobre a inconstância da alma selvagem. *Revista de Antropologia* 35: 21–74.

———— 1993. Alguns aspectos da afinidade no dravidianato Amazônico. In *Amazônia: Etnologia e história indígena*, E.Viveiros de Castro and M.Carneiro da Cunha (eds). São Paulo: Núcleo de História Indígena e do Indigenismo da USP.

Watson, C.W. (ed.) 1999. *Being there: fieldwork in anthropology*. London: Pluto Press.

Watson, J.L. (ed.) 1977. *Between two cultures: migrants and minorities in Britain*. Oxford: Blackwell.

Webber, J. (ed.) 1994. *Jewish identities in the New Europe*. Oxford Centre for Hebrew and Jewish Studies. London and Washington: Littman Library of Jewish Civilization.

Weber, M. 1946 [1922]. Science as a vocation. In *From Max Weber: essays in sociology*, H.H. Gerth and C. Wright Mills (trans. and eds). New York: Oxford University Press.

———— 1949 [1904]. 'Objectivity' in social science and social policy. In *Max Weber on the methodology of the social sciences*, E.A. Shils and H.A. Finch (trans. and eds). Glencoe, IL: The Free Press.

Weiner, M. 1997. *Japan's minorities: the illusion of homogeneity*. London: Routledge.

White, G. and Goodman, R. 1998. Welfare orientalism and the search for an East Asian welfare model. In *The East Asian welfare model: welfare orientalism and the state*, R. Goodman, G. White and Huck-ju Kwon (eds). London and New York: Routledge.

Wilder, W. 1971. Purum descent groups:some vagaries of method. In *Rethinking kinship and marriage*, R. Needham (ed.). London: Tavistock.

Willis, J. 1993. *Mombasa, Swahili and the making of the Mijikenda*. Oxford: Clarendon Press.

Wolf, D.L. 1996. *Feminist dilemmas in fieldwork*. Boulder, CO: Westview.

Wolf, E. 1982. *Europe and the peoples without history*. Berkeley, CA: University of California Press.

Wulff, H. 1998. Perspectives towards ballet performance: exploring, repairing, and maintaining frames. In *Ritual, performance, media*, F. Hughes-Freeland (ed.). ASA Monographs 35. London: Routledge.

Yoshida, T. 1981. The stranger as god: the place of the outsider in Japanese folk religion. *Ethnology* 20: 87–99.

Yoshino, K. 1992. *Cultural nationalism in contemporary Japan: a sociological enquiry*. London: Routledge.

INDEX